Environment, energy, and economy

Environment, energy, and economy: Strategies for sustainability

Edited by Yoichi Kaya and Keiichi Yokobori

United Nations University Press

TOKYO · NEW YORK · PARIS

United Nations University Press
The United Nations University, 53-70, Jingumae 5-chome, Shibuya-ku, Tokyo 150, Japan
Tel: (03) 3499-2811   Fax: (03) 3406-7345
Telex: J25442   Cable: UNATUNIV TOKYO

UNU Office in North America
2 United Nations Plaza, Room DC2-1462-70, New York, NY 10017
Tel: (212) 963-6387   Fax: (212) 371-9454   Telex: 422311 UN UI

United Nations University Press is the publishing division of the United Nations University.

Cover design by Joyce C. Weston

Printed in the United States of America

UNUP-911
ISBN 92-808-0911-3

Library of Congress Cataloging-in-Publication Data

Environment, energy, and economy : strategies for sustainability /
  edited by Yoichi Kaya and Keiichi Yokobori.
      p.   cm.
  "This document represents the proceedings of the Tokyo
Conference on 'Global Environment, Energy, and Economic
Development' held at the United Nations University
Headquarters in Tokyo, 25–27 October 1993"—Preface.
  Includes bibliographical references and index.
  ISBN 9280809113 (pbk.)
  1. Sustainable development—Congresses. 2. Economic devel-
opment—Environmental aspects—Congresses. 3. Environmen-
tal policy—Congresses. I. Kaya, Yoichi, 1934–   . II. Yokobori,
Keiichi, 1940–   . III. Tokyo Conference on "Global Environ-
ment, Energy, and Economic Development" (Tokyo, Japan : 1993)
HC79.E5E5726   1997
333.79—dc21   97-21167
                                                   CIP

Contents

Contents

Preface

This document represents the proceedings of the Tokyo Conference on "Global Environment, Energy, and Economic Development" held at the United Nations University Headquarters in Tokyo, 25–27 October 1993.

The conference was organized jointly by the United Nations University and the International Development Center of Japan to examine strategies for sound economic development while conserving global environmental protection, in which energy plays a key role. This conference was intended to be the first international meeting at the new Headquarters Office of the United Nations University to address the global consensus on sustainable development reached at the United Nations Conference on Environment and Development in June 1992, particularly the Energy Chapter of Agenda 21. The aim was also to encourage communication among scholars of differing disciplines and government and business decision makers on issues related to energy, the environment, and economic development. The conference received sponsorship from the Japanese Ministries of Foreign Affairs and International Trade and Industry, from the Japanese Agencies of Economic Planning and Environment, as well as from the Japanese Federation of Electric Power Companies.

Preface

The two-and-a-half-day conference discussed both short-term and long-term policy measures for the economy and the directions of development in developing countries as well as industrialized countries, and touched on various facets of the interrelations among the environment, energy requirements, and economic development. The Introduction will present the key issues and provide summaries of the presentations.

The publication of the proceedings is long overdue. Since the conference, such major developments as the First Conference of the Parties (COP–1) to the Framework Convention on Climate Change (FCCC), March–April 1995, and the publication of the Second Assessment Report of the Intergovernmental Panel on Climate Change (SAR–IPCC) have taken place. However, these developments do not invalidate the various views and findings presented at the conference, because key issues and concerns surrounding the global environment, energy, and economic development continue to be discussed. The views and findings of the conference will also provide some background insights in understanding the discussions at the COP–1 and the IPCC SAR.

We are grateful to Professor A. Amano and Dr. K. Yamaji for their active participation from the preparatory stage to the fruitful discussions at the conference and to the UNU rector, Professor Heitor Gurgulino de Souza, and to Dr. Fu-chen Lo, Dr. Victor Kuipers, and Ms. Hiromi Suzuki at the UNU for their dedication and initiatives from the preparations for the conference to the publication of this volume. Our gratitude should be extended to the session chairpersons, speakers, discussants, participants, and many other people, including those in the sponsoring organizations and governmental agencies.

Yoichi Kaya
Keiichi Yokobori

1

Introduction

Yoichi Kaya and Keiichi Yokobori

This volume contains the major discussions presented at the United Nations University's Tokyo Conference on "Global Environment, Energy, and Economic Development" held at its Headquarters from 25 to 27 October 1993. The presentations are grouped into six parts and the main issues and conclusions are summarized below.

Part 1 introduces the key issues to be addressed in the subsequent discussions. All three authors discuss the interrelations among the environment, economy, and energy (the three "Es"). Environmental problems are caused by intensifying use of natural resources, in particular fossil fuels (the major form of energy used and produced), which in turn results from growing human economic activities. At the same time, economic development can also promote the development and use of environmental protection technologies. Further, economic development, energy use and production, and environmental degradation are taking place on a global scale. Thus, their interrelations are discussed in this part both in theoretical terms and in practical terms.

Giuseppe Sfligiotti (chap. 2) presents a perspective on these matters based on his experience as an energy industry executive. He states that until the early 1980s the availability of energy, particularly oil, in sufficient quantities and at competitive prices constituted the main preoccupation of business and government leaders in the industrialized countries in order to ensure economic development. In contrast, environmental concerns, which had not much affected the actions and behaviour of businessmen, governments, or consumers in general, have become more apparent in recent years. While he recognizes the growing concerns about the environment as entirely justified, he regards the diminishing energy concerns as dangerously complacent in light of the inevitable increase in world energy consumption and the more acute imbalance between the geopolitical areas of production and supply, especially in the case of oil and gas. He argues "the problems related to energy, the environment, and economic development, in their growing global interdependence, cannot be coped with by adopting an ideological approach, be it based on the ideas of Karl Marx or on those of Adam Smith." He cites many cases where the "free market" has been conditioned by government. He contends that "a 'Sustainable Society' cannot be brought about without rational government intervention to complement and correct market forces." He recognizes both the need to "internalize" environmental costs and the difficulties inherent in this process. Despite such difficulties, he concludes that "it is essential to go ahead with all the necessary precautions, but with determination, before the present trend of irrational development makes it more difficult and painful to 'change course' towards sustainable development."

Sozaburo Okamatsu (chap. 3) provides the perspective of a government official responsible for industrial, technology, and trade policy on sustainability. At the outset, he underscores the importance of harmonizing the "three Es." Although he recognizes that expanding economic activities and growing world population damage the environment and deplete abundant natural resources, he focuses on global warming for its distinctive difference from other environmental issues. Its major cause, CO_2, inevitably arises from the use of fossil fuels, on which depends world economic development. Economic growth not only increases the environmental burden but also provides the conditions necessary to protect the environment. He notes that the effectiveness of a variety of environmental countermeasures depends on the availability of appropriate technologies. He also argues that the reduction of atmospheric CO_2 from the level accumulated over the past two centuries to the pre-Industrial Revolution level will not be made without the development of truly revolutionary technologies, which will take time. This concept of the "New Earth 21," a phased approach combining deployment of available technologies with development of new technologies, was presented at the White House Conference on Science and Economic Research Related to Global Change (17–18 April 1990). There were two subsequent developments. First, following the 1993 Tokyo Summit Economic Communiqué, the major industrialized countries and the secretariat of the International Energy Agency (IEA) and the OECD pursued the TREE (Technology Renaissance for Environment and Energy) concept to initiate international joint research projects. (This project was followed up by such meetings as the 1994 IEA/OECD High Level Meeting on Development and Deployment of Technologies to Respond to Global Climate Concerns.) Secondly, Okamatsu explains, Japan launched the Green Aid Plan to facilitate the transfer of existing environmental protection technologies to developing countries in a relatively short time. This plan consists of two steps: policy discussions between Japan and recipient countries with regard to energy and environmental policies, and the implementation of a comprehensive support plan. The second step is further composed of technical cooperation and demonstration projects. To facilitate the effective implementation of the Green Aid Plan, a Centre for Energy and Environmental Technologies was established in Bangkok. Okamatsu stresses the importance of dialogues with developing countries to support self-help. He concludes with a plea for cooperation by all humanity to respond to environmental challenges and indicates the possibility of expanding the Japan–USA bilateral cooperation framework to other countries.

Yoichi Kaya (chap. 4) also addresses the challenging issue of balancing the three "Es." He argues that the present environmental degradations result from violation of Herman Daly's three conditions for physical sustainability; i.e. consumption rates of renewable resources are higher than their recovery rates; consumption rates of non-renewable resources are higher than the rates of increase in the supply of renewable resources; and pollutant emissions are beyond nature's capacity to absorb them. Kaya also recognizes many barriers to the implementation of a strategy to recover sustainability, differing economic development being the most serious. He asks the developed and the developing countries to undertake different tasks. Developed countries should reduce their resource consumption through technological and social efforts substantially to improve energy- and resource-use efficiencies and through the introduction of clean resources such as solar energy. Developing countries should introduce energy- and resource-efficient technologies as long as they are economically viable for them as a "no regrets strategy." The feasibility of such a strategy depends very much on the future availability of technological measures with a large potential for improving energy efficiency, recycling resources, reducing pollution emissions, or producing biomass. He believes it is feasible and suggests serious feasibility studies of "heat cascading" and the production of recyclable products (such as automobiles and office equipment) as prime candidates. Kaya urges the developed countries to promote such innovative technologies both for their own sake and for developing countries, which would be enabled to buy energy and resources much more cheaply.

In summary, these three authors commonly underscore the needs for:

- a resolve to act by politicians or decision makers;
- an extended perspective
  - to consider the needs of future generations, and
  - to sustain efforts progressively to implement response actions and research for new initiatives, including technologies;
- international cooperation and coordinated action, reflecting sectoral and regional differences; and
- supplementation of the role of markets by government orientation of actions.

Part 2 discusses the energy-related climate change issue in the context of the global environment from two angles: first by looking at climate change from the scientific aspect; and secondly by examining deforestation and desertification in developing countries.

Tatsushi Tokioka (chap. 5) discusses the climate change predictions of climate models and their limitations, reflecting the assessment conducted by Working Group I of the Intergovernmental Panel on Climate Change (IPCC). The carbon dioxide and other greenhouse gases trap infra-red radiation from the earth to raise the earth's surface temperature by about 33K from 255K ($-18\,°C$) to 288K ($15\,°C$). Tokioka states that interactions among the earth's climate system components (the atmosphere, the ocean, the land surface, the cryosphere, and the biosphere) are complex and involve mutual dynamic, physical, chemical, and biospheric processes with differing time-scale patterns to reach a new equilibrium after being disturbed. The present understanding of those interactions is still limited.

Despite the divergence of modelling approaches, three-dimensional global atmosphere–ocean general circulation models (AOGCMs) serve the purpose of predicting transient, regional climate change. However, Tokioka points out the sensitivity of model predictions to the treatment of certain feedbacks. For example, different treatments of cloud feedbacks produce a spread of $1.9°–5.2°C$ in the average surface temperature increase under doubled CO_2 concentration in the atmosphere.

Climate models also indicate the importance of oceanic circulations in determining transient response and local climate change. For example, Manabe and Stouffer (1993) show marked weakening in the thermohaline circulation and thus marked changes in the thermal and dynamic structure of the ocean in the quadrupled-CO_2 climate, leading to a $7°C$ increase in the globally averaged surface temperature (William Cline also discusses this observation by Manabe and Stouffer in chap. 7). However, lack of observed data prevents full verification of such indications.

Tokioka notes that, despite the different predictions as regards the regional details of climate change, there is general agreement among model predictions on many larger-scale aspects, such as a warmer troposphere and cooler stratosphere, a spread of $1.5°–4.5°C$ in the average temperature increase under doubled CO_2, the dominant temperature increases being in winter at high latitude, acceleration of the hydrological cycle, such as a 3–15 per cent increase in global average precipitation and evaporation, and likely soil moisture decreases in the summer at mid-latitudes. He calls for further studies on processes that are currently inadequately understood, thus leading to uncertainties in predicting possible future climate change: clouds and other elements of the atmospheric water budget, ocean influences on the timing and pattern of climate change, land surface processes and feedbacks, sources and sinks of greenhouse gases and aerosols and their atmospheric concentrations, and polar ice sheets.

Radjendra K. Pachauri and Rajashree S. Kanetkar (chap. 6) look at deforestation and desertification, two of the major terrestrial degradations affecting the planet. They point out the difficulty arising from the imprecise or broad terminology (deforestation is not limited to the quantitative loss of vegetation) and the lack of available statistics showing their wide scope of severity. Deforestation, both in many tropical developing countries and in many developed countries, results from many factors: human population growth, agricultural expansion, and resettlement, especially shifting agriculture in developing countries; grazing and ranching (e.g. livestock owners forced into forest areas by the spread of irrigated and cultivated land in India);

exploitation of fuelwood and charcoal in tropical and subtropical woodlands; timber exploitation; plantation of tropical crop trees (rubber, oil palm, eucalyptus, etc.); atmospheric pollution, with a large volume of circumstantial evidence on the rain threat; and other human activities such as large dam constructions. Desertification too results from the human pressure of population increases in dry zones combined with a consequential growth in demand for natural resources for food, water, fuel, etc. that exceeds the carrying capacity of the land, and also from protracted drought in recent years, which has exacerbated the human pressure.

Pachauri and Kanetkar note that the environmental hazards of desertification and deforestation provide mutual feedbacks and have similar implications, involving changes in microclimates and ecology, adverse effects on agricultural productivity, human and livestock health, and economic activities such as eco-tourism, as well as higher resource requirements to combat these adverse impacts. They describe citizen action to counter deforestation and desertification such as the Chipko Movement in India. Recognizing the magnitude and complexity of desertification, they discuss the multiple benefits of forestry in the development of arid lands – for example, soil and water maintenance, livestock production, the provision of fuelwood, charcoal, and other forest products. They attribute the Indian deforestation to the progressive expansion of reserved forests and the emphasis on a few commercially valuable species such as Teak during British rule and under the institutions subsequently introduced after independence. They also discuss several Indian programmes to counter desertification and deforestation and the achievement of the Tata Energy Research Institute's Joint Forest Management Programme in the State of Haryana. They review international undertakings and note the limited success of the Plan of Action to Combat Desertification (PACD) adopted by the United Nations Conference on Desertification in 1977. They describe various efforts by multinational development agencies and philanthropic foundations to encourage management by small groups and to give them responsibility for forests in good condition as well as for degraded land.

Pachauri and Kanetkar have qualified confidence in the possibility of damage prevention and the reversal of damage that has already occurred. Strategies would have to include a recognition of the true value of finite natural resources, institutional responsibility for forest management linked with a matching accountability for results, and better knowledge of the extent, quality, and potential of resources.

They conclude that the success of programmes to counter deforestation and desertification will depend on the institutional arrangements, the dissemination of information, the creation of awareness, the development of assessment methodology, and adaptive research. These programmes must be fully integrated into programmes of socio-economic development, instead of being considered only as rehabilitation measures, and the affected populations will have to be fully involved in their planning and implementation.

Mohamed Kassas comments on the presentations by Tokioka and Pachauri and Kanetkar. Kassas first notes the interrelationship between climate change and land degradation. Apart from the role of deforestation in the global carbon cycle and its addition to the atmospheric load of carbon dioxide, land degradation impacts on climate will include: the effects of atmospheric dust from desert and desertified territories; the effects of impoverishment of plant cover on ground surface, energy budget, and the temperature of the near-surface air; reduced roughness of the surface as a result of reduced plant cover; reduced availability of organic particles in the atmosphere; and reduced rainfall. He urges the expansion of global sinks for carbon dioxide and related greenhouse gases through afforestation and revegetation and the reclamation of desertified areas. Kassas further points out the negative implications of the loss of biodiversity arising from both desertification and deforestation for the agricultural sector, medicines, and economic values. He differentiates "systemic" global environmental issues, whose causes may be local but whose effects are global, from "cumulative" issues, whose causes and effects are both global. He emphasizes the urgency of action on desertification, which is an actual threat, whereas the climate change issue is shrouded in uncertainties and its damaging impacts are likely to appear within 50–70 years.

In summary, the discussions in part 2 point to the uncertainties of analyses, involving a lack of data and complex interrelationships among the factors involved in environmental problems. As regards deforestation and desertification, it is their socio-economic factors and implications that are important.

Part 3 reviews several economic issues associated with the reduction of greenhouse gases, especially CO_2. These include the cost of emission reduction measures (e.g. a rate of a carbon tax), the macro-economic impacts of such reductions, and their sectoral or trade implications. The issues associated with the use of models in such analysis are also discussed.

William Cline (chap. 7) presents a cost–benefit analysis of green-house gas emissions using models and compares his findings with other studies. He first assesses the economic damage of climate change, then estimates the cost of reducing the emission of green-house gases and further examines the issue of the proper time dis-count rate. With the conventional doubling of the carbon dioxide concentration in relation to pre-industrial levels, for which the IPCC "best guess" estimate of equilibrium mean global warming was 2.5 °C, he places damage to the US economy in a range of 1–2 per cent of GDP, of which 0.3 per cent results from damage to agricul-ture. He compares his estimates with those of Titus (much larger potential damage in forest loss of 0.8 per cent of GDP) and Frank-hauser (a GDP loss of 1.3 per cent for the United States and an average of a modest 1.4 per cent globally). In the latter's case, a GDP-weighted measure masks the relatively higher damage in de-veloping countries.

Cline argues that, without policy intervention, much higher atmo-spheric concentrations (threefold by 2100 and ninefold by 2300) of carbon dioxide could occur, resulting in greater global warming (for example, 10 °C by 2300). Recent simulations of Princeton Uni-versity's Geophysical Fluid Dynamics Laboratory (GFDL) general circulation model by Manabe and Stouffer tend to confirm Cline's very-long-term baseline. They examined the effects of a quadrupling of pre-industrial carbon dioxide equivalent by 140 years from now, to which Tokioka also referred. With a modest degree of non-linearity (an exponent of 1.3) for damage, Cline expects very-long-term dam-age with 10 °C warming to cost between 6 and 12 per cent of GDP. He also notes that Manabe–Stouffer simulated a "catastrophe," namely, the shut-down of the ocean conveyer belt, of the flow of the Gulf Stream, and of the large reservoir function of the deep ocean as a sink for carbon dioxide, resulting from the complete cessation of the thermohaline circulation and from the deeper thermocline. How-ever, these catastrophic cases are not included in the subsequent analyses.

Cline surveys economic models on the costs of reducing carbon dioxide emissions. Their central range of results indicates some 2–3 per cent of gross world product (GWP) as a cost of reducing emis-sions by 50 per cent from their business-as-usual baseline by 2050. The OECD investigation of standardized simulations of several car-bon abatement models assumes, in an aggressive intervention scenario, an annual 2 per cent reduction from their business-as-usual time-path, such that by 2050 emissions would be at 70 per cent below baseline and by 2100 at 88 per cent below baseline. Costs range from 1.3 per cent of GDP (OECD's "GREEN" model) to about 2.6 per cent (Manne–Richels and Rutherford models). Despite the non-linearity of the costs of emission reductions, Cline argues, economic costs could be reduced by a two-phased approach, with more moderate action in the first decade pending further scientific confirmation and wider availability of technological alternatives, referring to studies of Manne–Richels and the US National Academy of Sciences. Economic costs could be also reduced by removing market failures, such as information costs and utility pricing distortions, and by using carbon tax revenues to correct distortions in fiscal structure.

Cline then examines the benefit–cost trade-off over time for an aggressive action programme to cut global carbon emissions by one-third and to hold them constant thereafter. He also distributes risk weights with 0.375, 0.125, and 0.5 for the high-damage, low-damage, and central cases, respectively, to capture risk aversion. He concludes his aggressive action programme justified despite higher net costs early in the time-horizon. He compares his analysis with Nordhaus's Dynamic Integrated Climate-Economy (DICE) model, which finds net social costs of 0.7 per cent of discounted future consumption resulting from freezing emissions at their current level. He attributes the major difference to the use of the time discount rate, which he sets to zero, whereas Nordhaus uses 3 per cent. Adjusting this and another difference in an elasticity of marginal utility, Cline gets a DICE estimate of about 50 per cent cutback from the baseline by 2100, much bigger than the 14 per cent cut identified by Nordhaus. The remaining gap between Cline and Nordhaus could arise from such factors as a higher marginal cost curve for carbon reduction in DICE, incorporation of the risk of higher-damage cases, and imposition of a backstop-technology ceiling in abatement costs. Cline uses DICE to identify the shadow price of carbon (optimal carbon tax), which rises from US$45 per tonne of carbon equivalent (tC) initially to US$84/tC by 2025, US$133 by 2055, and US$243 by 2105.

Considering the policy implications of these comparisons, Cline finds a convergence of the various analyses on action in the first decade, i.e. a cut-back of 10–15 per cent from baseline emissions and a carbon tax rate of US$20–25/tC. He recognizes, however, the sharper divergence in policy prescriptions beyond the first decade. Cline calls for intensive scientific research during this initial decade, to narrow discrepancies among general circulation models on cloud feedback,

9

etc., and on the very-long-term prospects for warming and damage. He feels that economists' insistence on discount rates has discouraged scientists from looking at horizons beyond a century. He also advocates much more extensive analysis of the benefits and costs of greenhouse gas abatement for developing countries. Although it may be appropriate to concentrate abatement efforts in the industrialized countries in the first phase, in the long run the seriousness of global warming will require a ceiling on emissions in developing countries.

Akihiro Amano (chap. 8) presents, first, a comparison of various model simulations of the magnitudes of the macroeconomic costs of limiting carbon dioxide emissions, second, an examination of the side-effects of abatement measures, particularly the international implications, and, thirdly, estimates of the macroeconomic costs associated with optimal response approaches. He compares four models studied in the OECD comparative studies – the Manne–Richels model (MR), Rutherford's Carbon Rights Trade Model (CRTM), the Edmonds–Reilly model (ER), and OECD's GREEN model – together with six Japanese models (Goto, Ban, Mori, Yamaji, Ito, and Yamazaki). As Cline mentioned, the four models used in the OECD exercise produce carbon dioxide emission reductions of 2 per cent per annum from the baseline, using the same set of exogenous assumptions and the same methods of perturbing the system. Their results are fairly similar, especially for the developed countries, with two notable exceptions: larger impacts in the longer term in the ER model owing to a smaller role of backstop technologies; and smaller effects in CRTM owing to the effects of emission trading. They suggest, in general, a 0.02–0.05 per cent decrease in GDP for a 1 per cent reduction in carbon emissions in industrialized countries and corresponding carbon tax rates of some US$2–10/tC. Despite somewhat diverse results for non-OECD countries, relatively larger output effects are observed and fairly low carbon taxes are seen for the former USSR and China because of their subsidized low energy prices. Whereas two similarly constructed Japanese models (Goto and Ban) give comparable outcomes to those in the OECD study, other Japanese models, which differ in type from those in the OECD study, produce substantially larger estimates. Besides the difference in the nature of the models, temporary deviations from full employment caused by higher energy prices and a lack of tax revenue recycling in the short-run models could explain the difference.

Amano concedes that actual policy may not follow the suggestions of model simulations because of many side-effects. Among such side-effects, Amano considers that appropriate policy instruments could accommodate domestic regressive distributional implications. He therefore focuses on the implications for international competitiveness. First, uneven internalization of external environmental costs may induce "trade-diversion effects." He notes a Hoeller and Wallin study showing fairly large differences in implicit carbon tax rates among major OECD countries and expects more efficient energy and carbon uses by eliminating these distortions. Secondly, he examines the issue of "carbon leakages": high carbon taxes introduced in some countries could depress world energy prices and increase energy consumption and carbon emissions in countries without carbon taxes. Whereas Rutherford estimates 100 per cent offsetting carbon emission increases from non-participating countries in response to a unilateral OECD 3 per cent reduction in CO_2 emission increases, the OECD GREEN model postulates moderate leakage of 2.5 per cent and Manne shows overall results falling in between. Amano concludes that carbon leakages may be at most a medium-term issue. He also suggests that disaggregated analyses of industries could reveal the differential burden of adjustments among industries, and notes the almost negligible effects of tax exemption of energy-intensive industries in terms of leakage rates and of changes in sectoral output in an OECD GREEN study. Third, he refers to the possible impact of an international carbon tax scheme on terms of trade in favour of carbon-energy-importing countries. The OECD GREEN model has shown such effects on real incomes of non-negligible magnitudes.

Amano then examines the issue of the social costs of carbon dioxide emissions. He also compares the aforementioned analyses of Nordhaus and of Cline. With a discount rate of 0.5 per cent, Amano indicates that Nordhaus's estimate of the social costs of carbon emissions would come closer to Cline's estimate. He argues, however, that differing discount rates can explain only a part of their differences, owing to some cancelling effects, and that climate and damage parameters also affect the nature of the optimal paths. However, these would not justify optimal abatement paths of immediate emission stabilization at current levels. Some other social valuation functions incorporating much broader non-market values or taking a serious view of uncertain, catastrophic situations in the distant future will be needed.

John Ferriter (chap. 9) discusses possible energy market responses to carbon taxes, energy efficiency standards, and other measures, drawing on the results of the IEA's World Energy Outlook Model.

11

His presentations focus on energy market impacts, including regional and sectoral ones. He also points out the historical energy use and price data constraints and further needs for energy market analyses, especially in the residential/commercial and transport sectors. Ferriter compares four scenarios: a reference scenario, in which energy demand grows by 48 per cent from 1990 to 2010 in the world and by 28 per cent in the OECD region, and annual carbon emissions rise by 46 per cent in the world and by 28 per cent in the OECD region; two OECD-wide carbon tax cases with annual gradual increases to reach US$100 and US$300 per tonne of carbon emitted, respectively; and an accelerated energy efficiency improvement case.

The 2010 OECD level of carbon dioxide emissions compared with the 1990 level is higher by 17 per cent in the US$100 tax case, and slightly higher (by less than 10 per cent) in both the US$300 tax case and the efficiency-driven scenario (EDS). But the 2010 levels under the two tax cases are lower by 9 per cent and by 17 per cent than the reference case, respectively. Regionally, Ferriter points out, primary coal and gas prices and the taxes on energy products are lower in North America than in other OECD regions so that a given level of carbon tax leads to larger percentage increases in end-use prices in the former. In all three sensitivity cases, over 50 per cent of the OECD emissions reductions occur in North America, about one-third in Europe, and the rest in the Pacific region. The EDS is more effective at reducing energy use than the US$300 carbon tax, although the US$300 case is slightly more effective than the EDS in achieving emissions reductions. Sectorally, the two tax cases give roughly the same proportions of emissions reductions: changes in power generation provide some 50 per cent of emissions reductions; final fuel use in industry some 25 per cent; the transport and residential/commercial sectors the rest. The EDS differs significantly in its sectoral effects from the tax cases. Changes in the electricity sector account for some 55 per cent; the transport and domestic sectors account for 40 per cent of the reduction in emissions from final energy use; and industry the rest. One of the reasons for the insensitivity of transport and domestic energy demand to high-level taxes is the relatively modest impact of the taxes on the actual prices paid by consumers.

Ferriter cautions against generalizing about the effects of CO_2 reduction policies on energy commodity markets, which differ from other world commodity markets because of their specific characteristics and factors, such as the role of oil as the price leader, the importance of regional markets, and present and future prospects of government control and subsidies. On specific markets, he notes uncertainties in the coal market, including disproportionately greater demand reductions resulting from further fuel switching, lower pre-tax coal prices inducing coal demand and emission increases outside the OECD region, and possible offsetting policies by large coal-producing countries. He also notes uncertainties about oil-exporting countries' reactions, possible infrastructure constraints on greater gas use, the impacts of lower-priced spot cargoes on the Pacific LNG markets, the stability of hydrocarbon supplies from Russia and other newly independent states, and possible moves away from coal and nuclear in the former COMECON region.

Ferriter lists a series of areas for further study, including further elaboration of the IEA model to incorporate technical possibilities, the use of several different analytical approaches, linkages with other modelling efforts, and in-depth analyses of questions such as the distribution of the costs of carbon taxes among parties, possible OPEC reactions, the implications of historical relations between crude oil prices and oil product prices, and the effect of changing government interventions. He concludes that a US$300/tC tax might be able to re-duce carbon dioxide emissions nearly to 1990 levels in 2010, although such high-level taxes have not been seriously discussed in any inter-national forums; that institutional and transitional issues require careful consideration on a national and regional basis; that a mix of policies may be the most effective approach to reducing emissions; that a hedging strategy would contain a balance of measures to improve energy-use efficiency and a heavier emphasis on R&D to make renewable energy sources competitive earlier; that realistic and palatable policies are needed not only for the OECD but also for relations between the OECD and the rest of the world; and that much reform of local and regional energy policies is required within countries.

Lawrence R. Klein warns about the uncertainties associated with statistical model exercises on environmental issues. The models are based on meagre data samples, often with large measurement errors, so that the estimated confidence intervals are quite large. The main sources of error and uncertainty result from the estimation of the rate and volume of emissions from prevailing technologies; reactions of consumers and producers to price changes in energy use; a flawed global database; and effects of climate and other natural conditions that are not well understood. Klein calls for findings to be described in general terms with both point values and regions of uncertainty.

This could be done, first, by maximum use of statistical methods for the estimation of standard errors of extrapolation or projection, and, second, by the calculation of stochastic simulations of the associated models. A minimal first or preliminary step should be to make a sensitivity analysis of the effect of assigning very different values, in a plausible range, to key parameters of the system. One-at-a-time estimates of different parameters should be avoided because of mutual correlations among many of them. However, use of the "error-cancellation" phenomenon can save efforts for the examination of deviations from baseline cases. This process will help to restrain the inherent degree of uncertainty. Klein, further, points out that the very long time taken by many environmental phenomena to reach serious magnitudes entails growing uncertainty and errors of extrapolation.

Warwick McKibbin comments on the papers by Cline, Amano, and Ferriter and also presents results of the analysis of a G-Cubed model jointly developed with Peter Wilcoxen. He agrees with Cline's arguments on the need for more aggressive action to combat carbon dioxide emissions, the failure of standard calculations of costs and benefits to recognize the potential for a major disaster, and his policy prescription for the next decade to introduce a carbon tax of US$20–25/tC along with more investment in scientific research. He disagrees with his estimate of the cost-effectiveness of planting trees to absorb CO_2 and his criticism of a 3 per cent time discount rate. McKibbin attaches greater importance to the extent of baseline emissions, the existence of backstop technologies, and the mode of recycling tax revenues in analyses. He agrees with many points raised by Amano, including the sources of differences between short-run Japanese models and models in the OECD study, the relevance of tax revenue recycling and trade diversion, and the need for a model with disaggregated sectoral detail. However, he differs from Amano who infers that a 1 per cent reduction in CO_2 requires a carbon tax of US$2–10/tC. McKibbin questions Ferriter's model results because of a lack of feedback from the change in energy prices after tax to aggregate GDP and then back to energy demand. He also finds a carbon tax of US$300/tC by 2010 as the stabilizing level for the United States to be higher than other model results. He suspects that the lack of feedback in the model causes a higher estimate for a tax. McKibbin then presents his G-Cubed model, a multi-sector (12 sectors) dynamic general equilibrium model with seven economic regions, and some results for the impact of a permanent US$15/tC tax. The simulations are made on the assumed introduction of a tax in 1993 through 2022 and on five alternative assumptions about tax revenue recycling (deficit reduction; a lump-sum rebate to households; an investment tax credit to all sectors except housing; a cut in the household income tax rate; and a cut in the corporate tax rate). GNP impacts are different: a lump-sum rebate will hold GNP below baseline well beyond 2022, whereas an investment tax credit will restore it to baseline by 1995. Each case reduces emissions effectively. McKibbin concludes that there need not be a linear relationship between carbon emissions and GNP because of sectoral substitution possibilities plus the differential impact across sectors of policies. On leakage, he finds that a unilateral US carbon tax reduces US emissions by about 15 per cent less than when all OECD countries impose a tax. He concludes that there is evidence of some offset from unilateral action but nowhere the complete offset suggested by Amano.

Kenji Yamaji makes three comments on the three presentations. His first comment is that the varying evaluations of the macro-economic costs of a carbon tax depend on several factors, such as time-horizons, the type of model, and the treatment of tax revenues. His view is that the general equilibrium type model and a more explicit optimization model tend to produce a smaller economic cost than simulation models, judging from actual past performances. He also regards the higher marginal CO_2 emission reduction costs as a factor influencing the higher cost estimate in his Japanese simulation. His second comment concerns the policy implications of integrated economic analysis. Although great uncertainties associated with climate change may make an optimal control path very close to the business-as-usual cases, the choice of discount rates and a longer time-horizon could make CO_2 emission reductions more optimal. He also points out the possibility of a catastrophic positive feedback and of lower cost estimates arising from the inclusion of eventual technological development. His third point concerns interregional equity and the likely leakage effect in non-participating countries associated with unilateral emissions reductions by developed countries. He also notes that joint implementation has mostly been discussed in qualitative terms, not in quantitative terms. He hopes more analyses on the global perspective will reduce pessimistic views of abatement.

Part 3 also includes an appendix by Hung-yi Li, Peter Pauly, and Kenneth Ruffing examining the macroeconomic effects of CO_2 emission reductions with the project LINK world econometric model. Li et al. find two problems in most simulations of the impact of carbon taxes using macroeconomic models and energy models. First, macroeconomic models treat the level of economic activity as an exogenous variable and energy models do so for energy demand. Second, many models assume a constant pattern of international trade and exogenous energy prices. These limit the models' ability to evaluate a carbon tax because they fail fully to capture the effects of a carbon tax on international trade and on the economic activity of countries with and without such a tax and the quantity of emissions abated by the carbon tax. The simulation using the world econometric model of Project LINK with the trace gas accounting system (TGAS) aims at endogenously generating these impacts of a carbon tax.

The LINK model is a multi-country model linking separate national econometric models by means of models of merchandise trade, exchange rates, and commodity prices. The LINK baseline projects an annual increase in overall CO_2 emissions from the G7 countries of 3.3 per cent (cumulatively 30 per cent) from 1993 to 2000, with annual growth in their aggregate GNP of 2.7 per cent. With the introduction of a carbon tax, whose rate was initially US$30/tC to reach US$100/tC in 2000, the G7 emissions would be 8 per cent lower than the baseline in 2000 with a 2 per cent reduction in GNP. Among the G7 countries, the percentage reductions in emissions vary from 3 per cent in Japan to 11 per cent in the United States. The estimated level of tax required to induce significant emission reductions appears higher than in other studies. Li et al. then present a simulation of a uniform US$40 carbon tax with an endogenous oil price response, where the oil price will be about US$3 per barrel (bbl) below the original scenario's by 2000 and the emission reductions are lower by 1.5–4.7 per cent. They conclude that a unilateral G7 carbon tax would reduce carbon dioxide emissions in these countries, with varying effects on non-OECD emissions ranging from a slight reduction to increases up to 15 per cent; that a tax induces a medium-term reduction in the real price of oil by some US$2/bbl; that reduced oil prices positively stimulate G7 economies, reducing their short- to medium-term GNP loss; that the trade balance improves in oil-importing G7 countries at the expense of G7 oil exporters and non-participating countries; and that the results are sensitive to assumptions about the strategic behaviour of energy producers, particularly of OPEC. They consider that the elimination or reduction of the negative activity effects of a carbon tax is possible through the recycling of revenues and parallel stabilizing policies.

The discussions in part 3 suggest the following common findings: uncertainties surrounding economic simulations of environmental impacts; different simulation results from differences in models and assumptions (e.g. social discount rates, technological progress, tax revenue recycling, energy–economy interactions); the need for more data collection and analytical work to reduce uncertainties; the desirability of phased approaches; policy ineffectiveness or "leakages" owing to market distortions, uneven internalization of externalities, and uncoordinated global policy actions.

Part 4 deals with technological potential options and perspective for preventing climate change.

Chihiro Watanabe (chap. 10) discusses the role of technologies in improving the interface between energy and economy, with reference to Japanese experience. He emphasizes the role of technology in replacing limited resources in order to achieve sustainable development and presents the New Sunshine Programme of Japan's Ministry of International Trade and Industry (MITI) from this perspective. He demonstrates the parallel movements of economic development and energy supply requirements from 1880 to the early 1970s, which is in contrast to their decoupling after the two oil crises of the 1970s. He also compares energy efficiency improvements with the rather stable materials intensity in the manufacturing sector. He attributes energy efficiency improvements largely to oil price increases and technology stocks rather than to autonomous energy efficiency improvements (AEEI). He sees the substitution of technology (an unconstrained factor) for energy (a constrained factor) as improving energy efficiency.

Watanabe states that the heavy concentration of material-intensive and energy-intensive industries and population in Japan's Pacific belt area resulted from the expansion of the heavy and chemical industries in the 1960s and caused serious environmental pollution problems. *MITI's Vision for the 1970s* proposed a shift toward a knowledge-intensive industrial structure by the substitution of technology for energy and materials. A concept of "Industry–Ecology" emerged in 1972 aimed at optimally balancing the ecosystem by creating an environmentally friendly energy system. The first oil crisis confirmed the need for a policy to solve basic energy problems through R&D on new and clean energy technology. The Sunshine Project was thus created in 1974, followed by the Moonlight Project for R&D on energy conservation technology in 1978. Later, the Global Environmental Technology Programme was initiated. However, declining oil prices and the upsurge of the Japanese economy (the "bubble economy") discouraged energy efficiency improvements and increased environmental stresses such as carbon dioxide emission increases, which were exacerbated by reduced R&D efforts, in particular for environmental protection and energy. Watanabe claims that this prompted MITI to integrate the three previous energy R&D programmes into a New Sunshine Programme, encouraging more efficient and effective use and mutual supplementation of technologies such as catalysts, hydrogen, high-temperature materials and sensors for technologies for new energy, energy conservation, and environmental protection. The new programme entails acceleration of R&D on innovative technologies, international collaboration on large-scale R&D projects, and cooperative R&D on appropriate technologies for technology transfer. Watanabe suggests that the Japanese experience and ongoing efforts would provide useful suggestions concerning the role of technology in the pursuit of a sustainable development path.

Thomas Johansson (chap. 11) discusses the potential role of renewable-energy sources in meeting future energy needs with reduced carbon dioxide emissions. He reviews the recent progress in renewable-energy technologies and systems, which have benefited from developments in electronics, biotechnology, materials sciences, and other energy areas such as gas turbine combustion advanced by jet engines. He also notes the advantages of the small size of most renewable-energy equipment in faster, easier, and less costly applications. Johansson then presents a renewable-intensive global energy scenario for the years 2025 and 2050, assuming the removal of market barriers by comprehensive national policies. The assumed energy demand levels for electricity and for solid, liquid, and gaseous fuels were the same as those in the IPCC's Working Group II's high economic growth and accelerated policy case. Further, the scenario was subject to conditions allowing sustainable biomass production, land-use restriction for wind power, limited penetration of intermittent power generation such as wind, solar–thermal, and photovoltaic power, and environmental and social constraints on hydro potential. Johansson postulates global renewable resources consumption equivalent to 318 exajoules (EJ) per year of fossil fuels by 2050, a comparable rate to total present world energy consumption. With this, he claims, the world could expect to have adequate supplies of fossil fuels well into the twenty-first century. He cautions, however, that the transition to renewables will not occur at this pace if existing market conditions remain unchanged. He calls for the removal of subsidies artificially reducing the price of fuels competing with renewables, policy instruments to ensure full-cost pricing, including environmental and other externalities, governmental R&D supports for renewable-energy technologies, etc. He stresses the need in the decades ahead to frame economic policies simultaneously satisfying both socio-economic development and environmental challenges.

William Chandler, Marc Ledbetter, Igor Bashmakov, and Jessica Hamburger (chap. 12) discuss the energy-efficiency potential in Eastern Europe, the former Soviet Union, and China and possible policy measures to materialize such potential. They recognize that energy-efficiency technology transfer is a high priority in cooperation programmes for these countries, whose energy intensity ranks high by any standard. They emphasize the importance of market restructuring supplemented by such measures as market-pull programmes and integrated resource planning (IRP).

In reviewing the energy-efficiency prospects, they note that low energy efficiency constrains economic growth in Eastern Europe and that the countries of the region have had varying degrees of success in lowering energy intensity. Their energy-efficiency potential amounts to 15–25 per cent of current energy use, or 4 EJ. The former Soviet Union consumes three-quarters as much energy as the United States to produce only 30–50 per cent as much economic value. Its high energy intensity resulted from its reliance on heavy industry and energy-intensive materials as well as outdated technologies. Its potential energy saving could exceed 15 EJ with positive macroeconomic and environmental impacts (e.g. avoided investments up to 1.8 trillion roubles and 10 per cent reductions in atmospheric pollutant emissions). China, the world's third-largest energy consumer, is characterized by a dominance in industrial energy use, high energy intensity (twice the average level of other developing countries and three times that of Western Europe), and low per capita consumption. Even considering gains in energy efficiency and the initiation of energy-efficiency measures in addition to price reforms and ownership changes, the efficiency potential must be viewed in terms of a reduction in demand growth from a baseline and could amount to a cut in demand to 50 EJ from a projected level of 75 EJ in 2025. Chandler et al. note many energy-efficient technologies available to these countries, such as combined-cycle and gas-turbine system generation of electricity.

For policy options, Chandler et al. recommend Eastern Europe to give priority to such areas as the application of IRP, energy-efficiency loans to consumers, building domestic capability in the manufacture and installation of energy-efficient equipment and materials, energy-efficiency labelling of appliances, and more attractive public transportation. For the former Soviet Union, their suggestions include the promotion of competition through the regulation of monopolistic utilities, international financial assistance for energy-efficiency measures, and IRP in the utility sector. For China, facilitating joint ventures through business information exchange and demonstration projects would contribute to its economic development and environmental protection. Chandler et al. conclude that technology transfer to these countries requires significant new efforts in the energy sector, such as establishing market prices and freer markets for energy, adopting cost-effective energy-efficiency policies and programmes, satisfying new energy demand in the medium term with natural gas, and developing renewable energy supplies over the long term.

Nebojša Nakićenović (chap. 13) observes the long-term dynamic transformation and structural change of the energy system towards less carbon intensity and expects this trend to continue into the next century. Although global consumption of primary energy and energy-related emissions and other environmental effects have been growing during past decades, he notes declines in both CO_2 emissions per unit of energy and energy intensity per unit of value added in most countries. Nakićenović further examines the carbon intensity trends of primary energy, final energy, and energy conversion for selected countries. He observes declining trends in the carbon intensity of the first two factors and mixed trends in the last, i.e. increased intensity in the developing countries and decreasing intensity in the industrialized countries. He also notes some degree of decarbonization arising from lower energy intensities. However, to offset absolute increases in emissions, structural changes in energy systems towards carbon-free energy sources should complement decarbonization and lower energy intensity. Nakićenović notes the role of natural gas as a bridge to a non-fossil-fuel energy future and as an element in a minimum-regret option.

In summary, part 4 shows that technology has a role to play in offering wider future energy options for sustainable development. Past history also demonstrates the potential for more efficient and cleaner energy use and for technology transfer. But these technological improvements also depend on non-technological factors such as energy prices, freer markets, and other institutional and policy elements.

Part 5 discusses the energy challenges faced by developing countries. Two of the presentations address the issues of rural energy, while the third paper looks at the implications of growing energy demand in the developing world.

Kunio Takase (chap. 14) discusses the crisis of rural energy, with a special emphasis on fuelwood, in developing countries on the basis of the ongoing four-year study of "Global Environment and Agricultural Resource Management" entrusted by the Japanese Ministry of Agriculture, Forestry, and Fisheries to the International Development Centre of Japan (IDCJ). The IDCJ believes technical innovation, financial resources, and implementing capacity, supported by political will and people's participation, to be minimum requirements to prevent environmental destruction and to maintain compatibility between development and environment. Takase reviews world forest resources and notes that in recent years forest areas have slightly increased in developed countries and have decreased in developing countries. The present rate of afforestation is judged inadequate. Whereas industrial wood use accounts for 80 per cent of harvesting in developed countries, fuelwood use accounts for the same ratio in developing countries. Despite local differences in fuelwood demand, the present forest areas in developing countries fall short of satisfying the demand of the growing population in developing countries. Takase examines the potential of more efficient use of fuelwood (e.g. by improved cooking stoves) and alternative energy sources (charcoal, renewables, fuelwood thermal power generation) and identifies their respective constraints. He also identifies basic problems for sustainable fuelwood management, which include lack of reliable information and data, conflict of interests among parties, and competing land-use demand. He calls for a comprehensive international collaborative research programme with a mix of short-term and long-term development strategies. He presents a scenario for narrowing the gap between rich and poor countries in GNP per capita by 2040, because poverty alleviation is the first step to solving environmental problems, including the crisis of rural energy in developing countries. In conclusion, he suggests the need for a new philosophy of a "strategically planned market economy."

Anthony Churchill (chap. 15) discusses the energy production and consumption patterns of the developing world and the resulting implications. He challenges the assumptions of the "consensus view," such as held in the World Energy Council's Commission's Report, *Energy for Tomorrow's World*. He argues that increased energy efficiency resulting from a more market-oriented pricing structure and other policies could increase rather than reduce energy demand, as the increased energy efficiency reduces the service price and could increase the quantity consumed. Further, as most empirical studies suggest, income elasticity of energy demand ranging from 1.5 to 3.0 is likely to apply in developing countries. Demand for energy-intensive services is likely to be income elastic at the stage of growing income in developing countries. Even assuming modest income and price elasticity and a conservative rate of growth, developing countries' energy demand could be much larger than contemplated in a high scenario in the "consensus view." Such high energy demand growth may not be constrained by either supply or financing constraints. The reserve base of coal and oil, cost reductions from the combination of improved efficiency and technology, and emerging substitutes would satisfy demand at prices not too different from today's price. The challenge in finance exists in mobilizing the resources that economic growth and appropriate policies will generate. A fundamental restructuring of institutions necessary to mobilize domestic resources is taking place. Churchill is optimistic about dealing with environmental pollution except for greenhouse gas emissions, for which there is no immediate solution. He argues that, if global warming proves to be a serious problem, it should be dealt with using tomorrow's technology, guided by the historical evidence of continuous technological changes. In most developing countries, however, the greatest benefits will come from using already tried and true technologies.

Jike Yang (chap. 16) deals with the challenge of Chinese rural energy development. First, he notes the energy consumption patterns of rural households, such as high biomass fuel consumption (one-third of total energy consumption in China), high energy intensity in terms of agricultural output (close to heavy industry's average), low heat conversion efficiency of biomass burning, and adverse economic and ecological effects of biomass burning. Corrective actions include the greater use of straw- and fuelwood-saving stoves and of biogas digesters, the development of fuelwood forestry, rotating use of plains land for crops, forestry, and forage grasses, and greater use of solar energy. He recognizes the following issues as being relevant to the implications of growing township enterprises for rural economies and environment: low energy consumption in agriculture, due to a high dependence on manual and animal labour and to low consumption of commercial fuels, higher energy intensity of township enterprises' consumption, the value of low-energy intensive household handicraft industry, and growing labour inflows from rural areas into cities, increasing energy supply shortages in city industry which would also keep rural energy demand unfilled, the value of emerging service industries in towns absorbing excess labour, the potential energy output of human and animal power, and the benefits of small-scale hydropower plants. Yang then describes the benefits of energy-efficiency improvements and the use of renewable sources: the reduced use of synthetic fertilizers, the maintenance of soil quality, increased rural incomes from backyard-farming, amelioration of the energy shortage, the development of rural agro-industry, the dispersion of culture and industry from urban centres, reduced energy intensity, and other socio-economic, environmental, and resource benefits. Yang concludes that, despite good starts in the development of renewable energies in rural areas, much more work has to be done on sustainable land development.

Yujiro Hayami, in commenting on Takase's presentation, stresses the importance of designing institutions that provide incentives to local people to conserve natural resources in developing countries and cites two examples of forest conservation programmes in South-East Asia. The first case is a programme to privatize forest land management in Viet Nam by transferring management from co-operatives to individual households. The positive effects so far observed indicate the system's potential for solving the difficult problem of how to achieve socially optimum conservation of forest resources while producing current income and employment for local people not only in Viet Nam but also in other developing economies. The opposite case of institutional design miscalculating local people's incentive mechanisms is a reforestation programme in the Philippines where the payment of a fee per seedling planted was used to mobilize local people. Despite initial speedy reforestation, the local people's fear about eventual unemployment drove them to destroy the seedlings. Hayami underscores the importance of a full understanding of human behaviour and incentive systems in local communities.

In summary, part 5 notes the increase in demand for energy, in particular in rural areas, which could exceed the present high estimates. Afforestation and biomass energy can play an important role alongside efficiency improvements. The need for institutions that properly motivate local initiatives is emphasized.

Part 6 addresses issues of long-term energy strategies in support of sustainable development. The papers are by prominent scholars and experts from developing countries.

José Goldemberg (chap. 17) discusses the possibility of developing countries' adopting leapfrogging strategies to delink environmental degradation, energy demand increases, and economic growth. He recognizes that the historically observed linkage of economic growth and energy consumption growth and pollution production has been broken in OECD countries through the saturation of consumer goods markets, shifts towards less energy-intensive materials and more efficient fuels, and the adoption of more energy-efficient technologies. Such delinking has important implications for developing countries whose economic growth has yet to occur. Goldemberg observes that energy intensity initially grew with economic growth, reached a peak, and then declined in many industrialized countries but also that the latecomers had lower peaks than their predecessors. Energy intensity in most developing countries is rising (although it is declining in China). The introduction of energy-efficient technologies earlier in the development process, or technological leapfrogging, would decouple energy growth from economic growth, thereby avoiding greater environmental stress in developing countries. Goldemberg notes mixed success in delinking GDP growth and pollution increases, e.g. successes in emissions of particulates, lead, and sulphur oxides, and failure in the case of nitrogen oxides. Greater progress in the future will require phased and progressive strategies such as those advocated earlier by Okamatsu and Watanabe.

Amulya Reddy (chap. 18) also proposes an energy strategy compatible with sustainable development. He suggests that the achievement of reduced pollutant emissions is compatible with economic and social development through a combination of energy efficiency and greater use of advanced biomass-based fuels. Reddy recognizes the present industrial countries' large contribution to greenhouse gas emissions and the rapidly increasing contribution of developing countries. He also points out the difference in the nature of the contribution to environmental degradation of the poor and the élites within developing countries. Despite the lack of precise data on the breakdown of emissions by income group, he suspects that the poor contribute marginally. He also supports a step-by-step environmental approach, starting with local problems, then gradually tackling wider regional, national, and global problems.

Reddy notes that energy systems in developing countries involve environmental, capital, and equity crises. These crises and the environment–development conflict stem from the conventional energy paradigm based on the energy–GDP correlation. Reddy argues that the new challenge to the energy systems of developing countries is to decouple GDP growth and energy consumption by identifying and implementing a least-cost mix of saving and generation options for increasing energy services, particularly for the poor. He proposes a development-focused end-use-oriented service-directed (DEFENDUS) approach. He illustrates this with three examples. First, he cites the Pura Community Biogas Plants system in India, which provided safer water and better illumination as well as economic and environmental benefits. He then describes a DEFENDUS scenario that led to the shelving of the Long-Range Planning of Power Projects (LRPPP) by the Karnataka State government for 1986–2000. The scenario was based on a mix of efficiency measures and decentralized electricity generation requiring a final installed capacity of 4,000 MW, an annual bill of US$618 million, and lower environmental impacts, compared with LRPPP projections of 9,400 MW and US$3.3 billion, respectively. Reddy's third illustration is a proposed strategy for reducing Indian oil consumption – which is a major source of India's balance-of-payments deficits – by a combination of more efficient use of oil products, shifting passenger traffic from private vehicles to public transportation, home electrification, the removal of subsidies on diesel and kerosene, and the replacement of oil with non-oil fuels, particularly those derived from biomass. Reddy underscores two crucial basic needs of poor households: efficient energy sources for lighting and for cooking. He concludes that the pursuit of development objectives via energy-efficient strategies is tantamount to addressing local and global environmental concerns.

Fengqi Zhou (chap. 19) describes the main challenges for China in balancing the needs for economic development and energy and protection of the environment. He refers to China's transition from a low-efficiency and highly centralized planned economy to a high-efficiency market economy to establish a socialistic market system with Chinese characteristics. Assuming GDP annual growth of 8–9 per cent and a reduction in energy–GDP elasticity from 0.56 in the 1980s to 0.45 in 2000, China's total primary energy consumption will grow from 987 Mtce (million tons of coal equivalent) in 1990 to 1,450 Mtce in 2000. Zhou considers that the main environmental problem in China is urban air pollution (particulates and SO_2), largely caused by coal use, as well as soil erosion caused by biomass overconsumption. He regards energy-efficiency improvements as the best means of harmonizing the development of energy and protection of the environment and notes the continuous reduction in energy intensity, which needs to decline further by at least 35–40 per cent by 2000. Zhou expects the importance of coal as China's main energy source to continue and views the clean coal technologies as the best way to reduce pollutant emissions.

Hoesung Lee, in commenting on part 6, agrees with the energy-efficient growth path involving technological leapfrogging for developing countries, as suggested by Goldemberg and Reddy. His comments pertain to the practical barriers to achieving this strategy. In particular, he argues that subsidized energy costs lead to an energy-intensive industrial structure. Lee recognizes the difficulties of removing energy subsidies because they involve complex economic, social, and political interdependencies. On the basis of Korean experience, he calls for the supplementary role of greater competition and energy-efficiency regulations to encourage higher efficiency in a situation of low energy prices.

Part 6 thus presents the possibility that developing countries can avoid the bitter experience of the industrialized countries. Improved energy efficiency could be achieved through technology leapfrogging, but there would have to be the political determination to set prices that reflect market levels.

Conclusions

During the conference several issues were raised by many, if not all, speakers. These are listed below to serve as a summary of the main discussions:

- Energy demand and the associated environmental burdens are likely to increase with the growing emergence of the present-day developing countries.
- Carbon dioxide emissions will increase and the standard case of the doubling of CO_2 concentrations is not likely to be the equilibrium situation. Concentrations could increase to a much higher level.
- The introduction of high carbon taxes alone may not be effective in reducing carbon dioxide emissions to a desired level.
- Many methodological questions remain to be addressed. The development of methodologies, including climate models and econometric models, is important, and the results of differing approaches should be carefully assessed. There remain many analytical issues that require further research.
- Deforestation and desertification are also important global environmental issues, which are directly or indirectly associated with energy-related environmental issues.

- On the other hand, technology options to contribute to environmental protection are available at present. The full technological potential is unlikely to be utilized in the real world. The differing countries and sectors will have differing technological options and capabilities. Technology leapfrogging opportunities exist for the developing countries in addressing their environmental and energy challenges.
- There are differing potentials for alleviating environmental problems, for example depending on the type of environmental question (as illustrated by Professor Goldemberg).
- Future technological developments and their market acceptance will be needed.
- Obstacles to the achievement of full technical potential include:
  - distorted energy and other prices;
  - failure to internalize social and environmental concerns; and
  - technological drawbacks and lack of information.
- The removal of these barriers or obstacles will require political resolve or courage, although their specific forms will differ in some circumstances or be the same on other occasions.
- The role of analysts will be to prepare the basic information to enable policy or decision makers to make sound decisions.

Reference

Manabe, S. and R. J. Stouffer. 1993. "Century-scale effects of increased atmospheric CO_2 on the ocean–atmosphere system." *Nature* 364, 15 July: 215–218.

Part 1
Global issues and response strategies: Overview

2

Past issues and new problems: A plea for action

Giuseppe M. Sfligiotti

Much has been written, and possibly more has been said, in recent years on the subject of economic development, energy, and the environment. So when I was invited to give a keynote speech at this conference, I must admit that I had some qualms about accepting. The fact is, I do not feel that I have a particularly profound, specialized knowledge of any of the subjects being discussed here and I was afraid that anything I could offer would be a case, as the English say, "of bringing coals to Newcastle." In the end, I decided to accept the honour because, as I see it, a keynote speech does not necessarily have to deal in detail with any one particular problem, but it can – or even should – set forth some considerations of a general and global nature on the links between economic development, energy, and the environment; the whole – at least in my case – seen in the light of experience gained inside a large industrial group operating in the energy sector and which, therefore, has had to face the problems that are the subject of this conference: "Global Environment, Energy, and Economic Development."

I have worked for 35 years in a large Italian industrial group [ENI] that is very active both nationally and internationally in the energy sector (oil and gas in particular) and in fields of engineering related to the energy sector, as well as in chemicals and other industrial sectors. Looking back over my own professional experience, I can see that in the 1950s and 1960s our group was mainly concerned with contributing to the economic development of my country by supplying, in particular, energy required to fuel this economic and industrial growth.

I do not, for a moment, think that this concern was unique to my group. It was – and still is – a characteristic that can be found in energy companies all over the world. Perhaps in ENI the trait was accentuated by some elements peculiar to the situation in Italy. Like in Japan, Italy's entire productive system (industry, infrastructure, services) had been massively destroyed during the Second World War. The overriding need, therefore, was for rapid reconstruction. To do this and to fuel the productive system it was necessary to have ever-growing quantities of energy – a problem common to all countries, but one that was particularly acute in Italy, which, historically and throughout its struggle to industrialize, had always suffered from a chronic lack of domestic energy sources.

However, in its reconstruction and development during the decades following the war, the country found itself able to take advantage of the large quantities of cheap oil available during the 1950s, 1960s, and early 1970s. One might even say that Italy's historical disadvantage of not possessing domestic coal resources, as compared with other European countries such as the UK, Germany, Belgium, and France, turned to its advantage in that it could profit of the worldwide availability of oil at very competitive prices.

With the first oil crisis in 1973–1974, and then the second in 1979–1980, all the oil-importing industrialized countries woke up to the fact of just how delicately balanced and vulnerable their position had become due to their heavy dependence on imported fuels. Being heavily dependent on oil imports means that the availability of supplies can be at risk and that the trade balance has negative repercussions, with all the consequences that these factors can have on the country's economic growth, employment, and inflation. In the case of Italy, three-quarters of the country's total energy demand in 1974 was satisfied by oil, and almost all this oil was imported from North Africa and the Middle East. The impact on the balance of payments when the price of oil quadrupled between October 1973 and January 1974 was simply enormous: in 1974 as much as 30 per cent of Italy's export earnings went to cover the nation's oil bill. It was only logical, therefore, that the oil-importing countries began to implement a policy aimed at reducing dependence on oil imports so as to decrease the negative effects on their balance of payments, the inflation rate, and employment.

A clear and unmistakable testimony to the worry the two oil crises generated within governments of the industrialized oil-importing countries can be found in the declarations of the G7 summit meetings held in those years. Here is what the Heads of State of the Governments of France, the Federal Republic of Germany, Italy, Japan, the United Kingdom, and the United States (Canada was not present) declared at their first meeting at Rambouillet, France, in November 1975:

World economic growth is clearly linked to the increasing availability of energy sources. We are determined to secure for our economies the energy resources needed for their growth. Our common interests require that we continue to cooperate in order to reduce our dependence on imported energy through conservation and the development of alternative sources. Through these measures as well as international cooperation between producer and consumer countries, responding to the long-term interests of both, we shall spare no effort in order to ensure more balanced conditions and a harmonious and steady development in the new world energy market. (G7 Economic Summit, 1975)

From this first summit onwards, references to energy under the double aspects of cost and security of supply were constant in the declarations of the G7.

I do not wish to take up your time here with too many quotations but I would just like to add that anyone who goes back to look at these declarations will be struck by the intense atmosphere of uncertainty about the future and the preoccupation felt by the Heads of State and Government of the major industrialized countries regarding the safety and cost of their energy supplies. I shall limit myself here to making two further brief quotations.

The first is from the Tokyo Summit of 1979, which – like many others – devoted ample space to the energy problem: "Higher oil prices and oil shortages have reduced the room for maneuver in economic policy in all our countries. They will make inflation worse and curtail growth, in both industrial and developing countries. The non-oil developing countries are among the biggest sufferers."

The second comes from the Venice Summit Meeting held in June 1980 during the second oil crisis. This declaration had a long chapter dedicated to energy and began with the following words of warning and concern: "In this, our first meeting of the 1980's, the economic issues that have dominated our thoughts are the price and supply of energy and the implications for inflation and the level of economic activity in our countries and for the rest of the world as a whole. Unless we can deal with the problem of energy, we cannot cope with the other problems."

Attention to the energy problem, at least in its security and cost aspects, diminished gradually over the first half of the 1980s, in step with an improvement worldwide in the general petroleum situation. In 1986 the excessive supply of oil on the market brought about a sudden drop in oil prices, and something like a "counter oil shock" took place. An actual or potential scarcity of oil and gas, and the corresponding high prices, seemed a thing of the past, although there was no lack of experts ready to exhort the public, and their governments, to keep in mind that the structure of the world supply of and demand for petroleum was such that a return to another crisis was by no means to be excluded. At any rate, the Gulf crisis of 1990–1991 was easily overcome without any serious problems regarding both physical availability of energy (oil) and prices.

The availability of energy at a reasonable price – the twin problems that were the source of greatest concern and had raised doubts about the possibility of being able to maintain the pace of economic growth – now seemed no longer to be difficult problems along the road of steady human progress. The reality, however, was quite different because another problem was gradually emerging and taking shape: the impact of energy on the environment in the various phases of production, processing, and end use. Thus, while the lack of energy, or its excessively high cost, may be obstacles to economic development, the impact on the environment of its production, processing, and use can prove to be a hindrance of equal magnitude.

The problem of the environment is certainly not a new one, but until a few years ago it was not widely perceived as a source of major concern. In the report published by the Club of Rome more than 20 years ago (Meadows et al., 1972), and entitled *The Limits to Growth*, the environmental consequences of continuous economic development were examined, together with other specific development problems such as the availability of food, raw materials, energy, etc. This report by the Club of Rome was widely publicized and gave rise to heated debates, but it is fair to say that it did not leave much effect on the actions of industry and business at large, or on governments' policies or on the behaviour of consumers in general. Consumers continued quite happily as before to consume energy and other goods and services without excessive worries about the environment. The only restraint they balked at was the increase in price. As for industrialists, their main worry still was the availability of energy and its cost. There was, of course, concern for the environment, but in all honesty – except in a few special cases – it does not seem to me that protection of the environment became a top priority among entrepreneurs and businessmen. Even in the case of governments, I also have the impression that any serious interest in the environment is a recent phenomenon.

One demonstration of the low priority attached to environmental matters can be found in the previously mentioned declarations of the G7 summits. In fact, it is only at the fourth summit, held in Bonn in 1978, that we come across the first rather timid reference (barely two lines) to the environmental question: "In energy development, the environment and human safety of the population must be safeguarded with the greatest care." And that is all!

In the following summit, which was held in Tokyo in June 1979, the environmental issue received more than lip-service: "We need to expand alternative sources of energy, especially those which will help to prevent further pollution, particularly increases in carbon dioxide and sulfur dioxides in the atmosphere." By contrast – and this should be noted – ample space is given to the problem of energy supply and oil prices. It is worth quoting a few lines dealing with the problem of oil prices: "We deplore the decisions taken by the recent OPEC Conference. We recognise that relative moderation was displayed by certain of the participants. But the unwarranted rise in oil prices nevertheless agreed are bound to have very serious economic and social consequences. They mean more worldwide inflation and less growth. That will lead to more unemployment, more balance of payments difficulties and will endanger stability in developing and developed countries of the world alike. We remain ready to examine with oil-exporting countries how to define supply and demand prospects on the world oil market."

I have made frequent references to the G7 summit meetings because there is little doubt about the fact that their declarations accurately reflect both the importance of the problems themselves and what governments think about them and the way they would like to resolve them at the international level. It is quite interesting, therefore – by glancing through the various summit declarations – to see just how, at a certain particular moment, the environmental problem began to acquire – together with other important international problems – a growing importance, while the concern for the issue of energy supply and oil prices, which had been of such importance in the 1970s, began to wane. Starting in the early 1980s, as you may recall, the worry about secure oil supplies disappeared and the rapid decline in the price of crude began. The drop in prices reached its lowest point in July 1986 when the price of Arabian Light, which had been US$41.25 per barrel (bbl) in November 1980, dropped to US$8.69/bbl (expressed in current dollars).

The problem of energy, therefore, gradually became less important, while the attention being paid to the environment increased. So, in the declaration of the Bonn Summit in May 1985, we find no reference to energy, while a whole ad hoc chapter is dedicated to "Environmental Policies" and at the beginning of it we read: "Economic progress and the preservation of the natural environment are necessary and mutually supportive goals. Effective environmental protection is a central element in our national and international policies."

Subsequently, more and more attention was focused on the environmental issue, not only at the G7 summits. The latter, in any case, only reflect world problems as they are perceived and felt by politicians, experts, entrepreneurs, industrialists, and ordinary citizens, all of whom, in recent years, have recognized the environmental question – or, to be more precise, the question of compatibility between development and the environment – as *the* problem for future generations as well as ours. We are all aware that in these last few years there has been a dramatic change in emphasis regarding the gravity and urgency of coping with the issue of sustainable development. The real issue at stake is not so much whether the world will have enough food, energy, and other raw materials to meet the requirements of present and future generations, but rather, whether, in spite of having enough food, energy, and raw materials, the environment will be able to stand up to the impact that the production, transformation, and consumption of such food, energy, and other raw materials will have on our planet.

This shift in the priority of our concerns is entirely justified. But I am afraid, as regards energy, that this new attitude may be revealed to be inadequate in the long term. I do not believe, in fact, that the present situation of plentiful oil and low prices should allow us to think that the problems of the physical availability and the price of energy have been definitely resolved. In spite of the progress made in the fields of energy conservation through improved efficiency, the inevitable increase in world energy consumption that will accompany the ongoing growth in world population will, sooner or later, give rise to tensions in the physical supply of energy, even if only for the fact that the present imbalance between the geopolitical areas of consumption and the geopolitical areas of production (especially in the case of oil and natural gas) is bound to become more acute. It would be a serious error if we were to assume that the problems of the physical availability and cost of energy have been solved, and that we can concentrate, therefore, all our attention on the problems of the environmental impact of production, processing, and the end use of energy.

A balanced and more realistic attitude towards the intertwined problems of energy and the environment has been set forth recently (June 1993) by the Governing Board at the Ministerial Level of the International Energy Agency [IEA]:

The member countries established the IEA in 1974 as a forum in which to cooperate in enhancing their collective energy security. The challenges faced in the energy sector have evolved over the past two decades. The goal of energy security, which remains a primary one, has been complemented in recent years by increasing awareness of the significance for energy policy, and for energy security, of two further factors: concern over the environmental impact of energy-related activities, and the growing globalisation of energy issues, as different countries' economies and energy markets become increasingly interdependent.

The list of IEA "shared goals" that, according to the ministers, must "provide a basis for developing their energy policies" is sensible and worth noting. I do not have the time here to comment on these decisions taken by the IEA ruling body, but there is one point in particular that I believed should be noted.

The Governing Board of the IEA, the G7, as well as many governments of the industrialized countries and various other experts on the subject, all make frequent reference to the need to base energy policies on the "free and open market," or to rely on the "free forces of the market," and so on and so forth. Quite frankly, I get the impression that these references to "free market forces" are another case of lip-service being paid to an institution that is dear to the hearts of all of us in the developed countries and that, for quasi-ideological reasons, can only be the subject of praise – praise that now seems all the more justified in the light of the recent disasters of the Soviet-type planned economies in Eastern Europe.

Nevertheless, I think we should be more intellectually honest on this matter and admit that the problems related to energy, the environment, and economic development, in their growing global interdependence, cannot be coped with by adopting an ideological approach, be it based on the ideas of Karl Marx or on those of Adam Smith.

Already back in 1945, a well-known scholar of the oil industry, paraphrasing the words of George Clemenceau, said that: "Oil is too serious an affair to be left to oilmen." In any case, what has happened over the past decades in the field of energy, and of oil in particular, has shown quite clearly that the rules of the "free market" have often been violated by various governments for reasons of foreign policy and security, or to protect the interests of national companies. The examples that come to mind are the acquisition by the British government of control over Anglo Persian that Winston Churchill so much wanted in 1914, and the "open door" policy that the US administration pursued during the 1930s in the Middle East. There are plenty of other examples available to show that quite often the energy policies of governments have diverged completely from the "golden rule" of the free market (we may as well recall here the "proration" and the "import quotas," both introduced in the oil industry by the US administration).

One recent and very eloquent example of how heavily the "free market" was conditioned by governments can be found in the way the 1990–1991 Gulf crisis was handled. As many of you will recall, the Yom Kippur crisis in 1973–1974 and the Iranian crisis in 1979–1980 both resulted in sharp oil price rises even though there was no great imbalance in the energy market between supply and demand. On both these occasions, the absence of any political will to face up to the emergency in an organic and coordinated way permitted the market to react in total freedom, with deplorable results that were evident to all. But the Gulf crisis was handled differently. Here, too, the market played a fundamental role, but it did not operate "freely"; it was heavily conditioned by two important factors. The first of these was the political decision of some producing countries to increase production, thus forgoing the opportunity to profit from the free play of market forces. The second conditioning factor was the political decision of the government members of the IEA to adopt and implement a "contingency plan," which prevented all forms of speculation and helped maintain an overall global balance between the supply and demand for energy. In fact, far from shooting up, the price of oil, which prior to the outbreak of war was over US$30/bbl, dropped to around US$21/bbl when the hostilities actually began. This marked a considerable success not only for the market, which was able to face the new emergency, but also for all those forces that conditioned the market by preventing it from behaving according to its natural logic and inclination, which, as in the oil crises of the 1970s, would have resulted in a jump in prices and, even worse, in difficulties in supply.

If it is now acceptable that the energy market may in the real world be conditioned by government decisions, then this same principle should work when we move to the fields of economic development and the environment; in other words, to the field of "sustainable development." In my view, whether we like it or not, a "Sustainable Society" cannot be brought about without rational government intervention to complement and correct market forces. My conviction is based on the following three arguments.

First, the market frequently reacts far too slowly and, paradoxically, the time-span of its outlook is too short. The seriousness and the urgency of the problems posed by sustainable development suggest that the famous warning of Lord Keynes should always be borne in mind: "In the long run we are all dead."

Second, the free market does not always behave in a way that can be considered to be for the general good. You will agree that the reactions of the market during the first and second oil crises caused serious difficulties that could certainly have been eased, or even avoided, if the market itself had been corrected by appropriate actions by governments, as happened later at the time of the Gulf Crisis.

Third, the market itself does not have at its disposal all the necessary inputs to be able, spontaneously, to arrive at the most rational and appropriate solutions. External environmental costs are not yet part and parcel of the fundamental inputs on the basis of which the market "fixes" prices and, more generally, reaches its decisions. In other words, we are already using up our planet without making any allowance for this in our costs. What would happen to a businessman who decided on his company's business strategy (prices, investments, etc.) without making allowances in his production costs for such items as depreciation of plant and equipment? The answer is easy: he would soon go bankrupt.

This problem of the ability, or rather the "inability," of the market to provide the accurate and complete inputs required for rational decision-making was recently taken up by the Business Council for Sustainable Development. This is an organization made up of around 50 large international corporations that drew up a report for the UN Conference on Environment and Development that was held in Rio de Janeiro in June last year [1992]. The title of the report itself – *Changing Course* – is quite revealing and its content points out how companies and governments can render the ecological imperatives an integral part of those same market forces that govern production, investments, and business.

The Business Council's report contains important statements on the need for companies to adopt profoundly different attitudes, and a new way of doing business, if sustainable development is to be achieved. Since the enterprise is the principal promoter of world economic development, I think it would be worth our while to take note of the points of view expressed by some prominent business leaders on the subject of sustainable development in their report *Changing Course:*

So long as creating wealth ranked far above protecting nature as the major objective of society, markets guided economic actors such as consumers and producers toward maximizing wealth creation without concern for the resulting degradation of nature.

Today the world's nations – to different degrees and with different priorities – appear ready to base a reassessment of their long-term objectives on the realisation that economic progress can only be achieved amid plentiful environmental resources and within healthy global eco-systems.

Changing course in accord with this new realisation does not imply abandoning a system that has proved its merits. But it does mean that economic actors need the right signals to steer them toward the new objective.

The fundamental signals guiding market decisions are prices reflecting the relative scarcity of goods based on supply and demand.

This basic mechanism has never been given a real chance to work for the environment. The use, exploitation and degradation of nature has not created signals of scarcity because those who "own" nature and its services – society, expressing its wishes and intentions through government – have tended to give away environmental resources and services for free. (Schmidheiny, 1992)

It is necessary, therefore, to make due allowance for environmental costs; even if, as the same report points out, "it will be a long and complex task to make prices reflect the ecological impact of resource use and the production of goods and services. This task is also laden with difficulties: assessing values and determining unknown costs associated with ecological impacts; changing basic elements of existing industrial structures; introducing potentially distorting elements into international trade, which may put a higher burden on the poor and tempting governments to abuse a potentially important source of revenue, by using it for purposes other than guiding choices toward sustainable development."

These extensive quotations from the Business Council report *Changing Course* are justified in my view because the business community is often perceived to be rather reluctant to accept a new approach to doing business. A new attitude is apparently taking shape and it cannot but be of great help in solving the complex and intricate problem of sustainable development.

Here I should like to underline, in particular, the difficulties inherent in the process of "internalizing" environmental costs. These are not theoretical difficulties either. To introduce such a system, which can only be international in character, will mean overcoming enormous obstacles since the process will evidence the contrasts that exist between the diverse economic sectors and different countries: "just demands," economic vested interests, various types of "sacred national selfishness," will all meet head on during the definition of the rules for such an international agreement for sustainable development, as well as during the actual control and enforcement of it. Nevertheless, in spite of all the difficulties of a theoretical and practical nature, it is essential to go ahead with all the necessary precautions, but with determination, before the present trend of irrational development makes it even more difficult and painful to "change course" towards sustainable development.

Being conscious of the difficulties must not, in Hamlet's words, "make cowards of us all," or allow "the native hue of resolution [to be] sicklied o'er with the pale cast of thought." In this difficult but absolutely essential undertaking of saving our planet for future generations, rather than give way to the doubts and fears of Shakespeare's Hamlet, we must be spurred on by the teaching of the Roman philosopher Seneca, who said: "Multa non quia difficilia sunt non audemus, sed quia non audemus sunt difficilia." Which can be translated as follows: "Many deeds we do not dare, not because they are difficult; rather they are difficult because we do not dare."

References

G7 Economic Summit. 1975. *Declaration of Rambouillet.* Rambouillet, France.

IEA (International Energy Agency). 1993. *Communique. Meeting of Governing Board at Ministerial Level.* Paris: IEA.

Meadows, D. L., et al. 1972. *The Limits to Growth. A Report for the Club of Rome's Project on the Predicament of Mankind.* New York: Universe Books.

Schmidheiny, S., ed. 1992. *Changing Course. A Global Business Perspective on Development and the Environment.* Cambridge, Mass.: MIT Press for the Business Council for Sustainable Development.

3

Policy measures for global environmental problems: A Japanese perspective

Sozaburo Okamatsu

Let me thank the organizers of this conference for giving me the honour to address this distinguished audience on a subject of great interest and concern to all of us: global environmental problems.

In my current post as the Vice Minister for International Affairs at the Ministry of International Trade and Industry, I am responsible for all external policies, including environmental policies. However, a few years ago, I was serving as Director General of the Environmental Protection and Industrial Location Bureau, and in that capacity I was directly involved in the planning and formulation of Japan's environmental policies. The critical importance which environmental issues have for the world has been increasing rapidly in recent years. Today, I would like to show how we in Japan are working to meet the global challenges that environmental issues place before us.

Before proceeding, however, I would like first to emphasize the importance of harmonizing the "three Es" which appear in the title of this conference: environment, energy, and economic development. Should the proper balance between the "three Es" be lost, this certainly would give rise to some very unfortunate developments for humankind.

The history of humankind is also the history of its increasing demands on the global environment. While having benefited from the increase in living standards propelled upward by a quantum leap in industrial activities, particularly since the Industrial Revolution, we have been using up at an ever-increasing pace the wealth of the earth's natural resources, which has resulted in environmental damage all over the world.

The first problem was industrial pollution, i.e. the pollution of our atmosphere and contamination of water arising from pollutants emitted by factories and other manufacturing operations. Industrial pollution has long been a serious problem for both developing and industrialized countries. Industrial pollution is, however, generally a local phenomenon, having effects on a limited area only. Moreover, many of the means of dealing with industrial pollution and handling industrial polluters are well established. For example, desulphurization technologies and water treatment technologies are well established and widely available, making resolution of industrial pollution largely a domestic matter for the country concerned.

However, explosive growth in both the scale of economic activity and the world's population in recent years has changed the basic nature of environmental problems. As human activities expand, their impact on the environment transcends national boundaries and spills over to future generations. Global environmental problems today include the following: global warming, the destruction of the ozone layer, acid rain, the endangerment of animal and plant species, desertification, deforestation, marine pollution, transboundary movement of hazardous waste, and environmental problems in developing countries. Among these, the first three are of special concern, while the issue of global warming deserves our most critical attention.

I intend to focus my talk today on global warming and present an outline of the Japanese perspective on this problem.

First, I wish to emphasize the nature of global warming and set it apart from other environmental issues. For instance, take the destruction of the ozone layer and acid rain. One is caused by chlorofluorocarbons (CFCs), while the other is caused by sulphur oxides (SOx) and nitrogen oxides (NOx). CFCs are synthetic substances and certain advances have already been made in developing substitutes. As for SOx and NOx, we already have well-established technologies for filtering out these compounds and preventing their build-up. Therefore, the present discussion is centred on the practical application of these technologies. In other words, on acid rain and the destruction of the ozone layer, we are already committed to policies of stopping the manufacture and preventing the generation of these problem-causing substances. What is more, the crucial problem-solving technologies already exist, and we are now at a stage of grappling with the issues of implementation.

But on global warming, on the contrary, the major cause is carbon dioxide (CO_2). CO_2 is a compound which has been with us since the beginning of humankind. And humankind has continued to produce carbon dioxide since we first learned to use fire. Humankind has depended on fossil fuels in its quest for ever-increasing amounts of energy to meet the demands of a rapidly growing world economy, and growing CO_2 emissions are an inevitable by-product. Energy consumption negatively affects the environment by increasing CO_2 emissions but, at the same time, we cannot enjoy economic development without energy consumption.

The important thing here is maintaining a proper balance between the "three Es," which I mentioned earlier. Striking this balance distinguishes global warming from the other issues. Suppose we were to choose one of the "three Es" – for instance, the environment – and assign absolute importance to it. This, in itself, would be very easy to do. The problem, however, is that humankind will continue to aspire toward further economic development. As a practical matter, we are unable to concentrate solely on the environment at the expense of all future growth.

Economic growth does not merely increase the burden on the environment. Economic growth also provides the conditions that are necessary to protect the environment by making it possible to bear the costs of environmental protection.

So, environmental protection and economic growth, far from each other, should be thought of as interrelated concepts. It is fundamental, therefore, that maximum effort be exerted to secure the coexistence of these two notions, under the concept of "sustainable development."

But this is not easy to do. The "New Earth 21" which we have been advocating is aimed at developing some solutions to this difficult problem. Its basic concepts are promotion of energy conservation, introduction of cleaner energy sources, technology transfer, and innovative technological breakthroughs with a view to coping with population growth and increasing CO_2 emissions.

The earth today is inhabited by 5.6 billion people. A review of past trends shows that the time it has taken to increase the global population by an additional 1 billion has been shortened from 13 years to 12 years to 11 years. This trend can be expected to continue in the future. According to UN projections, the global population is expected to pass the 10 billion mark some time around the year 2050. This population growth, accompanied by rising standards of living, is raising carbon dioxide emissions.

A breakdown of total CO_2 emissions in 1987, expressed in terms of the weight of carbon, shows that the advanced industrialized countries generated 2.7 billion tons, the former Soviet Union and the Eastern bloc generated 2.1 billion tons, and the developing countries generated 1.2 billion tons, totalling 6.0 billion tons. On a per capita basis, these figures translate into 3.3 tons per capita per year in the advanced industrialized countries, as opposed to 1.4 tons and 0.5 tons in the Eastern bloc and developing countries, respectively.

Let's go back to population. Based on current trends the population distribution among these three groups of nations in the second half of the twenty-first century, when the global population reaches 10 billion, will be as follows: the advanced industrial countries will have a population of 900 million, the former Eastern bloc countries will have 2.3 billion, and the developing countries will have 6.8 billion. Let us assume that per capita emissions remain unchanged for the advanced countries, while increasing by 50 per cent and 100 per cent in the Eastern bloc and developing countries, respectively. This means that, by the second half of the twenty-first century, annual CO_2 emissions would amount to 3.0 billion tons in the advanced nations, 5.0 billion tons in the Eastern bloc countries, and 6.2 billion tons in the developing countries. It is surprising that the figure for the developing countries alone exceeds the world total of CO_2 emissions in 1987.

Demanding an immediate reduction in these figures means the denial of future improvements in living standards. This is not realistic. Energy conservation and the introduction of cleaner energy sources will certainly help to improve living standards while maintaining a balance among the "three Es." At the same time, major technological breakthroughs are indispensable in the search for truly effective solutions. What the world must do is to develop and exploit new technologies which hold out the promise of acceptable solutions to this dilemma.

How can we do this? Some people advocate a tax on CO_2. Let us suppose that the CO_2 tax is adopted. Responding to the introduction of such a tax, enterprises would move to promote energy conservation and the use of renewable-energy sources, including changes in the product/process technology mix in order to reduce the amount of fossil fuels consumed. If there was existing technology that would allow manufacturers to reduce fossil fuel consumption without reducing production output, then companies would weigh the cost advantages of simply paying the CO_2 tax versus the cost of such technology. If such technology did not exist, companies might cut production as a way to reduce their fossil fuel consumption. Therefore, availability of appropriate technologies will influence the effectiveness of a variety of environmental countermeasures.

Two hundred years have already passed since the inception of the Industrial Revolution. The reduction of the atmospheric level of CO_2 which has accumulated over the past two centuries and the restoration of the atmosphere to pre-Industrial Revolution conditions will require the development of truly revolutionary technologies. This also cannot be achieved immediately.

Therefore, we must first challenge ourselves to develop the necessary new technologies which can be used to return the atmosphere to the conditions of 200 years ago. The next 50 years, say, could be spent in developing the technologies. Then the next 50 years would be given to the practical deployment of these technologies. This 100 years would be spent in returning the atmosphere to its previous condition. This is the basic concept of the "New Earth 21" approach.

We presented this concept to the global community at the White House Conference [on Science and Economic Research Related to Global Change] held in Washington D.C. three years ago [17–18 April 1990]. Since that time, our approach has attracted wide attention, both at home and abroad. We have no intention of allowing our concept to end as a "noble dream." To realize its objective, we have divided our task into two areas, where we have already begun working. The first area is called the TREE concept (an acronym for Technology Renaissance for Environment and Energy). The essential idea here is that the advanced industrialized countries should come together and cooperate to develop new technologies in the area of energy and the environment, assuming around 2050 or 2100 as the final stage. The second area of action is the Green Aid Plan, which is aimed at transferring to the developing countries the environmental protection technologies already possessed by the advanced nations from a relatively short-term perspective.

Let me go into these two concepts in some greater detail.

Regarding the TREE concept, we presented our proposals in the preparatory sessions for the [1993] Tokyo Summit [of the G7] and believe that we have gained a certain degree of understanding and appreciation from other countries. This is reflected in the 1993 Tokyo Summit Economic Communiqué, which stated that "We welcome the analysis being done by OECD/IEA on the contribution of environment and energy technologies in meeting global environmental concerns." This indicates the acceptance of our proposal.

Pursuant to this, a working group meeting of the major advanced nations and the OECD/IEA secretariat will be held in Tokyo on Thursday and Friday of this week [28 and 29 October 1993]. Following the discussions of this working group, the OECD/IEA secretariat is scheduled to draw up a blueprint for the implementation of the TREE concept. Based on this blueprint, steps will be taken toward initiating international joint research projects, which will be conducted through existing international organizations. Heading up to the discussions on Thursday and Friday, I would like to explain Japan's basic stance on the fundamental aspects of the TREE concept as we prepare to engage in this discussion. First of all, solutions to global environmental problems must be found within a framework which provides for both environmental protection and economic growth. So, we consider the development of innovative new technologies, in the area of environment and energy, indispensable to any viable solution. Second, the development of environment- and energy-related technologies is the common responsibility of the advanced countries, which possess the necessary scientific knowledge, manpower, and financial resources. Given our limited resources and the urgency of the problem, it is essential that the advanced countries reach a common understanding and become involved in a co-operative programme for technological development. This is the most efficient approach. Third, we believe that it is appropriate to go step-by-step with international cooperation, since this is long-term cooperation and may require substantial financial resources. In this step-by-step process, we might, for example, first come up with commonly shared concepts by the international community and then make a blueprint or work programme, based on those concepts, to be followed by actual implementation of international cooperation.

Let me next turn to the Green Aid plan. This plan was first advocated by the Ministry of International Trade and Industry in August 1991 and is primarily geared toward supporting the self-help efforts of the developing countries in the area of environment- and energy-related problems. Specifically, based on our own past experiences in the area of pollution control, Japan is offering to undertake energy and environmental improvement projects in the developing countries in response to their particular needs.

In the latter half of the 1960s, as the Japanese economy shifted into high gear, severe industrial pollution problems, including air pollution caused by sulphur emissions, emerged. However, due to the development of exhaust gas desulphurization technology backed by both public and private sector efforts and its widespread dissemination by means of government regulation and support, Japan reached the highest level of environmental protection. During this period (1970–1992), Japan maintained an average annual GDP growth rate of 4.4 per cent, thus attaining continuous high economic growth while increasing environmental protection. The Green Aid Plan is intended to assist developing countries in improving their environmental situations based on such Japanese experience.

Four specific areas of pollution control are targeted in the Green Aid Plan: preventing the pollution of waterways; preventing atmospheric pollution; waste disposal and recycling; and energy conservation and utilization of alternative energy sources.

When undertaking a project, of course we will have to take into account the needs of the developing country and avoid forcing our environmental policies upon that country. To do so, we will take a two-step approach consisting of extensive policy discussions and the implementation of a comprehensive support plan for energy and environmental policies.

Allow me to comment briefly on the first step: the policy discussions. The policy discussions are aimed at reaching a common understanding between Japan and the developing country with regard to energy and environmental policies, and consist of high-level discussions between the responsible offices designed to promote effective implementation of the programme.

The second step is the implementation of a comprehensive support plan. That is based on the conclusions reached in preceding policy discussions, and is aimed at implementing energy and environmental assistance projects which fit the specific needs and conditions of that country. The second step is itself divided into two areas: technical cooperation and demonstration projects.

In the area of technical cooperation, we would dispatch specialists to and accept trainees from participating developing countries, in order to foster the human resources necessary for effectively coping with energy and environmental problems. This part of our programme is also aimed at undertaking joint research projects in areas of special interest to developing countries, such as the development of energy and environmental technologies suited to the needs of these countries. We are also involved in undertaking feasibility studies for energy and environmental measures being considered by the developing countries.

In the area of demonstration projects, we are involved in various experiments in developing countries aimed at identifying optimal technologies from the perspective of the host country and its specific needs. Such demonstration projects are focused on desulphurization methods, improvement of energy efficiency, and the development of clean energy sources.

In addition, we have established a Centre for Energy and Environmental Technologies in Bangkok, which functions as a communications and administrative centre to effectively implement the Green Aid Plan and we plan to build the same type of facility in other countries.

We believe that there are some important key points to the successful promotion of the Green Aid Plan. We ourselves must take the initiative to begin a dialogue with the developing countries. From that point on, the self-help efforts of the developing countries are at the heart of our approach. We would stand ready to help in the formulation of policies and to provide the necessary support.

Allow me to summarize the main points of my presentation. Firstly, global environmental problems today have become very critical international issues which form a common theme for all nations. The Environmental Summit held last year [1992] in Rio de Janeiro especially served to heighten interest in global environmental problems, not only of the leading nations of the world but also of the developing countries. What we must do now is to find ways of translating this newly found consciousness and concern into action.

Japan and the United States concluded the so-called framework agreement [for bilateral economic talks] at the July [1993] Summit [of the G7]. One of the most important aspects of this agreement is bilateral "cooperation" in coping with international issues and problems. The first theme for this bilateral cooperation is the environment. This bilateral cooperation was discussed by our two sides at the first framework meeting held in Washington D.C. on September 9 [1993]. At that meeting, I made the following proposal to the US government and received the support of the American side: "This scheme for bilateral cooperation is not solely limited to our two countries. Through this cooperation, let us take the leadership in calling on the rest of the world to join in this cooperative effort. Let us work together to promote the cooperative framework among the leading nations."

As I have stated, several actual projects are already under way. Let us expand the scope of these projects, and I would like to leave you with this message: through the cooperation of all humanity, let us take action now to "win back the green earth."

Thank you very much.

4

Environment, economy, energy, and sustainable development

Yoichi Kaya

Global environmental degradation is one of the most serious threats facing humankind as a result of the expansion of its activities around the globe. One of the international responses to global environmental problems – the Framework Convention on Climate Change – was ratified and came into effect in March 1994. The convention aims not only at stabilizing CO_2 emissions in developed countries but also at ultimately reducing man-made CO_2 emissions globally so as to stabilize the global climate. However, with fossil fuels comprising nearly 90 per cent of primary energy sources in the world, the final target of the framework convention seems very ambitious.

Environmental degradation cannot be singled out as an independent matter among various global issues. Also important are the interactions among economic development, stable energy supplies, and global environmental conservation. In the next few decades fossil fuels will continue to be the principal source of energy driving economic development. The source of fossil fuels is stable and their extraction is affordable. Attempts to restrict the use of fossil fuels for environmental reasons are likely to have a negative impact on economic development and the overall availability of energy. The objective of this volume is to present papers focusing on the "three Es" –

environment, energy, and economic development – to offer readers a way to comprehend the complexity of the problems involved and to elaborate possible measures for mitigating those problems.

I offer here a strategy for mitigating "three Es" issues, that is, a strategy for environmentally sustainable economic development. Herman Daly's well-known three conditions for sustainability are as follows:

1. The consumption rate of renewable resources is not higher than its recovery rate.
2. The consumption rate of non-renewable resources is not higher than the rate of increase in renewable resource supply.
3. The emission of pollutants is within the absorption capacity of the environment. (Daly, 1990: 1–6)

Unfortunately these conditions have been violated for years. Examples of respective violations typically include deforestation, the depletion of fossil fuels, and the increase in CO_2 concentration in the air. Such violations may be hard to reverse in the short term but, unless long-term remedial action is taken, present global development trends will not be sustainable. In particular, a substantial reduction in resource consumption and emissions of pollutants is essential for the development of a sustainable human society on this planet.

There are, however, a number of barriers that impede the adoption of strategies to realize sustainable development. The most serious among them is the wide disparity in levels of economic development around the world. For instance, whereas overeating is a health concern in some Western countries, malnutrition and poverty are at a crisis point in other parts of the world – developing countries that hope to alleviate their social ills through substantial economic development. It is neither appropriate nor possible to ask such developing countries simply to reduce their consumption of resources if this would result in their economic development being handicapped.

What, then, are promising strategies for the entire world to restore Daly's three conditions? One answer is for developed countries to reduce their resource consumption through technological and social policies aimed at substantial gains in energy- and resource-use efficiencies and through the introduction of clean resources such as solar energy. Complementing this, developing countries should introduce energy- and resource-efficient technologies wherever this is economically viable. The latter requirement essentially means that developing countries adopt what is known as a "no regret" strategy – that is, one that contributes to their economic development without causing unacceptable damage to the environment.

The essence of this strategy is for both rich and poor parts of the world to undertake efforts to their own advantage that also contribute positively to the global realization of the conditions of sustainable development as suggested by Daly. Developed countries would need substantially to improve their use of energy and other resources, and then to reduce resource consumption even under conditions of higher economic growth. Developing countries, for their part, would need to be sensible and flexible enough to introduce resource-efficiency technology and other economic lessons, where applicable, from the developed world.

The feasibility of such a strategy depends very much upon the future availability of technological innovations that have potential application for improving energy efficiency, recycling resources, reducing pollution emissions, and increasing biomass production. The outlook is positive, and below I introduce two technologies as typical examples.

The first is the use of heat cascading, both within industries and between industries and residential/commercial sectors. The basic concept is simple: demands for heat energy differ not only in quantity but also in quality. For example, a metal-melting process may require a certain amount of heat energy where temperatures reach 1,000 °C or more. A water-heating process, on the other hand, under normal pressure may require the same amount of heat energy but only at temperatures of 100 °C or lower. Utilization of waste heat from the metal-melting process in the water-heating process would halve the total energy required for the two processes combined.

Such a heat cascading process has already been put into practice in various forms. A typical example is combined-cycle power generation where natural gas is burned in a gas turbine at a temperature of more than 1,100 °C, producing, in turn, steam, which drives a second turbine. The total efficiency of the plant is about 20 per cent higher than the efficiency of a normal, simple gas-fuelled power plant.

The concept of heat cascading can also be applied to other systems in various sectors of society – with the collaborative efforts of energy customers, producers, and government. Of course, the appropriate location of complementary users of heat energy is essential for the effective realization of heat cascading. It is not easy to find such complementary sets of users within a single factory and this is the main reason heat cascading has so far not been widely used. The idea of a "heat combine" will arise where industries try to locate their factories so as to utilize heat as efficiently as possible through cascading. A combine could also include residential/commercial users who require only low-temperature heat. Owing to the relatively low price of energy, such a heat combine has yet to be established. Nevertheless, taking into account the importance of both energy resources and the environmental impacts of energy use, the idea of heat combines should be seriously investigated as an effective means of improving energy efficiency.

The second technology is the development of recyclable products. Nowadays most industrial goods, except certain materials such as steel, are discarded after their first use. Such disposal often occurs regardless of whether the material is still physically reusable or not, because goods and materials are recycled only when it is economically viable to do so. Needless to say, resource-use efficiency will be enhanced with more recycling. What, then, are possible ways to make recycling more economically viable?

Of course, the cooperation of the public in the process of recycling is indispensable. From a technological point of view, however, a basic change is needed in design concepts to enable the easy decomposition of industrial products into their component materials. If still physically usable, the component materials can be utilized again in new products after any necessary treatment process. This idea has already been partly implemented in automobile industries. A key problem with a comprehensive recycling process is the development of production technologies that can produce products with sufficient mechanical strength while at the same time being easily decomposable. This is a new challenge for mechanical engineers engaged in the design of most industrial products, because mechanical strength and easy decomposability are in most cases contradictory requirements. Nevertheless, efforts at meeting these two requirements are currently being undertaken in various industrial sectors such as the manufacture of automobiles and office automation devices.

The above technologies are just examples of what are needed for substantial improvements in resource-use efficiency. I strongly urge developed countries to develop these innovative technologies. The results would be profitable not only for developed countries but also for developing countries through more efficient resource use, and for the global community through reductions in waste discharge and resource depletion.

Reference

Daly, H. 1990. "Toward some operational principles of sustainable development." *Ecological Economics* 2: 1–6.

Part 2
The status of the global environment

5

Climate changes due to the increase in greenhouse gases as predicted by climate models

Tatsushi Tokioka

1. Introduction

There is widespread concern that continual man-made emissions of "greenhouse gases" are resulting in global atmospheric warming, local climate changes, and sealevel rise, with the prospect of consequent serious environmental, social, and economic impacts. This paper describes some of the issues involved in modelling the climate system and the model-based predictions currently obtained.

The most comprehensive scientific assessment of climate change was conducted by Working Group I of the Intergovernmental Panel on Climate Change (IPCC), which is organized jointly by the World Meteorological Organization (WMO) and the United Nations Environment Programme (UNEP). The results (Houghton et al., 1990, 1992) are the most authoritative and strongly supported statement on climate change that has ever been made by the international scientific community. Most of the points discussed briefly in this paper are addressed more fully in the IPCC reports.

2. The greenhouse effect

Suppose there were no atmosphere on earth, incoming solar radiation would be reflected at the surface and some of it would be ab-

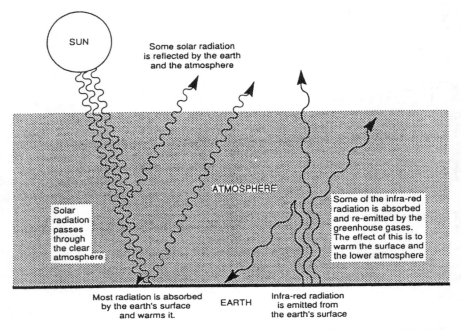

Fig. 5.1 **A schematic diagram illustrating the greenhouse effect (Source: Houghton et al., 1990)**

sorbed. The earth, in turn, would emit radiation at a longer wavelength, because the surface has a lower temperature than that of the sun, and this would escape to space. For the earth to be in equilibrium in energy, the absorbed solar radiation has to be balanced by the outgoing longwave radiation. At equilibrium the effective radiating temperature of the earth is about 255K ($-18\,°$C). This would be the earth's surface temperature in the absence of atmosphere (see fig. 5.1).

Actually, the earth has an atmosphere, the major components of which are nitrogen and oxygen. However, it also contains water vapour, CO_2, and CH_4, although their amounts are very small. The radiative properties of these gases for the shorter solar wavelengths are quite different from those at the infra-red wavelengths. Some of the infra-red radiation from the surface is absorbed by these gases within the lower atmosphere and then it is re-emitted, both downwards – warming the surface and lower atmosphere – and upwards. To establish an equilibrium state, there must be radiative balance at the top of the atmosphere and energy balance at the surface and within the atmosphere. These gases effectively trap infra-red radiation that would otherwise escape from the earth and are termed "greenhouse gases." The mechanism that influences the temperature of the surface and the atmosphere is called the "greenhouse effect." The effect of the greenhouse gases is to raise the surface temperature by about 33K to 288K (15 °C) (see fig. 5.1).

3. Climate models

The earth's climate is determined not only by the atmosphere but also by the ocean, the land surface, the cryosphere, and the biosphere. This entire system is called the "climate system." Figure 5.2 schematically shows the earth's climate system and the complexity of interactions between components of the system. The earth's climate is regulated by interactive dynamic, physical, chemical, and biophysical processes. The characteristic time-scales for each component to recover its equilibrium state after being disturbed differ a great deal, ranging from one to two months for the atmosphere, a few months for the mixed layer of the ocean, several decades for the upper part of the ocean, a few thousand years for the deep ocean, to tens of thousands of years or more for the ice sheet. Mutual interactions produce varying time-scales of climate variation. However, our understanding of those interactions, obtained mainly through numerical experiments with climate models, is still very limited.

Climate models numerically predict or determine the physical states of these components on the basis of physical laws. There are many different modelling approaches, ranging from simple vertically one-dimensional radiative–convective models to the full complexity of three-dimensional coupled atmosphere–ocean general circulation models (AOGCMs). Figure 5.3 shows an example of a grid-box representation of a three-dimensional atmospheric model. The representative physical state of each box is numerically predicted with the use of relevant physical laws.

In order to predict transient, regional climate changes, the models used must allow in some way for the influences of the various components of the climate system and for the significant interactions between them. The type of model that meets this purpose is the one developed from existing three-dimensional global AOGCMs. These provide an effective framework for testing new hypotheses about climate sensitivity and change.

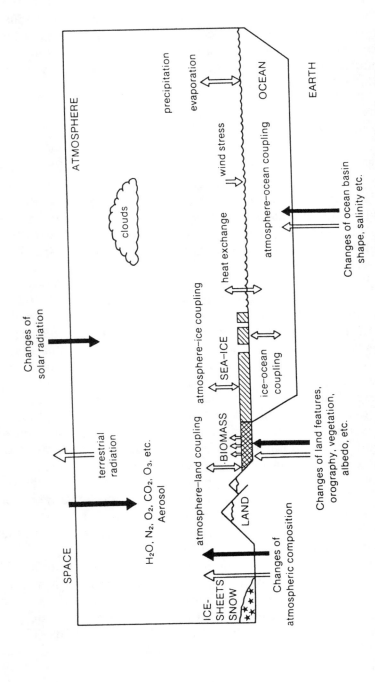

Fig. 5.2 **Schematic illustration of the coupled atmosphere–ocean–ice–land climate system (Note: The full arrows are examples of external processes; the open arrows are examples of internal processes in climate change. Source: Houghton et al., 1990)**

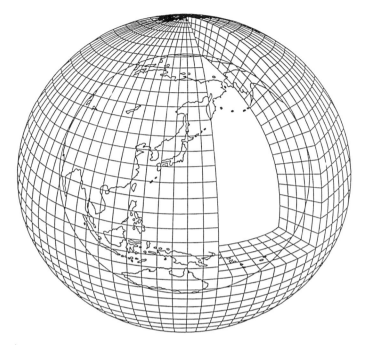

Fig. 5.3 **An example of a grid representation of a three-dimensional atmospheric model. Representative physical states of each box are predicted numerically on the basis of relevant physical laws**

4. Climate feedback processes

The earth's climate system is characterized by complicated inter-actions between the various components of the system. When some change is introduced into the climate system, such as the increase in the atmospheric concentration of CO_2, it is fairly easy to evaluate its direct effect through changes in the radiative heating rate. Warming of the tropospheric temperature will follow. However, this warming causes other (indirect) changes in the climate system. After a chain of changes, the initial direct change will be affected again so as to enhance it (positive feedbacks) or to suppress it (negative feedbacks).

As an example of a positive feedback, temperature–water vapour feedback is explained briefly. The maximum amount of water vapour allowed in the air depends on pressure and temperature. Under con-stant pressure, it increases with the increase in air temperature. Be-cause water vapour is one of the greenhouse gases, the increase in atmospheric water vapour due to the increase in air temperature will enhance the greenhouse effect of water vapour, resulting in a further increase in air temperature.

In discussing global warming due to the increase in greenhouse gases, there are other important positive feedbacks such as snow–albedo feedback and sea ice–albedo feedback. "Albedo" is the total reflectivity of solar radiation. A temperature rise will decrease both the snow-covered area and the sea-ice area. Because snow and sea-ice are good reflectors of solar radiation, the decrease in these areas allows more absorption of solar energy by the earth's surface. This will lead to a further rise in the surface air temperature.

Cloud is recognized as a very important and complicated element in discussing feedbacks. When climate changes, it is not only the amount of cloud that changes but also cloud height and the optical property of clouds. If the cloud amount decreases under global warming, the gain in solar energy at the surface surpasses the loss in long-wave radiation as the albedo of the entire air column decreases except when the surface is covered either by snow or by sea-ice. So this is a positive feedback.

The cloud albedo usually increases either when cloud water increases or when cloud particles change from the ice-phase to the water-phase. These changes are likely to occur under global warming. Because the increase in cloud albedo reduces the increase in surface temperature, this is a negative feedback.

Sensitivity experiments on the treatment of clouds performed so far demonstrate both positive and negative roles depending on the treatment (Senior and Mitchell, 1993). Where a standard, simple cloud prediction scheme based on relative humidity was adopted, the globally averaged surface temperature increase under doubled CO_2 was 5.2 °C. In another case where cloud radiative properties were allowed to depend on the predicted liquid water content of the clouds, the temperature increase was only 1.9 °C. This spread, 1.9 °–5.2 °C, represents a factor of 2.7 in the response to changing the representation of clouds in the model. The uncertainty about how to formulate clouds poses a formidable obstacle to reliable climate prediction even in the sense of an equilibrium global mean, let alone in the context of transient, regional predictions.

Feedback processes involving biogeochemical or biogeophysical processes have not been clarified yet either. Currently, only the physical aspects of the biomass, i.e. evapotranspiration, albedo, and roughness, are considered in the model. No other processes are considered.

Table 5.1 **Model sensitivities to the effects of internal feedbacks on equilibrium warming in response to a doubling of CO$_2$**

Process	Warming
No feedback	1.2 °C
Allow water vapour feedback	1.9 °C
Allow snow and sea-ice feedback	2.3–3.2 °C
Allow cloud feedback	5.2 °C

Poor understanding in these areas might also introduce uncertainties in climate change prediction.

Table 5.1 summarizes model sensitivities to the effects of internal feedbacks on equilibrium warming in response to a doubling of CO$_2$.

5. Transient climate response and the ocean

Greenhouse gases are increasing year by year, in the case of CO$_2$ at the rate of 1.8 parts per million by volume (ppmv) per year currently. It takes some time for the earth's climate system to adjust to these changes, because the characteristic or relaxation time of the ocean (the time required for it to return to its former balanced state after being forced to move to an unbalanced state) is not short but several decades for the upper part of the ocean and a thousand years or more for the deep ocean. The total energy required to raise the entire air column by 1 °C is equivalent to the energy required to raise 2.5 m of sea water by 1 °C. As the mean depth of the ocean is about 4,000 m, the thermal inertia of the ocean is about 1,600 times as great as that of the atmosphere based on this simple energy consideration. The ocean, in this sense, is very important in determining the transient climate response. Once the oceanic surface temperature is determined, the atmosphere will respond to it very quickly, say within a month or two.

It is known that gyres exist in the ocean, such as the Kuroshio, the Gulf Stream, the California current, and so on. These currents are closely connected with the surface wind, are directed horizontally, and transport heat in a north–south direction. Another type of circulation in the ocean is thermohaline circulation. The density of sea water is determined by temperature, salinity, and pressure. As a result of differences in temperature and salinity, large-scale density difference is created in the ocean to drive meridional circulations. The full extent of these circulations has not yet been observationally confirmed. However, three-dimensional oceanic circulation models unanimously show very deep thermohaline circulation in the southern hemisphere along the Antarctic continent. Also shown is the very deep circulation in the north-eastern part of the North Atlantic. Deep thermohaline circulation transports energy in a vertical direction, contributing to a delay in the rise in sea surface temperature in those areas through vertical mixing.

Transient response studies by AOGCMs (Stouffer et al., 1989; Cubasch et al., 1992; Manabe et al., 1991; Murphy, 1992; Meehl et al., 1993) show a substantial delay in warming in the southern hemisphere compared with the northern hemisphere (see fig. 5.4), owing to the dominance of the oceanic area in the southern hemisphere. They also show a further delay in warming in the area where deep thermohaline circulations are dominant, i.e. circum-Antarctic ocean and the north-eastern part of the North Atlantic (see fig. 5.4). Manabe et al. (1991) show that the increase in precipitation and thus the dilution of surface salinity in those areas also contribute to delay warming in those areas.

A study of century-scale effects of increased CO_2 on the earth's climate by Manabe and Stouffer (1993) shows marked weakening in the thermohaline circulation and thus marked changes in thermal and dynamic structure of the ocean in the quadrupled-CO_2 climate, leading to a $7\,°C$ increase in the globally averaged surface temperature.

The AOGCM studies have clearly demonstrated the importance of oceanic circulations in determining transient response and local climate changes. However, the current oceanic general circulation models adopted in these AOGCM studies have not been fully verified because of a lack of observed data, especially in deep circulations. Considering the large impact of the ocean on the transient response of the climate system, further observations of the ocean are urgently needed.

6. Possible climate changes predicted by models

Although the predicted climate changes differ from model to model as regards regional details, they agree on many larger-scale aspects. These are summarized as follows:

Temperature
- The troposphere warms, whereas the stratosphere cools.
- The global mean surface temperature increase, when CO_2 is doubled, is $1.5–4.5\,°C$. The best estimate is about $2.5\,°C$.

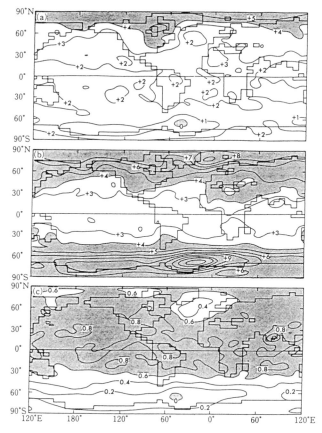

Fig. 5.4 **(a) The time-dependent response of surface temperature (°C) in the coupled ocean–atmosphere model to a 1 per cent per year increase in atmospheric CO_2. (b) The equilibrium response of surface air temperature (°C) in the atmosphere–mixed-layer ocean model to a doubling in atmospheric CO_2. (c) The ratio of the time-dependent response to the equilibrium response (Source: Manabe et al., 1991)**

• The surface warming is greatest in high-latitude winter; least in the tropics.

The hydrological cycle
• Global average precipitation and evaporation increase by 3–15 per cent when CO_2 is doubled.
• Soil moisture increases in high-latitude winter.
• Many models predict a decrease in soil moisture in mid-latitude summer.

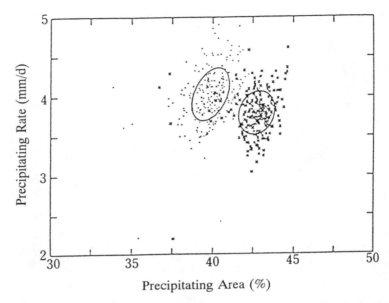

Fig. 5.5   **Scatter diagram of the precipitation rate (mm/day) versus the ratio of the precipitating area to the global domain (%) for 1–10 January (Note: Ellipses drawn with thick and thin solid lines denote the root mean square scattering for $1 \times CO_2$ and $2 \times CO_2$, respectively. Data points for $1 \times CO_2$ and $2 \times CO_2$ are denoted by crosses and dots, respectively. Source: Noda and Tokioka, 1989)**

- Cumulus-type precipitation increases, while stratus-type precipitation decreases in the low and middle latitudes, resulting in a decrease in the precipitating area and an increase in high-intensity precipitation (Noda and Tokioka, 1989); see fig. 5.5.

Transient response
- Temperature increase in the southern hemisphere lags behind that in the northern hemisphere.
- Temperature increase lags especially in those areas where deep thermohaline circulations are dominant, such as the circum-Antarctic area and the north-eastern part of the North Atlantic. An increase in precipitation and a melting of sea-ice also help to delay warming in those areas.
- When the atmospheric CO_2 concentration is increased at the rate of 1 per cent per year, the globally averaged surface temperature increase realized in the model is about 60 per cent of the warming

expected in the equilibrium state under the given concentration of
CO_2 (Stouffer, et al., 1989; Murphy, 1992).

7. Future problems

Uncertainties in predicting possible future climate changes exist in
our inadequate understanding and thus inadequate treatment of the
following processes (Houghton et al., 1992):
- clouds (particularly their feedback effect on warming induced by
greenhouse gases, as well as the effect of aerosols on clouds and
their radiative properties) and other elements of the atmospheric
water budget, including the processes controlling upper-level water
vapour;
- oceans, which, through their thermal inertia and possible changes in
circulation, influence the timing and pattern of climate change;
- land surface processes and feedbacks, including hydrological and
ecological processes that link regional and global climates;
- sources and sinks of greenhouse gases and aerosols and their atmospheric concentrations (including their indirect effects on global
warming);
- polar ice sheets (whose response to climate change also affects predictions of sealevel rise).

References

Cubasch, U., K. Hasselmann, H. Hock, E. Maier-Reimer, U. Mikolajewicz, B. D.
Santer, and R. Sausen. 1992. "Time-dependent greenhouse warming computations
with a coupled ocean–atmosphere model." *Climate Dynamics* 8: 55–69.

Houghton, J. T., G. J. Jenkins, and J. J. Ephraums (eds.). 1990. *Climate Change. The
IPCC Scientific Assessment.* Cambridge: Cambridge University. Press.

Houghton, J. T., B. A. Callander, and S. K. Varney (eds.). 1992. *Climate Change
1992. The Supplementary Report to the IPCC Scientific Assessment.* Cambridge:
Cambridge University Press.

Manabe, S. and R. J. Stouffer. 1993. "Century-scale effects of increased atmospheric
CO_2 on the ocean–atmosphere system." *Nature* 364: 215–218.

Manabe, S., R. J. Stouffer, M. J. Spelman, and K. Bryan. 1991. "Transient responses
of a coupled ocean–atmosphere model to gradual changes of atmospheric CO_2.
Part I: Annual mean." *Journal of Climate* 4: 785–818.

Meehl, G. A., W. M. Washington, and T. R. Karl. 1993. "Low-frequency variability
and CO_2 transient change. Part 1. Time-averaged difference." *Climate Dynamics*,
8: 117–133.

Murphy, J. M. 1992. *A Prediction of the Transient Response of Climate.* Climate
Research Technical Note, CRTN32, Hadley Centre, Meteorological Office, London Road, Bracknell, Berkshire RG12 2SY.

Noda, A. and T. Tokioka. 1989. "The effect of doubling the CO_2 concentration on convective and non-convective precipitation in a general circulation model coupled with a simple mixed layer ocean model." *Journal of the Meteorological Society of Japan* 67: 1057–1069.

Senior, C. A. and J. B. F. Mitchell. 1993. "Carbon dioxide climate: The impact of cloud parameterization." *Journal of Climate* 6: 393–418.

Stouffer, R. J., S. Manabe, and K. Bryan. 1989. "Interhemispheric asymmetry in climate response to a gradual increase of atmospheric carbon dioxide." *Nature* 342: 660–662.

6

Deforestation and desertification in developing countries

R. K. Pachauri and Rajashree S. Kanetkar

1. Introduction

This paper takes a fresh look at two of the major environmental hazards affecting the planet, namely deforestation and desertification, in terms of the nature and magnitude of the problem as faced by the developing world, and their causes and effects. The Indian scenario and the various measures that have been adopted so far to combat the problem are reviewed. The role of forestry in controlling desertification and strategies for sound economic development while conserving the global environment are also discussed.

Much of the earth is degraded, is being degraded, or is at risk of degradation. Marine, freshwater, atmospheric, near-space, and terrestrial environments have suffered and continue to suffer degradation. This paper focuses on terrestrial degradation – which may be defined as the loss of utility or potential utility or its reduction, or the loss or change of features or organisms that cannot be replaced (Barrow, 1991) – and on deforestation and desertification in particular.

The processes of deforestation and desertification, which are widespread, discrete when caused by human actions, and continuous when they occur naturally, are two of the major environmental concerns that are addressed by Agenda 21 developed for the United Nations

Conference on Environment and Development (UNCED) in June 1992.

2. Deforestation

The forests that occupy more than a quarter of the world's land area are of three broad types – tropical moist and dry, temperate, and degraded. The rapid loss of tropical forests, due to competing land uses and forms of exploitation that often prove to be unsustainable, is a major contemporary environmental issue. The main concern globally is with tropical forests that are disappearing at a rate that threatens the economic and ecological functions that they perform. Deforestation in developing countries is more recent, with tropical forests having declined by nearly one-fifth so far in this century. Areas of forests and woodlands at the end of 1980 as assessed by the Food and Agriculture Organization of the UN (FAO) are shown in figure 6.1.

Deforestation is a much-used, ill-defined, and imprecise term that tends to imply quantitative loss of woody vegetation. There can also be qualitative changes in forests, from, say, species-diverse tropical forests to single-species eucalyptus or pine plantations, or to less species-rich secondary (regrowth) forests. Each year, around 4 million hectares (ha) of virgin tropical forests are converted into secondary forests (Barrow, 1991). However there is little distinction in

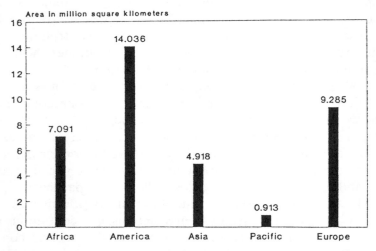

Fig. 6.1   **Area of forests and woodlands by continent, end 1980 (km² million)**

most of the literature between vegetation loss that will "heal" and that which will not.

Deforestation profiles – No simple stereotypes

According to the 1989 *World Development Report* (World Bank 1989), the 14 developing countries in South America, Africa, and South-East Asia where more than 250,000 ha of tropical forests are destroyed annually represent a wide range of third world development problems. They defy easy stereotypes: populations ranged from 11 million in Ecuador to 853 million in India; the percentage of the total population living in rural areas ranged from 15 per cent in Argentina to 82 per cent in Thailand; per capita GNP ranged from US$170 in Zaire to over US$2,600 in Argentina; total debt owed to foreign institutions varied from US$9 billion by Zaire to over US$110 billion by Brazil; and this debt as a percentage of total GNP ranged from 31 per cent in Peru to 140 per cent in Zaire (Wood, 1990).

More recent statistics on deforestation suggest that, for tropical forests, the overall annual rate in the 1980s was 0.9 per cent. This is also the rate in Latin America, with Asia's rate somewhat higher (1.2 per cent) and Africa's somewhat lower (0.8 per cent) (World Bank, 1992). However, current rates of deforestation do not provide an indication of the current conditions of forests on these continents because historically damage may already have taken place at a very high level in the past, leaving highly devastated areas wherein scope for further damage is low.

Figures 6.2 and 6.3 illustrate the extent of forest cover and deforestation rates in developing countries in the Asia and Pacific region.

The causes of contemporary deforestation

Severe human pressures on forests in many tropical developing countries, especially those resulting from a need to provide for the welfare of numerous poor rural dwellers, will continue to threaten the existence of these resources. In parallel, forests continue to be lost in many developed countries owing to over-harvesting, inadequate regeneration, clearance for agriculture and urbanization, and air pollution. The major causes of deforestation are discussed below.

Human population growth, agricultural expansion, and resettlement
Forest degradation and loss from the spontaneous expansion of people's activities into forest lands is notoriously difficult to quantify.

The status of the global environment

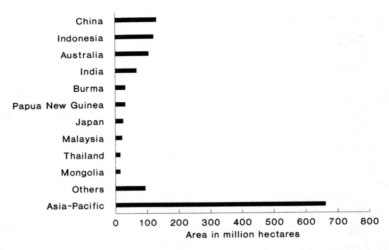

Fig. 6.2 **Area of forests and woodlands in the top 10 countries in the Asia and Pacific region, 1983 (million hectares)**

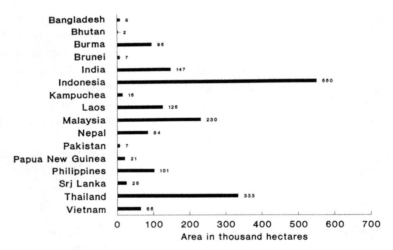

Fig. 6.3 **Annual deforestation by country in the Asia and Pacific region, 1976–1980 ('000 hectares)**

Shifting agriculture is the primary cause of deforestation, accounting for about 45 per cent of the 7.5 million ha losses in tropical forests in 1976–1980. In 1980 it accounted for 35 per cent of deforestation in Latin America, 70 per cent in Africa, and 49 per cent in South-East Asia (notably Sri Lanka, Thailand, north-east India, Laos, Malaysia, and the Philippines) (Tolba et al., 1992).

74

Grazing and ranching
Domestic animals in tropical woodlands and forests reduce regeneration through grazing, browsing, and trampling. India alone has about 15 per cent of the world's cattle, 46 per cent of its buffaloes, and 17 per cent of its goats. The spread of irrigated and cultivated land in India has forced livestock owners into forest areas, where 90 million of the estimated 400 million cattle now reside, whereas the carrying capacity is estimated at only 31 million (Government of India, 1987).

Fuelwood and charcoal
Exploitation for fuelwood and charcoal is mainly a problem of tropical and subtropical woodlands, although there are examples of closed forests being severely affected (notably in India, Sri Lanka, and Thailand).

Timber exploitation
On a global scale, increasing demand for industrial roundwood accounts for marginally less exploitation than fuelwood, although it remained high at around 1.7 billion m^3 in 1989 (Barrow, 1991).

Plantations
A smaller, but none the less significant, reason for the removal of natural forests is the planting of tropical tree crops such as rubber, oil palm, and eucalyptus, more so because the rate of plantation establishment is less than rates of deforestation.

Atmospheric pollution
The overall stress of pollution brings about nutrient deficiencies thereby rendering the vegetation vulnerable to droughts, insects, and pests. The growth, development, and decline of forests have always reflected the integrated effects of many variables. Acid rain has now been added to this list. It may not be possible to establish definite proof of the link between acid precipitation and damage to vegetation. The body of circumstantial evidence is large, however, and supports the view that the terrestrial environment is under some threat from acid rain.

In addition to the above, the expansion of communication, the construction of large dams, the failure to assist the poor, and climatic anomalies of fire and drought only aggravate this problem further.

3. Desertification

The development of desert-like conditions where none existed previously has been described in many ways. Definitions of desertification are usually broad, including losses of vegetative cover and plant diversity that are attributable in some part to human activity as well as the element of irreversibility. These definitions are not confined to advancing frontiers of sand that engulf pastures and agricultural land, as often shown visually in the media. Various indicators of this phenomenon are listed in table 6.1 (Barrow, 1991).

Table 6.1 **Indicators of desertification**

Physical indicators	Decrease in soil depth
	Decrease in soil organic matter
	Decrease in soil fertility
	Soil crust formation/compaction
	Appearance/increase in frequency/severity of dust sandstorms/dune formation and movement
	Salinization/alkalinization
	Decline in quality and quantity of ground and surface water
	Increased seasonality of springs and small streams
	Alteration in relative reflectance of land (albedo change)
Biological indicators	
Vegetation	Decrease in cover
	Decrease in above-ground biomass
	Decrease in yield
	Alteration of key species distribution and frequency
	Failure of species successfully to reproduce
Animal	Alteration in key species distribution and frequency
	Change in population of domestic animals
	Change in herd composition
	Decline in livestock production
	Decline in livestock yield
Social/economic indicators	Change in land use/water use
	Change in settlement pattern (e.g. abandonment of villages)
	Change in population (biological) parameters (demographic evidence, migration statistics, public health information)
	Change in social process indicators – increased conflict between groups/tribes, marginalization, migration, decrease in incomes and assets, change in relative dependence on cash crops/subsistence crops

Sources: Reining (1978) and Kassas (1987).

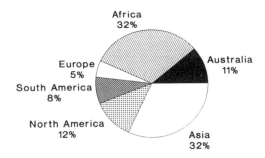

Fig. 6.4   **World arid lands by continent (Source: UNEP, 1991)**

The nature and scope of the problem

The UNCED defined desertification as land degradation in the arid, semi-arid, and sub-humid areas resulting from various factors, including climatic variations and human activities. These areas are subject to serious physical constraints linked to inadequate water resources, low plant formation productivity, and general vulnerability of biological systems and functions. Whereas on an individual basis animal and plant species are each a model of adjustment and resistance, ecological associates and formations are easily disturbed by the pressures exerted by rapidly growing populations and their livestocks. Desertification has become a longstanding and increasingly severe problem in many parts of the world, and in developing countries in particular.

According to a UNEP (1984) estimate, 35 per cent of the earth's land surface (4.5 billion ha) – an area approximately the size of North and South America combined – and the livelihoods of the 850 million people who inhabit that land are under threat from desertification. Currently, each year some 21 million ha are reduced to a state of near or complete uselessness. Projections to the year 2000 indicate that loss on this scale will continue if nations fail to step up remedial action (World Bank, 1992).

The distribution of the world's arid lands by continent is shown in figure 6.4.

Trends in desertification

Global statistics on trends in desertification are scanty. However, estimates of trends are possible for areas where detailed assessments

Table 6.2 **Some examples of desertification trends**

Kenya	At Lake Baringo, an area of 360,000 ha, the annual rate of land degradation desertification between 1950 and 1981 was 0.4%. At Marsabit, an area of 1.4 million ha, it was 1.3% for the period 1956–1972.
Mali	In the three localities of Nara, Mordiah, and Yonfolia, with a total area of some 195,000 ha, the average annual rate of loss during the past 30–35 years has been of the order of 0.1%.
Tunisia	The annual rate of desertification during the past century was of the order of 10% and about 1 million ha were lost to the desert between 1880 and the present.
China	The present average annual rate of desertification/land degradation for the country is of the order of 0.6%, while in such places as Boakong County, north of Beijing in Hebei Province, it rises to 1.3%, and to 1.6% in Fenging County.
USSR	The annual desertification/sand encroachment rate in certain districts of Kalmykia, north-west of the Caspian Sea, was recently estimated at a level as high as 10%, while in other localities it was 1.5–5.4%. The desert growth around the drying-out Aral Sea was estimated at about 100,000 ha per year during the past 25 years, which gives an annual average desertification rate of 4%.
Syria	An annual rate of land degradation of 0.25% was found in the 500,000 ha area of the Anti-Lebanon Range north of Damascus for the period 1958–1982.
Yemen	The country's average annual rate of abandonment of cultivated land owing to soil degradation increased from 0.6% in 1970–1980 to about 7% in 1980–1984.
Sahara	An analysis using a satellite-derived vegetation index shows steady expansion of the Sahara between 1980 and 1984 (an increase of approximately 1,350,000 km^2) followed by a partial recovery up to 1990 (Tucker et al., 1991).

Source: UNEP (1991).

have been made at the national or local level. These are highlighted in table 6.2 (Tolba et al., 1992).

The causes and the process

Much damage has been inflicted on the economic activities in the arid regions, leading to a great deal of hardship for the majority of the people there. Very few parts of the arid zone have been spared. What accounts for this unhappy situation?

The answer is twofold. Firstly, human pressure in the dry zones has grown enormously in recent decades owing to an increase in population. The needs for food, water, fuel, raw materials, and other natural resources have grown accordingly, exceeding the carrying capacity of the land in most cases. Secondly, many recent years have seen protracted drought, sometimes lasting for over 20 years. Under natural conditions, such failures of expected rainfall would have had little effect, but coupled with the human pressures they have produced disastrous results.

Soil erosion caused naturally by prolonged droughts and by various activities that abuse and over-exploit the natural resources are, in essence, responsible for the advance of deserts. Advancing deserts provide negative feedbacks to the root causes, thereby accelerating the process of desertification further. This is illustrated in figure 6.5.

Whatever the causes, the processes of degradation or desertification involve damage to the vegetation cover.

4. The implications of deforestation and desertification

The environmental hazards of desertification and deforestation, though distinct, provide mutual feedbacks and are far from being independent of each other. They consequently have similar implications and solutions.

Desertification and deforestation involve a drastic change in microclimates. For instance, if shrubs and trees are felled, the noonday sun will fall directly on hitherto shaded soil; the soil will become warmer and drier, and organisms living on or in the soil will move away to avoid the new harshness. The organic litter on the surface – dead leaves and branches, for example – will be quickly oxidized, the carbon dioxide being carried away. So too will be the small store of humus in the soil.

All these changes in microclimate also bring about ecological changes. The ecosystem is being altered, in most cases adversely. Hence, these processes result not only in a loss of biological productivity but also in the degradation of surface microclimates. Phenomena such as global warming and the greenhouse effect, which have their origin in deforestation and desertification, among many other causes, are more serious, global in scope, and therefore potentially more threatening.

Deforestation and desertification adversely affect agricultural productivity, the health of humans as well as of livestock, and economic activities such as eco-tourism. Hence, they have serious socio-economic implications too. In Asia, some 30 million people living in the coldest zones of the Himalayas were unable to ensure their energy supply

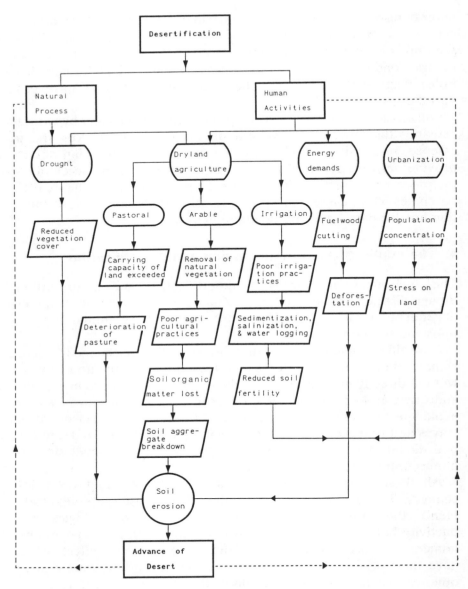

Fig. 6.5 **The causes and development of desertification**

in 1980, according to estimates for that year, despite overutilization of all the wood available. Approximately 710 million people were in a situation of decidedly inadequate fuelwood supplies, mainly in the highly populated zones of the Ganges and Indus plains and in the lowlands and islands of South-East Asia. It is estimated that by the year 2000, if present trends continue, 1.4 billion people in this region will be living in zones where fuelwood supplies are completely in-adequate to cover their minimum energy needs (World Bank, 1992).

Another indirect implication of these two hazards is that the re-sources needed to combat them are going to be very large. In 1982, it was estimated that between then and A.D. 2000, US$1.8 billion per year would be required to combat desertification (Tolba, 1987). Ahmad and Kassas (1987) estimated that a 20-year worldwide pro-gramme to arrest desertification would cost (at 1987 prices) roughly US$4.5 billion a year, US$2.4 billion of that needed in developing countries. Such sums are well beyond 1987 levels of donor assistance to the third world for everything.

5. Citizen action to counter deforestation and desertification

The Chipko Movement in India, which began in 1972, is a people's ecology movement professing non-violence and non-cooperation. It has been significant in protecting forest and woodland on the Indian subcontinent. Also in India, a centuries-old practice is being rediscovered, adapted, and promoted. Deeply rooted, hedge-forming vetiver grass, planted in contour strips across hill slopes, slows water run-off dramatically, reduces erosion, and increases the moisture available for crop growth. Since 1987 a quiet revolution has been taking place, and today 90 per cent of soil conservation efforts in India are based on such biological systems.

In the Philippines, non-governmental organizations (NGOs) and the Catholic Church have been active in supporting and promot-ing citizen groups seeking to protect existing trees and to plant new forests.

In the Sahel, simple technologies involving the construction of rock bunds along contour lines for soil and moisture conservation have succeeded where sophisticated measures once failed. Bunded fields yield an average of 10 per cent more produce than traditional fields in a normal year, and in the drier years almost 50 per cent more.

6. The role of forestry in combating desertification

The problem of developing arid lands and improving the well-being of the people living on them is one of both magnitude and complexity – magnitude in terms of the large area involved and complexity in that their development cannot be dissociated from their ecological, social, and economic characteristics.

Forestry has a major role to play in such a development strategy:
- one of its fundamental roles is the maintenance of the soil and water base for food production, through shelterbelts, windbreaks, and scattered trees, and through soil enrichment;
- it contributes to livestock production through silvipastoral systems, particularly the creation of fodder reserves or banks in the form of fodder trees or shrubs, to cushion the calamities of drought;
- it produces fuelwood, charcoal, and other forest products through village and farm woodlots;
- it contributes to rural employment and development through cottage industries based on raw materials derived from wild plants and animals and the development of wildlife-based tourism;
- it provides food from wildlife as well as from plants in the form of fruits, leaves, roots, and fungi.

Scenario of deforestation and desertification in India

During the British rule, the area under reserved forests was progressively increased at the cost of the areas set aside to meet the needs of village populations. Increasing population pressure, shrinking areas of land accessible to meet the domestic requirements of agriculture and animal husbandry, and, above all, the creation of open access meant continuing degradation of these areas. Simultaneously, in the reserve forests, the whole emphasis was on a few commercially valuable species such as Teak. The trend everywhere was to harvest the more accessible larger timber that had commercial value, with little thought for long-term sustainability. Making biomass available to influential groups in society (merchants, contractors, etc.) at highly subsidized prices was carried to its extreme after independence when the forest-based industry, originated under the British rule, really took off (Gadgil, 1989).

The latest statistics related to forest cover in India show that 19.44 per cent of the total geographical area (639,182 km^2) is covered by forests (Government of India, 1991). The estimated annual rate of deforestation during 1981–1985 was 147,000 ha and the area annually deforested as a percentage of the total forest area in the country was 0.25 per cent (Maheshwari, 1989).

The arid zone of India covers about 12 per cent of the geographical area including 31.9 billion km^2 of hot desert located in parts

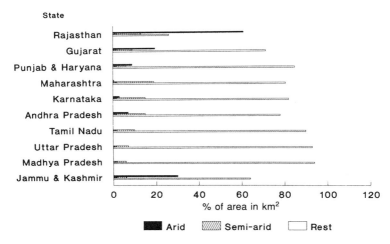

Fig. 6.6   **Arid and semi-arid zones in India, by state (Source: Maheshwari, 1989)**

of Rajasthan (61 per cent), Punjab and Haryana (9 per cent), and Andhra Pradesh and Karnataka (10 per cent). The cold arid tracts are located in the north-west Himalayas, namely Ladakh, Kashmir, and Lahaul Spiti (Himachal Pradesh). The Indian arid zone is by far the most populated arid zone in the world. The statewise distribution of arid zones in India is shown in figure 6.6, and they are mapped in figure 6.7.

The programme for combating desertification in India was started in 1977–1978 and is being implemented in 18 affected districts of Rajasthan, Gujarat, Haryana, Jammu & Kashmir, and Himachal Pradesh. During recent years there has been growing recognition of the failure of traditional forest management systems in India. The social forestry programme of the State Forest Departments and various community and agro-forestry projects, funded internally as well as internationally, are actively countering deforestation.

Looking at the potential of participatory forest management, the Tata Energy Research Institute (TERI) is implementing the Joint Forest Management Programme (JFMP) in the State of Haryana in collaboration with the Haryana Forest Department (HFD) and with the active participation of the local communities. After completing the first three-year phase successfully, implementation of the second phase has now begun. TERI's primary objectives in implementing this programme are:

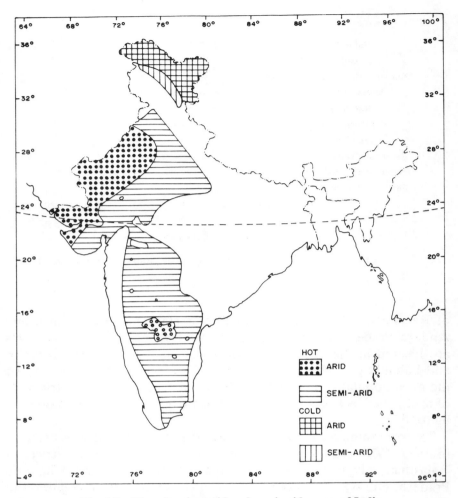

Fig. 6.7 **Map showing arid and semi-arid zones of India**

- to facilitate the development of participatory forest management systems for adoption by the HFD;
- to orient the forestry staff and local communities to bring in attitudinal changes regarding JFMP through regular meetings, workshops, training, and extension activities;
- to assist in research on the institutional, economic, social, and ecological aspects of joint forestry management;
- to disseminate information concerning the effects of joint forestry management on ecological regeneration, economic productivity, and environmental security.

84

Various strategies and incentive mechanisms adopted for implementing the programme are:
- the provision of various non-timber forest products to local communities at concessionary rates;
- the organization of meetings, field training and workshops emphasizing micro-planning and women's participation to sensitize, motivate, and orient the target groups;
- regular documentation, and dissemination of publicity and extension material.

So far, 38 Hill Resource Management Societies have been formed in villages adjoining the forests in Haryana Shiwaliks (lower Himalayas). The target group comprises marginal farmers and traditional graziers. Since 1990, there has been a remarkable change in the livestock pattern (the numbers have gone down whereas quality has improved), shifting the emphasis from open grazing to stall feeding. Agricultural yields have increased up to fourfold owing to the provision of irrigation water through the construction of water-harvesting structures. There has been significant increase in the yield of commercial as well as fodder grasses as a result of social fencing offered by the local communities in return.

Measures undertaken to counter the problems of deforestation and desertification

The FAO and United Nations Development Programme (UNDP) have been mapping and monitoring deforestation and desertification, especially since 1979. The Geographical Information System (GIS) is being used to map and monitor the amount and degree of damage caused by these hazards and extensive databases are being established.

In 1977, the United Nations Conference on Desertification (UNCOD) adopted a Plan of Action to Combat Desertification (PACD), which was endorsed by the UN General Assembly in the same year. The worldwide programme was aimed at stopping the process of desertification and at rehabilitating affected land. In 1985, the World Resources Institute, the World Bank, and the UNDP published a Tropical Forestry Action Plan (TFAP). This had taken several years to prepare through the combined efforts of governments, forestry agencies, UN agencies, and NGOs.

These plans, however, stated only what *should* be done, but not how it could be achieved, and efforts undertaken so far have not been adequate to cope with the magnitude of the problem. So the damage continues. The general conclusion is that the plans failed to generate enough political support, although the proposals were probably quite sound.

Despite the limited success of PACD, several countries have adapted their national plans to come within the scope of PACD implementation. Particularly significant measures have been undertaken in the countries of the Sudano-Sahelian belt of Africa, and in India, China, Iran, and the former USSR.

In both developed and developing countries much could be achieved through a change in attitudes toward forests – from one of seeing the potential for exploitation to one of seeing the need and desirability to conserve and make exploitation more rational and sustained and less wasteful. Various multinational development agencies and philanthropic foundations (e.g. the FAO, the World Bank, the Ford Foundation) are now supporting efforts to encourage management by smaller groups more closely associated with particular forest tracts, and to give them responsibility for forests in good condition, as well as for degraded land. For example, the Joint Forest Management Programme in India, implemented in 12 states since 1990, is being funded by such organizations and aims at evolving and establishing systems of sustainable forest management jointly by the government and the local people.

7. Possible solutions

In face of the above hazards, with all the social, economic, political, and environmental problems that they imply, it is inevitable that two questions have received increased attention in recent years: Can the damage be prevented? Can the damage that has already occurred be reversed? The answer to both is a qualified yes.

Preventive measures for combating drought and halting the spread of the deserts, as highlighted by the UNCED in *Agenda 21*, include:
- strengthening the knowledge base and developing information and monitoring systems for regions prone to desertification and drought, including the economic and social aspects of the fragile ecosystems;
- combating land degradation through, *inter alia*, intensified soil conservation, afforestation, and reforestation activities;
- developing and strengthening integrated development programmes for the eradication of poverty and the promotion of alternative livelihood systems in areas prone to desertification;

- developing comprehensive anti-desertification programmes and integrating them into national development plans and national environmental planning;
- developing comprehensive drought-preparedness and drought-relief schemes, including self-help arrangements for drought-prone areas and the design of programmes to cope with environmental refugees;
- encouraging and promoting popular participation and environmental education, focusing on desertification control and management of the effects of drought (UNCED, 1992).

The overriding need of the next few decades is to evolve strategies that inextricably tie conservation and development together. Policies for resource management will have to include the following essential components:

- a recognition of the true value of natural resources, because they ultimately are in finite supply;
- institutional responsibility for resource management hand in hand with a matching accountability for results;
- better knowledge of the extent, quality, and potential of the resource base while accelerating the diffusion of existing technology that can expand output in environmentally sound ways.

In developing countries, where the actions of local people are the root cause of deforestation, the various alternatives that offer some hope for slowing tropical deforestation, and at the same time are cheap and fast enough to be worthy of consideration, are: conservation to help natural forests regenerate, better management of forests, better fire control measures, reforestation and afforestation, fuelwood/energy plantations and woodlots, agro-forestry, farm and village woodlots, cash-crop tree farming, and, last but not least, non-conventional methods of forest management.

The causal chain of land degradation and possible interventions at various stages to reverse the process are illustrated in figure 6.8. As is evident in this figure, the development of science and technology occupies a prominent position in the possible interventions. Land-use planning, dryland cropping strategies, appropriate forest management technologies optimizing their resource potential, the standardization of harvesting techniques for non-timber forest products, fuelwood-supply plantations, and renewable energy technologies are some of the potential areas for research that need more probing.

The following are a few suggestions appropriate for immediate action to fight against deforestation and desertification in a reasonably long-term perspective:

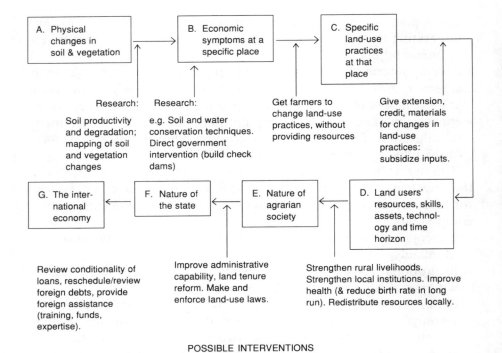

POSSIBLE INTERVENTIONS

Fig. 6.8 Interventions related to the causation of land degradation (Source: Winpenny, 1990)

- strengthen the planning and organization of ecological, silvicultural, and socio-economic research;
- strengthen research on particular subjects (such as certain social and cultural aspects of rural life, natural resource accounting, etc.) that appear to be weak at present in view of development and resource conservation objectives;
- strengthen research on non-traditional methods in forestry, e.g. community forestry programmes emphasizing people's participation like the JFMP, the use of biotechnology in the breeding of tree species for desired characteristics;
- decentralize research work according to ecological and socio-economic conditions;
- determine and carry out a systematic programme for the advanced training of research workers and research administrators.

To assume that massive aid inflows coursing through the multi-lateral development banks and bilateral agencies for international development can solve the developing countries' problems is to ignore decades of documentation demonstrating that such aid has compounded environmental degradation. The history of development assistance suggests that its success depends on getting it to the right people. NGOs such as TERI, which are actively involved in a participatory approach at the grass roots, research on biomass, and biotechnology could all play a vital role in developing and implementing the above strategy.

The urgency of the problem is accentuated by the fact that the pressure on natural resources is fast getting out of hand owing to unprecedented population growth and increasing densities. The time for action is running out as the environmental damage rendered by deforestation and desertification expands, threatening new areas and new societies, while countermeasures tend to be long term and time consuming. The cost of countermeasures is escalating from year to year because the area affected is growing, the degree of damage is growing, and world prices of rehabilitative measures are rising. Off-site (and social) costs too continue to increase. Other environmental and economic problems are likely to become serious, tending to distract the attention of international funding agencies to other issues (e.g. sealevel rise). However, if the process of desertification and deforestation is not arrested soon, the world shortage of food will increase dramatically.

Past experiences show that the success of programmes to combat desertification and deforestation will depend on the institutional arrangements, the dissemination of information, the creation of awareness, the development of assessment methodology, and adaptive research. Funding and implementing agencies, both national and international, must give priority to programmes for combating desertification and countering deforestation, both nationally and internationally. The necessary assistance – in cash as well as in kind – will have to be provided to developing countries affected by these hazards. Any countermeasures will have to be fully integrated into programmes of socio-economic development, instead of being considered only as rehabilitation measures, and the affected populations will have to be fully involved in the planning and implementation of these programmes.

References

Ahmad, Y. J. and M. Kassas. 1987. *Desertification: Financial Support for the Biosphere*. West Hartford, Conn.: Kumarian Press.

Barrow, C. J. 1991. *Land Degradation – Developments and Breakdown of Terrestrial Environments*. Cambridge: Cambridge University Press.

Gadgil, M. 1989. "Deforestation: Problems and prospects." Foundation Day Lecture, Society for Promotion of Wastelands Development, 12 May, New Delhi. Centre of Ecological Sciences and Theoretical Studies, Indian Institute of Science Bangalore.

Government of India. 1987. *State of Forest Report 1987*. Forest Survey of India, Dehradun.

────── 1991. *State of Forest Report, 1987–1989*. Forest Survey of India, Dehradun.

Kassas, M. 1987. "Drought and desertification." *Land Use Policy* 4(4): 389–400.

Kemp, D. D. 1990. *Global Environmental Issues – A Climatological Approach*. London: Routledge.

Maheshwari, J. K. 1989. *Processing and Utilization of Perennial Vegetation in the Arid Zone of India in Role of Forestry in Combatting Desertification*. Rome: FAO Conservation Guide 21, pp. 137–172.

Reining, P. 1978. *Handbook on Desertification Indicators*. Washington, D.C.: American Association for the Advancement of Science.

Tolba, M. K. 1987. *Sustainable Development: Constraints and Opportunities*. London: Butterworth.

Tolba, M. K., O. A. El-Kholy, et al. 1992. *The World Environment 1972–1992. Two Decades of Challenge*. London: Chapman & Hall.

Tucker, C. J., H. E. Dregne, and W. W. Newcomb. 1991. "Expansion and contraction of Sahara Desert from 1980–1990." *Science* 253.

UNCED (United Nations Conference on Environment and Development). 1992. *Agenda 21. United Nations Conference on Environment and Development, Brazil, June 3–14, 1992*. Brazil: UNCED.

UNEP (United Nations Environment Programme). 1984. *General Assessment of Progress in the Implementation of the Plan of Action to Combat Desertification, 1978–1984*. GC-12/9.

────── 1991. *Status of Desertification and Implementation of the United Nations Plan of Action to Control Desertification*. Nairobi: UNEP.

Winpenny, J. T. (ed.). 1990. *Development Research: The Environmental Challenge*. Boulder, Colo.: Westview Press, for the ODI.

Wood, W. B. 1990. *Tropical Deforestation. Balancing Regional Development Demands and Global Environmental Concerns*.

World Bank. 1989. *World Development Report 1989*. Oxford: Oxford University Press.

────── 1992. *World Development Report 1992*. Oxford: Oxford University Press.

Comments on part 2

Mohamed Kassas

My first comment concerns the relationship between the two topics dealt with in chapters 5 and 6, that is, the possible impacts of land degradation (as a result of deforestation and desertification) on the global climate system and the possible impacts of climate changes on the processes of deforestation and desertification (see Hulme and Kelly, 1993). Apart from the role of deforestation in the global carbon cycle and its adding to the atmospheric load of carbon dioxide, land degradation impacts on climate relate to several processes:

1. Desert and desertified territories are sources of atmospheric dust, which modifies the scattering and absorption of solar radiation in the atmosphere. Its effect on temperature would depend on the altitude at which it is borne (Bryson, 1972). The climatic impact of suspended particulate substances in the atmosphere may be no less than that of other pollutants, including the greenhouse gases.

2. The effects of an impoverishment of plant cover on the ground surface energy budget and the temperature of near-surface air have been the subject of many studies (Jackson and Idso, 1975; Balling, 1988, 1991; Schlesinger et al., 1990). Two processes are involved: increased surface albedo (especially with desertification)

and reduced removal of moisture by evapotranspiration (reduction of plant cover).

3. The reduction of plant cover reduces the roughness of the surface. Surface roughness (tree growth in moist territories or scrub growth in drylands) exerts a "drag effect" that dissipates wind energy. Numerical models indicate that a less rough surface could diminish rainfall (Hare and Ogallo, 1993).

4. There is evidence indicating that reduction of plant cover reduces the availability of organic particles in the atmosphere. These particles are potential condensation nuclei and their reduction may cause a reduction in rainfall.

5. It has also been suggested that much of the rainfall in Africa's arid and semi-arid inland territories derives from nearby forested regions (e.g. the Zaire–Congo basin); deforestation reduces rainfall and exacerbates aridity further leewards.

My second comment relates to the global balance of outputs and sinks of carbon dioxide and related greenhouse gases. The world's drylands (about 40 per cent of the land surface of the ice-free earth) contribute very little to the sink capacity of the earth. Desertification further reduces this contribution. But drylands provide the available space for enhancing the global sink capacity. Programmes of afforestation and revegetation for combating desertification and reclaiming desertified areas would entail the expansion of the global sinks for greenhouse gases.

One aspect common to both deforestation and desertification (degradation of biota) is loss of biodiversity. This is evident in deforestation especially in tropical forests and woodlands. Here a wealth of species (known and unknown) are lost daily. The number of species to be lost in the world drylands is less; but many crop (wheat, barley, sorghums, millets, etc.) and fodder (medicagos, trifoliums, etc.) species that form the backbone of world agriculture and pasture husbandry have their origin in arid and semi-arid territories (Vavilov, 1949; Barigozzi, 1986). Hundreds of wild species native to drylands are sources of valuable medicinal materials (UNESCO, 1960). The loss of populations of these plants and their wild relatives represents a loss of valuable genetic materials. The impact of desertification on the loss of germplasm resources may be, from the economic aspect, no less severe than the impact of deforestation.

When we discuss issues of climate changes (chap. 5) and deforestation and desertification (chap. 6) the issue of what is a global environmental problem poses itself. The Inter-governmental Negotiating

Committee for Elaboration of an International Convention to Combat Desertification (Geneva session, 13–24 September 1993) spent some time debating whether desertification was a "global environmental problem," and hence whether or not projects for combating it would qualify for support by the Global Environmental Facility (GEF).

Botkin (1989) and Turner et al. (1990) differentiate between two classes of global environmental issues: systemic and cumulative. Systemic global issues affect a physical system: its attributes at any locale can affect its attributes elsewhere because they influence the global state of the system. These need not be caused by a worldwide scale of activity. Examples include climate change and depletion of stratospheric ozone. The causes may not be global but the effects are. In cumulative global issues, the causes are geographically widespread and the impacts are also worldwide. Examples include land degradation, deforestation, desertification, population, and urbanization. As I have noted, desertification and deforestation qualify to be included in both categories because they are geographically worldwide and they may influence a physical system (the global climate).

Forest degradation goes back to the early history of humankind. Fire was an agent that inadvertently extended human impacts beyond the initial site. The impacts accelerated as population pressures increased (with the expansion of agriculture) and as world needs for timber and other forest products escalated. Matthews (1983) estimates the total area of world forests in the pre-agricultural era at 46,280,000 km^2; the FAO (1991) estimates the present area of world forests at 36,245,000 km^2, which represents a loss of 10 million km^2 of forests in all continents and in all climatic regions. Land degradation in the world drylands is the result of excessive human pressures (overgrazing of rangelands, overcultivation of rain-fed farmlands, mismanagement of irrigation and drainage systems in irrigated farmlands, over-cutting of woodlands, etc.). Dregne et al. (1991) give the following estimates of the extent of degradation:

World drylands	61.5 million km^2
Agriculturally used drylands	51.6 million km^2
of which: degraded	35.6 million km^2

Degraded agriculturally used drylands prevail in all world continents.

Here we have examples of worldwide problems that directly undermine the life-support system of billions of people and that indirectly affect the whole globe.

There is, however, one element of difference between the climate issue and the land degradation issue that needs to be considered when world policies are set. For instance, the world community found it suitable to address the former issue with a United Nations Framework Convention on Climate Change. Would it be suitable to address the desertification issue with a framework convention, or do we need an action-oriented convention? There are evident differences between the two issues. First, the climate change issue is still shrouded in uncertainties, including new uncertainties identified in the IPCC report published in 1992 (Houghton et al., 1992), that is, after the Convention had been elaborated (see also section 7 in chap. 5). Secondly, the damaging impacts of climate change (global warming and its consequences) are foreseen as likely to be manifest within 50–70 years. By contrast, desertification is an actual menace that has been actively occurring during the past 50 years, is already damaging the life support system of some 900 million people, and is associated with recurrent droughts that have caused the loss of millions of head of livestock in Africa and the uprooting of millions of people, who flee their homelands and swarm across political borders (10 million environmental refugees in Africa in 1984/85). Here, action is urgently needed.

References

Balling, R. C. 1988. "The climate impact of Sonoran vegetation discontinuity." *Climate Change* 13: 99–109.
——— 1991. "Impact of desertification on regional and global warming." *Bulletin of the American Meteorological Society* 72: 232–234.
Barigozzi, C. (ed.). 1986. *The Origin and Domestication of Cultivated Plants*. Amsterdam: Elsevier.
Botkin, D. B. 1989. "Science and the global environment." In: D. B. Botkin et al., *Global Change*. New York: Academic Press, pp. 1–14.
Bryson, R. 1972. "Climate modification by air pollution." In: N. Polunin (ed.), *The Environmental Future*. London: Macmillan, pp. 133–174.
Dregne, H. E., M. Kassas, and B. Rozanov. 1991. "A new assessment of the world status of desertification." *Desertification Control Bulletin*, no. 20: 6–18.
FAO (Food and Agriculture Organization). 1991. "Protection of land resources: Deforestation." UNCED Prepcomm., 2nd session, Doc. A/CONF. 15/PC/27.
Hare, F. K. and L. A. J. Ogallo. 1993. *Climate Variation, Drought and Desertification.* WMO-No. 653. Geneva: WMO.
Houghton, J. T., B. A. Callander, and S. K. Varney (eds.). 1992. *Climate Change 1992. The Supplementary Report to the IPCC Scientific Assessment.* Cambridge: Cambridge University Press.
Hulme, M. and M. Kelly. 1993. "Exploring the links between desertification and climate change." *Environment* 35(6): 5–11, 39–45.

Jackson, R. D. and S. B. Idso. 1975. "Surface albedo and desertification." *Science* 189: 1012–1013.

Matthews, E. 1983. "Global vegetation and land use: New high-resolution databases for climatic studies." *Journal of Climate and Meteorology* 22: 474–487.

Schlesinger, W. H., et al. 1990. "Biological feedback in global desertification." *Science* 247: 1043–1048.

Turner, B. L., et al. 1990. "Two types of global environmental changes: Definitional and spacial-scale issues in their human dimensions." *Global Environmental Change* 1: 14–22.

UNESCO. 1960. "Medicinal plants of arid zones." *Arid Zone Research* 13.

Vavilov, N. I. 1949. *The Origin, Variation, Immunity and Breeding of Cultivated Plants*. Waltham, Mass.: Chronica Botanica.

Part 3
Energy–economy interactions in stabilizing CO_2 emissions

7

Modelling economically efficient abatement of greenhouse gases

William R. Cline

1. Introduction

Cline (1992a) sets forth a comprehensive economic analysis of the greenhouse problem. That study develops estimates of the damage that may be expected from global warming; reviews other model estimates of the costs of abatement; and, after an in-depth examination of appropriate discounting methodology, presents cost–benefit calculations that find it is socially efficient to pursue an aggressive international policy of abatement of greenhouse gases (GHGs). The study suggests a two-phase policy approach, with more moderate action in the first decade pending further scientific confirmation.

Subsequent papers synthesize these findings and extend the analysis in various directions (North–South policy interaction, in Cline, 1992c; optimization using the Nordhaus, 1992a, DICE model in Cline, 1992b and 1992d; and a review of new benefits estimates, a survey of abatement cost models, and policy synthesis in Cline, 1993). To minimize duplication of these earlier studies, this paper presents only a summary statement of the cost–benefit analysis in Cline (1992a), and invites the reader to consult that study directly for further elaboration.

The emphasis here is on the evolving shape of the analytical debate. Recent scientific work tends to confirm the emphasis in Cline (1992a) on the much greater warming and damage that may be expected over a very long horizon (three centuries). New scientific results also underscore the risks of sudden and catastrophic effects. New damage estimates widen the menu of conceptual and regional effects even for the conventional doubling of CO_2. Ongoing comparisons of models provide a clearer emerging picture on the side of abatement costs as well.

For the overall cost–benefit comparison, it is becoming increasingly clear that the rate of time discounting is the single most important source of difference between analyses showing aggressive action to be socially efficient (Cline, 1992a) and conclusions in the opposite direction (Nordhaus, 1992b). Accordingly, this paper presents new estimates applying differing discount rates to the Nordhaus (1992a) optimization model, and incorporating backstop technology into that model as well. The analysis here also identifies the corresponding field of "carbon shadow prices," representing the socially efficient penalties for carbon emissions over time.

2. Damage from 2xCO₂ benchmark warming

The primary benefits of GHG abatement are the value of global warming damage thereby avoided. There are also secondary benefits, principally the reduction of urban pollution as a side-effect of reducing fossil fuel combustion. Most analyses examine these effects for the "equilibrium" warming associated with the doubling of carbon dioxide above pre-industrial levels ("2xCO₂").[1]

For this conventional benchmark, and the corresponding equilibrium mean global warming of 2.5 °C (the "best guess" estimate of the Intergovernmental Panel on Climate Change, IPCC, for the climate sensitivity parameter Λ), Cline (1992a) places damage to the US economy in a range of 1–2 per cent of GDP. The greatest damage occurs in agriculture (losses of 0.3 per cent of GDP), where careful attention to the appropriate allowance for "carbon fertilization" tends to leave greater net damage than is sometimes suggested.[2] Other major damage categories include the costs of increased energy for the excess of higher air-conditioning requirements over savings on heating (0.17 per cent of GDP); sealevel rise (0.12 per cent); losses in water supply (0.12 per cent); and increased losses of human life (0.1 per cent). On conservative valuations, forest loss, species loss, and increased air pollution from warmer temperatures (tropospheric ozone) add another

0.18 per cent of GDP to damage. More liberal allowances for species loss might place this damage alone on the order of 0.7 per cent of GDP. The secondary benefit of reduced air pollution could be of a comparable magnitude.

The 1 per cent of GDP damage estimate for $2xCO_2$ in Cline (1992a: table 3.4) is thus best viewed as a moderate central value, with the figure easily reaching 2 per cent of GDP. Moreover, if upper-bound warming ($\Lambda = 4.5\,°C$) is applied, and with even modest non-linearity (damage exponent $= 1.3$), the corresponding range for damage reaches 2-4 per cent of GDP.

Important additional damage estimates have been made by Titus (1992) and Fankhauser (1992). For the United States, Titus suggests extremely large potential damage in forest loss (0.8 per cent of GDP) and in increased water pollution associated with decreased stream flow (0.6 per cent of GDP, for a damage category not even considered in Cline, 1992a). The larger figure for forest loss incorporates a broader concept of the consumer value of forest use, whereas the much smaller estimate in Cline (1992a) is based narrowly on the market value of lumber forgone.

For his part, Fankhauser (1992) extends the damage estimates to other countries, estimating them at 1.5 per cent of GDP for the European Communities, 0.7 per cent for the former Soviet Union, a remarkably high 6.1 per cent for China, and 2.8 per cent for non-OECD countries overall.[3] His estimate for the United States is 1.3 per cent of GDP, which is comparable to the range in Cline (1992a). Fankhauser's estimate of an average of 1.4 per cent of GDP damage globally is comparable to that used by Nordhaus (1993b). It should be emphasized, however, that this is a GDP-weighted measure. Because of the relatively higher damage in developing countries, weighting by population would give a higher global estimate.

3. Very-long-term warming and damage

Cline (1992a) places heavy emphasis on the fact that, in the absence of policy intervention, global warming is likely to extend far beyond the amount associated with a doubling of pre-industrial atmospheric concentrations of carbon dioxide. A doubling of the carbon dioxide equivalent of all GHGs is expected to occur as early as 2025 (IPCC, 1990). In contrast, the proper time-horizon for analysis is at least three centuries. Thus, Sundquist (1990) estimates that the atmospheric concentration of carbon dioxide may be expected to rise until

101

the end of the twenty-third century, after which time mixing into the deep ocean could cause a limited reversal.

As calculated in Cline (1992a), with reasonable baselines for population and economic activity and given abundant coal resources, global emissions would multiply approximately threefold by 2100 and ninefold by 2300. With the atmospheric retention ratio at its recent level of approximately 50 per cent of emissions, over this horizon atmospheric concentrations of carbon dioxide could multiply some eightfold. Taking other GHGs into account, and applying the radiative forcing relationships identified in IPCC (1990), the implication is a central warming projection of $10\,°C$ by 2300 for the IPCC's "best guess" climate sensitivity parameter of $\Lambda = 2.5\,°C$. This would take the earth back to the climate of the mid-Cretaceous period 100 million years ago, when mean temperatures were an estimated $6\,°C$ to $12\,°C$ higher than today (Hoffert and Covey, 1992). If instead the upperbound climate sensitivity parameter is applied ($\Lambda = 4.5\,°C$), verylong-term warming could reach approximately $18\,°C$.

Recent simulations of the GFDL (Geophysical Fluid Dynamics Laboratory) general circulation model (GCM) at Princeton University tend to confirm the central very-long-term baseline in Cline (1992a). Manabe and Stouffer (1993) examine the effects of a quadrupling of pre-industrial carbon dioxide equivalent by 140 years from now. They note that this level amounts to a 1 per cent annual increase in CO_2-equivalent concentration, and is consistent with the IPCC "business-as-usual" scenario. The equilibrium mean surface air temperature increase reaches $7\,°C$.[4] This estimate turns out to be slightly more severe than that in my study (a central estimate of $7\,°C$ warming commitment by the somewhat later date of 2150; Cline, 1992a: 52).[5]

Manabe and Stouffer do not argue that atmospheric concentrations will in fact stop rising after 140 years. Instead, their interest is in examining the consequences of this specified century-scale scenario. They find that the sealevel rise from thermal expansion alone reaches 1.8 metres by the 500th year, and would presumably be much greater if the effect of melting of ice sheets were taken into account. In contrast, the IPCC's estimate for the sealevel rise by 2100 is only twothirds of a metre (IPCC, 1990: fig. 9.6).

Damage is highly likely to be non-linear in warming. As just one example, water runoff is a residual between precipitation (which rises with global warming but primarily in the high latitudes) and evapotranspiration, which rises more than linearly with warming. Cline

(1992a) uses a relatively modest degree of non-linearity for most effects: an exponent of 1.3. (In contrast, Nordhaus, 1993b, applies a quadratic damage function.) The Cline (1992a) estimate of very-long-term damage corresponding to 10 °C warming is in the range of 6–12 per cent of GDP for central estimates. Even with moderate non-linearity, the damage reaches an average of 20 per cent of GDP for higher-damage cases (upper-bound warming; with base damage for $2xCO_2$ at 1 or 2 per cent of GDP).

4. Catastrophic effects

One of the most disturbing findings of the new Manabe–Stouffer simulation for $4xCO_2$ is that:

... the ocean settles into a new stable state in which the thermohaline circulation has ceased entirely and the thermocline deepens substantially. These changes prevent the ventilation of the deep ocean and could have a profound impact on the carbon cycle and biogeochemistry of the coupled system. (Manabe and Stouffer, 1993: 215)

In other words, the GFDL model simulated for just $4xCO_2$ finds that in the *base case* one of the feared "catastrophes" occurs: the ocean conveyor belt shuts down, and along with it presumably the flow of the Gulf Stream that keeps Northern Europe from being as cold as its latitudinal peer, Canada's Hudson Bay region.[6] Moreover, the same phenomenon would largely close off the potential large reservoir of the deep ocean as a sink for carbon dioxide, presumably raising the atmospheric retention ratio and accelerating atmospheric build-up as a consequence.

Other recent evidence on the risk of catastrophe comes from the climate records in Greenland ice cores, which suggest that warming can come in extremely compressed periods. Thus, there was an estimated 7 °C (local) warming within the space of only 50 years in the Younger Dryas period some 12,000 years ago (Dansgaard et al., 1989); and a collapse and rebound of temperature by 14 °C within a 70-year period near the end of the last (Eemian) interglacial period before the present (Holocene) interglacial, some 115,000 years ago (Anklin et al., 1993). The extreme speed of such warming would seem highly likely to increase the non-linearity of damage, perhaps to catastrophic levels.

In the benefit–cost analyses examined below, these and other catastrophic scenarios are simply absent. The possibility of catastrophic outcomes must be kept in mind as a consideration that could warrant more aggressive abatement than indicated by the central benefit–cost analysis.

5. The costs of greenhouse gas abatement

Cline (1992a: chap. 4) provides a survey of economic models of the cost of reducing carbon dioxide emissions. Conceptually this cost equals the output loss imposed by restricting the use of a productive input, energy, in the "production function" for economic output. The central range of results in these models indicates that, by 2050, it would cost some 2–3 per cent of gross world product (GWP) to reduce emissions by 50 per cent from their business-as-usual baseline. This range is consistent with the production function approach.[7]

The OECD has investigated standardized simulations of several of the carbon abatement models (Dean, 1993). In an aggressive intervention scenario in which carbon emissions are reduced by 2 per cent annually from their business-as-usual time-path, by 2050 emissions would stand 70 per cent below baseline; and by 2100, 88 per cent below baseline. This scenario is broadly consistent with the aggressive action plan examined in Cline (1992a), where emissions are cut by one-third from present levels and then held constant at 4 billion tons of carbon (4 GtC) annually.[8]

The results of this standardized exercise show that, for the United States, the costs of the aggressive reduction by 2050 are in a range of 1.3 per cent of GDP (OECD's "GREEN" model) to about 2.6 per cent of GDP (the Manne–Richels, MR, model; and the Rutherford model). The extremely deep cut by 2100 imposes costs of 3.1 per cent of GDP in the MR model and 2.6 per cent of GDP in the Rutherford model (Dean, 1993: 11).[9]

For global costs, the models show somewhat (but not dramatically) higher costs. The simple average for these three models is a cost of 2.9 per cent of GWP for the 70 per cent cut from baseline by 2050, and 4.2 per cent of GWP for the 88 per cent cut from baseline by 2100. For the former Soviet Union, China, and other developing countries, costs are in the range of 4.0–5.5 per cent of GDP for the deep cuts by 2100 (MR and Rutherford models). Importantly, the somewhat higher costs of abatement for developing countries parallel the relatively higher damage of greenhouse abatement suggested by Fankhauser (as noted above), implying that for developing countries the benefit–cost trade-off may be comparable to that in industrial countries but at higher levels on both sides of the ledger.

Although costs can be substantially non-linear with respect to the depth of emissions cut-back at a given technology, they need not be so if it is recognized that the deeper reductions tend to come later in the time-horizon when the array of technological alternatives is wider. In particular, the advent of a "backstop technology" providing unlimited non-carbon-emitting energy at a fixed price premium above fossil fuels makes a critical difference to the cost of deep carbon cut-backs late in the horizon. Manne and Richels (1992) estimate that such technologies (e.g. advanced nuclear, solar, or biomass) should be available by about 2030, at a premium of about US$200 per ton of carbon (in 1990 dollars) above the opportunity cost of energy from carbon-emitting backstop technologies (e.g. synthetic fuels from coal).

Cline (1992a: chap. 5) emphasizes that abatement costs can be held lower initially through two strategies: forestry measures; and a move to the efficiency frontier using existing technology (as stressed in the "bottom–up" models). Reduced deforestation can remove carbon emissions at a cost of less than US$10 per ton. Afforestation can sequester carbon at costs under US$20 per ton (Moulton and Richards, 1990). However, additional carbon is sequestered only during the forest's growing stage, suggesting that afforestation is primarily an option for the first three decades or so.

The National Academy of Sciences (NAS, 1991) has estimated that, by moving to the efficiency frontier of existing technology, it would be possible to reduce US carbon emissions by 10–40 per cent at zero or very low cost. Information costs, utility pricing distortions, and other market failures help explain the gap between actual practice and potential efficiency. It is important to emphasize, however, that closing this gap is a one-time proportionate gain. Once the economy has moved to an "efficient" baseline, the new path *parallels* the original business-as-usual baseline at a lower absolute level that none the less still rises over time. It is unrealistic to expect a constant succession of additional movements to ever-shifting efficiency frontiers at zero cost, because the market failures in the revised baseline have already been removed. This is particularly so if the business-as-usual baseline already incorporates a widening array of technological alternatives (as in the Manne–Richels 1992 model). Thus, adherents of the bottom–up school cannot reasonably expect cost-free carbon abatement over the whole time-horizon.

Finally, costs can be substantially reduced if revenues from a carbon tax are used to correct existing distortions in fiscal structure. Existing taxes (e.g. on income and capital gains) impose disincentives that result in an economic loss of about 30 cents for each dollar of revenue collected (estimates for the United States by Jorgenson and Yun, 1990). Similarly, McKibbin (1992: 41) estimates that whereas an OECD-wide tax of US$15 per ton of carbon reduces US GDP by about 0.4 percentage points from baseline over the next two decades, if the revenues are used to reduce the budget deficit (rather than returned in a "lump sum" to households) the adverse output effect would be reduced to a 0.3 per cent reduction from baseline. The reason is that a lower fiscal deficit would reduce interest rates and stimulate investment and growth.

6. Benefit–cost comparison

Figure 7.1 shows the benefit–cost trade-off over time that emerges for an aggressive action programme that cuts global carbon emissions by one-third (to 4 billion tons of carbon annually) and then holds them constant over time (Cline, 1992a: chap. 7). In lieu of specific estimates for other countries, the figure assumes that the US damage profile is representative globally.

The benefits of abatement are set at only 80 per cent of the damage from baseline warming, on the grounds that even with aggressive action warming cannot be avoided completely. Similarly, abatement costs are expanded by 20 per cent above those for carbon alone, to take account of other GHGs. The cost curve is low at first, because of a 20 per cent "free" reduction assumed for the move to the efficiency frontier, as well as the availability of forestry measures. The abatement cost time-path then peaks at about 3.5 per cent of GWP, and thereafter declines to a plateau of about 2.5 per cent, because the cost function in Cline (1992a) allows for lower cost at later dates as the consequence of widening technological alternatives.[10]

Over the horizon, the benefits of abatement as a percentage of GWP substantially exceed costs in the high-damage case but are moderately below costs on average in the moderate central case. Moreover, the costs of abatement tend to be concentrated early in the horizon, whereas the greenhouse damage and thus benefits of abatement occur later. As a result, two factors drive the cost–benefit comparison: risk weighting, and the time discount rate for comparison across different points in time.

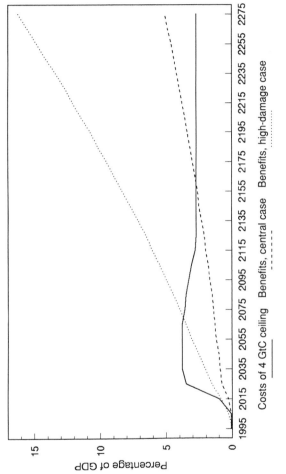

Fig. 7.1 **The costs and benefits of aggressive abatement of greenhouse warming**

107

Cline (1992a) places heavier weight (0.375) on the high-damage case than on the low-damage case (0.125) in aggregating with the central case (weight of 0.5) to capture risk aversion. Perhaps the single most important methodological issue, however, is the proper rate for time discounting.

The discount rate

When consumption is available at alternative time-periods, the proper discounting procedure applies a "social rate of time preference" equal to:

$$r = \rho + |\alpha| g, \tag{1}$$

where g is the rate of growth of per capita income, α is the elasticity of marginal utility of consumption, and ρ is the rate of *pure* time preference (Cline, 1992a: chap. 6; Nordhaus, 1992b: 1319). That is, the term α (< 0) tells how rapidly marginal utility drops off as per capita income rises; and the term ρ tells how much society prefers consumption today rather than tomorrow even for an unchanged level of per capita income.

Cline (1992a) adopts the classic view of Ramsey (1928) and others that the rate of pure time preference (ρ) should be set to zero for the purposes of social welfare analysis. Especially for intergenerational comparisons, from the point of view of society it makes no sense to value a dollar of consumption for the future at less than a dollar of consumption today when per capita consumption is held constant between the two periods. In contrast, utility-based discounting for income and consumption growth is appropriate, and is incorporated in the second term ($|\alpha| g$).

Many econometric studies use a logarithmic utility function, which sets the elasticity of marginal utility (α) equal to -1.0 (Blanchard and Fischer, 1989). Two specific investigations of the elasticity of marginal utility independently place it at -1.5 (Fellner, 1967; Scott, 1989), indicating a somewhat more rapid drop-off in marginal utility than in the usual logarithmic utility function.

Cline (1992a) sets per capita income growth over the three-century horizon at about 1 per cent annually. With $\rho = 0$, $|\alpha| = 1.5$, and $g = 1$, the result is a social rate of time preference of 1.5 per cent per annum. Even at this rate, which some economists would consider low,

US$1 of consumption today equates with US$20 (in real terms) 200 years in the future.

Following modern discount theory, Cline (1992a) further incorporates the influence of the portion of resources diverted from capital investment (on which the rate of return is higher) by applying a shadow price on capital and converting these resources to consumption equivalents. The overall effect is a discount rate of about 2 per cent.

Returning to figure 7.1, when this discounting procedure is applied, and when greater weight is applied to the high-damage case than to the low-damage case (not shown), the result is that the risk-weighted benefit/cost ratio for aggressive policy action comfortably exceeds unity (at 1.3). Thus, the economic benefits of the aggressive abatement of greenhouse gases would appear to warrant the corresponding economic costs, adding an economic basis for action to any case that might be made on ecological or scientific grounds alone.

Optimal emissions paths and the DICE model

In sharp contrast, Nordhaus (1992b) finds that even freezing emissions at their current level would have net social costs equivalent to 0.7 per cent of discounted future consumption. His optimal path would cut emissions by only 10 per cent *from baseline*, rising to 15 per cent in the next century. Because baseline emissions multiply more than threefold by 2100, his result indicates that it is economically efficient to allow the great bulk of emission increases to proceed unhindered.

To reach these conclusions, Nordhaus uses his Dynamic Integrated Climate-Economy (DICE) model (Nordhaus, 1992a). The DICE model is a potentially important advance in economic analysis of greenhouse policy. The model directly integrates emissions and global warming with savings, investment, and growth over time. The model appropriately takes a very-long-term view of the problem, as its simulations span 400 years (although Nordhaus, 1992b, reports results only through 2105). In principle the model provides the basis for identifying an optimal path of emissions over time, although in practice this path is extremely sensitive to assumptions.

Cline (1992b) implements the DICE model and examines its sensitivity to key parameters. As might be expected for an analysis over such a long horizon, the *time discount* rate turns out to be the prin-

cipal reason for the sharp divergence between the Nordhaus results
and those of the cost–benefit analysis in Cline (1992a).

In the DICE model, utility-based discounting (equivalent to the
term $|\alpha|g$ discussed above) takes place through the combined effect
of the logarithmic utility function (in which a 1 per cent rise in per
capita income causes a 1 per cent decline in the marginal utility of
consumption), on the one hand, and the model's optimal allocation
of resources between present consumption and capital formation
through saving (which drives the per capita growth rate, g), on the
other. The model then explicitly further discounts by incorporating
the rate of pure time preference, ρ. Its objective function is thus:

$$Max \sum_{t=1}^{T} P_t \ln(c_t)[1 + \rho]^{-t},\tag{2}$$

where P is population, c is per capita consumption, t is the year, and
T is the final year in the horizon (400 in DICE).

Alternative simulations with DICE

The impact of alternative discount rates
Figure 7.2 reports the results of simulating DICE with alternative
values for the rate of pure time preference, ρ. The figure shows the
proportionate cut of carbon emissions from baseline (business as
usual). For comparison, the path of proportionate cuts implied by the
ceiling of 4 GtC annually is also shown, identified as "Cline."

The lowest path of cut-backs in the figure represents results setting
the rate of pure time preference at 3 per cent, the value assumed by
Nordhaus. As indicated, the implementation here successfully repli-
cates the Nordhaus result of optimal cut-backs limited to only 10–15
per cent over the first 100 years when $\rho = 3$ per cent. However, the
figure also shows that, if lower values are assigned to ρ, the DICE
model itself generates much more aggressive optimal abatement
paths. Indeed, if the rate of pure time preference is set equal to zero
on the grounds argued above, the optimal abatement path in DICE
becomes approximately equivalent to the 4 GtC ceiling of the
aggressive abatement programme found to have a favourable risk-
weighted benefit–cost ratio in Cline (1992a).

For comparability with the results in Cline (1992a), the appropriate
value for the rate of pure time preference in figure 7.2 is in the range
of 0.5 per cent per annum. The reason is that the DICE model applies

110

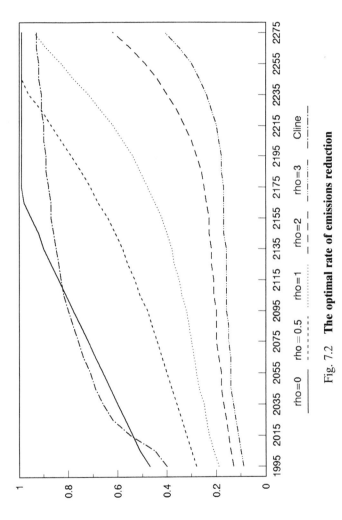

Fig. 7.2 **The optimal rate of emissions reduction**

rho=0   rho = 0.5   rho=1   rho=2   rho=3   Cline

a lower elasticity of marginal utility ($\alpha = -1$ instead of -1.5). This difference can be approximately compensated for by raising the rate of pure time preference (ρ) from the conceptually appropriate level of zero to 0.5 per cent.[11]

As may be seen in figure 7.2, if the rate of pure time preference is set at 0.5 per cent per annum, the optimal cut-back from baseline reaches about 50 per cent by 2100. Although this reduction is far greater than the optimal cut-back of 14 per cent identified by Nordhaus (1993b) for that period, the reduction remains considerably smaller than that implied by the aggressive international programme of limiting emissions to 4 GtC. However, adjustment of other elements of the DICE model could easily close this gap, including incorporation of the risk of higher-damage cases and imposition of a backstop-technology ceiling on abatement costs (as discussed below).

It should come as no surprise that the most profound policy decision that must be made on greenhouse policy turns on the rate of pure time preference, or how much weight we place on our own consumption in preference to that of our descendants. Global warming is inherently a problem involving small sacrifice in the present for large damage avoided for future generations. The 3 per cent value for ρ assumed by Nordhaus would seem to give far too little weight to future generations. This rate means that, under conditions of equal per capita income today and 200 years in the future, we can justifiably ask our descendants to give up US$370 in consumption to permit us to enjoy just US$1 of extra consumption today (in constant price dollars).

In this debate, Nordhaus (1993a) has replied that a zero rate of pure time preference is "lower than would be consistent with observed real interest rates." Even if this were true it would not be the proper basis for policy determination. Society would be irresponsible to impose a US$370/US$1 trade-off against our descendants even if the markets today stated that this rate is what currently obtains in financial transactions. Policy should seek to correct market distortions where they exist, and a rate of 3 per cent for pure time preference would strongly imply a severe distortion in the intertemporal consumption and assets markets. Indeed, it would be inconsistent to rule out the application of second-best pricing to compensate for market failure on the key analytical parameter – the discount rate – in addressing a policy issue that takes as its point of departure the need for second-best correction of market failure on another central price – that of carbon (for which the market price does not incorporate the external diseconomy of greenhouse damage).

Moreover, it is by no means clear that observed market behaviour places a rate as high as 3 per cent on pure time preference. The closest asset to this concept is the real rate of return on Treasury bills, which involve no risk. This rate has averaged only 0.3 per cent over the past 60 years (Cline, 1992a: 258).[12]

Nordhaus himself has examined the sensitivity of the DICE results to the discount rate (Nordhaus, 1993b). However, his sensitivity test is a weak one, because he maintains the sum of the pure rate of time preference (ρ) and the "growth discounting" ($|\alpha|g$) constant at 6 per cent. In his base case, $\rho = 3$ per cent, and growth rate, g, under "today's conditions" equals 3 per cent; so that, with $\alpha = -1$ (logarithmic utility), the left-hand side of equation (1) above equals 6 per cent, which he judges is the market rate for the present "real interest rate on goods." When he reduces the rate of pure time preference from 3 per cent to zero for purposes of sensitivity analysis, he compensates by increasing the elasticity of marginal utility from -1 to -2, so that the left-hand side of (1) remains 6 per cent with today's growth rate at $g = 3$ per cent. The result is that setting the rate of pure time preference to zero only increases optimal abatement from a 12.5 per cent cut-back from baseline in 2050 to a 25 per cent reduction; and from a 14.3 per cent cut-back by 2100 to a 28 per cent reduction (Nordhaus, 1993b: table 6-4). Moreover, even this increase in optimal abatement stems solely from the fact that growth is decelerating in Nordhaus's baseline. If growth were constant, there would be no change in optimal emissions, because the reduction of pure time preference would be wholly offset by the increase assumed for the elasticity of marginal utility.

As discussed above, insistence that equation (1) above must equal a "market" rate of 6 per cent would appear misguided. As noted, it is highly doubtful that the proper concept, the consumption rate of time preference, is anywhere near this high. Moreover, a "second-best" approach would consider the social rate of time preference rather than an observed market rate, as argued above.

Other model assumptions
There are other assumptions in DICE that may warrant change as well. The model's near-cubic cost curve for carbon reduction causes an extremely high marginal cost for deep cut-backs. This pattern stems in part from the fact that the cost curve has no time variable:

the sacrifice for a 70 per cent cut-back of carbon from baseline is identical whether the cut-back occurs today or in the latter part of the next century.[13]

The high cost of deep carbon reductions in DICE is revealed by considering the "shadow price" on carbon (the marginal cost of reducing carbon by 1 ton) under alternative simulations. Figure 7.3 reports these prices. It is evident that, with the much steeper optimal carbon reductions identified with lower rates of pure time preference, it is optimal to pay even very high marginal costs for carbon reduction (and thus very high carbon taxes). At $\rho = 0$, the optimal carbon tax reaches about US$220 per ton by 2025, and US$590 per ton by 2105.

These marginal costs would appear to overstate the expense of reducing carbon emissions. In particular, the marginal costs in the DICE model can rise far above the level of about US$200 per ton of carbon identified by Manne and Richels (1992) as an appropriate range for the ceiling associated with backstop technology.

Cline and Hsieh (1993) show that the imposition of a backstop-technology ceiling on the marginal cost of avoiding carbon emissions causes the optimal abatement path to jump to nearly complete elimination of carbon at the period when the shadow price of carbon (and thus the marginal benefit of its removal) begins to exceed the backstop price. Thus, with a ceiling of US$200 per ton of carbon removed, and with a rate of pure time preference of 1 per cent, the optimal cut-back from baseline jumps from 33 per cent in 2125 to 45 per cent in 2145 and nearly 100 per cent in 2155, compared with an optimal cut-back of only 43 per cent at the latter date in the absence of the backstop ceiling.

Another crucial source of understatement of optimal abatement in the Nordhaus (1992b) DICE results is that they do not incorporate the risk of upper-bound warming and upper-bound damage in the damage function. The analysis is strictly central-case, yet the essence of the greenhouse problem is dealing appropriately with risk.[14] Indeed, without risk weighting, the Cline (1992a) analysis shows a benefit/cost ratio for aggressive action of only 0.7. Moreover, both analyses omit the potential of catastrophic impact. Thus, neither Nordhaus (1992b) nor Cline (1992a) quantifies the economic damage that would result from a shutting down of the "ocean conveyor belt" that generates the Gulf Stream. Similarly, the damage functions are at most quadratic, and assume gradual warming.

The Nordhaus formulation of DICE would also appear to under-

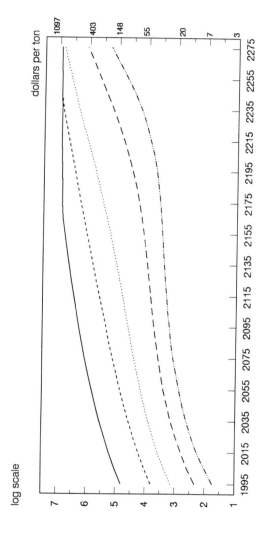

Fig. 7.3 **The shadow price of carbon with alternative discount rates**

115

state baseline carbon emissions, and thus prospective warming. The model sets business-as-usual emissions at 25 GtC by 2100 and only 31 GtC by 2275. In contrast, Cline (1992a) places emissions at 21 GtC by the first date and 56 GtC by the second. For their part, Manne and Richels (1992) set baseline emissions at 39 GtC already by 2100. The principal reason for the low emissions late in the horizon in the Nordhaus baseline is his assumption of low economic growth, driven by decelerating technological change (as discussed in Cline, 1992b).

Moreover, the climate module in DICE would appear to understate the prospective extent of even central-case warming. The global mean temperature rise never exceeds 5.5 °C over four centuries in the model as specified; yet the IPCC (1990: chap. 6) places the commitment to global warming at 5.7 °C already by 2100 under business as usual. One reason for the low very-long-term warming is the low emissions baseline, as noted. Another reason for the apparent understatement is that DICE specifies a low contribution of greenhouse gases other than carbon dioxide, which at their maximum add only 1.24 watts/m² (wm⁻²) in radiative forcing as opposed to the level of 3.06 wm⁻² already by 2100 estimated for these gases by the IPCC (1990: table 2.7).[15] Still another reason would appear to be that the DICE specification involves a declining atmospheric retention ratio for carbon dioxide emissions, which falls to only 37 per cent by 2100, 29 per cent by 2200, and 26 per cent by 2270 (Cline, 1992b). Yet Wigley has indicated that, under business as usual, a relatively constant atmospheric retention ratio of about 45 per cent can be expected to persist.[16]

Shadow prices and carbon taxes

Returning to figure 7.3, the alternative simulations with DICE provide a basis for identifying appropriate penalties to assign for carbon emissions. For a given point in time and a specified rate of pure time preference, the "shadow price" tells the marginal benefit of reducing emissions by an additional 1 ton of carbon and thereby reducing global warming; or, equivalently, the marginal economic cost of doing so. Accordingly, the shadow price also tells the optimal marginal carbon tax, because only a tax of this amount will send the proper price signal to economize on carbon emissions.

As indicated in figure 7.3, for a rate of pure time preference of 0.5 per cent, the shadow price of carbon (optimal carbon tax) rises from US$45 per ton initially to US$84 per ton by 2025, US$133 by 2055, and US$243 by 2105. As suggested above, this range for p corresponds roughly to the assumptions in Cline (1992a), albeit still with understatement of abatement from the standpoint of not incorporating the risk of upper-bound warming or cost limits from backstop technology.

In comparison, Fankhauser and Pearce (1993) identify a lower and flatter trajectory for the shadow price of carbon, rising from US$20 per ton in 1991–2000 to US$28 per ton by 2021–2030. An important source of the difference is that Fankhauser and Pearce use a probabilistic approach to the range of discount rates, thereby including considerable weight on rates substantially higher than suggested here. Conceptually their method differs as well, because it seeks to identify the shadow price on a basis of discounted greenhouse damage under probability-weighted scenarios of public action and inaction, rather than by identifying an optimal emissions path that takes account of the costs of abatement.

7. Policy implications

The analysis in Cline (1992a) recommends an aggressive programme of international abatement of greenhouse gases. However, it suggests a two-phase strategy. In the first decade, more moderate measures would be applied. Thereafter, pending further scientific confirmation, policy measures would be intensified to limit emissions to a path similar to that of a 4 GtC ceiling.

In the event, industrial countries essentially committed at the Earth Summit in Rio de Janeiro in 1992 to return greenhouse gas emissions to 1990 levels by the year 2000. In view of the rising business-as-usual path, this commitment is equivalent to a cut-back somewhere on the order of 10–15 per cent.

There is a surprising convergence of the various analyses on action approximately consistent with this degree of restraint in the first decade. The Cline (1992a) aggressive action programme is a reduction of one-third; but, with a milder first phase, cut-back from baseline by some 10–15 per cent in the first decade is consistent with the overall strategy. The Nordhaus (1992b) optimal cut-back of 9 per cent by 1995 is not far from the same outcome. Similarly, the hedging strategy of Manne and Richels (1992) also leads to a cut-back from baseline of about 12 per cent by the year 2000.

Similarly, the carbon tax tends to converge for this initial period.

117

Thus, the range suggested here of US\$45 per ton in the 1990s (fig. 7.3 at $\rho = 0.5$ per cent) suggests that something like US\$20–25 per ton might be appropriate in the initial decade of more moderate action pending further scientific confirmation. This range is consistent with the Fankhauser–Pearce initial shadow price (optimal carbon tax) of about US\$20 per ton of carbon. This tax is even within reach of the Nordhaus Monte-Carlo results. Those sensitivity results place Nordhaus's optimal carbon tax at an expected value of about US\$12 per ton of carbon in 1995, and as high as US\$45 per ton at the 95th percentile of the distribution. Considering the suggestion of Yohe (1992) that incorporation of risk recommends "focusing on a scenario which describes something around the 75th percentile of potential economic damage," an intermediate point between the two Nordhaus Monte-Carlo estimates would also tend to converge in the US\$20–25 per ton range for 1995. The policy prescriptions would begin to diverge more sharply only beyond the first decade, assuming scientific confirmation of the seriousness of the problem.

During this first decade, in addition to the moderate cut-backs and carbon taxes suggested here for the first phase, there should be intensive scientific research. One important area is in the narrowing of discrepancies among general circulation models on cloud feed-back, the principal source of divergence generating the IPCC range of Λ from 1.5 °C to 4.5 °C. However, another key area for further research is on the very-long-term prospects for warming and damage. It would appear that, until recently, the scientific community may have been discouraged from looking at horizons beyond a century by the presumed tyranny of the economists' discount rate. That is, more distant results may have been thought to matter little because of time discounting in the policy process. However, as suggested here (and in Cline, 1992a), proper discounting methodology can leave room for serious damage even after a century to play a significant role in the analytical outcome. Economists should encourage the scientists to extend their analyses to these longer horizons (as in Manabe and Stouffer, 1993), rather than discourage such analysis.

In addition, there is a need in the coming decade for much more extensive analysis of the benefits and costs of GHG abatement for developing countries. Most of the economic analyses to date have been for the United States and other industrial countries. However, the fragmentary evidence for developing countries suggests that the stakes for limiting global warming may be even higher in these regions. Confirmation of this diagnosis, and its broader dissemination, could help the international community move toward a more global response in a second phase of policy action. It may be appropriate that abatement efforts in the first phase be concentrated in the industrial countries (including "joint" measures they might undertake with developing countries). In the longer run, however, ceilings on emissions in China and other developing countries will be necessary as well, if the problem of global warming is to be seriously addressed (Cline, 1992a: 336–342; Manne and Richels, 1992: 91).

Notes

1. Because of ocean thermal lag, equilibrium warming occurs perhaps some three decades after the corresponding radiative forcing from the increase in atmospheric concentrations of GHGs above pre-industrial levels. "Transient" or actual warming is thus less than the "commitment" to equilibrium warming at a point in time, unless atmospheric concentrations have been at a stable plateau for several decades.
2. Because of other trace gases, there is much less than twice the amount of carbon dioxide in the atmosphere when $2xCO_2$-*equivalent* radiative forcing is attained.
3. The high estimate for China is driven by damage amounting to about 2 per cent of GDP each in two categories: agriculture and human mortality. The former reflects the large share of the agricultural sector in GDP. The latter is the consequence of applying a statistical value of life for China at US$150,000 – only about one-tenth the typical range for industrial countries but relatively high compared with per capita income.
4. The actual transient warming by the 140th year is 5 °C.
5. Note that the GFDL GCM has $\Lambda = 3.5$ °C; Cline (1992a) uses $\Lambda = 2.5$ °C.
6. The argument is that, with greater high-latitude precipitation and glacier melting, the waters near Greenland would become less saline and therefore less dense. In addition, warming (which would be much greater at this latitude than the global mean) would reduce the gradient of the thermocline. Together, the changes could mean that the cold surface waters there might no longer sink into the deep ocean as they currently do, shutting down the ocean conveyor belt.
7. Energy claims some 6–8 per cent of GDP. Economic theory states that this "factor share" is also the "elasticity" of output with respect to the factor. The models tend to show that a 50 per cent cut-back in carbon requires only a 25 per cent cut-back in energy. The resulting output loss would be $25\% \times 0.07 = 1.75$ per cent of GDP, based on the factor elasticity approach.
8. Thus, the average baseline in the OECD survey is about 15 GtC by 2050 and 27 GtC by 2100 (Dean, 1993: 8).
9. The study also reports much higher cost estimates from simulations by Barns, Edmonds, and Reilly. However, those estimates apply an unreliable "GDP feedback parameter" in the Edmonds–Reilly model. Unfortunately, the OECD survey did not use the methodologically preferable variant in the model, which instead estimates costs by integrating the area under the marginal carbon tax curve – a method that gives much lower costs. See the discussion in Cline (1992a: 160–161).
10. Indeed, a floor is set on costs to prevent this influence from reducing them to extremely low levels late in the horizon.
11. Note also that the Nordhaus DICE technical change parameter generates an optimal growth path with considerably less per capita consumption growth than in Cline (1992a). Per capita consumption grows at 1.1 per cent in the first 50 years, 0.5 per cent in the second

119

50 years, and more slowly thereafter, with average growth of 0.4 per cent over three centuries (compared with 1 per cent in Cline, 1992a). Note further that there is an inherent compensation for this difference in the growth-discounting effect. Slower growth depresses late-period GDP and therefore the economic base to which the proportionate excess of damages over abatement costs present late in the horizon applies (fig. 7.1). In compensation, the growth-discounting component of the discount rate, $|\alpha|g$, is lower because of the lower growth rate, g. The lower discount rate enhances the importance of later periods, neutralizing their diminution from the standpoint of the size of the economic base. Finally, note that the use of pure time preference at $\rho = 0.5$ per cent to compensate for a lower elasticity of marginal utility probably introduces an upward bias in the discount rate for DICE compared with Cline (1992a). That is, with the low growth rate of 0.4 per cent in DICE, the appropriate discount rate would be: $r = 0.4 \times 1.5 + 0 = 0.6$ per cent (equation 1). Instead, the approximation suggested as comparable in figure 7.2 here is $\rho = 0.5$, so that $r = 0.4 \times 1 + 0.5 = 0.9$ per cent.

12. It is true that observed real rates of return on capital of as much as 8 per cent imply that there is a large wedge between the social rate of time preference to savers in equation (1) and the return on capital. Under perfect markets, we would have the rate of return on capital i equal to the social rate of time preference r, or: $i = r = \rho + |\alpha|g$. However, private capital return includes substantial project risk, and in addition includes a wedge representing marginal tax rates. As a result, $i = r + w$, where w is a wedge incorporating risk, tax distortions, and other market imperfections. Importantly, it is practically inconceivable that real return on capital could remain as high as 8 per cent over three centuries. Such a rate is strictly inconsistent with the size of GWP in both the Nordhaus and Cline projections. Thus, an investment of just 1 per cent of today's GWP, or US$200 billion, earning a steady 8 per cent real return would grow to 1.3 million times projected GWP at the end of the 300-year horizon. What these considerations do suggest is that there may be undersaving and underinvestment in a wide range of areas from society's viewpoint. However, the existence of such underinvestment is no justification for a social decision to underinvest in greenhouse abatement, where the consequences build up to proportionately much greater magnitudes because of the extremely long time-horizon.

13. The Nordhaus cost function is: $c = 0.0686z^{2.887}$, where c is cost as a fraction of GDP and z is the proportionate cut-back of carbon emissions from baseline.

14. Although the subsequent version in Nordhaus (1993b) does conduct sensitivity analysis and address risk aversion through "Monte-Carlo" runs in which parameters are varied, that approach does not identify the optimal path under risk aversion with the key discount rate parameters set at $\rho = 0$ and $\alpha = -1.5$. Even so, the sensitivity estimates indicate somewhat more forceful optimal action. Thus, in Nordhaus's base case, the optimal carbon tax is only US$5.32 per ton in 1995, rising to US$13.68 by 2045, and US$21.03 by 2095. The corresponding rates of reduction from baseline are 9 per cent, 12.5 per cent, and 14.3 per cent, respectively. In contrast, with 400 Monte-Carlo runs, the expected (probability-weighted) carbon tax is US$11.83 per ton by 1995; and the tax for the 95th percentile in the distribution is US$42 per ton in that year.

15. Adjustment for the more recent findings that radiative forcing from CFCs tends to be neutralized by reduced forcing from the stratospheric ozone stripped by CFCs would not alter this estimate by much.

16. T. M. L. Wigley, University of Colorado, personal communication, 16 July 1993, using the model described in Wigley (1993). Note that Wigley has warned that his model may not provide reliable estimates for atmospheric concentration and retention for concentration levels above 1,000 ppm, because of the possible effect of a large increase in the ocean sink from the influence of dissolution of oceanic carbonates and near shore sediments. However, Eric Sundquist of Woods Hole Oceanographic Institute has indicated that the three-century horizon investigated here is too short for this influence to have much effect on atmospheric concentration. Personal communication, 5 February 1993.

References

Anklin, M. et al. 1993. "Climate instability during the last interglacial period recorded in the GRIP ice core." *Nature* 364, 15 July: 203–207.

Blanchard, O. J. and S. Fischer. 1989. *Lectures on Macroeconomics.* Cambridge, Mass.: MIT Press.

Cline, W. R. 1992a. *The Economics of Global Warming.* Washington, D.C.: Institute for International Economics, June.

——— 1992b. "Optimal carbon emissions over time: Experiments with the Nordhaus DICE model." Washington D.C.: Institute for International Economics, August.

——— 1992c. "Greenhouse policy after Rio: Economics, science, and politics." Paper presented at International Workshop on Costs, Impacts, and Possible Benefits of CO_2 Mitigation, 28–30 September, International Institute for Applied Systems Analysis, Laxemburg, Austria.

——— 1992d. "Socially efficient abatement of carbon emissions." Paper presented at the Second CICERO Seminar on Climate Change, 29 November – 2 December, Oslo.

——— 1993. "Costs and benefits of greenhouse abatement: A guide to policy analysis." Paper presented at the OECD/IEA International Conference on the Economics of Climate Change, 14–16 June, Paris.

Cline, W. R. and C.-T. Hsieh. 1993. "Optimal carbon emissions in the Nordhaus DICE model under backstop technology." Washington, D.C.: Institute for International Economics, mimeo, July.

Dansgaard, W., J. W. C. White, and S. J. Johnsen. 1989. "The abrupt termination of the Younger Dryas climate event." *Nature* 339, 15 June: 532–534.

Dean, A. 1993. "Costs of cutting CO_2 emissions: Evidence from 'top–down' models." Paper presented at the OECD/IEA International Conference on the Economics of Climate Change, 14–16 June, Paris.

Fankhauser, S. 1992. "Global warming damage costs: Some monetary estimates." London: Centre for Social and Economic Research on the Global Environment, mimeo, August.

Fankhauser, S. and D. W. Pearce. 1993. "The social costs of greenhouse gas emissions." Paper presented at the OECD/IEA International Conference on the Economics of Climate Change, 14–16 June, Paris.

Fellner, W. 1967. "Operational utility: The theoretical background and a measurement." In: *Ten Economic Studies in the Tradition of Irving Fisher.* New York: John Wiley, pp. 39–74.

Hoffert, M. I. and C. Covey. 1992. "Deriving global climate sensitivity from paleoclimate reconstructions." *Nature* 360, 10 December: 573–576.

IPCC (Intergovernmental Panel on Climate Change). 1990. *Scientific Assessment of Climate Change: Report Prepared for IPCC by Working Group I.* New York: WMO and UNEP, August.

Jorgenson, D. W. and K.-Y. Yun. 1990. *The Excess Burden of Taxation in the US.* Cambridge, Mass.: Harvard Institute of Economic Research, Discussion Paper No. 1528, November.

McKibbin, W. J. 1992. *The Global Costs of Policies to Reduce Greenhouse Gas Emissions.* Washington D.C.: Brookings Institution, Discussion Papers in International Economics No. 97, October.

Manabe, S. and R. J. Stouffer. 1993. "Century-scale effects of increased atmospheric CO$_2$ on the ocean–atmosphere system." *Nature* 364, 15 July: 215–218.

Manne, A. S. and R. G. Richels. 1992. *Buying Greenhouse Insurance: The Economic Costs of CO$_2$ Emission Limits*. Cambridge, Mass.: MIT Press.

Moulton, R. J. and K. R. Richards. 1990. *Costs of Sequestering Carbon through Tree Planting and Forest Management in the United States*. Washington, D.C.: US Department of Agriculture, Forest Service.

NAS (National Academy of Sciences). 1991. *Policy Implications of Greenhouse Warming*. Washington, D.C.: National Academy Press.

Nordhaus, W. D. 1992a. "The 'DICE' model: Background and structure of a dynamic integrated climate–economy model of the economics of global warming." New Haven, Conn.: Yale University, mimeo, February.

———— 1992b. "An optimal transition path for controlling greenhouse gases." *Science* 258, 20 November: 1315–1319.

———— 1993a. "Climate and economic development: Climates past and future." Washington, D.C.: World Bank, Annual Conference on Development Economics.

———— 1993b. "Managing the global commons: The economics of climate change." New Haven, Conn.: Yale University, mimeo, 7 June.

Ramsey, F. P. 1928. "A mathematical theory of saving." *Economic Journal* 38(152): 543–559.

Scott, M. F. 1989. *A New View of Economic Growth*. Oxford: Clarendon Press.

Sundquist, E. T. 1990. "Long-term aspects of future atmospheric CO$_2$ and sea-level changes." In: R. R. Revelle et al., *Sea Level Change*. Washington, D.C.: National Research Council, National Academy Press, pp. 193–207.

Titus, J. 1992. "The cost of climate change to the United States." In: S. K. Majumdar et al. (eds.), *Global Climate Change: Implications, Challenges and Mitigation Measures*. Pennsylvania Academy of Science.

Wigley, T. M. L. 1993. "Balancing the carbon budget: Implications for projections of future carbon dioxide concentration changes." *Tellus* 45B(15): 409–425.

Yohe, G. W. 1992. "Sorting out facts and uncertainties in economic response to the physical effects of global climate change." Paper presented to the Workshop on Assessing Climate Change Risks, Resources for the Future, 23–24 March, Washington, D.C.

8

Macroeconomic costs and other side-effects of reducing CO_2 emissions

Akihiro Amano

1. Introduction

More than 150 nations signed the Framework Convention on Climate Change in June 1992 at Rio de Janeiro, revealing their determination to start coping with the global warming issue. Although the agreements were not as aggressive as had been expected in advance, the extensive guiding principles brought together in Agenda 21 represent a big step forward. One clear message is that more use is to be made of economic measures to combat global warming and other environmental problems. The question we now face is to decide the extent to which we should apply these measures with respect to the abatement of carbon dioxide and other greenhouse gas emissions. The nations that agreed to the Convention have not yet decided about it explicitly except for some environmentally advanced Northern European countries.

In this paper I shall first discuss, in section 2, the magnitudes of the macroeconomic costs of limiting carbon dioxide emissions. By comparing the results of the OECD global model comparison project and those of Japanese studies, I shall point up the importance of understanding the model structures behind these simulation experiments. Besides the macroeconomic costs, economic measures such as carbon taxes (and to a large extent other market-oriented measures as well) will have other side-effects both domestically and internationally. In section 3, some of these problems will also be addressed.

Assessment of mitigation costs alone cannot determine the optimum scale of measures against global warming. Recently, there have been interesting discussions concerning the size of optimal carbon taxes. In section 4, I shall attempt to discern the factors affecting the size of carbon taxes in the optimal abatement path, or the social costs of carbon emissions. Section 5 closes the paper with a summary and conclusions.

2. The macroeconomic costs of reducing CO_2 emissions

When the OECD convened an international workshop in 1991 to compare the simulation results of representative global models on cost estimates of limiting carbon dioxide emissions, one of the objectives was to investigate the reasons such diverse figures had been obtained. Intensive comparative studies of six global models of greenhouse gas emissions culminated in a number of OECD working papers and *Economic Studies* articles, and many important findings explaining the determinants of macroeconomic costs have been obtained. (See Dean, 1993, for a survey of the workshop.)

Table 8.1 is constructed from the simulation results of four dynamic, long-term models: the Manne–Richels model (MR), Rutherford's Carbon Rights Trade Model (CRTM), the Edmonds–Reilly model (ER), and the OECD GREEN model (GREEN). The figures in the table have been derived from the simulation results involving CO_2 abatement in terms of a 2 per cent reduction in annual rates of increase compared with the business-as-usual scenarios.

The left-hand panel of table 8.1 reports the ratio of percentage reductions in real GDP to those in CO_2 emissions (i.e. percentage GDP losses caused by a one percentage point reduction in CO_2 emissions relative to the baseline), and the right-hand panel reports the ratio of carbon tax rates (measured in dollars per ton carbon) to percentage reductions in CO_2 emissions (i.e. the amount of carbon taxes required to achieve a 1 per cent reduction in CO_2 emissions).

Because these simulation exercises were performed on the same set of exogenous assumptions and on the same method of perturbing the systems, the results turned out to be fairly similar, especially for developed countries. There are a couple of notable differences, however. The Edmonds–Reilly model reports relatively larger impacts

Table 8.1 **The macroeconomic costs of CO$_2$ emission reduction**

Year	Percentage reduction in GDP[a]					Carbon taxes (US$/tC)[b]				
	United States	Other OECD	Former USSR	China	Other regions	United States	Other OECD	Former USSR	China	Other regions
MR										
2000	0.05	0.03	0.10	0.11	0.18	7	7	11	12	12
2020	0.05	0.03	0.07	0.06	0.11	8	5	7	6	9
2100	0.04	0.02	0.06	0.06	0.06	2	2	9	2	2
CRTM										
2000	0.01	0.00	0.04	0.04	0.13	10	9	9	9	12
2020	0.03	0.01	0.03	0.04	0.06	7	5	7	7	9
2100	0.03	0.02	0.05	0.04	0.05	2	2	9	1	2
ER										
2000	0.03	0.03	0.03	0.05	0.05	4	6	3	3	6
2020	0.04	0.04	0.02	0.06	0.05	8	8	2	4	10
2100	0.10	0.05	0.04	0.07	0.06	31	14	8	8	23
GREEN										
2000	0.02	0.02	0.02	0.02	0.06	7	9	1	1	5
2020	0.03	0.03	0.04	0.02	0.09	5	5	2	1	4
2050	0.02	0.02	0.05	0.02	0.06	5	4	3	1	5

Source: Dean and Hoeller (1992).

a. The percentage change in GDP relative to the business-as-usual scenario for a 1 per cent reduction in CO$_2$ emissions, also relative to the business-as-usual scenario.

b. Carbon taxes required for a 1 per cent reduction in CO$_2$ emissions relative to the business-as-usual scenario.

Table 8.2 **Carbon tax simulations of Japanese models**

Model	Final year	Percentage reduction in GNP	Carbon taxes ($/tC)
Goto	2030	0.02	3
Ban	2000	0.05	6
Mori	2020	0.22	17
Yamaji	2005	0.23	19
Ito	2010	0.29	17
Yamazaki	2010	0.41	19

Source: Amano (1992a,b).

in the longer term, because backstop technologies do not play a large role compared with other models. The Rutherford model, on the other hand, reports smaller effects, because this model allows for opportunities to trade energy-intensive products and carbon emission rights. Noting these special cases, however, we may say that a 1 per cent reduction in carbon emissions generally requires a 0.02–0.05 per cent decrease in GDP in developed countries. The corresponding carbon tax rates are around US$2–10 per ton carbon (tC).

For non-OECD countries the results are somewhat diverse, but I can make two observations. First, all models show relatively larger output effects in these countries, especially in the "rest of the world" region, which includes energy-exporting countries. Secondly, carbon taxes for the former USSR and China are fairly low in the GREEN and Edmonds–Reilly models, because these models take into account the subsidized, low domestic energy prices in these countries.

Table 8.2 presents the results of similar simulation studies conducted in Japan. I report this additional information because it clearly shows that the objectives of model-building and the methods of simulation experiments can both influence the results substantially. The figures in table 8.2 are constructed in the same way as those in table 8.1.

We can distinguish two groups in this table. The first group (the Goto and Ban models) obtained comparable results to those of table 8.1 with respect to both GDP/GNP reductions and carbon taxes. The results of the second group, however, are surprisingly similar to each other, but they are much larger than other estimates in either table 8.2 or table 8.1.

126

Three reasons can explain these differences. First, the models in the second group have been developed by combining econometric forecasting models of the demand-determined type with some form of energy model, and most of them have usually been used for projection and simulation exercises. The role expected of such models is to make precise short- to medium-term projections and not to draw a clear picture of the distant future. On the other hand, computable general equilibrium (CGE) models can generally treat the long-run responses more explicitly and adequately with smoother adjustments in various sectors. As the above results indicate, the long-run and short-run responses captured by these two sets of models can give rise to notable differences.

The second reason for the difference is that short-run models involve temporary deviations from full employment resulting from higher energy prices, which are absent in CGE models by assumption. Of course, this does not mean that short-run adjustment problems are unimportant. There are, however, regular anti-cyclical measures in the policy arsenal, and these measures should be and will be integrated in the policy package at the level of actual implementation.

The third point relates to the treatment of tax revenue. In general equilibrium models, carbon tax revenue is usually recycled to the public to make the carbon tax revenue neutral. However, this is not true for the second group of models in table 8.2; the results reported in the table were based on an assumption of no change in public sector behaviour. This assumption, combined with the demand-determined type of macroeconometric model, can lead to a large decline in output with the imposition of carbon taxes.

These considerations suggest that policy simulation results should be presented and interpreted with care. Analysts try to identify the effects of some factors by isolating the disturbance as far as possible. But the way of isolating an event depends a great deal on how that factor is modelled. Therefore, the results of such simulations must be presented and interpreted with a clear understanding of the model structure.

In fact, actual policies may not be implemented as suggested by the model simulations we have just seen. Assignment of the same percentage reduction in emissions to all countries is not an efficient way of formulating a global or an international policy. An efficient policy would require that the rate of carbon tax be the same for all countries. The way in which tax revenue is recycled may vary from one country to another, reflecting differing public deficits. To say the same thing from a different angle, real policy simulations should be based on combinations of policy measures with realistic policy responses to expected unfavourable side-effects. Ordinary "policy simulations" are often not carried out in this way.

3. Some side-effects of reducing CO_2 emissions

The kind of consideration mentioned at the end of the last section provokes discussion concerning the various side-effects of economic measures to mitigate global warming (such as carbon taxes), including the regressive distributional effects within a country and undesirable effects upon international competitiveness when other countries do not adopt similar measures. There is some empirical evidence to support the first point (see, e.g., Poterba, 1991, and Smith, 1993), but these authors also indicate that there are policy instruments that can offset the socially undesirable distributional consequences of carbon taxes.

The question of international competitiveness seems to involve at least three points. First, when the external costs associated with carbon emissions are internalized, changes in the relative cost structure may lead to alterations in the pattern of the international division of labour. If an international carbon tax scheme is adopted with a uniform tax rate, then an efficient international division of labour will not be distorted, although ordinary short-term adjustment problems will accompany any change in comparative cost structures. Rather, international resource allocation will be improved because the price structure now reflects social costs rather than mere private costs. However, if only a subset of countries participate in this scheme, or if the tax rates vary substantially among countries, then "trade-diversion effects" may result. The supply sources of carbon-intensive goods may shift from more efficient and more benign-to-the-environment countries to less efficient and less benign-to-the-environment countries. In such circumstances, exemption from carbon taxes may be justified. It should be noted, however, that this argument applies only to those industries that suffer from the trade diversion, not to all industries suffering from a loss of international competitiveness.

In this connection, Hoeller and Wallin (1991) show that there exist fairly large differences in implicit carbon tax rates among major OECD countries, and Burniaux et al. (1992) subjoin that the differences are even wider if we consider the world economy as a whole. World energy and carbon uses would be made much more efficient if these distortions could be eliminated.

Secondly, when carbon taxes are introduced in some countries to the extent that world energy prices are depressed, then energy consumption or carbon emissions in other countries not participating in the carbon tax scheme will increase, and this tends to lessen the initial reduction in carbon emissions. This effect, combined with the off-setting influence resulting from trade-diversion effects mentioned above, is called "carbon leakages." Rutherford (1992) reported that the leakage effects are fairly large, especially when carbon limitation becomes very stringent. According to his model simulation, when OECD countries alone attempt to reduce the annual rate of increase in carbon emissions by 3 per cent, the leakage rate, i.e. the proportion of unilateral abatement effects that are offset by the expansion of carbon emissions in non-participating countries, will approach 100 per cent (see Rutherford, 1992). If this conclusion is correct, then any international unilateral action that might affect international energy prices should involve some arrangements to minimize such carbon leakage effects.

On the other hand, simulation analyses performed by the OECD GREEN model suggest that the carbon emission stabilization scheme unilaterally adopted by the OECD countries will lead to carbon leakages of only 2.5 per cent (see Burniaux et al., 1992, and Nicoletti and Oliveira-Martins, 1992). On the average for the period 1990–2050 the greatest reduction in the production of energy-intensive sectors occurs in Japan (-2.6 per cent) and the smallest reduction in the United States (-0.4 per cent). These results are in sharp contrast to those of Rutherford.

Manne (1993) also examined the extent of carbon leakages with a global model incorporating international trade in crude oil, natural gas, energy-intensive products, and tradable emission permits. According to his simulation results, carbon leakages through the channel of oil trade seem unimportant except perhaps in the initial period. However, international trade in energy-intensive products creates a broad conduit for carbon leakages. The leakage rate starts from around 20 per cent in 2000, increasing to a level slightly above 30 per cent in 2050. Trade in natural gas also raises the leakage ratio in the medium term, but it tends to moderate the leakage in the longer run as world natural gas prices are capped at the backstop level. The overall results seem to fall between Rutherford and the GREEN model results.

Even with these leakage effects, however, Manne concludes that unilateral carbon limitations by the OECD nations would be effective in that they could reduce global emissions for some time. At the same time, he also stresses the finding that, beyond 2020 or so, emissions from non-OECD countries will become quite important. These two major conclusions seem to suggest that carbon leakages are at most a medium-term issue, if relevant at all. In the longer term, many energy-intensive activities will move to the non-OECD region anyway, irrespective of the introduction of carbon taxes in OECD countries, and emission reductions in the non-OECD region will become a central issue. Effective arrangements to contain the vast increase in emissions expected from this region will become imperative under most plausible scenarios.

All three models mentioned above aggregate industries into energy-intensive and energy-non-intensive sectors, but a more disaggregated approach would be needed to verify the results. Quantitative studies of the impacts of carbon taxes upon more disaggregated sectors, such as Jorgenson et al. (1992) for the United States and Kuroda and Shimpo (1992) for Japan, have shown that output responses brought about by the imposition of carbon taxes will be concentrated in a rather small number of energy-related industries such as coal mining, crude oil, electric utilities, gas utilities, and refining. The effects on energy-intensive manufacturing sectors such as iron and steel and paper and pulp products, however, are not as marked as in the energy industries. Therefore, the distinction between energy-intensive and energy-non-intensive sectors does not really indicate the uneven distribution of sectoral impacts upon output. Of course, aggregation does not affect the size of the total impact upon carbon dioxide emissions, so that the implications of simulation results concerning carbon leakages will remain unaffected. However, the distinction masks the differential burden of adjustments among industries which should somehow be taken into account in formulating an appropriate policy package.

Another interesting study applies the GREEN model. Oliveira-Martins et al. (1992) examined the effects of tax exemption of energy-intensive industries, in order to see if such measures can protect these industries from a loss of international competitiveness. Their results show, quite interestingly, that the effects of tax exemption are almost negligible in terms both of leakage rates and of changes in sectoral output. It appears that it is not the loss of competitiveness due to the imposition of the tax but a contraction in the market in question that hits these particular industries.

The third question related to the international competitiveness issue concerns the effects of changes in the terms of trade caused by an international carbon tax scheme. As discussed in relation to the second problem, the international application of carbon taxes, be they unilateral or worldwide, would most probably lead to changes in the international terms of trade of carbon energies in favour of energy-importing countries and against energy-exporting countries, implying large-scale international income transfers. There are not many global models that examine this question, but the OECD GREEN model has shown that the terms of trade effects upon real incomes are of non-negligible magnitudes (see Burniaux et al., 1992). In international negotiations to apply economic measures to mitigate global warming, due consideration will have to be given to this issue.

4. The social costs of CO_2 emissions

One of the important questions remaining unresolved in the discussion of how to cope with the global warming issue is the extent of the desirable, or socially optimal, strategy to reduce greenhouse gases. On the one hand, the group of scientists associated with the Intergovernmental Panel on Climate Change (IPCC) confirmed their earlier recommendation that in order to stabilize climatic change it would be necessary to reduce the current level of emissions of CO_2 by 60 per cent (IPCC, 1992). On the other hand, William Nordhaus has been maintaining in a series of papers that climatic stabilization or even emission stabilization is far from optimal from the socioeconomic viewpoint, and that the socially optimal abatement path is much closer to the uncontrolled path (Nordhaus, 1990a,b, 1992a,b). According to his view, percentage rates of reduction of greenhouse gases along the optimal path will be as low as 10 per cent in around 2000 and 14 per cent in around 2100. The levels of carbon taxes will also be moderate along the optimal path, ranging from about US$6/tC in 2000 to a little above US$20/tC in 2100.

William Cline (1992), on the other hand, considers that a more aggressive policy of stabilizing current CO_2 emissions at an annual rate of 4 billion tons of carbon (GtC) would be justified if (a) future benefits are given higher weights by means of a lower social rate of time discount, and if (b) the risk-averse stances of policy makers are taken into account. Although Cline's conclusions are not based on an optimization model, they are derived from a detailed global cost–benefit analysis. If we reconstruct his cost–benefit model, we can calculate the carbon taxes required for the aggressive policy to obtain US\$50/tC in 2013, US\$100/tC in 2020, US\$200/tC in 2025, and US\$250/tC in 2054 and after. These rates are much higher than those of Nordhaus.

At an OECD/IEA international conference, Fankhauser and Pearce (1993) reported that their estimates of the social costs of CO_2 emissions, measured as the discounted sum of future incremental damages, are US\$20/tC in 1991–2000, US\$23/tC in 2001–2010, US\$25/tC in 2011–2020, and US\$28/tC in 2021–2030. These estimates fall between those of Nordhaus and Cline, although Fankhauser and Pearce did not present estimates beyond 2030.

In this section I shall examine the factors affecting the magnitude of the shadow prices or social costs of carbon dioxide emissions by means of a small economy–climate model of the Nordhaus type (see the appendix at the end of the chapter for a brief description of the model).

I first performed simulation experiments in order to substantiate the wide differences between Nordhaus's results and those assuming stabilization of CO_2 emissions or of temperature rise. The first five columns of tables 8.3–8.7 present cases where (a) a 3 per cent annual social discount rate is used, as in Nordhaus's analysis, except for Case O' as will be explained below, (b) the IPCC's central estimate of 3 °C is used for the climate sensitivity parameter (i.e. the temperature increase at the benchmark condition of doubling carbon dioxide concentration in the atmosphere relative to the pre-industrial level), and (c) the damage function is such that the damage parameter (i.e. the percentage reduction in world GDP at the benchmark climate of $2 \times CO_2$) is 1 per cent and the function is quadratic.

In these simulations, world output is influenced by climate change through the damage function, which reflects both the macroeconomic costs of emission control and the damage arising from a temperature increase (or the benefits of preventing temperature increase through emission control). The "Uncontrolled" case, however, refers to a situation where these cost–benefit interactions between climate and the economy are completely neglected. In what follows I shall call this the "Business as Usual" (BaU) case.

As expected, the characteristics of Case O are very similar to those of Nordhaus. Optimal percentage reductions in carbon emissions start from 7 per cent in 2000 and remain below 20 per cent all the time. Carbon taxes are also low, starting from US\$5/tC and rising to US\$13/tC in 2050 and to US\$25/tC in 2100. Reflecting such low emission control, the pattern of temperature rise is very similar to

Table 8.3 **Percentage reductions in CO$_2$ emissions**

Year						Case				
	U	O	O′	E	T	LT	MT	HT	LL	HH
2000	–	7	23	20	29	19	23	32	14	48
2010	–	7	25	32	34	20	25	34	15	52
2020	–	8	25	45	40	20	25	35	15	54
2050	–	8	26	55	60	20	26	37	14	59
2100	–	12	33	76	92	22	33	46	16	79
2150	–	15	37	86	92	23	37	53	17	95
2200	–	18	36	92	94	21	36	52	17	100

U: Uncontrolled
O: Optimization (3% discount)
O: Optimization (0.5% discount)
E: Emission stabilization
T: Temperature rise stabilization

LT: Low temperature rise
MT: Medium temperature rise
HT: High temperature rise
LL: Low damage, etc.
HH: High damage, etc.

Table 8.4 **Carbon taxes (US$/tC)**

Year						Case				
	U	O	O′	E	T	LT	MT	HT	LL	HH
2000	–	5	60	46	94	41	60	117	23	263
2010	–	7	76	130	146	50	76	149	27	344
2020	–	8	89	280	219	56	89	174	30	415
2050	–	13	129	571	697	72	129	254	36	672
2100	–	25	200	1,116	1,704	91	200	401	47	1,214
2150	–	42	255	1,474	1,712	96	255	526	55	1,830
2200	–	58	244	1,700	1,777	64	244	514	52	2,268

Table 8.5 **Carbon emissions (GtC)**

Year						Case				
	U	O	O′	E	T	LT	MT	HT	LL	HH
2000	7.6	7.0	6.1	6.0	5.4	6.4	6.1	5.4	6.6	4.2
2010	8.9	8.2	7.3	6.0	5.8	7.7	7.3	6.3	7.7	4.2
2020	11.0	10.2	9.0	6.0	6.6	9.7	9.0	7.8	9.0	6.1
2050	16.6	12.5	11.1	6.0	5.2	12.1	11.1	9.4	9.4	7.9
2100	26.2	23.0	19.3	6.0	1.9	22.5	19.3	15.3	12.1	10.7
2150	47.2	39.4	32.3	6.0	3.3	39.9	32.3	23.8	16.0	5.5
2200	82.9	65.8	56.6	6.0	4.7	71.3	56.6	41.3	28.2	0.2

Table 8.6 **Temperature rise (°C)**

Year	Case

Year	U	O	O'	E	T	LT	MT	HT	LL	HH
2000	1.1	1.1	1.1	1.1	1.1	0.6	1.1	1.7	0.6	1.7
2050	1.5	1.4	1.4	1.3	1.3	0.7	1.4	2.0	0.7	1.9
2100	2.4	2.3	2.1	1.6	1.5	1.1	2.1	2.9	1.0	2.6
2150	3.8	3.6	3.3	1.9	1.5	1.8	3.3	4.3	1.4	3.5
2200	5.7	5.2	4.7	2.2	1.5	2.6	4.7	6.1	1.8	3.9

Table 8.7 **Percentage change in world GDP relative to "business-as-usual" scenario**

	Case									
Year	U	O	O'	E	T	LT	MT	HT	LL	HH
2000	–	−0.2	−0.4	−0.4	−0.6	−0.4	−0.4	−0.9	−0.3	−1.6
2050	–	−0.4	−0.9	−2.9	−3.3	−0.7	−0.9	−1.7	−0.5	−3.3
2100	–	−0.8	−1.5	−5.8	−9.3	−1.2	−1.5	−2.9	−0.8	−6.2
2150	–	−2.0	−2.6	−7.9	−9.0	−1.9	−2.6	−4.7	−1.3	−10.1
2200	–	−3.7	−4.2	−9.3	−7.5	−2.8	−4.2	−7.0	−1.7	−12.0

that of the BaU scenario. In other words, a large-scale reduction in CO_2 emissions would not be optimal, and the optimal control path under these conditions almost implies the maintenance of the status quo as far as global warming is concerned.

The contrasting assumptions often adopted in the mitigation scenarios are cases of stabilizing emissions or temperature increases. In Case E, the annual level of CO_2 emissions is stabilized at the 1990 level, and, in Case T, the temperature rise from the pre-industrial level is constrained below or equal to 1.5 °C. The required emission reductions in these two cases are, of course, substantial. The carbon taxes required in Case E, for instance, are US$46/tC in 2000, US$130/tC in 2010, US$280/tC in 2020, and so on; and in Case T they are somewhat higher in the near term and register US$697/tC in 2050 and US$1,704/tC in 2100. The rate of reduction in world GDP in 2100 is a mere 0.8 per cent in Case O, but it is much higher in Cases E and T (5.8 per cent and 9.3 per cent, respectively).

Against the view that deems continuing global warming optimal, there can be a criticism that it discriminates against future generations. Indeed, Cline argues that the application of a 3 per cent discount rate is inappropriate. On the basis of the facts that the elasticity of marginal utility of consumption is around 1.5 and that the long-term rate of growth of per capita income is roughly 1 per cent per annum, he considers that the annual rate of social time discount should be around 1.5 per cent. He also points out that, if a logarithmic utility function is used, the elasticity of marginal utility with respect to consumption is unity so that consumption growth at an annual rate of 1 per cent implies built-in discounting of 1 per cent per annum.

Case O' in tables 8.3–8.7 reports the results where only the rate of time discount is changed, from 3 per cent per annum to 0.5 per cent per annum, all other conditions being kept unchanged as in Case O. It can be seen that both the rates of emission reduction and carbon taxes are higher now, although the rates of emission reduction hardly exceed 40 per cent even in the 22nd century. Moreover, the time profile of temperature rise does not change very much. When the rate of social discount is lowered, a larger weight is given to the utility from future consumption. Therefore, when optimization involves savings–investment decisions, as in the present model, this change tends to induce larger investments and hence larger future output and CO_2 emissions. On the other hand, the lower discount rate also attaches a larger weight to future damage, so that it raises rates of emission reduction in the nearer term. Because these two opposing forces cancel each other out, the two scenarios look very similar as far as physical conditions are concerned. This means that lowering the discount rate can explain only a part of the differences between the Nordhaus and Cline results.

Let us now turn to the remaining five cases of tables 8.3–8.7. In these cases, I set the rate of discount at 0.5 per cent per annum. The first three cases distinguish climate sensitivity and the extent of damage from global warming as follows:

LT – low climate sensitivity parameter (1.5 °C) and low damage parameter (1 per cent with the degree of non-linearity 1.3);

MT – medium climate sensitivity parameter (3.0 °C) and medium damage parameter (1 per cent with the degree of non-linearity 2.0);

HT – high climate sensitivity parameter (4.5 °C) and high damage parameter (2 per cent with the degree of non-linearity 3.0).

The central case, MT, is identical to Case O'. Comparing the results for these three cases, we can observe that climate and damage parameters can change the nature of optimal time paths substantially. Emission reduction rates and carbon taxes are higher in Case HT than in Case MT, with smaller emissions but larger temperature increases and larger output reductions in Case HT. The reverse holds for Case LT. However, none of the three cases would satisfy those who prefer stabilizing emissions or temperature rise. The temperature increases in 2200 lie in the range of 2.6–6.1 °C, which is much higher than in Cases E and T.

In the last two columns of tables 8.3–8.7, I take up two extreme cases: for Case LL I assigned the lowest parameter values for climate sensitivity and output damage as well as for the rates of population growth, and similarly for Case HH I assigned the highest set of parameter values. I can point out two interesting similarities. First, Case LL has many points in common with Case O. This means that the application of rather high time discount rates is tantamount to assuming the most favourable global climate conditions in many important aspects: low temperature increases, little damage, less severe non-linearity of damage, and low rates of population growth. Second, Case HH, in turn, has many similarities with Cases E and T. CO_2 emissions are severely controlled by high carbon taxes, resulting in fairly large output losses in the long run. However, there is one important difference: even with such severe emission controls global warming will not be mitigated in Case HH as sufficiently as in cases E and T.

One might think that if the expected damage caused by global warming were much more substantial, then further stringent emission controls would lessen global warming. Thus, I considered two higher-damage scenarios in table 8.8: one with a higher degree of non-linearity of the damage function (power 3.5) and the other with an even higher damage parameter (4 per cent of world output at 2 × CO_2). In both cases carbon tax rates in 2100 are in the range of US\$1,200–\$1,500/tC, and rates of emission reduction in 2200 become 100 per cent. Indeed, in the case where damage is 4 per cent, the extent of temperature rise becomes lower than that in Case HT or HH. However, it is still larger than those of Cases E and T. Thus we must conclude that, even enlarging the size of the damage parameter by twice the most pessimistic estimate and making other assumptions most amenable to substantial damage, we cannot obtain optimal

Table 8.8 **Two high-damage scenarios**

Year	Emission reduction (%)		Carbon tax (US$/tC)		Emissions (GtC)		Temperature rise (°C)	
	Power 3.5	Damage 4%	Power 3.5	Damage 4%	Power 3.5	Damage 4%	Power 3.5	Damage 4%
2000	47	56	257	357	4.2	3.5	1.7	1.7
2010	52	60	338	461	4.9	4.0	1.7	1.7
2020	54	62	409	551	6.2	5.0	1.7	1.7
2050	59	67	671	868	7.9	6.3	1.9	1.8
2100	79	86	1,235	1,467	10.3	6.9	2.6	2.3
2150	96	100	1,874	2,075	4.4	0.1	3.5	2.8
2200	100	100	2,365	2,572	0.2	0.2	3.8	2.7

abatement paths that would justify immediate emission stabilization at about current levels. It appears that we need some other sort of social valuation function that incorporates much broader non-market values, or that takes a more serious view of uncertain, catastrophic situations in the distant future.

As I mentioned at the beginning of this section, Fankhauser and Pearce arrived at the conclusion that the social costs of carbon emissions for the period 1990–2030 are in the range of US$20–30/tC. I shall conclude this section by summarizing my own estimates in table 8.9. It is clear that Case O, which attempts to reproduce the Nordhausian situation, does not seem to be normal when we apply the discount rate of 0.5 per cent per annum. My MT scenario gives slightly higher estimates than those of Fankhauser and Pearce, but it should be noted that these numbers are only for a relatively short period. My Case MT shows that the estimates would rise as we move further into the future, and will approach US$200/tC by 2100.

I add one more simulation in table 8.9 within brackets. This case is based on exactly the same assumptions as Case MT, but the terminal year is 2250 rather than 2300. Thus, shortening the time-horizon tends to reduce the social costs of carbon emissions. Since the problem of global warming arises from stock externality, higher discounting of the future will make the social costs smaller. By shortening the time-horizon, we simply discount the events beyond the time-horizon by an infinite discount rate. We must therefore take a fairly long view in evaluating the social costs of greenhouse gas emissions.

Table 8.9 **The social costs of carbon emissions (US$/tC)**

Scenario	2000	2010	2020	2030
Optimization *à la* Nordhaus	5	7	8	11
Emission stabilization	48	130	280	375
Stabilization of temperature rise	94	146	219	331
Low temperature rise	41	50	56	62
Medium temperature rise	60	76	89	103
(With shorter time horizon	54	69	80	92)
High temperature rise	117	149	174	201
Low population growth, etc.	23	27	30	32
High population growth, etc.	263	344	415	497
High damage: power 3.5	257	338	409	493
High damage: damage parameter 4%	357	461	551	655

5. Summary and conclusions

In this paper I first examined the magnitudes of the macroeconomic costs of carbon emission reductions based upon the OECD project of global model comparisons. I found that a 1 per cent reduction in carbon emissions generally requires a 0.02–0.05 per cent decline in GDP in developed countries, and that corresponding carbon tax rates are around US$2–10/tC.

I also showed that many Japanese research results had found much larger macroeconomic costs, because these models are fairly short term in scope involving demand-determined output responses. Also, the treatment of tax revenue is different. These findings suggest that interpretation of simulation results should be based upon clear understanding of the nature of the model.

Economic measures to limit carbon dioxide emissions, such as carbon taxes, usually have some side-effects as well. There is some empirical evidence that carbon taxes would have regressive distributional implications, but there seem to exist appropriate instruments to accommodate these undesirable domestic side-effects.

International side-effects need careful distinction. Any change in the structure of comparative advantage induced by an efficient, international scheme to internalize the external costs of carbon emissions should not be counteracted. Sectoral adjustment problems should be handled as in many other cases of changing environments. Carbon leakages resulting from trade diversion and from changes in international energy prices can theoretically be large enough to negate the initial effort of limiting carbon emissions, but the available evidence seems to suggest that unilateral action by OECD countries, for example, will still be largely effective. Finally, due consideration should be given to the possibility of an international scheme to limit carbon emissions causing large-scale international redistribution of income against fossil-fuel-exporting countries.

In contrast to the macroeconomic cost estimates based upon some sort of stabilization objectives for the emission or atmospheric concentration of greenhouse gases, the optimal response approach suggested by William Nordhaus has led to the conclusion that optimal abatement paths are much closer to the business-as-usual scenario path than to stabilization paths. The questions of the appropriate rate of time discount and of proper estimates of damage from global warming do not seem to resolve the wide gap between the optimization approach and the stabilization approach. It appears that we need to investigate further if we are to broaden our scope of non-market values and take a more serious view of uncertain, catastrophic situations in the distant future.

Appendix: A simple Nordhaus-type model of climate and the world economy

This appendix gives a short summary of a simple Nordhaus-type model of climate and the world economy to evaluate optimal emission control paths under various alternative assumptions. The model consists of the following 12 equations:

1. Max. $U = \Sigma_{t=1}^{N} L_t \log(C_t/L_t)(1 + \rho)^{-t}$
2. $C_t + I_t \leq GDP_t$
3. $K_t = I_t + (1 - \delta_K) \cdot K_{t-1}$
4. $GDP_t = \Phi_t A_t K_t^{\pi} L_t^{1-\pi}$
5. $A_t = A_0(1 + g_A/100)^t$
6. $E_t = \alpha_t(1 - \mu_t)GDP_t$
7. $\alpha_t = \alpha_{t-1}(1 + g_\alpha/100), t \leq 2050; \ \alpha_t = \alpha_{t-1}, t > 2050$
8. $AC_t = \kappa E_t + (1 - \delta_M)AC_{t-1}$
9. $T_t^e = 6.3 \log(AC_t/AC_P) \cdot 0.3 \cdot \beta$
10. $\beta = T_B^e/(6.3 \log(2.0) \cdot 0.3)$
11. $T_{t+1} - T_t = \lambda(T_t^e - T_t)$
12. $\Phi_t = (1 - \gamma_1 \mu_t^3)/(1 + \gamma_2 T_t^\theta)$

Variable and parameter names and parameter values as well as initial conditions are as given below.

Variables

A_t:	production technology factor	Φ_t:	damage factor
AC_t:	atmospheric stock of carbon dioxide	I_t:	investment
C_t:	consumption	K_t:	capital stock
E_t:	carbon dioxide emissions	L_t:	population
GDP_t:	gross domestic product	T_t:	temperature rise
g_A:	annual growth rate of A	T_t^e:	equilibrium temperature rise
g_α:	annual rate of change in α	U:	discounted sum of consumption utility
α_t:	emission factor	δ_K:	capital depreciation rate
μ_t:	emission control variable	δ_M:	fraction of CO_2 transferred to deep ocean

Parameters

a: percentage loss of world GDP due to GHG abatement

b: percentage loss of world GDP due to global warming damage

AC_P: pre-industrial level of atmospheric stock of carbon dioxide

N: time horizon

T_B^e: temperature rise at the benchmark

β: feedback parameter

θ: power of the damage function

γ_1, γ_2: coefficients in the damage function

κ: fraction of CO_2 remaining in the atmosphere

λ: adjustment coefficient

π: share of capital

ρ: social discount rate

Parameter values and initial conditions

$a = 1\%$

$AC_P = 580 \text{ (GtC)}$

$AC_0 = 750 \text{ (GtC)}$

$A_0 = GDP_0 / K_0^\pi / \Phi_0 / L_0^{(1-\pi)}$

$b = 1\% \text{ or } 2\%$

$E_0 = 6.003 \text{ (GtC)}$

$g_A = 0.85\% \text{ p.a.}$

$g_\alpha = -1.0\% \text{ p.a.}$

$GDP_0 = 25.8 \text{ (tril. \$)}$

$T_B^e = 1.5, 3.0, \text{ or } 4.5$

$\alpha_0 = E_0 / GDP_0$

$\gamma_1 = a/100/0.5^3$

$\gamma_2 = [1/(1 - b/100) - 1]/(T_B^e)^\theta$

$\delta_K = 0.05$

$\delta_M = 0.002$

$\theta = 1.3, 2.0, \text{ or } 3.0$

$\kappa = 0.5$

$\lambda = 0.2$

$K_0 = 70.32$ (tril. \$) $\qquad\qquad$ $\pi = 0.25$

$L_0 = 5.292$ (bil.) $\qquad\qquad$ $\rho = 0.005$ or 0.03

$N = 2300$

Acknowledgements

The author thanks Kenji Yamaji of the University of Tokyo and Tsuneyuki Morita of the National Institute of Environmental Studies for helpful comments and valuable suggestions. Of course, the author is solely responsible for any remaining errors.

References

Amano, A. (ed.). 1992a. *Global Warming and Economic Growth: Modeling Experience in Japan.* Tsukuba, Japan: Center for Global Environmental Research, National Institute for Environmental Studies.

———— 1992b. "Economic costs of reducing CO_2 emissions: Modeling experience in Japan." Paper presented at the IIASA Workshop, September.

Burniaux, J.-M., J. P. Martin, G. Nicoletti, and J. Oliveira-Martins. 1992. *The Costs of Reducing CO_2 Emissions: Evidence from GREEN."* Paris: OECD, Economics Department Working Papers No. 115.

Cline, W. R. 1992. *The Economics of Global Warming.* Washington, D.C.: Institute for International Economics.

Dean, A. 1993. "Costs of cutting CO_2 emissions: Evidence from top–down models." Paper presented at the OECD/IEA International Conference on the Economics of Climate Change, 14–16 June, Paris.

Dean, A. and P. Hoeller. 1992. *Costs of Reducing CO_2 Emissions: Evidence from Six Global Models.* Paris: OECD, Economics Department Working Papers No. 122.

Fankhauser, S. and D. W. Pearce. 1993. "The social costs of greenhouse gas emissions." Paper presented at the OECD/IEA International Conference on the Economics of Climate Change, 14–16 June, Paris.

Hoeller, P. and M. Wallin. 1991. *Energy Prices, Taxes and Carbon Dioxide Emissions.* Paris: OECD, Economics and Statistics Department Working Papers No. 106.

IPCC (Intergovernmental Panel on Climate Change). 1992. *Climate Change: The 1990 and 1992 IPCC Assessments, IPCC First Assessment Report Overview and Policymaker Summaries and 1992 IPCC Supplement.* World Meteorological Organization/United Nations Environment Programme, June.

Jorgenson, D. W., D. Slesnick, and P. J. Wilcoxen. 1992. *Carbon Taxes and Economic Welfare.* Cambridge, Mass.: Harvard Institute of Economic Research, Discussion Paper No. 1589, April.

Kuroda, M. and K. Shimpo. 1992. *Stabilization of CO_2 Emissions and Economic Growth.* Keio Economic Observatory Occasional Paper J.No. 27, November (in Japanese).

Manne, A. S. 1993. "International trade – The impact of unilateral carbon emission limits." Paper presented at the OECD/IEA International Conference on the Economics of Climate Change, 14–16 June, Paris.

141

Nicoletti, G. and J. Oliveira-Martins. 1992. *Global Effects of the European Carbon Tax*. Paris: OECD, Economics Department Working Papers No. 125.

Nordhaus, W. D. 1990a. "Greenhouse economics: Count before you leap." *The Economist*, 13 July: 19–22.

—— 1990b. "An intertemporal general-equilibrium model of economic growth and climate change." In: D. O. Wood and Y. Kaya (eds.), *Proceedings of the Workshop on Economic/Energy/Environmental Modeling for Climate Policy Analysis, October 22–23, 1990*. Washington, D.C., pp. 416–433.

—— 1992a. *The "DICE" Model: Background and Structure of a Dynamic Integrated Climate–Economy Model of the Economics of Global Warming*. Cowles Foundation Discussion Paper No. 1009, February.

—— 1992b. "An optimal transition path for controlling greenhouse gases." *Science* 258, 20 November: 1315–1319.

Oliveira-Martins, J., J.-M. Burniaux, and J. P. Martin. 1992. "Trade and the effectiveness of unilateral CO_2 abatement policies: Evidence from GREEN." *OECD Economic Studies*, No. 19 (Winter): 123–140.

Poterba, J. M. 1991. "Tax policy to combat global warming: On designing a carbon tax." In: R. Dornbusch and J. M. Poterba (eds.), *Global Warming: Economic Policy Responses*. Cambridge, Mass.: MIT Press, chap. 3.

Rutherford, T. 1992. *The Welfare Effects of Fossil Carbon Restrictions: Results from a Recursively Dynamic Trade Model*. Paris: OECD, Economics Department Working Papers No. 112.

Smith, S. 1993. "Who pays for climate change policies? Distributional side-effects and policy responses." Paper presented at the OECD/IEA International Conference on the Economics of Climate Change, 14–16 June, Paris.

9

The effects of CO_2 reduction policies on energy markets

John P. Ferriter

1. Introduction

Numerous studies have now been completed on the macroeconomic effects of policies (mostly carbon taxes) to reduce greenhouse gas emissions.[1] These analyses show a range of economic effects that might be expected in the long term. But most long-term analyses are unable to give detailed descriptions of the next 10 to 20 years. This is the period for which governments have set CO_2 reduction or stabilization targets. It is a difficult period for policy makers. The risks and costs associated with climate change may remain uncertain for at least 20 years to come, and these uncertain costs have to be balanced against the possible costs to the economy of early intervention to reduce CO_2 emissions. In this context, policy makers have been eager to find "no-regrets" strategies, which reduce CO_2 emissions but which would be fully justified by other policy objectives. Even a carbon tax, ostensibly aimed at reducing CO_2 emissions, might be justified as a "no-regrets" strategy if it showed other benefits. These could include reduced dependence on imported fuel, the stimulation of technical progress in industry, reduced local pollution, and reductions in other taxation. Nevertheless, recent discussions about the BTU tax in the United States and the carbon/energy tax in Europe give an indication of the uncertainties about the timing and manner in which any tax might be introduced.

This paper examines some of the issues that might arise in energy markets during the next 20 years, using results from modelling by the International Energy Agency (IEA) of world energy markets over the period 1990–2010. Fuel markets will be the main focus of policies to reduce emissions of CO_2. Most policy measures will aim either to limit or reduce the amount of energy consumed, or to change the form of energy used to acquire a given energy service.

As has frequently been stressed (Hoeller and Coppel, 1992; IEA, 1993b), carbon-based fuels are not currently priced or taxed to reflect their relative carbon content. Governments already intervene in energy markets for reasons including energy security, the local environment, social welfare, employment, and industrial competitiveness. Any policy to reduce energy demand or encourage fuel switching will be applied on top of a host of other measures and may have only marginal effects in some sectors. Without coherent action to deal with all of the policy objectives associated with energy use, we therefore start from a less than optimum position. Thus suboptimal economic efficiency of policy impact is to be expected and counter-intuitive consequences should not surprise us.

Approximations and simplifications are inherent in almost all modelling efforts and the IEA model is no exception. One of the most difficult areas to treat effectively in such models is the process of technical change, especially during times of rapid transition. Although we can use econometrics to relate energy efficiency to income and energy price, such a relationship cannot take account of the potential for technical breakthroughs or switching to fuels and energy sources that have not been widely used in the past.

It is similarly impossible to account in an econometric model for the uncertainties associated with the politics of fuel supply and for some of the unexpected results that may occur because of the way policy measures are implemented. World market prices for fuels in the IEA model are exogenously determined and these issues have been considered in choosing the price trajectories. Sensitivity analysis gives some idea of the effect of the variability of world market prices.

A further area that has been modelled at a minimal level of detail is the effect of changing market structure. Energy demand and prices, as well as the price elasticities of demand, are likely to be changed by the moves towards open energy markets and private ownership.

In analysing the results from the IEA model, this paper does not pretend to be giving a "correct" view of the effects of government policy in energy markets. It does give a view of the sectors and regions where different types of policy are likely to be most effective, and it identifies areas where further investigation is needed to improve our understanding of the effectiveness of policies.

2. Background – Energy markets and policies

Energy markets are dynamic, complex, interdependent systems, built on massive capital investments and relying on fuel supply systems that are in part commodity markets and in part dedicated transportation and conversion systems. Energy suppliers meet a constantly evolving and very broad spectrum of demand for energy services.

Markets for different energy forms are interdependent in a variety of ways. For example, gas and coal prices are often linked to the oil price in contracts; substitutable energy forms such as gas and electricity will have their prices linked through market forces; in other cases where energy products are co-produced, cross-subsidies can occur, one product having a highly variable price while the other's price is constant. These effects can confound efforts by governments to intervene in the market. To the extent that human behaviour is unpredictable, surprising effects can come from decisions made by fuel producers, commodity speculators, and energy service consumers.

The fuel mix in a regional market will depend greatly on the resource endowment of a region and the cost of extraction. It will also depend on the mix of demands for specific energy services, such as transport or refrigeration, where particular forms of energy are preferred. Thus, heterogeneity of energy markets is the point of departure for any analysis of their response to policy interventions.

Our definition of CO_2 reduction policies covers a broad range of government interventions. Parts of the energy industry are regulated to a greater or lesser extent, involving significant government ownership and/or direction in some countries. However, the focus in analysis of CO_2 reduction policy has been on market measures such as carbon taxes or energy efficiency standards rather than on measures to alter institutional factors. Market measures are more easily modelled than institutional changes and we view carbon taxes, or other price signals, as the most efficient way to induce the optimum response. Yet a broad spectrum of policy measures must ultimately be considered. Those most often mentioned in the CO_2 reduction context are: fuel-use restrictions; taxes and other fiscal instruments (including changes

145

in fuel and technology subsidies and in R&D spending); regulations such as energy efficiency standards; and voluntary agreements with industry. Companion policies, such as emissions trading or joint implementation, are often advocated to improve the economic efficiency with which national or regional emission targets are met. Other policies of an economic reform nature, such as opening up access to electricity or gas transmission, have been mentioned in the context of climate change as "no-regrets" strategies. OECD countries already have considerable experience with all of these approaches to energy policy.

Policies to reduce emissions from the energy sector can do so by causing: (i) a reduction in fuel used without altering the quality of energy service (increased efficiency); (ii) a reduction in fuel used through a reduction in the service or in its quality (conservation); and/or (iii) a switch to a fuel with less or no carbon content while delivering the same service. Using carbon-stripping technologies is another response, but one that is currently not commercially available. See the appendix at the end of the chapter for a summary of the main policy types discussed in relation to CO_2 emission reduction.

3. The World Energy Outlook: A reference scenario

The IEA has updated its *World Energy Outlook* (WEO) using its medium-term energy econometric model (IEA, 1993a). Simultaneously, we decided to use the model to investigate the effects of certain CO_2 reduction policies on energy markets. To do this we used the WEO model itself as a reference case and then created three policy scenarios: two carbon tax cases and one efficiency-driven case. The reference case assumes no major policy changes. We describe this case in some detail below.

Our results are similar to those from other models for energy and emission trends. In the WEO model, world energy demand grows by 48 per cent from 1990 to 2010. Three regions are defined in the model: (1) the OECD member countries (OECD); (2) the newly independent states and the Central and Eastern Europe economies in transition (NIS/CEE); and (3) the rest of the world (ROW). Over the period modelled, both OECD and NIS/CEE shares of energy consumption fall *vis-à-vis* ROW: OECD drops from 53 per cent to 46 per cent, NIS/CEE drops from 21 per cent to 15 per cent, and ROW rises from 26 per cent to 39 per cent (see fig. 9.1).

The use of fossil fuels grows significantly over the period: coal consumption rises by 44 per cent, oil by 33 per cent, and gas by 66 per

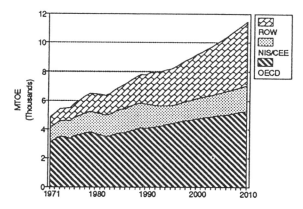

Fig. 9.1   **World total primary energy demand, 1971–2010 (Source: IEA, 1993a)**

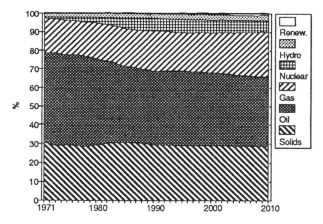

Fig. 9.2   **World primary energy shares, 1971–2010 (Source: IEA, 1993a)**

cent. Of the increase in total fuel use, coal represents 27 per cent in energy terms, oil 39 per cent, and gas 30 per cent. Fuel shares change less dramatically than they did over the period 1971–1990 (see fig. 9.2).

World trends mask some opposing trends in the three regions. For example, ROW and OECD coal growth is somewhat offset by reductions in coal consumption in the NIS/CEE. About 85 per cent of the net growth in coal demand occurs in the ROW. Oil growth is 72 per cent ROW and 26 per cent OECD. Gas growth is 48 per cent ROW and 44 per cent OECD. World electricity production grows 73 per cent. Electricity's share of primary energy continues its growth (from

25 per cent in 1971 in both the OECD and the World to 42 per cent and 38 per cent respectively in 2010). The shares of fuel for electricity generation continue to change between 1990 and 2010, with oil down 5 percentage points, gas up 8 percentage points, and nuclear down 5 percentage points.

Growth in OECD energy demand is greater in 1990–2000, slowing down during 2000–2010. The highest growth rate is in the OECD Pacific region, followed by OECD Europe and then North America. Although growth in ROW energy demand shows a similar slow-down in 2000–2010, the absolute growth rates are over three times higher in ROW than in OECD. Energy intensity declines worldwide, more in OECD than elsewhere and less where economies are in transition. Increasing electrification leads to a decrease in total final consumption (TFC) in relation to GDP, e.g. electricity demand growth is faster in North America during 2000–2010 than in 1990–2000. Lack of infrastructure in ROW retards the penetration of gas, and limited financial resources in both the ROW and NIS/CEE limit the uptake of more efficient technologies. Continued growth in the transport sector accounts for almost all of the incremental oil demand in the OECD.

Under the reference case assumptions, annual world carbon emissions rise from 5,880 million tonnes in 1990 to 8,600 million tonnes in 2010, or 46 per cent (see fig. 9.3). OECD carbon emissions rise from 2,830 million tonnes to 3,600 million tonnes by 2010, or 28 per cent. Increases vary among the OECD regions, rising 25 per cent in OECD North America, 48 per cent in the OECD Pacific region, and 24 per cent in OECD Europe. The faster rise in the OECD Pacific is due to a higher expansion of energy demand, occurring through a higher rate of economic growth than in North America and Europe, and despite the significant further addition of nuclear power plants in Japan.

Carbon emissions from the NIS/CEE region follow the same path as energy consumption, first falling and then returning to the 1990 level of 1,300 million tonnes by 2010. Carbon emissions from the ROW countries increase from 1,750 million tonnes to 3,700 million tonnes of carbon in the same period, or a rise of 111 per cent. By the end of the projection period, therefore, more carbon originates in ROW countries than in the OECD region. The major reason for this is the much faster rate of growth in energy demand in ROW countries cited earlier. Moreover, the major energy input into power generation in two of the most important and fastest-growing non-OECD countries – India and China – is coal, the most carbon intensive of the

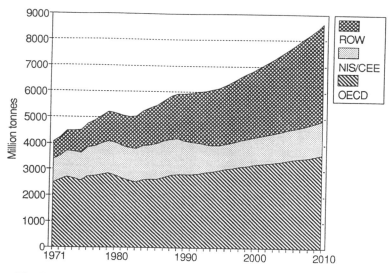

Fig. 9.3 **World carbon emissions, 1971–2010 (Source: IEA, 1993a)**

fossil fuels. In the absence of the improvement in efficiency of power generation that has been assumed in the reference case for these countries, their growth in emissions could be even faster. These two countries also account for 45 per cent of the world's population additions by 2010.

The robustness of the carbon emissions in the reference case was tested against alternative economic growth assumptions and lower oil and gas prices. Even under rather pessimistic economic growth assumptions, world carbon emissions over the projection period grow by at least 38 per cent. Under a scenario of low oil and gas prices (based on flat US$20 per barrel to 2010), emissions from OECD exceed those of the reference case by only about 3.7 per cent. Emissions from the ROW countries rise by some 5 per cent above the reference case if lower prices prevail.

4. Two carbon tax cases

Two carbon tax sensitivity cases (US$100 and US$300 per tonne of carbon emitted) were simulated with the WEO model.[2] In both cases, nearly one-third of the tax is imposed in 1993 with the remainder added in annual increments of almost US$4 in the US$100 case and US$12 under the US$300 case. These taxes are in addition to any

149

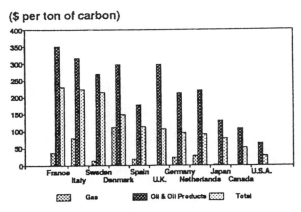

Fig. 9.4   **Implicit carbon taxes, 1988 (Note: Coal is taxed only in Sweden)**

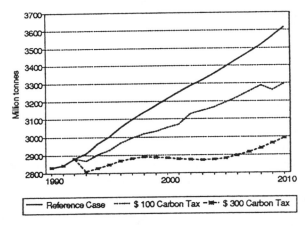

Fig. 9.5   **OECD carbon emissions: Carbon tax cases relative to reference case, 1990–2010**

excise or other taxes currently in place (see fig. 9.4) and are applied to final energy prices in the model. It must be emphasized that we are using these two cases to investigate the effects of large carbon taxes, not to represent any existing government policies. In the real world, carbon taxes are not likely to be introduced so soon, or with such high starting levels.

Figure 9.5 illustrates the emissions growth for the two tax cases and the reference case described above.[3] Emissions in 2010 under the US$100 tax reach 3,300 tonnes, compared with 3,620 tonnes in the reference case (a 9 per cent reduction). This is still well above the

150

1990 level of 2,830 million tonnes per year. Under the tax of US$300 per tonne of carbon, emissions reach 2,990 tonnes in 2010, somewhat above the 1990 level and 17 per cent below the reference case.

The use of all fossil fuels is reduced in both tax cases (except natural gas under the US$100 tax), as shown in table 9.1. The reduction in contribution to total primary energy supply (TPES) is greatest for coal, then oil, and finally gas. Reductions in final energy use are greatest for oil, then coal, then electricity, and then gas. Contributions to CO_2 emission abatement follow the same ranking, as shown in table 9.2. Tripling the level of carbon tax only doubles the emission reduction, reflecting the diminishing scope for substitution between fuels in the medium term and implying that the effectiveness of the carbon tax is reduced as the tax gets higher.

5. An efficiency-driven scenario

An "efficiency-driven" scenario (EDS) has also been constructed. Under this scenario, the efficiency of energy conversion and use improves faster than in the reference case. The improvement rates are exogenous to the model and are based on the introduction of commercially available technology over the period (IEA, 1991, 1992a). In the reference case, the rate of take-up of technology is based on historical trends. Waste heat in power generation is also assumed to be utilized to a much greater extent than at present in all OECD regions. Table 9.3 details the efficiency assumptions used to construct this case. It is not suggested that these improvements would arise exogenously or that they would follow naturally from market factors. Implicitly these accelerated efficiency gains are achieved through some form of regulation or behaviour changes, which we have not specified.

By 2010 energy use is reduced relative to the reference case by 25 per cent in the residential/commercial sector, 7 per cent in the industrial sector, and 10 per cent in the transport sector. By our own assumptions, the EDS's effects involve no fuel switching in the industry or residential/commercial sectors. We have assumed some switching from gasoline to diesel cars in the transport sector.

Under these assumptions, emissions in Europe and North America by 2010 return almost to 1990 levels while in OECD Pacific some growth in emissions still occurs. Emissions for the OECD grow on average by less than 0.4 per cent per annum, compared with 1.2 per cent per annum in the reference case (see fig. 9.6). Whereas emissions

151

Table 9.1 **The effects of tax cases on fuel use relative to reference case**

	In TPES				In TFC			
	US$100		US$300		US$100		US$300	
Fuel	Mtoe change	% of reference case use	Mtoe change	% of reference case use	Mtoe change	% of reference case use	Mtoe change	% of reference case use
Coal	−230	−20	−306	−26	−57	−22	−100	−39
Oil	−96	−5	−250	−13	−96	−5	−233	−13
Natural gas	+6	0	−148	−12	−36	−5	−94	−13
Electricity	–	–	–	–	−41	−5	−96	−12

Table 9.2 **The effects of tax cases on CO_2 emissions associated with fuel use (MtC change relative to reference case)**

	Emission change	
Fuel	US$100	US$300
Coal in TFC	−62	−109
Oil in TFC	−81	−196
Natural gas in TFC	+23	−60

Table 9.3 **Efficiency assumptions for reference case and efficiency-driven scenario**

	Reference case	Efficiency-driven scenario
Use of heat produced as co-product in power generation		
North America	6%	12%
OECD Europe	6%	12%
Japan	1%	7%
Residential/commercial sector energy efficiency improvement		
All regions	–	1.5% p.a. energy savings (extra 25% in 2010)
Industrial sector energy efficiency improvement		
All regions	–	0.4% p.a. energy savings (extra 7% in 2010)
Transport sector energy efficiency improvement		
Air transport		
All regions	1% p.a.	2% p.a.
Freight transport		
North America and OECD Europe	0.5% p.a.	1% p.a.
Japan	1% p.a.	1.5% p.a.
New car improvement by 2010		
North America	19%	43%
OECD Europe	15%	47%
Diesel share in passenger transport		
OECD Europe	14%	28%
North America	1%	14%

in the reference case grow almost in line with primary energy, under this scenario they increase at just over half the energy demand growth rate of 0.6 per cent per annum. This is due to the growing proportion of non-fossil fuels in electricity base-load: non-fossil capacity grows

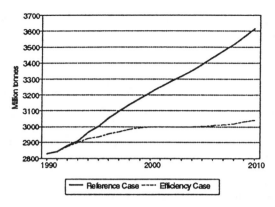

Fig. 9.6 **OECD carbon emissions: Efficiency case relative to reference case, 1990–2010**

at 1.6 per cent per annum in all cases, so that reduced electricity demand results in a reduction in fossil fuel use only.

6. Regional and sectoral differences in the three policy cases

Regional differences

Primary coal and gas prices and the taxes on energy products are lower in North America than in other regions, so that a given level of carbon tax leads to larger percentage increases in end-use prices. Prices combine with other factors such as economic structure, current fuel use patterns, and growth rates in their effect on carbon emissions. Nevertheless, under the US$300 tax, emissions stay close to 1990 levels in North America, rise slightly in Europe, and are about 13 per cent higher in OECD Pacific, reflecting the assumed, sustained higher growth rates in that region.

In all three sensitivity cases using the IEA model, over 50 per cent of the OECD emissions reductions occur in North America, about one-third in Europe, and the rest in the Pacific region, mainly Japan (fig. 9.7). These are roughly the regional shares of primary energy use in 1990. The EDS is more effective in reducing energy use than the US$300 carbon tax, although the US$300 case is slightly more effective than the EDS in achieving emissions reductions (see figs. 9.8 and 9.9.)

In the carbon tax cases there is more regional variation in energy savings than in emissions reductions. The US$300 tax leads to 17 per

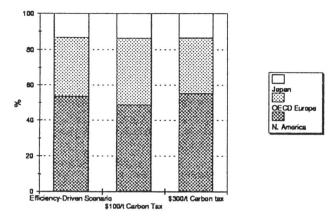

Fig. 9.7 **Carbon emission reductions, OECD 2010: Three cases regional breakdown**

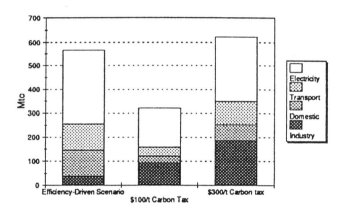

Fig. 9.8 **Carbon emission reductions, OECD 2010: Three cases sectoral breakdown**

cent final energy savings in North America, but only 6 per cent in Europe. The Japanese savings are slightly more than in Europe. The OECD's GREEN model and other modelling produce generally the same results. The reasons for these regional differences are examined below.

Figure 9.10 shows a comparison between the Commission of the European Communities' (CEC) model, looking at the effect of the CEC's proposed energy/carbon tax, and the IEA model output for Europe. The CEC tax has much less effect than any of the WEO cases because the tax is much lower (equivalent to roughly US$70 on oil per tonne of carbon), and is introduced gradually over the period to

155

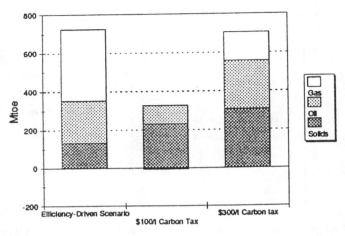

Fig. 9.9   **Energy use reductions, OECD 2010: Three cases breakdown by fuel**

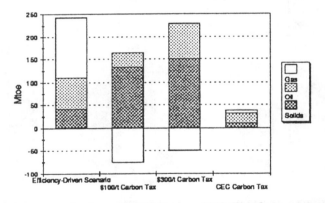

Fig. 9.10   **Energy use reductions, OECD Europe 2010: The three cases and the CEC carbon tax case**

2000. The tax is disproportionately higher on gas and nuclear, but lower on coal, than a pure carbon tax. In the CEC model, gas use decreases with the tax, with gas for power generation going down as well as in end use. With the US$100 tax, the WEO produces increases in gas use for electricity generation in all regions. It produces a decrease only in the higher tax case.

Sectoral effects

In examining the responses of energy consumers to policy measures, there are important distinctions between individuals such as car-

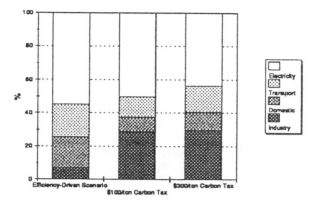

Fig. 9.11   **Carbon emission reductions, OECD 2010: Three cases sectoral break-down**

drivers and home-owners making personal decisions, and industrial or corporate decision makers. For personal decisions, lifestyle and personal values can often have more influence on fuel-use decisions than price signals, whereas industry is generally expected to be more price responsive. Industrial consumers generally have better access to information about alternative technologies and to the capital needed to invest in them.

Figure 9.11 presents breakdowns by sector of carbon emissions reductions for the three cases. The sectoral emissions reductions in the two tax cases are in more or less the same proportions. Changes in power generation provide roughly 50 per cent of emission reductions, final fuel use in industry roughly 25 per cent, and the transport and residential/commercial sectors the rest.

The EDS differs significantly in its sectoral effects from the carbon tax cases. Changes in electricity generation account for roughly 55 per cent of emissions reductions and there are significant differences in end-use sectors. Excluding electricity, the transport and domestic sectors each account for roughly 40 per cent of the reduction in emissions from final energy use, while industry provides the rest (20 per cent). The EDS is far more effective in the "problem" residential/commercial sector.

Figure 9.12 shows the breakdown of emissions reductions by sector for each region in the US$300 tax case. The differences in the sectoral contribution to each region's emission abatement are mostly explained by differences in the sectoral shares in emissions in the reference case.

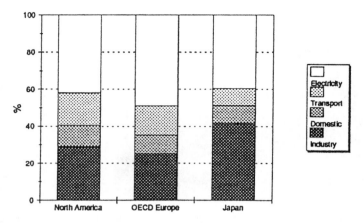

Fig. 9.12 **Carbon emission reductions, OECD 2010: Regional and sectoral break-down, US$300 tax case**

Even the percentage changes in transport energy use are similar in North America, Japan, and Europe, which may seem surprising given the higher reference case fuel price in Europe and Japan to which the tax is added. Different turnover rates and saturation of vehicle-miles travelled in North America account for the closeness of the reductions. Fuels are affected differently according to sector. Faced with carbon taxes, industry tends to reduce electricity use more than gas, whereas the residential/commercial sector reduces gas more than electricity.

The relationship between primary energy prices and consumer energy prices
One reason for the apparent insensitivity of energy demand in the transport and residential/commercial sectors to high levels of carbon taxes is the relatively modest impact of the taxes on the prices that consumers actually pay. Whereas the imposition of a US$100 carbon tax is likely to increase gasoline prices by about 20 per cent in the United States, prices would increase by less than 8 per cent in Europe and Japan. Similarly, the impact on the price of residential gas is around 22 per cent in the United States, 12 per cent in Europe, and less than 6 per cent in Japan. Whereas a US$100 carbon tax is greater than the primary coal price by 2010, its impact on the price of electricity, by far the largest consumer of coal, would be less than 10 per cent in Europe and Japan. Thus, unless carbon taxes are set at a very high level, the reaction of energy consumers is expected to be moderate.

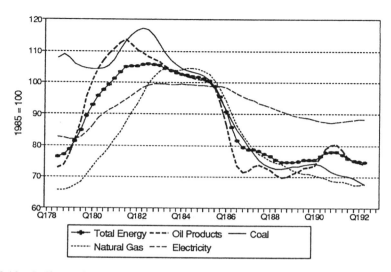

Fig. 9.13 **Indices of real energy end-use prices: Total OECD (Note: 1985 = base year for "total energy" price; further moving averages of 4 quarters are used. Source: International Energy Agency, Paris)**

7. The effects of CO_2 reduction policies on energy commodity markets

The nature of energy commodity markets

Crude oil is the largest single commodity traded on world markets in dollar terms. It represents 75 per cent of the world trade in fossil fuels partly because of its ease of transport, storage, and use. Markets for gas tend to be organized regionally; in the case of coal, sources are linked to particular users. Although the coal industry has made great strides in developing preparation and blending techniques to increase the number of potential buyers, improved coal products make up a very small percentage of coal in international trade. Because of its ubiquitousness and flexibility of use, oil tends to be the price leader, with coal and natural gas following (see fig. 9.13).

Energy commodity markets are not entirely distinct, but major regional markets are recognized in North America, Western Europe, Central and Eastern Europe and the newly independent states, and the Asia/Pacific region. Some national economies are virtually self-sufficient in energy, especially for gas and coal.

There is a high degree of government ownership in many regional

159

markets, whether developed countries, economies in transition, or developing countries. Government control is especially prominent in the utility sector but it is also significant in natural gas and oil production and transformation. Government control generally inhibits the efficient functioning of the markets for these fuels, for example in limiting market access and competition among suppliers or by ensuring cross-subsidies to certain consumer sectors.

Concurrently it will be important to understand the strength of other changes that have been set into motion in energy commodity markets. Examples are the effects of a global trend (particularly in a number of large ROW and NIS/CEE greenhouse gas emitters) to eliminate energy subsidies and to open up markets to greater competition.

The effects of removing subsidies should not be overestimated. In competitive situations, producers may not be able to raise prices to cover the loss of former subsidies. In situations with other types of government control, the removal of subsidies alone might not "free" the producer from other regulations that constrain fuel choice.

Although the elimination of consumer subsidies is expected to lead to a reduction in demand for some fuels, greater competition in energy markets could reduce prices and raise demand. In some regions, including parts of OECD Europe, protection of indigenous coal production is being reduced, allowing cheaper imports into the market. Coal prices could be reduced relative to those of oil and gas, resulting in a shift towards a fuel mix with a higher carbon content. Conversely, open access to electricity grids for power producers, especially small suppliers, could lead to an increase in co-generation and renewable energy use. Furthermore, the move away from government ownership and control could result in higher discount rates being used for energy-related investment. In electricity systems this might result in a move away from nuclear and coal toward less capital-intensive capacity such as oil- or gas-fired plant.

In an energy commodity market such as the Japanese market, even without direct fuel-use requirements, a considerable amount of "administrative guidance" creates a "price wedge" that keeps the prices of fuels higher than the world price although the fuels are not actually taxed. Although either the European or the Japanese case has the effect of a tax on demand, it is not clear what would happen if other policies were superimposed in order to reduce greenhouse gas emissions. One could easily imagine the wedge reducing somewhat in the face of new taxes, with the net result being a lower price than one might calculate taking the actual price and simply adding the tax to it.

Coal market issues

In all three CO_2 reduction policy cases using the IEA model, coal in OECD primary energy supply falls relative to the reference case. The 2010 level is below the 1990 level in the US$300 tax case. Carbon taxes are likely to have more effect on coal than on other fuels because coal contains more carbon per unit of energy. However, coal is also at a disadvantage relative to oil and gas in that it is mainly used in non-premium applications. Although some oil products (mainly heavy fuel oil) are sold in these non-premium markets, oil companies may be able to pass on most of the carbon tax to consumers of premium fuels in the transport sector. Similarly gas producers may be able to raise residential gas prices more than commercial contract prices. Fuel suppliers are likely to cross-subsidize their customers in this way to some extent, regardless of whether taxes are imposed on primary fuels or on final energy products. Thus, not only is coal more affected than other fuels by a carbon tax, it is also likely to be disproportionately more affected in the markets where fuel switching is easiest.

OECD carbon taxes could affect the coal market in the rest of the world. Reduced OECD demand could lead to a fall in the pre-tax price. However, if the tax is applied only in the OECD, rising demand in other regions may stabilize the market. Meanwhile the movement in the OECD and former Comecon countries away from domestic coal subsidies will increase demand for imported coal.

Countries typically have energy systems (especially electricity generation) based largely on their indigenous resources even when these take the form of relatively highly polluting coal. Most of the world's very large CO_2 emitters are also very large energy producers. Included in the top 10 CO_2 emitters are the United States, Russia, China, India, Ukraine, and Canada, which are large energy producers although some of these are not exporters (IEA, 1992b). Some governments might be expected to continue to shield certain fuels from the effects of carbon taxes, offsetting some of the demand-dampening effect of the CO_2 reduction policy.

Oil markets

It is not possible to predict how major oil-exporting countries would react to an OECD-wide tax. To date they have criticized such proposals as being an incursion on the rent that should be theirs as owners of the oil resources. They correctly point to the existing taxes on fossil fuels and note that premium oil products in most OECD countries already bear high taxes. Producers may attempt to increase volume to offset the revenue losses stemming from a carbon-tax-driven lower demand, or they may prefer to reduce exports to the OECD, given that markets are growing elsewhere.

Natural gas markets

Gas is the only fuel for which consumption is increased overall under any of the CO_2 reduction policy cases and electricity generation is the only sector in which this occurs for the OECD as a whole. There are some regional variations, and increases in gas used for electricity generation in Japan and Europe are masked by larger decreases elsewhere.

The trend towards the use of natural gas, particularly in Europe and Japan, leads to questions about the speed and cost at which fuel substitution could be achieved. In the European and Japanese markets, significant incremental gas supplies would have to be imported and preceded by major investment in production and transportation systems. Policies intended to encourage switching away from high carbon fuels could be frustrated, or their effects delayed, by a lack of infrastructure for natural gas, the regional concentration of resources, and the expense and time-lags to build the infrastructure to connect them to distant new users.

The Pacific gas market, where rapid growth in energy demand exists, will remain dominated by liquefied natural gas (LNG) for the next two or three decades at least. LNG markets are only beginning to go into their "second era": the first of the early 1970s' contracts are being renegotiated and, unlike the first contracts, formal contract re-opener or price review clauses have been introduced. In future there is likely to be more competition between LNG suppliers than in the past 20 years. As more markets open for LNG, and given variations in demand in different countries, there are greater prospects of lower-priced spot cargoes. Against this, LNG depends on large investments in terminals and no new projects are assured at current prices.

One of the biggest uncertainties in the European energy commodity market is the stability of the supply of oil and gas from Russia and other newly independent states. These countries are strongly motivated to export gas and oil to obtain Western currency, but political instability and poor infrastructure lead to uncertainties about the availability of the fuels. Deep economic recessions in recent years have led to declines in fossil fuel use, potentially freeing up supplies for export. Many of these countries are in the process of raising domestic energy prices, which will continue to have some dampening effect on demand. The European Energy Charter, with its emphasis on opening and improving the technical aspects of energy commodity trade, is also an important step in stabilizing the European energy commodities markets.

Other factors mitigate against the availability of oil and gas from the former Comecon region. Carbon taxes are not likely to be introduced by these countries in the near future, but some may move away from existing coal and nuclear energy use for environmental and safety reasons. In this case, domestic demand for gas, which is already significant, could increase rapidly. Oil demand is also likely to increase rapidly as a result of increasing car use.

8. Areas for further study

There is clearly a need for more work on the analytical base from which we make conclusions about the costs and effects of CO_2 reduction policies. For example, further elaboration of the IEA model could take account of the technical possibilities, including the introduction of non-fossil fuels and the retrofitting of existing energy-using equipment, especially in electricity generation, to use low-carbon fuels.

More importantly, several different analytical approaches are needed to comprehend the full range of effects on the economy, including the energy sector. Econometric modelling is only one of these tools – one that is particularly suited to examining the effects of policy measures in the short to medium term.

Linkages with other modelling efforts must continue. This will allow the analysis to incorporate the impacts of CO_2 reduction policies on economic activity and the important feedback effects of changes in economic activity on energy demand and prices, on fuel commodity markets, and on the rate of carbon leakage.

More questions have been raised than answered in this paper, but this was by design. More attention must be given to in-depth analysis of CO_2 reduction policies and energy markets. At the OECD/IEA Conference on the Economics of Climate Change in June 1993 in Paris, participants raised a number of questions for further analysis.
• How will the costs of carbon taxes be distributed between fuel producers, suppliers, and consumers? How is this affected by moving the point at which the tax is levied?

- How might OPEC react to carbon taxes or other CO_2 reduction policies?
- What does the historical relationship between crude oil prices and oil product prices tell us about the way carbon taxes would be passed on to consumers?
- How will changing government intervention in coal markets modify the effects of carbon taxes?
- What are the financial implications of the capital costs associated with switching to natural gas on a very large scale *vis-à-vis* interest rates and the financing of energy investments in general? On what time-scale?
- What are the options for moving natural gas to key markets, and what are the economic and political constraints on various source and/or transportation options?
- Will exporting countries (again) wish to retain significant natural gas supplies for domestic consumption, for both environmental and trade-competitive reasons?
- In choosing fuels for power generation, will utilities be able to select among fuels freely, taking into account not only price (including tax) but also supply security and other factors, or will price be the only determinant allowed by the regulators?
- How do emissions trading, power-wheeling, and other efforts to find least-cost approaches affect the cost-effectiveness of CO_2 reduction policies?

9. Conclusions

The IEA's energy modelling work has shown, within the assumptions applied, that a US$300 per ton carbon tax might be able to reduce OECD carbon emissions in 2010 nearly to 1990 levels. This level of tax is far beyond any that has been seriously discussed in international forums, yet governments already intervene to a greater extent, and in some instances at considerable cost to national budgets, in parts of the energy market.

Institutional and transitional issues require careful consideration on a national and regional basis. Opening up energy markets and reducing subsidies could reduce the economic costs of applying CO_2 reduction policies. The degree and timing of the implementation of a policy could be fine tuned to divert future investment toward more environmentally friendly fuels and technologies without resulting in excessive disruption in the economy.

The reader is strongly cautioned against concluding that either a regulatory approach, or the use of fiscal or financial incentives, could achieve CO_2 stabilization at little or no cost. Considerable further work should be done to develop a better understanding of the possible economic impact of regulations, taxes, and other fiscal measures before such a judgement is made.

The analysis presented here does suggest that a mix of policies may be the most effective, although not the most cost-effective, approach to reducing emissions. In the foreseeable future, it appears unlikely that OECD governments will adopt substantial carbon taxes. Voluntary agreements with industry are receiving increasing attention. All measures attempting to bring emissions back to 1990 levels by reducing demand or improving efficiency have to be continually strengthened to hold emissions at 1990 levels. The effects of achieved improvements in efficiency could lead to increased energy use elsewhere in the economy. Decreased GDP might suppress gains in energy efficiency through reduced capital replacement.

A hedging strategy would contain a balance of measures to improve the efficiency with which we use energy (e.g. through voluntary agreements, performance standards, and incentives), with a much heavier emphasis on R&D to make renewable energy sources competitive earlier. Two major questions brought out in an OECD/IEA model comparisons project relate to the rate of autonomous energy efficiency change and the availability of backstop technology. These both depend on clear policy signals such as encouragement of R&D and the creation of necessary market conditions.

The results of the IEA *World Energy Outlook* model also point to the need for realistic and palatable policies not only for the OECD but also for relations between the OECD and the rest of the world. This may include examining the potential for investment in clean energy supply and industry, but also programmes to facilitate local initiatives for the efficient and clean use of energy. For the OECD, energy efficiency standards or voluntary agreements may be needed to address energy use in the residential/commercial sector and for transport. Where taxes are effective, such as in industry and in affecting the electricity fuel mix, these might be the preferred route. Meanwhile we should not forget that governments themselves are a major wild card in the design and implementation of CO_2 reduction policies. Subsidies and fuel-use restrictions are still widespread inside as well as outside of the OECD. Thus, much reform of local and regional energy policies is required within countries, which could go a long way to reducing the severity of any eventual national or international policy actions needed to reduce CO$_2$ emissions.

Appendix: Commonly proposed CO$_2$ reduction policies

Instrument	General purpose	Specific GHG application
Economic or quasi-economic		
Taxes (carbon, BTU, or	Induce behaviour changes	Reduce CO$_2$ emissions, or reduce energy use, or both
combination)	Raise funds for programmes	R&D or grants for efficiency or renewables
Subsidies	Induce behaviour changes or provide funds for specific behaviour or R&D	Efficiency or renewable investments and development
Price supports	Increase use of "desirable" fuel	Increase use of non-fossil fuels
Other (regulatory and quasi-regulatory)		
Fuel-use require-ments and restrictions	Force users to move to more "desirable" fuel or prohibit use of "undesirable" fuel	Increase nuclear and renewables
Performance standards	Force greater efficiency or fuel switching	Decrease emissions
Voluntary programmes (for industry or individuals)	Induce beneficial actions, often by "carrot" (financial incentives) or "stick" (possibility of regulation or fines)	Allow end-user to choose means for emission reduction
Regulatory planning approaches	Require consideration of social good of fuels in supply planning	Shift fuel choices to less polluting fuels and give efficiency a better chance to compete
Joint implementa-tion and offsets/ credits	Reduce costs of compliance and accelerate beneficial actions	Induce action in non-OECD countries as well as within OECD countries

Notes

1. This paper is based on a study prepared by Mr. Robert Skinner, Director of the IEA Office of Long-Term Co-operation, with contributions from Ms. Connie Smyser, Head of the IEA Energy and Environment Division, and Mr. Laurie Michaelis, Administrator, Energy and Environment Division, and presented to the OCED/IEA Conference on the Economics of Climate Change, 14–16 June 1993 in Paris. It is further derived from research conducted by

Mr. Robert Reinstein, consultant, and Ms. Christina Shåhle, IEA Energy and Environment Division. Much of the discussion of the *World Energy Outlook* and the policy cases is derived from IEA (1993a). For more details on the IEA's model, see Vouyoukas (1992).

2. The results obtained from the IEA econometric model differ from those derived from the OECD GREEN model and from other models. This is because of the very different structures of the different models, the different time-periods considered, and the degree to which existing capital stock and capital stock turnover rates are explicitly modelled. The IEA model was designed to analyse the world energy markets. It was not designed to assess macro-economic questions and there is no feedback link for evaluating the impact of taxes such as those examined here on GDP.

The two carbon tax sensitivity cases differ from the reference case only in the taxes incrementally applied as described. GDP and fossil fuel supply costs were kept as in the reference case. The ability to resort to non-fossil alternatives such as hydro and nuclear was also constrained as in the reference case. The sensitivity analysis did not include effects on the NIS/CEE region or China.

3. The rise in emissions between 2001 and 2008 in the US$100 case is caused by a change in the merit order in the electricity generation submodel for Europe. This occurs as coal becomes cheaper with the opening up of European markets and increasing use of imported coal. Although in practice this effect might be smoothed, it draws attention to the possibility of unexpected changes in market conditions resulting in rises in emissions.

References

Hoeller, P. and J. Coppel. 1992. "Carbon taxes and current energy policies in OECD countries." *The Economic Costs of Reducing CO$_2$ Emissions*. Paris: OECD Economic Studies No. 19, Winter.

IEA (International Energy Agency). 1991. *Energy Efficiency and the Environment.* Paris: OECD.

——— 1992a. *Cars and Climate Change.* Paris: OECD.

——— 1992b. *Climate Change Policy Initiatives.* Paris: OECD.

——— 1993a. *World Energy Outlook to 2010.* Paris: OECD/IEA.

——— 1993b. *Taxing Energy: Why and How.* Paris: OECD.

Vouyoukas, L. 1992. *Carbon Taxes and CO$_2$ Emissions Targets: Results from the IEA Model.* Paris: OECD Economics Department Working Paper No. 114.

Comments on part 3

1. Lawrence R. Klein

Uncertainty in environmental analysis

Statistical model building is a natural procedure to use in studying environmental impacts on social activity and also in examining the effects of alternative environmental policies. There are, however, uncertainties in this, as in any other, approach. It appears to me that some of the discussion at the conference was based on the assumption that model findings are correct, and accurate beyond their abilities.

I simply want to caution those among us who would speak as though certain estimates – say, of CO_2 pollution or many other environmental measures – are quite correct. The discussion has been based on "point" estimates with more digits or decimals than can be justified, on the basis either of observational accuracy or of our precision in estimating technical or behavioural reactions.

The models that are being used are based on meagre data samples, often with large measurement errors. If the errors were to be evaluated by appropriate statistical formulas, we would undoubtedly find that the estimated confidence intervals, based on standard errors of extrapolation, are quite large. These intervals (or regions in higher dimensions) are often so wide that a surprisingly large number of qualitatively different social consequences could plausibly occur, yet I notice people speaking of societal results that are deceptively implied to be quite precise. For example, there is great uncertainty about the amount of carbon reduction in the atmosphere that would be associated with a given carbon tax.

My guess is that the interval of uncertainty, for a given degree of probability (such as two-thirds), is as great as 1,000 million metric tons. Those who confidently expect that emission levels can be held to the global amounts that prevailed in 1990 as a result of the imposition of a moderate tax of less than US$75/ton may well be wrong. It may require a much steeper tax to hold emissions at 1990 levels, and this good, in itself, would not be a very satisfactory outcome for the world. In fact, the different models that are used for the projection of CO_2 emissions come to very different conclusions as to the effectiveness of taxation in reducing emissions. The spread among different model estimates is as large as a carefully evaluated confidence interval based on any one model.

Some of the main sources of error and uncertainty are the following:
- the estimation of the rate and volume of emissions from prevailing technologies;
- reactions of consumers and producers to price changes, either by market forces or by tax changes, in the use of energy;
- a flawed global database, such that some magnitudes are not available and the combustion effects, on a global basis, from the burning of fuel are not precisely known;
- the effects of climate and other natural conditions in which the model is assumed to operate not being fully (or even "well") known.

There are formidable obstacles to accurate projections of the economy and the physical environment, in tandem. These obstacles do not mean that we can say nothing about the problem or that we should remain silent in the face of the obstacles. They do imply, however, that we should describe our findings in general terms, with both point values and regions of uncertainty.

How can this be done? In the first place, well-known statistical methods for the estimation of standard errors of extrapolation or projection should be employed as far as possible. In some cases, sample data will be too sparse to permit careful evaluation of the underlying estimates of error variances.

A second step involves the calculation of stochastic simulations of the associated models. The investigation must assess all entry-points in the model design that admit error, and use drawings of numerical disturbance values (random in many cases) for the computation of alternative extrapolations. If this process is replicated, over and over again, an entire *distribution* of extrapolations can be assembled. Error variances or ranges can be determined from the replicated set of extrapolations. Of course, a minimal first or preliminary step should be to make a sensitivity analysis of the effect of assigning very different values, in a plausible range, to key parameters of the system. These different parameter estimates should not be purely one-at-a-time, because many of the key parameter estimates are interrelated with one another. This is an important point that is frequently overlooked in sensitivity analysis.

There is one saving aspect in this approach. If analysts concentrate on the examination of *deviations* from baseline cases they can take advantage of the phenomenon of "error cancellation." To the extent that some of the underlying uncertainties are the same, both in the baseline case and in the scenario case, there will tend to be high correlation between the same magnitude extrapolated from the two cases.

In the well-known statistical formula for the variance of a difference,

$$\mathrm{var}(x^s - x^b) = \mathrm{var}\, x^s - 2\,\mathrm{cov}\, x^s x^b + \mathrm{var}\, x^b,$$

we find that large positive values for $\mathrm{cov}\, x^s x^b$ can help offset the cumulative effects of var x^s *plus* var x^b. In this formula, x^s stands for a scenario value, x^b for a baseline value, var for variance and cov for covariance. If x^s and x^b are highly correlated, as one might suspect, then $\mathrm{cov}\, x^s x^b$ will be large, relative to var x^s + var x^b.

This issue does not necessarily make the analysis accurate, in an absolute sense, but it does help to restrain the inherent degree of uncertainty.

It should also be noted that many environmental phenomena take a very long time to build up to serious magnitudes, i.e. serious for the quality of life. It is my conviction that the error of extrapolation grows with the length of the extrapolation horizon. Statements about the year 2020, or in some cases 2050, are extremely uncertain. We must try to look ahead, but we must be aware of the high degree of uncertainty associated with an attempt to extrapolate that far into the future.

2. Warwick J. McKibbin

The three papers in part 3 have a number of common themes. The central theme is the costs and benefits of implementing policies to reduce the expected increase in CO_2 emissions over the next 10–300 years. I found that all three papers offered useful insights on the issues that they address, but they also highlight the need for more detailed research and better modelling efforts in this area. I will raise comments on specific aspects of each paper and then present some results from a new report to the US Environmental Protection Agency that uses a model called G-Cubed that I have developed jointly with Peter Wilcoxen. This model has a time-horizon of 300 years but integrates the short-run macroeconomic adjustment process in a model with multiple sectors in production and trade. It also explicitly deals with the interaction of asset flows and goods flows in international trade which are ignored in all other models that examine carbon taxes. In addition, this model is participating in the next round of OECD model comparisons. Each of the authors refers to results from the last round of model comparisons and thus these new results from G-Cubed will supplement the discussion of these earlier studies.

The paper by William Cline presents further extensions to his important contributions over the past several years, related to the issue of the benefits of reducing greenhouse gas emissions. His main argument is that more aggressive action is needed to combat the emission of CO_2 than is likely to be implemented. His basic argument is that standard calculations of costs and benefits ignore the potential of a major disaster if nothing is done. In addition, economists have used discount rates that are high so that major problems that occur more than 100 years in the future are discounted away. Although I disagree with his arguments on this point, I agree with his policy prescription for the next decade. That is, to introduce a carbon tax of US\$20–25 per ton and to increase investment in scientific research so as to improve our understanding of where we are and where we may be going. In addition, at the end of these comments I will provide some evidence that will support Cline's position that more can be done to reduce carbon emissions by illustrating that there need not be a trade-off between carbon emission reduction and lower economic growth. It is possible to reduce CO_2 emissions with only short-term loss of GDP if the revenue that is generated by the tax is invested appropriately.

I would also like to raise several issues that Cline touches upon in his paper. First, in my opinion, the cost-effectiveness of planting trees to absorb CO_2 is significantly overestimated. The sort of estimates for the United States from the studies that Cline cites are that around 20 per cent of the arable land in the United States should be planted to significantly reduce net projected increases in US carbon emissions. The general equilibrium effects of this are potentially large, given that it will raise the price of land, especially in agriculture. These general equilibrium effects have been ignored in the studies to date. The G-Cubed modelling work to which I have referred is attempting to focus more on this issue. We do not yet have a clear picture of the cost-effectiveness of the tree-planting strategy on a scale sufficiently large to lead to a reduction in baseline emissions.

Cline is right to point out the important role played by the discount rate in cost–benefit calculations. But also of great importance in any of these evaluations are: the extent of baseline emissions; the existence of backstop technologies; and how the revenue from the carbon tax is used.

Specifically on the question of discount rates, I tend to agree with the standard economists' approach of using a pure rate of time preference closer to 3 per cent. Cline points out when criticizing Nordhaus's assumption of 3 per cent: "This rate means that, under conditions of equal per capita income today and 200 years in the future, we can justifiably ask our descendants to give up US$370 in consumption to permit us to enjoy just US$1 of extra consumption today (in constant price dollars)." But it can easily be countered that, with a 3 per cent marginal product of capital, why should we be expected to give up US$1 of extra consumption today so that our descendants 200 years from now will have US$370 in extra consumption? In standard intertemporal consumer theory, where we have a representative consumer who lives forever, it can be shown that the marginal product of capital (or the real interest rate) is driven to the pure rate of time preference in steady state. If the discount rate is greater than the real interest rate then it pays to borrow and raise consumption today because the forgone consumption is less valuable in terms of future utility. If the discount rate is less than the real interest rate then it pays to forgo consumption today, invest the saving in physical capital, and get a future return that in terms of utility makes you better off. As consumption is forgone, the capital stock rises and the marginal product of capital falls until the interest rate equals the rate of time preference. In terms of valuing per capita consumption between any two periods, then the rate of time preference equal to the marginal product of capital is the logical assumption to use (at least in steady state).

I remain unconvinced by Cline's argument about discount rates, although I agree with Cline that more should be done, especially in the United States, to limit the emission of greenhouse gases. My view is based on the argument below that there need not be a linear relationship between reductions in CO_2 emissions and GDP loss.

Professor Amano also addresses the consequences of reducing CO_2 emissions through carbon taxes. He does this by comparing results from the models used in the OECD global model comparison project with results from Japanese studies. He makes a number of important points with which I agree. I will provide evidence in support of his contentions below.

Amano argues that many of the Japanese models have a larger loss of GDP per unit of carbon tax than the models in the OECD study because they place more weight on short-run changes in aggregate demand. Secondly, the Japanese models allow for unemployed resources in the short run, which computable general equilibrium (CGE) models typically do not. Thirdly, he points out that what is done with the revenue from the tax is very important. In addition, he raises questions about the extent of trade diversion leading to leakage of the effects of a unilateral tax levied by one country. Amano argues that to capture the overall effects requires a model with disaggregated sectoral detail because the carbon tax does not fall uniformly across the economy.

As already mentioned, I agree with many of Professor Amano's points. One aspect of the paper with which I disagree is the link between GDP growth and carbon emissions. Despite making the point that the impact of a carbon tax falls differentially on different sectors of the economy, Amano then summarizes the model results, as many commentators in this debate do, by inferring that a 1 per cent reduction in CO_2 emissions requires a carbon tax of US\$2–10 per ton. This tax then implies a reduction in GDP of between 0.02 and 0.05 per cent. Below, I will show that in the G-Cubed model a 1 per cent reduction requires a carbon tax of around US\$8 per ton but the outcome for GDP depends crucially on how the revenue is used. By 2010 it could lead to a fall in GDP of 0.3 per cent if revenue is rebated back to consumers or to a rise of 0.4 per cent if the revenue is recycled to fund an investment tax credit.

In the final paper John Ferriter presents a baseline scenario out to the year 2010 from the International Energy Agency model. He then presents results for a US$100 per ton carbon tax, US$300 per ton carbon tax, and an increase in energy efficiency. I have little to argue with in the baseline scenario, but I question the usefulness of the model results. From my reading of the paper, it is assumed that between 1993 and 2010 there is no feedback from the change in energy prices after tax to aggregate GDP and then back to energy demand. This result is counter to most other model studies, including those of the models he refers to in his paper. I also found the results that a carbon tax of US$300 per ton by 2010 is the stabilizing level for the United States to be at the high end of the evidence from other models. Part of the reason a large tax is required is that there is no aggregate reduction in GDP that drives down the demand for energy.

I will now present some results for the impact of a US$15 per ton carbon tax in the G-Cubed model to add evidence to that presented by the three papers as well as to show the crucial importance of the assumption about how the revenue from the tax is used. In addition, the difference between short-run aggregate demand consequences and long-run production substitution that is pointed to by Professor Amano will be highlighted.

The G-Cubed model

The G-Cubed model is documented in McKibbin and Wilcoxen (1992). This model is a multi-sector dynamic general equilibrium growth model. The key features of G-Cubed can be summarized as follows:

- specification of the demand and supply sides of industrial economies;
- integration of the real and financial markets of these economies;
- intertemporal accounting of the stocks and flows of real resources and financial assets;
- imposition of intertemporal budget constraints so that agents and countries cannot forever borrow or lend without undertaking the resource transfers necessary to service outstanding liabilities;
- short-run behaviour is a weighted average of neoclassical optimizing behaviour and ad hoc "liquidity constrained" behaviour;
- disaggregation of the real side of the model to allow for the production and trade of multiple goods and services within and across economies;
- full short-run and long-run macroeconomic closure with macro-dynamics at an annual frequency around a long-run Solow/Swan neoclassical growth model;

• the model is solved for a full rational expectations equilibrium at an annual frequency from 1993 to 2200.

The model consists of seven economic regions – the United States, Japan, the European Economic Community (EUR), the rest of the OECD (ROECD), oil-exporting developing countries (OPEC), Eastern Europe and states of the former Soviet Union (EFSU), and all other developing countries (LDCs) – with 12 sectors in each region. There are five energy sectors – electric utilities, natural gas utilities, petroleum processing, coal extraction, and crude oil and gas extraction – and seven non-energy sectors (mining, agriculture, fishing, and hunting, forestry and wood products, durable manufacturing, non-durable manufacturing, transportation, and services). This disaggregation enables us to capture the sectoral differences in the impact of alternative environmental policies.

G-Cubed's seven regions can be divided into two groups: four industrial regions and three others. For the industrial economies, the internal macroeconomic structure as well as the external trade and financial linkages are completely specified in the model.

Figure 3C.1 presents results from McKibbin and Wilcoxen (1993a). This simulation shows the path of gross national product (GNP) in the United States after the imposition of a permanent US$15 per ton carbon tax in the United States commencing in 1993. The results are expressed as percentage deviations from the model baseline; thus zero implies no change in GNP relative to the baseline path. Each line in figure 3C.1 is for a different assumption about how the revenue from the tax is used. The five alternative assumptions are:
1. deficit reduction;
2. a lump-sum rebate to households;
3. an investment tax credit (ITC) to all sectors except housing;
4. a cut in the household income tax rate;
5. a cut in the corporate tax rate.

It is clear from figure 3C.1 that the consequences of the different assumptions are important. For example, with a lump-sum rebate of the revenue (which is the standard assumption many studies use) GNP remains below baseline well past the year 2022. However, by giving an investment tax credit, GNP is back to baseline by 1995. Secondly, in each case the aggregate demand consequence of the policy is important in the short run and the production substitution is important in the long run. This supports Professor Amano's argument.

Figure 3C.2 presents the consequences for carbon emissions of the alternative assumptions about the use of the tax revenue. Although

175

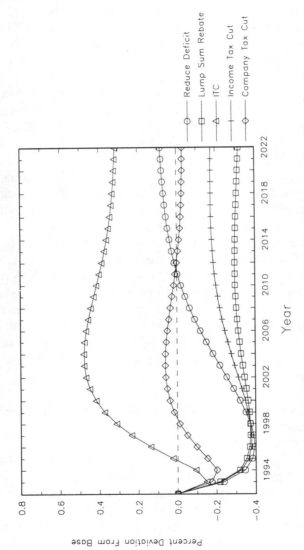

Fig. 3C.1 **Consequences for US real GNP of a US$15/ton carbon tax under alternative revenue recycling assumptions, 1993–2022 (Source: McKibbin and Wilcoxen, 1993a)**

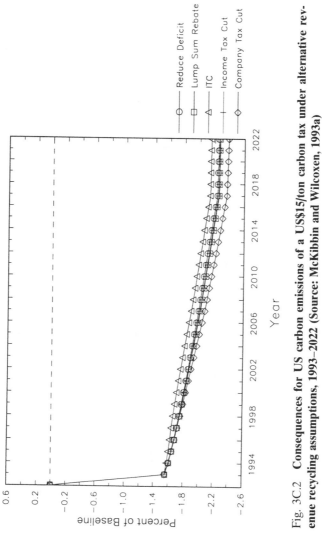

Fig. 3C.2 **Consequences for US carbon emissions of a US$15/ton carbon tax under alternative revenue recycling assumptions, 1993–2022 (Source: McKibbin and Wilcoxen, 1993a)**

there are some differences between the resulting paths for carbon emissions, it is clear that in each case the policy is effective in reducing emissions. The reason is that the dominant effect of the carbon tax is to reduce carbon, especially in the coal industry. None of the alternative revenue assumptions stimulates the coal industry sufficiently to negate the carbon tax in that industry, because the policies are economy wide rather than sector specific. Thus they can change economy-wide production and income but not carbon emissions that are concentrated in the coal, oil, and natural gas extraction industries. The two figures together show that there need not be a linear relationship between carbon emissions and GNP. This is because of the sectoral substitution possibilities plus the differential impact across sectors of the policies.

Finally, the question of offset through trade flows resulting from unilateral carbon taxes has been assessed using the G-Cubed model in McKibbin and Wilcoxen (1993b). In that paper, we show that a unilateral US carbon tax reduces carbon emissions in the United States by about 15 per cent less than when all OECD countries also impose a carbon tax. Thus there is evidence of some offset from unilateral action but nowhere the complete offset suggested by the estimates discussed in Amano's paper.

References

McKibbin, W. and P. Wilcoxen. 1992. *G-Cubed: A Dynamic Multi-Sector General Equilibrium Growth Model of the Global Economy: Quantifying the Costs of Curbing CO$_2$ Emissions*. Washington, D.C.: Brookings Institution, Discussion Paper in International Economics No. 98, September.

——— 1993a. "Global costs of policies to reduce greenhouse gas emissions II." Report prepared for the Office of Policy Analysis, US Environmental Protection Agency, on the 2nd-year results from a multi-year research grant.

——— 1993b. "The global consequences of regional environmental policies: An integrated macroeconomic, multi-sectoral approach." In: Y. Kaya, N. Nakicenovic, W. Nordhaus, and F. Toth (eds.), *Costs, Impacts and Benefits of CO$_2$ Mitigation*. Austria: International Institute for Applied Systems Analysis, CP-93-2.

3. Kenji Yamaji

Many interesting topics are raised and discussed in part 3. Dr. Cline makes a persuasive argument for his two-phase policy approach with the first phase of CO$_2$ stabilization through the application of "integrated" economic analysis. By "integrated" I mean that both the cost of greenhouse gas control and the damage resulting from climate change are treated.

Professor Amano is rather neutral in a sense. He surveys the macroeconomic cost evaluations of a CO_2 tax and studies of its side-effects, and he also talks about his own study on the sensitivity of the optimal climate control using a version of the integrated model originally developed by Professor Nordhaus.

Mr. Ferriter is the most pragmatic and cautious of the three. He introduces an IEA study on the carbon tax with relatively high rates and regulatory approach for promoting energy efficiency improvements. He suggests that the regulatory approach would have effects equivalent to those that can be expected with a carbon tax of US\$300/tC.

I would like to comment on three points related to these presentations.

The first point is the macroeconomic impact of a carbon tax. As Professor Amano points out, the macroeconomic cost varies depending on several factors, such as the time-horizons of the models and the treatment of tax revenues. He also mentions the difference in the types of model employed. I would like to emphasize here the influence of the basic structure of the models used. On the basis of actual past performances, the general equilibrium type model and a more explicit optimization model tend to produce a smaller macroeconomic cost compared with simulation models that simulate the performance of actual imperfect market functions.

My own study on carbon tax, which is included in Professor Amano's survey, is based on a simulation type model. The cost I obtained is rather high even when the tax revenue is assumed to be recycled through income tax reduction. Of course, there is also a regional difference. I think my result reflects the higher marginal cost of CO_2 reduction in Japan. But the difference of model type makes a more significant impact.

My second comment concerns the policy implications of integrated economic analysis, or optimal climate control with minimum total social cost. The uncertainties involved in damage cost evaluation are huge, particularly in the case of climate change. We have too little knowledge to do a full cost–benefit analysis of climate control. In this context, sensitivity analyses, as demonstrated by Dr. Cline and Professor Amano, are very interesting and important. However, optimal control may be very close to the business-as-usual case, and very far from CO_2 stabilization, which is the path many OECD countries (including Japan) are now choosing. But, as Dr. Cline says, CO_2 reduction, which is a more stringent control than CO_2 stabilization, could be the optimal path depending on the choice of discount rate and the time-horizon.

It is clear that more study should be done in this field. My personal feeling is that we should take action now to deal with climate change. There are two aspects that are not mentioned in the presentations: one is that there could be a catastrophic positive feedback such as triggering a burst of methane emission from tundra in Siberia, and the second is that technology development could, eventually, dramatically reduce the cost of CO_2 control. These issues are not short-term ones and therefore appear not to be suitable topics of discussion here. But I believe short-term policy should also be rooted in long-term considerations.

The last point I would like to raise is the global perspective of climate control, or more specifically the issue of "carbon leakage," which Professor Amano mentions as a side-effect. I think inter-regional equity is important as well as intergenerational equity. In this sense, the developed regions should take the lead in climate control and CO_2 limitation. However, unilateral efforts by developing regions are quite likely to be accompanied by leakage; i.e. CO_2 reductions in a developed region may result in CO_2 increases in other regions. And such leakages can be very large. On the other hand, the assertion that joint implementation between developed and developing regions can be one of the most effective and efficient schemes to reduce global CO_2 emissions is mostly maintained in qualitative terms; as far as quantitative analysis is concerned, there is not enough research in this field. Through analyses addressed to these global perspectives, pessimism about carbon leakage could be turned into positive opportunities.

Appendix to part 3
Examining the macroeconomic effects of curbing CO_2 emissions with the Project LINK world econometric model

Hung-yi Li, Peter Pauly, and Kenneth G. Ruffing

1. Introduction

Amid the considerable uncertainty surrounding the issue of global warming, two scientific facts are undisputed. The first is that carbon dioxide gas has been accumulating in the earth's atmosphere over the past 100 years. The second is that the gas traps heat from the sun's energy when it is absorbed by the earth and then re-radiated.

The first area of uncertainty is how much the earth's climate would heat up in response to the further accumulation of carbon dioxide in the earth's atmosphere. Most studies based on computerized climate models have attempted to examine the impact of a doubling of atmospheric carbon dioxide from 1990 levels by the year 2100 (a plausible rate of increase in the absence of significant policy change). A United Nations scientific advisory committee concluded in 1990 and again in 1992 that the average global temperature by 2100 would increase within the range of 3–8°F, with a central value of 4.5° (IPCC, 1990; Houghton et al., 1992). A study by researchers at New York University and Lawrence Livermore National Laboratory of two ancient climates, one much colder and one much warmer than the current global climate, concluded that a doubling of atmospheric carbon dioxide was associated with an increase of 4°F in the average temperature of the atmosphere (Martin Hoffert and Curt Covery, cited by Stevens, 1993). Despite numerous critiques of such studies faulting the reliability of the data and the models used, most climate researchers believe that there is a greater than 50 per cent chance that the climate will warm up by at least 3.5° over the next century.

The second area of uncertainty concerns the effects of the anticipated warming in the absence of measures to prevent it. These effects bear mainly on the impact on agriculture and forestry of changes in weather patterns and on the impact of a potential rise of about 2 feet in the sealevel from melting polar ice. Studies of potential impacts on the United States based on the physical consequences associated with a doubling of CO_2 equivalent concentrations of greenhouse gases have been done by the Environmental Protection Agency of the United States and used as the basis for alternative calculations by others. Recent estimates by Nordhaus (1993), Cline (1992), and Fankhauser (1992) range from 1 to 1.3 per cent of annual national income. Morgenstern (1991) provides arguments that support a figure closer to the "high" end of the range as the more plausible.

Schelling (1992) has pointed out that all the estimates of potential losses have relied on models of gradual change. He raises the possibility that "some atmospheric or oceanic circulatory systems may switch to alternative equilibria, producing regional changes that are both sudden and extreme." He admits that "insurance against catastrophes is ... an argument for doing something expensive about greenhouse emissions. But to pay a couple percent of GNP as insurance premium, one would hope to know more about the risk to be averted" (1992: 8), and he calls for climate research to focus on extreme possibilities rather than to continue to refine median projections.

Representative of the "no regrets" approach of policy advocates for modest action to curb carbon dioxide and other greenhouse gas emissions is the position of a panel of the US National Research Council. This body concluded in 1991 that "despite the great uncertainties, greenhouse warming is a potential threat sufficient to justify action now" (cited by Stevens, 1993). The emerging consensus on the seriousness of the threat of global warming and on the wisdom of adopting early measures resulted in the United Nations Framework Convention on Climate Change by which developed countries agreed to limit their CO_2 emissions in the year 2000 to their 1990 levels. The Convention entered into force on 21 March 1994.

The potential for emissions of carbon dioxide to change the global climate is prompting policy makers to examine the costs and benefits of a carbon tax. Research focuses on several aspects. Among the most important are: (a) the relation between the size of the tax and the quantity of carbon emissions that are abated and (b) the relation between the size of the tax and its effect on economic activity.

Understanding these aspects of a carbon tax is advanced considerably using computer simulation models (Weyant, 1993). Most often, the quantity of emissions abated by a tax is analysed using energy demand models, and the effect on economic activity is analysed using economic models. This schism is associated with the strengths and weaknesses of existing models (Beaver and Huntington, 1992). Energy demand models focus on the determinants of energy demand but many treat the level of economic activity as an exogenous variable. Conversely, economic models simulate economic activity endogenously but exogenize many of the important determinants of energy demand.

The use of energy demand models and economic models to analyse the quantity of emissions abated and the effect on economic activity forces the modellers to adopt several assumptions. Two of the most commonly used assumptions are that the pattern of international trade is constant and that energy prices are exogenous. These assumptions are required because most of the models cannot simulate endogenously how a carbon tax affects international trade or energy prices. One cause for the inability to simulate the change in trade is the geographic level of coverage and the level of aggregation. Many of the models used to analyse the effects of a carbon tax include one nation; therefore, these models cannot simulate the effects of trade. Conversely, models that include the entire world aggregate economic activity by countries into a few regions (Hoeller et al., 1990; Beaver and Huntington, 1992). Such aggregation prevents these models from simulating accurately the international pattern of trade. Finally, many models do not simulate energy supply, demand, or OPEC behaviour explicitly; therefore they cannot simulate energy prices endogenously.

The inability to simulate the pattern of international trade or the determinants of world energy markets limits the models' ability to evaluate a carbon tax. A carbon tax has significant short- and long-run effects on the economic system. In the short run, its price and budgetary effects are important for an economy's cyclical position; in that, it is no different from any other fiscal policy. In the medium to long term, it alters the competitive position of nations, which changes their structure of imports and exports and the composition of value added across sectors and the product spectrum. A carbon tax also changes the supply of and demand for energy and the price for energy, which affects the incidence of the carbon tax. These changes in trade and world energy markets have an important effect on the quantity of emissions abated by a carbon tax and the effect of a tax on economic activity. Models that cannot simulate the changes in international trade and world energy markets caused by a carbon tax tend to underestimate the quantity of emissions abated by the tax and misrepresent the effect of the tax on economic activity. For example, models that cannot simulate the determination of world energy prices endogenously cannot simulate the reduction in world energy prices due to the reduction in demand generated by a carbon tax, which offsets some of the incentive to lower carbon emissions. Similarly, models that cannot simulate the pattern of international trade endogenously cannot simulate the gains and losses to nations that do and do not adopt a carbon tax.

Part of this paper describes how changes in the pattern of international trade and changes in energy markets affect the quantity of carbon abated by a carbon tax and the effect of a carbon tax on economic activity. These effects are simulated endogenously using the world econometric model of Project LINK (LINK) with the trace gas accounting system (TGAS) (Kaufmann et al., 1991). In this system, the combination of a short- to medium-term globally consistent and complete international macroeconomic model with modules that endogenously simulate the world oil market (OIL-LINK) and international energy demands, inter-fuel substitution, and emission levels (TGAS) provides a modelling framework that is particularly suited to address problems of short- to medium-term adjustments to a carbon tax.

2. Carbon taxes, energy prices, and international trade

Most of the scenarios used to analyse the effectiveness of carbon taxes, and indeed the simulations presented in the next section, assume that the tax is adopted worldwide and that energy prices are exogenous. If these assumptions are relaxed, the forecast for economic activity and carbon emissions may change significantly. If carbon taxes are not adopted worldwide, the carbon tax may cause significant changes in the pattern of internal trade. If energy prices are determined endogenously by economic conditions, a carbon tax may cause significant changes in the pre-tax price of energy. Both of these changes have an important effect on the quantity of carbon emissions that are abated by a carbon tax and the effect of a carbon tax on economic activity.

The failure to simulate the effect of a carbon tax on the international pattern of trade causes models to omit an important mechanism that will determine, in part, the quantity of emissions abated by a carbon tax and the effect of a carbon tax on economic activity. A carbon tax affects the international pattern of trade regardless of the level of international cooperation. If all nations impose the same carbon tax, the fractional increase in the price of energy to end-users will vary among nations because of existing differences in energy taxes or subsidies (Kaufmann, 1991). Nations that have the highest level of existing taxes experience the smallest percentage increase in prices. Under these conditions, the competitive balance shifts slightly in favour of those nations that experience the smallest percentage increase in prices. But the effects on trade that result when the carbon tax is imposed universally are small compared with the effects that occur if only some nations adopt a carbon tax. Without global participation, energy prices rise significantly in nations that adopt a carbon tax (participating nations) relative to nations that do not impose a carbon tax (non-participating nations). This differential rate of change causes the cost of production to decline in non-participating nations relative to that in participating nations. *Ceteris paribus*, the change in costs tips the competitive balance among nations in favour of nations that do not adopt the carbon tax.

The shift in competitiveness generated by a carbon tax changes the pattern of international trade via two mechanisms. The relative decline in the cost of production allows non-participating nations to capture market share from participating nations. The differences in end-user energy prices generated by the carbon tax also induce some multinational firms to relocate production in non-participating nations. Both of these changes increase the level of exports and economic activity in non-participating nations relative to nations that adopt a carbon tax.

The failure to simulate world energy markets endogenously also causes existing models to omit an important mechanism that determines, in part, the quantity of emissions abated by a carbon tax and the effect of a carbon tax on economic activity. A carbon tax reduces the demand and/or price for energy. The effect on demand and/or price depends on the degree to which energy producers, especially members of OPEC, recognize and react to the change in demand. If producers do not recognize and/or anticipate the reduction in demand correctly and adhere to their original schedule for adding capacity, reduced levels of demand create excess capacity. This overhang exerts downward pressure on the wellhead price of oil, which also depresses the price for other forms of energy. Conversely, OPEC may recognize and/or anticipate the reduction correctly and slow its schedule for adding capacity. Under these conditions, lower levels of demand do not create over-capacity and prices may proceed along the path that was envisioned for a world without a carbon tax (Kaufmann et al., 1994).

The changes in the pattern of international trade and world energy markets that are generated by a carbon tax have an important effect on the quantity of carbon abated by a carbon tax and the effect of the carbon tax on economic activity. The effect on the quantity of emissions abated is measured by "leakages" from the tax. Leakages are defined as an increase in emissions by non-participating nations beyond levels that they would have emitted had no carbon tax been imposed. By definition, the quantity of carbon abated by a tax shrinks as the quantity of leakages increases. Leakages are minimized implicitly by models that treat the pattern of international trade and energy prices as exogenous variables. Endogenizing these variables allows a model to measure the size of leakages that are generated by several mechanisms. One important cause of leakages is the change in the pattern of international trade. The increase in economic activity by non-participating nations that is caused by expanding market share and location decisions by multinational firms increases carbon emissions by non-participating nations relative to a world in which there is no carbon tax. Another important source of leakages is the potential for changes in world energy markets. If energy producers do not recognize the reduction in demand and lower capacity accordingly, the reduction in price diminishes the incentive to reduce energy use per unit output, which increases carbon emissions relative to a world in which there is no carbon tax.

The changes in trade and world energy markets have offsetting effects on the impact of a carbon tax on economic activity. The increase in economic activity by non-participating nations exacerbates the negative effect of a carbon tax on economic activity in participating nations because the increase in economic activity is accomplished, in part, by moving production from participating nations to non-participating nations. On the other hand, the potential for lower energy prices may reduce the negative effect of the carbon tax on economic activity. If a carbon tax reduces energy prices, the reduction slows the transfer of money from energy-consuming nations to energy-producing nations. Retarding this flow increases income in energy-consuming nations, which increases demand and production (Marquez and Pauly, 1984). Even though trade effects offset the energy price effects, there is no a priori reason to believe that they cancel each other so that the net effect is small. As a result, models that do not simulate patterns of international trade and the formation of energy prices endogenously either underestimate or overestimate the negative effect of a carbon tax on economic activity by participating nations. In addition to overestimating the quantity of emissions abated by a tax and misrepresenting the effect of a carbon tax on economic activity, the failure to represent the effect of a carbon tax on the pattern of international trade and world energy markets causes the models to ignore the potential for strategic behaviours regarding a carbon tax. The potential for leakages from the tax reduces the effectiveness of the tax, but this loss of effectiveness creates winners and losers. Nations with the smallest rise in end-user prices or that do not adopt a carbon tax may "win" because they may reap the benefits of lower emissions while enjoying increased levels of economic activity and emissions. Conversely, nations with the largest rise in end-user prices may "lose" by reducing emissions less than they anticipated and suffering economic losses greater than they anticipated. The effect of a carbon tax on the world energy markets also creates winners and losers. Energy-consuming nations will "win" by shifting a portion of abatement costs to energy-producing nations, which will "lose" by paying for abatements accomplished by consuming nations via lower energy prices and/or lower levels of exports.

3. A policy simulation

The modelling framework

The LINK model has been described elsewhere, including in a paper prepared for the UNU Programme on Global Change and Modelling in 1991 (Hickman and Ruffing, 1991). It is a multi-country model that links separate national econometric models by means of models of merchandise trade, exchange rates, and commodity prices. We use the LINK-TGAS modelling system to study how changes in the pattern of international trade and world energy markets affect the quantity of emissions abated and the economic impact of a carbon tax. A detailed description of the basic structure of the system can be found in Kaufmann et al. (1991). The LINK-TGAS system is suited for this task because, in addition to standard domestic macroeconomic feedbacks and the modelling of energy use and emissions, it simulates endogenously the international pattern of trade, disaggregated by commodities, and world energy prices. The pattern of international trade is simulated on the basis of bilateral trade matrices by commodity groupings; trade shares can respond to technological changes, to changes in structures and preferences, as well as to changes in competitiveness. The LINK-TGAS system uses a combination of assumptions about monetary and fiscal policy, OPEC behaviour, and OPEC capacity to generate a forecast for economic activity and the pattern of imports and exports for the 79 nations and regions in the Project LINK modelling system. The modelling system also generates a forecast for carbon emissions by the 14 nations for which TGAS models are available (Canada, France, Germany, Italy, Japan, the United Kingdom, the United States, Brazil, China, Hungary, India, Korea, Mexico, and Poland). With the exception of the states of the former Soviet Union, this subset represents the most important emitters of CO$_2$. Finally, the modelling system also generates a forecast for energy prices. The effect of a carbon tax on the world energy markets is simulated endogenously and is based on the level of supply, demand, OPEC capacity, and OPEC behaviour (Kaufmann, 1995). Together, these variables constitute a baseline that can be compared with different scenarios to determine the effectiveness of a carbon tax.

The baseline scenario

One of the difficulties in constructing a baseline scenario is predicting CO$_2$ emissions for the next decade in the absence of additional policy measures. There are several reasons for this. First, there is the question of the overall rate of GDP growth that might be expected over the eight years to the year 2000. The LINK reference scenario was 2.7 per cent per year (2.4 per cent for the decade as a whole). This is close to the baseline scenario described together with high and low variants in a recent study by the United Nations (UN, 1992) making use of the Global Input–Output Model (GIOM). Secondly, over periods of a decade or more, the sectoral composition of output can be expected to change both within and among countries. Thirdly, the energy intensity of production in each sector can also be expected to change as economic agents continue to adjust with a long response lag to past changes in energy pricing policies and other measures.

As a consequence of the interplay of these factors, the United Nations study concluded that carbon from fossil fuels emitted by the developed market economies would increase only slightly under the baseline scenario, cumulatively by only 8 per cent between 1990 and 2000 (0.8 per cent per year) but by 36 per cent under the high-growth scenario (3.1 per cent per year). In the high-growth scenario, emissions of carbon dioxide per unit of GDP are assumed to fall by 16 per cent in the developed market economies between 1990 and 2000. This implies an overall income elasticity of 1.0. Without the change assumed in the energy intensity per unit of output, the income elasticity would be nearly 1.5. There are other studies that suggest low rates of growth of CO_2 emissions in the United States. Several widely quoted studies cited in Morgenstern (1991) suggest a rate of growth of only 0.9 per cent per year in the United States from 1987 to 2000 with current policy commitments. In the LINK baseline, overall CO_2 emissions by the G7 countries are projected to increase by 3.3 per cent per year from 1993 to 2000 (cumulatively by 30 per cent). Since the aggregate GNP of the same countries is projected to increase by 2.7 per cent per year over the same period, the implied income elasticity is about 1.2.

A macroeconomic policy simulation using the world econometric model of Project LINK

In the LINK policy simulation prepared for this paper, a carbon emission tax was imposed on each G7 country. The tax was set at US$30 per metric ton of carbon equivalent (tC) in 1993 and increased to US$100/tC in 2000. There are considerable variations in the percentage reductions in CO_2 emissions per country, ranging from a cumulative decrease of 3 per cent in the case of Japan to 11 per cent in the case of the United States. For the G7 countries as a group the reduction from the 2000 baseline figure is 8 per cent. This is not quite a third of the reduction that would be necessary to freeze emissions in 2000 to their 1990 levels. Yet the reduction in GDP would be about 2 per cent. Recently, Weyant (1993) reported that studies undertaken for the Energy Modeling Forum 12 suggest that the long-term costs of stabilizing global carbon emissions could be in the neighbourhood of 4 per cent of world GDP by the year 2100.

Several studies reviewed by Morgenstern (1991) estimate that a 10–20 per cent reduction from base levels would require a carbon tax of US\$10–75/tC. Some more recent studies suggest levels of carbon taxes toward the higher end of this range. The Edmonds–Reilly model, for example, calculated that a 14 per cent reduction in CO_2 emissions from baseline levels in OECD countries in 2005 would require a carbon tax of US\$55–56/tC in that year (Barns et al., 1992). The Global 2100 model developed by Manne and Richels calculated that an 11 per cent reduction in the baseline CO_2 emissions of OECD countries in 2000 would require carbon taxes in the range of US\$60–70/tC in the terminal year (Manne, 1992). The LINK calculations appear to be on the high side as far as the level of tax required to induce significant CO_2 emissions reductions is concerned. However, it should be borne in mind that most other studies employ a general equilibrium framework to calculate the fully adjusted response to a hypothetical tax, as if there were no adjustment lag. The smaller response suggested by a dynamic econometric model suggests that the task of reducing CO_2 emissions may be greater than commonly thought.

As may be seen from table 3A.1, the macroeconomic effects are fairly strong. A carbon tax that rises to US\$100/tC by 2000 would leave GDP in G7 countries 2 per cent lower than in the baseline. Growth elsewhere would also be reduced but by less because in this scenario no direct taxes were imposed on these countries. The fact that inflation increases by an average of only about 0.35 of a percentage point over a period to 2000, while unemployment increases by about 0.6 of a percentage point in 2000, suggests that there would be scope for offsetting reductions in other taxes to mitigate the negative impact of a carbon tax on output and employment.

Table 3A.1 **The LINK model scenario (impact expressed as percentage deviation from baseline)**

	GDP in world	GDP in G7 countries	World trade volume	Inflation in developed market economies	Unemployment in developed market economies	CO_2 emissions in G7 countries
1993	−0.19	−0.21	−0.24	0.69	0.09	−0.7
1994	−0.67	−0.87	−0.55	0.28	0.54	−3.7
2000	−1.39	−2.04	−0.76	0.47	0.59	−8.1

Note: A carbon tax of US\$30 per metric ton of carbon equivalent is imposed in 1993 rising to US\$100 in 2000.

The role of oil prices

The scenario described in the previous section compares the effects of a unilateral carbon tax on economic activity, carbon emissions, and energy prices. These results are generated via an exogenous tax assumption under exogenous energy prices, and we can identify the ways in which changes in the pattern of international trade and energy prices that are generated by a carbon tax affect the quantity of carbon abated by the tax and the effect of the tax on economic activity. The comparisons are also used to identify the gains and losses that are associated with adopting a carbon tax and the cost of emissions reductions borne by emitters as opposed to energy producers.

The following scenario uses all of the assumptions about monetary and fiscal policy from the reference scenario, but now is based upon a uniform US$40 carbon tax with an *endogenous oil price response*. This change in the size of the shock is of little consequence for the multiplier properties of the system. This scenario calculates the first-purchase price of energy endogenously using the assumptions about OPEC behaviour and capacity used in the reference scenario. The price of crude oil in this scenario is different from the price calculated in the reference scenario because the carbon tax changes the demand for oil. Demand is changed because the end-user price of energy increases in nations that impose a carbon tax and the increase in end-user prices changes the pattern of international trade, the level of economic activity, and the quantity of energy consumed per unit of economic activity.

In this scenario, all variables are solved endogenously. Because it uses the same assumptions about OPEC behaviour and additions to OPEC capacity, this scenario represents the effect of a carbon tax on world energy markets if OPEC ignores the effect of the carbon tax on oil demand. Under these conditions, oil prices fall owing to lower levels of capacity utilization. This reduction in energy prices allows the scenario to identify how changes in world energy markets affect the quantity of emissions abated by the tax and how changes in world energy markets affect the impact of the carbon tax on economic activity. The effect of a carbon tax on world energy markets and the impact of these effects on the quantity of carbon abated and the level of economic activity can be gleaned from this scenario in three steps. In the first step, the results from this scenario are used to determine the effect of a carbon tax on energy prices by comparing the price forecasts generated by this scenario with those of the reference scenario.

In the second step, the results of this scenario are used to determine the quantity of carbon abated by a tax and how changes in energy prices affect this quantity. The total amount of carbon abated by the tax is determined by the difference in total carbon emissions between the reference scenario and this scenario. The leakage from the tax through world energy markets is determined by subtracting the total amount of emission reductions forecast by this scenario from the total amount of emission reductions forecast by the reference scenario. A positive value indicates a leakage from the tax. A similar process is used to determine the effect of a carbon tax on economic activity. The total effect of a carbon tax on economic activity is determined by comparing the level of economic activity forecast by the reference scenario with the level forecast by this scenario. The effect of changes in world energy markets on the economic impact of a carbon tax is determined by subtracting the level of economic activity forecast by the reference scenario from the level of economic activity forecast by this scenario. A positive value indicates that changes transmitted through world energy markets reduce the negative effects of a carbon tax on economic activity.

The quantity of emissions abated by the tax depends on changes that occur in both participating and non-participating nations. In participating nations, the carbon tax reduces the quantity of carbon emitted by reducing emissions per unit output. This reduction may be reinforced or offset by changes in the level of economic activity by participating nations and by changes in the first-purchase price of energy. In non-participating nations, the carbon tax changes the quantity of emissions abated by changing the level of economic activity and by reducing the first-purchase price of energy. The sum of these effects determines the quantity of emissions abated *in toto*.

Endogenizing the oil price has several effects. The relative increase in G7 activity associated with a carbon tax *per se* would increase the oil price, but the tax provides incentives to substitute away from oil. On balance, this depresses the oil price. By the year 2000, the price path lies about US$3 per barrel below the exogenous price path of the original scenario. This exerts a slightly positive impact on the participating countries in terms of lower imported inflation, even though it depresses activity in non-participating energy-producing countries (mostly developing countries). In addition, the implied change in the relative price of energy induces an increase in the use of carbon energy sources and thus reduces the efficiency of the tax.

The quantity of emissions abated by participating countries is given by the level of emissions forecast by the endogenous scenario relative to the level of emissions forecast by the reference scenario. The size of these reductions varies from 1.5 to 4.7 per cent in 2000. The largest reductions occur in the United States and the smallest reductions occur in Japan and Germany. This differential rate of reduction is caused by differences in the fuel mix, the mix of economic activities, the size of the elasticities estimated from the historical record for individual nations, and differences in the percentage increase in end-user prices generated by the carbon tax. This last effect seems to be the most significant determinant of the reduction in emissions. For example, the United States has the largest percentage increase in end-user prices in 2000 whereas Japan and Germany have the smallest percentage increase in end-user prices.

The direction and size of the change in emissions depend on changes in economic activity caused by the tax, changes in world energy markets that reduce the first-purchase price of energy, and changes in economic activity caused by changes in world energy markets. The results of the three scenarios can be used to identify the change in emissions associated with each mechanism. Changes in the world energy markets that reduce the first-purchase price of energy are the second mechanism that changes the quantity of carbon abated by the tax. The effect of reductions in the first-purchase price of energy on the quantity of carbon abated is evaluated by calculating the percentage change in the emissions/GDP ratio forecast by the reference scenario relative to the ratio forecast by the endogenous scenario. An increase in the carbon emissions/real GDP ratio forecast by the latter relative to carbon emissions/real GDP ratio forecast in the former indicates that the reduction in first-purchase prices reduces the incentive to reduce energy use, which generates a leakage from the carbon tax in participating nations.

The third mechanism for leakages in participating nations is a change in economic activity caused by changes in world energy markets. The reduction in the first-purchase price of coal, oil, and natural gas changes economic activity (including imports and exports) and these changes affect emissions. The change in emissions caused by this effect is evaluated by calculating the percentage change in economic activity forecast by the endogenous scenario relative to the change forecast by the reference scenario.

Leakages in non-participating nations depend on the same mechanisms that cause leakages in participating nations: changes in economic activity caused directly by the carbon tax, changes in the first-purchase price of energy that cause changes in the quantity of carbon emitted per unit of economic activity, and changes in economic activity caused by changes in world energy markets.

The effect of a carbon tax on the international pattern of trade and world energy markets creates the potential for an array of strategic behaviours. Changes in trade make non-participating nations better off and their gains are reinforced by the negative effects of the tax on participating nations. Changes in world energy markets redistribute the costs of the tax such that a carbon tax reduces the economic well-being of energy-producing nations and, in some cases, energy-consuming nations are able to reduce the negative impacts of the tax by shifting a significant portion of the costs to energy-producing nations.

A carbon tax presents energy producers with a range of strategies that vary between two extremes. At one extreme, producers can ignore the effect of the tax on demand and add capacity at the rate that would have prevailed in a world without a tax. Under these conditions capacity utilization drops and the resultant overhang depresses the price of oil and other forms of energy. At the other extreme, producers can anticipate perfectly the effects of the tax on demand and retard additions to capacity so that utilization rates and real prices evolve along the same path that would have prevailed in a world without a tax. Under these conditions, the demand for oil and other forms of energy drops. Regardless of the strategy chosen, the economic well-being of energy producers is reduced. These issues are explored in detail in Kaufmann et al. (1993).

4. Conclusions

This study has been concerned with unilateral (non-global) carbon tax policies, and with an evaluation of the effects of the response on the world oil market on the efficiency of such a policy, i.e. the extent of oil-related carbon leakages and the short-run adjustment costs of such a policy. The results are based on simulations with the LINK-TGAS system, which combines a global macroeconometric model with modules for energy use and emissions analysis and energy price determination. The results are, of course, preliminary, but they confirm and complement studies of a longer-term nature (McKibbin and Wilcoxen, 1992; Piggott et al., 1993).

Among the findings of the study are the following:

- A unilateral (G7) carbon tax induces reductions in emissions in these countries; the effect of such a policy on non-OECD emitters is diverse, ranging from a slight reduction to increases up to 15 per cent.
- The results are critically dependent upon the responses of international energy prices, in particular the world oil price. A carbon tax in the G7 countries induces a medium-term reduction in the real price of crude oil by approximately US$2 per barrel.
- The oil price reduction generates a positive stimulus in G7 countries that significantly tends to reduce the short- to medium-term GNP loss to G7 countries.
- A unilateral G7 policy generates a trade balance improvement in these countries, at the expense of non-participating countries; oil-exporters among the G7 (Canada and the United Kingdom) experience deteriorations in the trade balance.
- The results are sensitive to assumptions about the strategic behaviour of energy producers, in particular of OPEC.

It is, of course, possible to reduce or even eliminate the negative activity effects of a carbon tax through the recycling of revenues and parallel stabilizing policies, such as a mild monetary expansion. In general, such policies increase the short-run effectiveness of a tax, but at a price of increased inflationary pressure. The results obtained in single-country analyses (Shackleton et al., 1992) have to be confirmed in future multi-country simulations. The present results already point towards a substantial potential for improvement in the efficiency of international carbon taxation through international cooperation.

References

Barns, D. W., J. A. Edmonds, and J. M. Reilly. 1992. *Use of the Edmonds–Reilly Model to Model Energy-Related Greenhouse Gas Emission*. Paris: OECD, Economics Department Working Papers No. 113.

Beaver, R. and H. Huntington. 1992. "A comparison of aggregate energy demand models for global warming policy analyses." *Energy Policy* 20(6): 569–574.

Cline, W. R. 1992. *Global Warming: The Economic Stakes*. Washington, D.C.: Institute for International Economics.

Fankhauser, S. 1992. "Global warming damage costs: Some monetary estimates." London: Centre for Social and Economic Research on the Global Environment, mimeo, August.

Hickman, B. G. and K. G. Ruffing. 1991. "Project Link: Past, present and future." UNU Conference on Global Change and Modelling, November, Tokyo.

Hoeller, P. A., A. Dean, and J. Nicolaisen. 1990. *A Survey of Studies of the Costs of Reducing Greenhouse Gas Emissions*. Paris: OECD, Working Paper.

Houghton, J. T., B. A. Callander, and S. K. Varney (eds.). 1992. *Climate Change 1992: The Supplementary Report to the IPCC Scientific Assessment*. Cambridge: Cambridge University Press.

IPCC (International Panel on Climate Change). 1990. *Policymakers' Summaries of the Scientific Assessment of Climate Change, Report prepared for IPCC by Working Group I*. Geneva, June.

Kaufmann, R. K. 1991. "Limits on the economic effectiveness of a carbon tax." *Energy Journal* 12(4): 139–144.

——— 1995. "A model of the world oil market for Project LINK: Integrating economics, geology, and politics." *Economic Modelling* 12(2): 165–178.

Kaufmann, R. K., W. Gruen, and R. Montesi. 1994. "Drilling rates and expected oil prices: The own price elasticity of US oil supply." *Energy Resources* 16: 39–58.

Kaufmann, R. K., H. Y. Li, P. Pauly, and L. H. Thompson. 1991. "Global Macro-economic Effects of Carbon Taxes: A Feasibility Study." Prepared for the US Environmental Protection Agency.

Kaufmann, R. K., H. Y. Li, P. Pauly, K. Seto, and J. Sweitzer. 1993. "A preliminary analysis of international aspects of a carbon tax: The role of the world oil market." Boston University and University of Toronto, mimeo, December.

McKibbin, W. J. and P. J. Wilcoxen. 1992. *G-CUBED: A Dynamic Multi-Sector General Equilibrium Growth Model of the Global Economy: Quantifying the Costs of Curbing CO₂ Emissions*. Washington, D.C.: Brookings Institution, Discussion Paper in International Economics No. 98, September.

Manne, A. S. 1992. *Global 2100: Alternative Scenarios for Reducing Carbon Emissions*. Paris: OECD, Economics Department Working Papers No. 111.

Marquez, J. and P. Pauly. 1984. "OPEC's pricing policy and the international transmission of oil price effects." *Energy Economics* 6(4): 267–275.

Morgenstern, R. D. 1991. "Towards a comprehensive approach to global climate change mitigation." *American Economic Review* 81(2): 140–145.

Nordhaus, W. D. 1993. "Reflections on the economies of climate change." *Journal of Economic Perspectives* 7(4): 11–26.

Piggott, J., J. Whalley, and R. Wigle. 1993. "How large are the incentives to join subglobal carbon-reduction initiatives." *Journal of Policy Modeling* 15: 473–490.

Schelling, T. C. 1992. "Some economics of global warming." *American Economic Review* 82(1): 1–14.

Shackleton, R., M. Shelby, A. Cristofaro, R. Brinner, J. Yanchar, L. Goulder, D. Jorgenson, P. Wilcoxen, and P. Pauly. 1992. "The efficiency value of carbon tax revenues." Washington, D.C.: US Environmental Protection Agency, Working Paper, mimeo, May.

Stevens, W. K. 1993. *The New York Times*, Tuesday, 14 September.

UN. 1992. "Structural change in the world economy: Implications for energy use and air emissions. Report of the Secretary-General." A/47/388, mimeo, 7 October.

Weyant, J. 1993. "Cost of reducing global carbon emissions." *Journal of Economic Perspectives* 7(4): 27–46.

Part 4
Long-term strategies for mitigating global warming

10

The role of technology in energy/economy interactions: A view from Japan

Chihiro Watanabe

1. Introduction

Over 20 years have passed since the publication of the international best-seller *The Limits to Growth* (Meadows et al., 1972), and the external factors that place restrictions on sustainable development have changed dynamically since the early 1970s. Indeed, only one year after the appearance of *The Limits to Growth*, the world faced a grave new situation, the first oil crisis. This crisis brought energy issues to the forefront around the world and completely changed global development theory. Key factors governing the sustainability of development changed from environmental capacity considerations to the quantitative and qualitative supply of energy. Since the decline of international oil prices in 1983, problems related to the world's energy supply have eased considerably. However, a new issue now governs the sustainability of development – the global environmental problem.

Japan successfully overcame a number of domestic environmental challenges in the 1960s and 1970s. Although the global environmental issue now facing the world is structurally different from that which faced Japan in the 1960s and 1970s, given the two-sided nature of the global environmental issue and energy consumption, Japan's experience in overcoming the two energy crises of the 1970s despite the fragile nature of its energy structure and while also maintaining sustainable development provides useful suggestions concerning the current worldwide question of how to sustain world development in the face of a grave situation such as global environmental constraints (MITI, 1992a).

The Japanese economy, despite many handicaps, achieved sustainable development in the face of various constraints by focusing efforts on improving the productivity of the relatively scarce resources of the time (Economic Planning Agency, 1980). Scarce resources were chiefly capital stock in the 1960s, followed by the supply of labour, environmental capacity constraints, and then the supply of energy after the first energy crisis in 1973 (Economic Planning Agency, 1980). The driving force behind this achievement was the development of manufacturing industry, and the rapid enhancement of productivity levels was most typically observed in the overcoming of constraints in the supply of energy by means of technological development. It is noteworthy that this enhancement was successful because of such means as substituting an unlimited resource (technology) for limited resources (energy) (Watanabe, 1992b). This success provides a new theory which can be applied to a "constrained economy." Attaining sustainable development by overcoming existing constraints is important for a constrained economy, and a positive solution can be expected through the contribution of technology (MITI, 1992a). Thus, a key point in the question of how technology and sustainable development interact with respect to global environmental constraints is how effectively resources that have become scarce owing to global environmental constaints can be substituted for by an unlimited resource, technology.

In this paper I first introduce Japan's technological development path over the past two decades – a path that aimed to overcome the energy crises by substituting an unlimited production factor (technology) for a limited production factor (energy), thereby resulting in a dramatic improvement in the nation's technology as a whole. I then introduce the Ministry of International Trade and Industry's (MITI's) new challenge of leading the way to sustainable development by overcoming energy and environmental constraints simultaneously through technological innovation that induces the substitution of limited production factors by technology in the new circumstances of increasing global environmental constraints in the face of economic stagnation. Section 2 explains Japan's sustainable development path, with special emphasis on energy constraints; section 3 explains MITI's

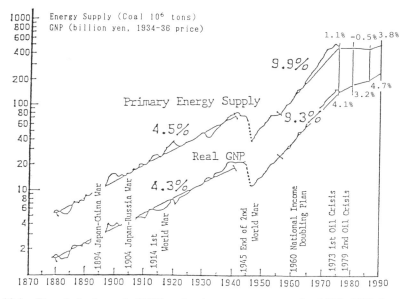

Fig. 10.1 **Trends in Japan's GNP and primary energy supply, 1880–1990 (average change rate, % p.a. Source: elaboration of data from the Institute of Energy Economics, Tokyo)**

efforts to encourage R&D aiming at freedom from energy constraints after the first energy crisis in 1973; section 4 analyses fears concerning an increase in energy and environmental constraints; section 5 explains MITI's new comprehensive approach for sustainable development by means of technological innovation; and section 6 explains the implications for sustainable development.

2. Sustainable development despite energy constraints: Japan's path

Parallel path between energy supply and development

Figure 10.1 illustrates trends in Japan's economic development and energy supply since 1880 (just after the Meiji Revolution in 1868). We can note the parallel path between economic growth and energy supply: the average rate of increase in real GNP over the period 1880–1940 (just before World War II) was 4.3 per cent, while the average rate of increase in the primary energy supply was 4.5 per cent. For the period 1955–1973 (the year of the first energy crisis),

201

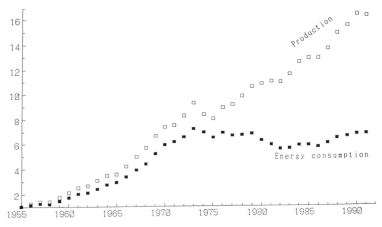

Fig. 10.2 **Trends in production and energy consumption in Japanese manufacturing industry, 1955–1990 (1955 = 1. Sources: Agency of Natural Resources and Energy, MITI,** *Comprehensive Energy Statistics*; **MITI,** *Annual Report on Indices on Mining and Manufacturing***)**

the average rates of increase were 9.3 per cent and 9.9 per cent, respectively. These data suggest that Japan was able to sustain its high rate of stable economic growth supported by a stable energy supply (MITI, 1982). Faced with the energy crises in 1973 and again in 1979, this stable energy supply disappeared and the fragile nature of Japan's energy structure was revealed.

Given the parallel paths of economic growth and energy supply, which provided a structural foundation for Japan's sustainable development before the energy crisis, Japan's economic growth should have declined as its energy supply decreased as a result of the energy crises. However, as illustrated in figure 10.2, despite a dramatic decrease in energy dependency, Japan was able to maintain sustainable development that was, among advanced countries (see figure 10.3), the most stable despite having the most fragile energy structure and incurring the most damaging impacts of the energy crises.

Trends in improvement in energy efficiency

Figure 10.4 illustrates trends in production (value added and index of industrial production (IIP)) and materials (intermediate inputs except energy) and energy consumption of Japan's manufacturing industry over the period 1970–1990. We can note the significant contribution

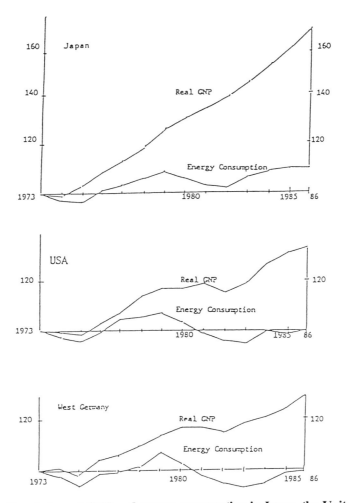

Fig. 10.3 **Trends in real GNP and energy consumption in Japan, the United States, and West Germany, 1973–1986 (1973 = 100. Sources: Real GNP: Japan – Economic Planning Agency,** *Annual Report on National Accounts*; **USA – US Department of Commerce,** *Survey of Current Business*; **West Germany – OECD,** *OECD Quarterly National Accounts*; **Energy: Japan – Agency of Natural Resources and Energy, MITI,** *Comprehensive Energy Statistics*; **USA & West Germany – OECD,** *Energy Balances of OECD Countries*)

of improvements in energy efficiency (the gap between IIP and energy consumption) to a dramatic decrease in energy consumption after the first energy crisis in 1973.[1] The average contribution of improvements in energy efficiency to the decrease in energy consumption in the

203

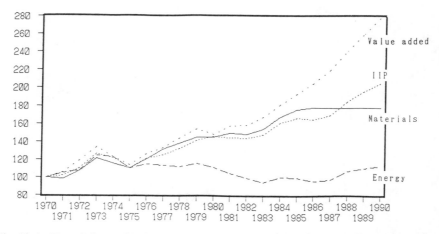

Fig. 10.4 **Trends in production and in energy and materials consumption in Japanese manufacturing industry, 1970–1990 (1970 = 100. Sources: See fig. 10.2)**

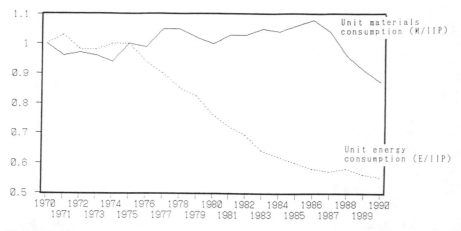

Fig. 10.5 **Trends in unit energy and materials consumption in Japanese manufacturing industry, 1970–1990 (1970 = 1. Sources: See fig. 10.2)**

period 1974–1990 was 64 per cent while the contribution of changes in industrial structure and the value added of production goods (the gap between value added and IIP) was 32 per cent. This dramatic improvement in energy efficiency can be clearly observed by looking at trends in unit energy consumption (energy consumption per IIP). Figure 10.5 illustrates trends in unit energy and materials consumption in Japanese manufacturing industry over the period 1970–1990,

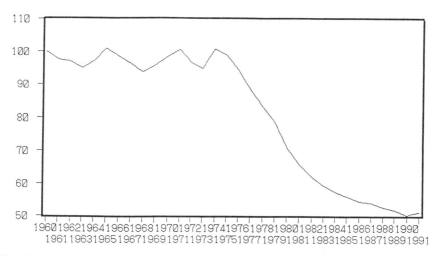

Fig. 10.6   **Trends in the ratio of energy consumption to the index of industrial pro-duction in Japanese manufacturing industry, 1960–1991 (1960 = 100. Sources: See fig. 10.2)**

and indicates a contrast between energy efficiency improvements and those of materials. Figure 10.6 demonstrates the clear structural change in energy efficiency after the first energy crisis.

The substitution of technology for energy

In order to identify sources contributing to a dramatic improvement in energy efficiency I first analysed the impact of oil prices. Figure 10.7 illustrates trends in international oil prices and derived changes in both energy and materials prices in Japanese manufacturing industry in the period 1970–1990. We can note that energy prices increased dramatically, influenced by a sharp increase in international oil prices owing to the energy crises of 1973 and 1979, whereas materials prices were stable despite the change in international oil prices. Figures 10.5 and 10.7 suggest that dramatic improvements in energy efficiency were made as a reaction to the sharp increase in energy prices. Second, I analysed the contribution of technology, which is largely independent of the constraints of energy price increases. Table 10.1 compares correlations between improvements in energy efficiency and (a) prices of energy, (b) autonomous energy efficiency improvements (AEEI) from autonomous productivity increases, and

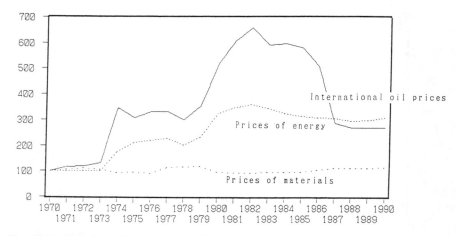

Fig. 10.7 **Trends in international oil prices and prices of energy and materials in Japanese manufacturing industry, 1970–1990 (1970 = 100. Sources: See fig. 10.2)**

Table 10.1 **Comparison of the contribution to energy productivity (*E/IIP*) improvements by autonomous energy efficiency improvement (*AEEI*) and technology stock (T) in Japanese manufacturing industry, 1974–1988**

	Adj. R^2	DW
AEEI[a]		
$\ln E/IIP = 81.24 - 0.04t - 0.13 \ln Pe$	.984	1.24
$(-16.74)(-2.68)$		
Technology stock[b]		
$\ln E/IIP = 3.52 - 0.50 \ln T - 0.14 \ln Pe$	.971	1.05
$(-12.19) \quad (-2.23)$		

a. $t =$ time trend; $Pe =$ energy prices.
b. Technology stock (T) is measured by the following equation:

$$T_t = R_{t-m} + (1 - \rho)T_{t-1},$$

where $R_{t-m} =$ R&D expenditure in the period $t - m$, $m =$ time-lag of R&D to commercialization, and $\rho =$ rate of obsolescence of technology.

(c) technology stock (endogenous technological change). Table 10.1 suggests that the contribution of technology stocks to improvements in energy efficiency was almost equivalent to the contribution of AEEI and more significant than the contribution of energy prices. These analyses suggest that endogenous technological change by means of an increase in technology stock made a great contribution to improvements in energy efficiency in Japan's manufacturing industry after the energy crises.

In the circumstances of a "constrained economy," it is generally pointed out that the majority of efforts aimed at overcoming constraints are directed towards substitution of a constrained (or limited) production factor by unlimited production factors (Christensen et al., 1973) similarly to an ecosystem in that, in order to maintain homeostasis (checks and balances that dampen oscillations), when one species slows down another speeds up in a compensatory manner in a closed system (substitution), whereas dependence on supplies from an external system tends to dampen homeostasis (complement) (Odum, 1963). This concept of "*substitution*" provides useful analogies in relation to a "constrained economy."

In this particular case, a constrained production factor is energy whereas technology is an unlimited production factor. Figure 10.8 illustrates trends in the substitution of energy by other production factors in Japanese manufacturing industry. These indicate that, in order to overcome sharply increased energy constraints resulting from the energy crises while maintaining sustainable development, intensive efforts to *substitute technology for energy* (such as energy conservation technology, alternative energy technology, and technologies for improving energy productivity) followed by efforts to *substitute capital for energy* (typically observed in investment in energy conservation) have been made in Japan's manufacturing industry over the past two decades. This substitution of energy by other production factors (chiefly technology and capital) was distinctive compared with the substitution of materials by other production factors. These analyses suggest that the Japanese economy was able to sustain its development in the face of sharply increased energy supply constraints by substituting technology for energy, and this substitution resulted in a dramatic improvement in Japan's technological level as a whole (MITI, 1988; Watanabe, 1992b).[2]

3. MITI's efforts to stimulate R&D that challenges energy constraints

Trends in MITI's energy R&D efforts

Japan has adopted different industrial policies at different stages of its economic development, and these policies have reflected the inter-

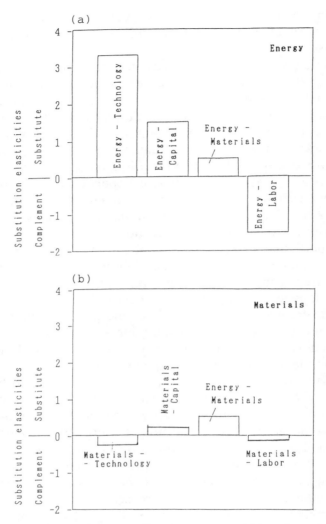

Fig. 10.8 **Comparison of the average substitution elasticities of energy and materials in Japanese manufacturing industry, 1974–1987. (a) Energy, (b) Materials (Sources: See fig. 10.2)**

national, natural, social, cultural, and historical environment of the postwar period (Watanabe, 1990). In the late 1940s and 1950s, Japan made every effort to reconstruct its war-ravaged economy and lay the foundations for viable economic growth. During the 1960s, Japan actively sought to open its economy to foreign competition by liberalizing trade and the flow of international capital. In the process, it achieved rapid economic growth led by the heavy and chemical industries. On the other hand, the heavy concentration of such highly material-intensive and energy-intensive industries and population in Japan's Pacific belt area led to serious environmental pollution problems (Ogawa, 1991). This necessitated a re-examination of industrial policy (MITI, 1972b).

Recognizing the need for a change in direction, MITI formulated a new plan for Japan's industrial development. This plan, which was published in May 1971 as *MITI's Vision for the 1970s* (MITI, 1971), proposed a shift to a knowledge-intensive industrial structure that would place a lesser burden on the environment by depending less on energy and materials while depending more on technology.[3]

In order to identify the required basic concept of industry and the industrial technology policies that would contribute to the establishment of the industrial structure proposed in its vision, MITI organized an ecology research group in May 1971, consisting of experts from ecology-related disciplines, to define an ecology science for studying the global environment. This research group then proposed the concept of *"Industry–Ecology"* as a comprehensive method for analysing and evaluating the complex mutual relations between human activities centring around industry and the surrounding environment (MITI, 1972b).

On the basis of its extensive research work, MITI attempted to develop a new policy principle to be applied to its industrial policy as well as a new policy system based on the principle. Efforts were directed to further developing R&D programmes to contribute to restoring the ideal equilibrium of the ecosystem by creating an environmentally friendly energy system[4] in the summer of 1973 (MITI, *Annual Report on MITI's Policy, 1973*).[5]

The first energy crisis occurred a few months later, which induced the reduction in redundancies by taking ecological considerations into account. The majority of MITI's efforts focused on how to secure an energy supply in the face of a dramatic increase in oil prices. Given such circumstances, a new policy was initiated, based on the basic principle of Industry–Ecology, namely securing a solution to basic energy problems by means of R&D on new and clean energy technology. This policy led to the establishment of a new programme, the Sunshine Project (R&D on New Energy Technology), which was initiated in July 1974.

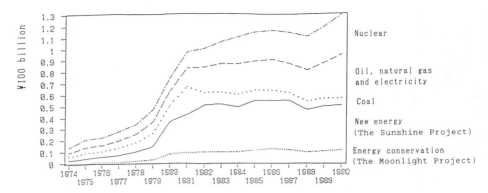

Fig. 10.9 **Trends in MITI's energy R&D budget, 1974–1990 (Source: *Annual Report on MITI's Policy*, MITI, 1974–1990)**

The basic principle of Industry–Ecology suggests that substitution among available production factors in a closed system should be the basic way to achieve sustainable development under certain constraints. The Sunshine Project initiated this approach by enabling substitution of technology-driven energy, which has unlimited potential, for limited energy sources, chiefly oil. Further substitution efforts needed to be made not only in the energy supply field but also in the field of energy consumption. Improvements in energy efficiency by means of technological innovation would contribute to a lower dependence on energy, and this process is simply the substitution of technology for energy. In line with this policy consideration, the Moonlight Project (R&D on Energy Conservation Technology) was initiated in 1978 (MITI, *Annual Report on MITI's Policy, 1978*).

The second energy crisis occurred in 1979, and MITI was able to implement policies capable of stimulating industrial dynamism conducive to sustainable development in the face of the damaging impact of the energy crises by means of the substitution of an unlimited resource, technology, for a limited resource, energy.[6] MITI's budget for the Sunshine Project and the Moonlight Project represented 14 per cent of MITI's total R&D budget in 1979, and in 1982 it increased to 29 per cent. It had been only 5 per cent in 1974 (figs. 10.9 and 10.10, and table 10.2).[7]

As international oil prices decreased and the "bubble economy" emerged, MITI's priority for energy R&D shifted to other policy

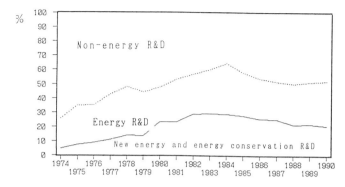

Fig. 10.10 **Trends in the share of MITI's energy R&D budget in its total R&D budget, 1974–1990 (Source: See fig. 10.9)**

Table 10.2 **R&D expenditures on energy and environmental technologies in Japan, 1990 (¥100 million)**

	Industry (Manuf. ind.)	Research institutions[a]	Universities	Total[b]
Energy technology	3,492 (2,819)	5,241	417	9,150
Nuclear	827 (660)	2,922	272	4,021
Non-nuclear	2,665 (2,159)	2,319	145	5,129
Energy conservation	1,882 (1,693)	1,754	66	3,702
Renewable	145 (120)	86	52	283
Coal	172 (117)	185	8	365
Oil & gas	294 (177)	198	10	502
Electric power	172 (52)	96	9	277
Environmental technology	1,428 (1,360)	–	–	–

a. Research institutions are organizations established by central or local governments or by private organizations that perform R&D.
b. Total R&D expenditure in 1990 (natural sciences): ¥11,993.5 billion (industry 9,267.2; research institutions 1,401.2; universities 1,325.2).

fields such as the Global Environmental Technology Programme, which was initiated in 1989 (Watanabe and Honda, 1992).

Stimulation of industry's energy R&D

MITI's efforts to engender the substitution of technology and technology-driven energy for energy and also for limited energy

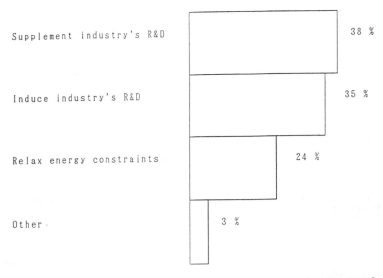

Fig. 10.11 **Expectations of MITI's energy R&D: Questionnaire to manufacturing firms (valid sample 54) involved in MITI's energy R&D programme projects (Source: Agency of Industrial Science and Technology, MITI, June 1993)**

sources stimulated industry's energy R&D. Figure 10.11 summarizes the outcome of a questionnaire to manufacturing firms involved in MITI's energy R&D programme projects regarding their expectations concerning these R&D projects. In addition to supplementation of industry's own R&D activities, a significant number of firms expressed the strong expectation that such projects would stimulate industry's R&D in relevant fields. Table 10.3 summarizes the outcome of an analysis with respect to correlations between MITI's energy R&D expenditure and expenditure on energy R&D initiated by Japan's manufacturing industry. We can observe a strong correlation between industry efforts and MITI's initiatives with respect to energy R&D. The correlations of R&D on energy conservation, renewable energy, and coal technologies led by both the Moonlight Project and the Sunshine Project are very clear, while the correlations of resource-constrained exhaustible energy technologies such as oil and gas R&D are relatively less clear. These analyses demonstrate that MITI's energy R&D programme projects such as the Sunshine Project and the Moonlight Project functioned well in stimulating related R&D activities initiated by industry.

Table 10.3 **Stimulating impact of MITI's energy R&D on energy R&D initiated by Japanese manufacturing industry, 1976–1990**

	Adj. R^2	DW	D
Energy R&D total			
$\ln(ERT) = 3.43 + 0.45\ln(SSML) + 0.24\ln(nSM) - 0.65\,D$ $\qquad\qquad\quad (4.21)\qquad\quad (1.31)\qquad\qquad (-5.67)$	.978	0.96	1976 = 1
Energy conservation			
$\ln(ERS) = 3.84 + 0.72\ln(ML + SSH) - 1.43\,D$ $\qquad\qquad\quad (12.82)\qquad\qquad\qquad (-8.36)$	.975	1.28	1976 = 1
Renewable energy			
$\ln(ERR) = 0.09 + 0.98\ln(SSS + SSG + SSO)$ $\qquad\qquad\quad (17.59)$	.957	1.75	
Coal			
$\ln(ERC) = -5.86 + 0.50\ln(SSC) + 1.13\ln(MC)$ $\qquad\qquad\quad\quad (18.07)\qquad\qquad (12.06)$	.972	2.18	
Oil and gas			
$\ln(EROG) = 0.46 + 0.92\ln(MOG) - 1.01\,D$ $\qquad\qquad\qquad (4.41)\qquad\qquad\quad (-2.24)$	.780	0.95	1976 = 1
Nuclear			
$\ln(ERN) = 3.17 + 0.56\ln(MN)$ $\qquad\qquad\quad (8.88)$	.848	2.16	
Electric power			
$\ln(ERE) = -2.59 + 1.53\ln(ME) + 1.34\,D$ $\qquad\qquad\qquad (9.76)\qquad\qquad (2.54)$	.870	1.07	1979 = 1

213

Table 10.3 (**cont.**)

	Adj. R^2	DW	D

MITI's energy R&D (¥100 m.)

Total (SSML + nSM) 1,299

SSML 512

Moonlight (ML) 116 — Energy conservation (ML) 116
  └ Hydrogen (SSH) 1

Sunshine (SS) 396
  ┌ Solar (SSS) 74
  Renewable ┤ Geothermal (SSG) 54
  └ Wind/ocean (SSO) 18
  Coal conversion (SSC) 249

nSM 787 Coal/Oil/Nucl./Elec.
  ┌ Coal (MC) 66
  │ Oil/gas (MOG) 256
  │ Electric power (ME) 119
  └ Nuclear (MN) 346

Manufacturing industry's energy R&D (¥100 m.)

Total (ERT) 2,819

Conservation (ERS) 1,693

Renewable (ERR) 120

Coal (ERC) 117

Oil and gas (EROG) 117

Electric power (ERE) 52

Nuclear (ERN) 660

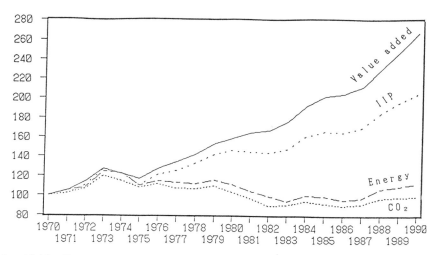

Fig. 10.12 **Trends in production, energy consumption, and CO_2 emissions in Japanese manufacturing industry, 1970–1990 (1970 = 100. Sources: See fig. 10.2)**

4. Fears of increasing energy and environmental constraints

Trends in factors contributing to change in CO_2 emissions

The global environmental consequences of CO_2 emissions resulting from energy use are causing mounting concern regarding the sustainability of development. Figure 10.12 illustrates trends in production, energy consumption, and CO_2 emissions in Japan's manufacturing industry over the period 1970–1990.[8] We can see that Japan's manufacturing industry was able to sustain steady development (the average growth rate of manufacturing production by value added between 1971 and 1990 was 5.1 per cent) despite the damaging impact of the energy crises on the energy supply. However, despite this big increase in production, CO_2 emissions were controlled at a mininum level (the average rate of increase in CO_2 emissions between 1971 and 1990 was 0.08 per cent), which was largely attributable to efforts to reduce dependency on energy.

Figure 10.13, which analyses the factors contributing to trends in CO_2 emissions in Japan's manufacturing industry, indicates that, over the period 1971–1990, 58 per cent of the reduction in CO_2 emissions was due to energy conservation (improvements in energy efficiency), 27 per cent was due to a change in industrial structure and production goods, and 12 per cent was due to changes in fuels.[9]

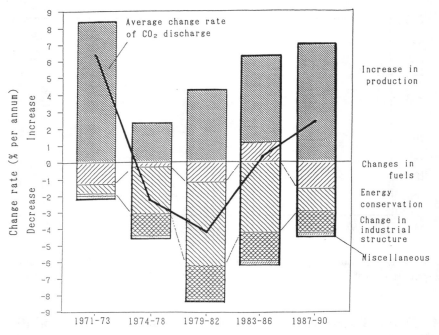

Fig. 10.13 **Factors contributing to changes in CO₂ emissions in Japanese manu-facturing industry, 1971–1990 (Note: Change in industrial structure includes changes in production goods and services in the same sector. Sources: See fig. 10.2)**

If we look at CO_2 emissions trends and the contributing factors by period, we find that the CO_2 emissions level fell dramatically after the first energy crisis in 1973 in line with an increase in energy conservation efforts. This was largely the result of the substitution of technology (energy conservation technology) and capital (energy conservation facility) for energy (see fig. 10.8), whereas the contribution made by a change in fuels (which also represents the outcomes of similar substitutions involving oil-alternative technologies and capital investment) was not so significant (only 6 per cent). This was considered to be due to an increasing dependency on coal as a promising alternative to oil. If we look at these trends carefully, we note that CO_2 emissions changed to an increasing trend after 1983 (the year when international oil prices started to fall) because of an increasing dependency on coal and slight decrease in energy conservation efforts. The decrease in energy conservation efforts became significant after 1987, the year of the start of Japan's so-called "bubble economy," resulting in further increases in CO_2 emissions.

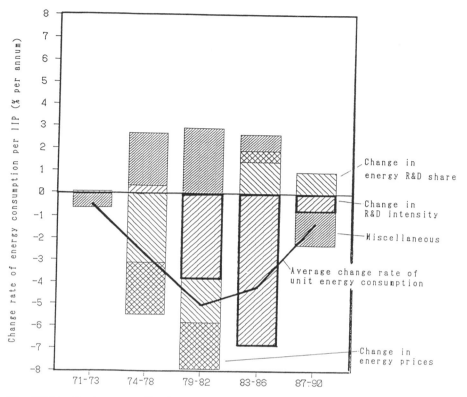

Fig. 10.14 **Factors contributing to changes in energy conservation in Japanese manufacturing industry, 1971–1990 (Sources: Agency of Natural Resources and Energy, MITI,** *Comprehensive Energy Statistics***; MITI,** *Annual Report on Indices on Mining and Manufacturing***;** *Annual Report on MITI's Policy,* **MITI, 1974–1990)**

Trends in factors contributing to changes in energy conservation

Figure 10.14 illustrates the outcome of analyses on trends and factors contributing to energy conservation in Japan's manufacturing industry over the period 1971–1990. We can note that a distinct decrease in energy conservation after 1987 was due chiefly to a decrease in R&D intensity.[10]

The following equation demonstrates the contribution to R&D intensity of technology substitution for other production factors in the period 1974–1990:

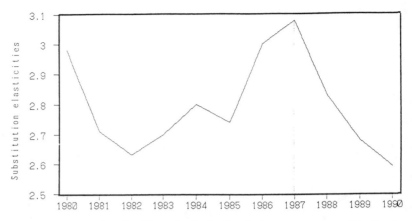

Fig. 10.15　**Trend in the elasticity of substitution between energy and technology in the 1980s (Source: See fig. 10.9)**

$$R/S = 1.4(\sigma_{tl} - 1)^{-0.18}(\sigma_{tk} - 1)^{-0.12}(\sigma_{tm} - 1)^{-0.73}(\sigma_{te} - 1)^{0.32}$$
$$(-2.53) \qquad (-1.81) \qquad (-9.72) \qquad (3.78)$$

Adj. R^2 .979　DW 1.68

where $R/S = $ R&D intensity and $\sigma_{tx} = $ elasticity of technology substitution for production factor x ($l = $ labour, $k = $ capital, $m = $ materials, and $e = $ energy).

This shows that efforts to substitute technology for energy made a significant contribution. The trend in elasticity of substitution between energy and technology in the 1980s is illustrated in figure 10.15. We can see that elasticities rose considerably up to 1986, whereas there was a dramatic decrease after 1987 as a result of a decreasing trend in international oil prices and the succeeding "bubble economy," causing, to a certain extent, a decrease in R&D intensity.

R&D intensity has a strong correlation with R&D's investment share of total investment, with a one- to two-year time-lag (see table 10.4). Considering the decreasing trend in R&D investment as a share of total investment illustrated in figure 10.16, it is strongly feared that R&D intensity may further decrease as a result of the bursting of Japan's "bubble economy" (see fig. 10.17).[11]

Table 10.5 compares the factors that stimulated energy R&D, R&D for environmental protection, and R&D for information technology in Japan's manufacturing industry over the period 1976–1990. We can note that R&D for environmental protection and energy R&D

Table 10.4 **Correlations between R&D investment share of total investment and R&D intensity in Japanese manufacturing industry, 1978–1990**

Industrial sector	Adj. R^2	DW	D
Chemicals			
$\ln(R/S) = -0.02 + 0.52\,\mathrm{Lag2}(\ln IR)$	.933	2.53	
$\qquad\qquad\qquad(12.96)$			
Iron & steel			
$\ln(R/S) = 0.07 + 0.30\,\mathrm{Lag1}(\ln IR) + 0.21\,D$	.907	1.58	$1985{-}1987 = 1$
$\qquad\qquad\quad(7.36)\qquad\qquad\quad(4.14)$			
Machinery			
$\ln(R/S) = -0.24 + 0.58\,\mathrm{Lag2}(\ln IR) + 0.06\,D$	.886	1.51	$1986{-}1990 = 1$
$\qquad\qquad\quad(8.74)\qquad\qquad\quad(2.66)$			

IR = R&D investment share of total investment, R/S = R&D intensity.

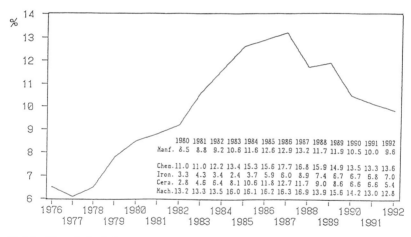

Fig. 10.16 **Trends in R&D investment share of total investment in Japanese manufacturing industry, 1976–1992 (Source: See fig. 10.9)**

are sensitive to the level of R&D intensity, in contrast to R&D for information technology.

Warning of a decrease in R&D intensity and its impact

The analyses in figure 10.17 and table 10.5 suggest that the R&D intensity of Japan's manufacturing industry will change to a decreasing trend in the near future, resulting in increases in both unit energy consumption and CO_2 emissions as estimated in figure 10.18. These

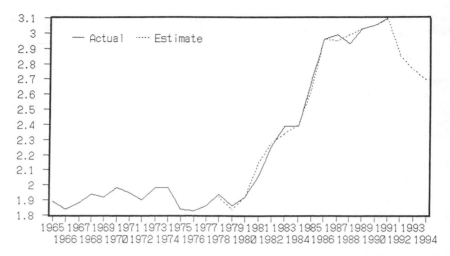

Fig. 10.17 **Trends in R&D intensity in Japanese manufacturing industry: Actual values, 1965–1991; estimated values, 1978–1994 (%, using constant prices. Source: See fig. 10.9)**

analyses also provide us with some warning that, despite its success in overcoming energy and environmental constraints in the 1960s, 1970s, and the first half of the 1980s, Japan's economy once again faces the prospect of constraints following the fall in international oil prices and the succeeding "bubble economy" (MITI, 1992a).

This prompted MITI to develop effective policy measures to reactivate efforts directed towards substituting technology for constrained production factors such as energy and environmental capacity. Moreover, MITI needed to develop a comprehensive approach based on *an integration of related programmes* (MITI, 1992b).

5. MITI's new comprehensive approach: The New Sunshine Programme

Principal countermeasures to global environmental constraints

Figure 10.19 illustrates the principal countermeasures to global environmental constraints that Japan's manufacturing industry has been taking and is also planning to take on a priority basis in the near future. We can note that waste treatment is currently the highest priority, followed by energy conservation and changes in fuels. Towards 1995, however, whereas priorities for energy conservation

Table 10.5 **Factors stimulating R&D on energy, environmental protection, and information technology in Japanese manufacturing industry, 1976–1990 (firms with capital of more than ¥100 million; 1985 constant prices)**

	Adj. R^2	DW	D	Multipliers of factors		
				R&D share by objectives	R&D intensity	Energy prices
Energy R&D $\ln ENERD = 2.12 + 0.77 \ln ENERS + 1.50 \ln R/S + 0.451 \ln Pe + 0.12 D$ $\quad\quad\quad\quad\quad (2.64)\quad\quad\quad (3.70)\quad\quad (1.29)\quad\quad\quad (1.34)$	.918	1.54	1990 = 1	0.77	1.50	0.45
R&D for environmental protection $\ln ENVRD = 2.86 + 1.07 \ln ENVRS + 2.08 \ln R/S + 0.21 \ln Pe - 0.14 D$ $\quad\quad\quad\quad\quad (7.94)\quad\quad\quad (8.97)\quad\quad (1.57)\quad\quad\quad (-1.77)$	.847	1.85	1986 = 1	1.07	2.08	0.21
R&D for information technology $\ln INFRD = 2.75 + 1.53 \ln INFRS + 0.87 \ln R/S + 0.27 \ln Pe$ $\quad\quad\quad\quad\quad (23.10)\quad\quad\quad (6.25)\quad\quad (4.92)$	.999	2.44		1.53	0.87	0.27

$ENERD$, $ENVRD$, and $INFRD$ = R&D expenditures on energy R&D, R&D for environmental protection, and R&D for information technology, respectively.

$ENERS$, $ENVRS$, $INFRS$ = the ratio of R&D expenditures on energy, environmental protection, and information technology, respectively.

R/S = R&D intensity.

Pe = energy prices.

221

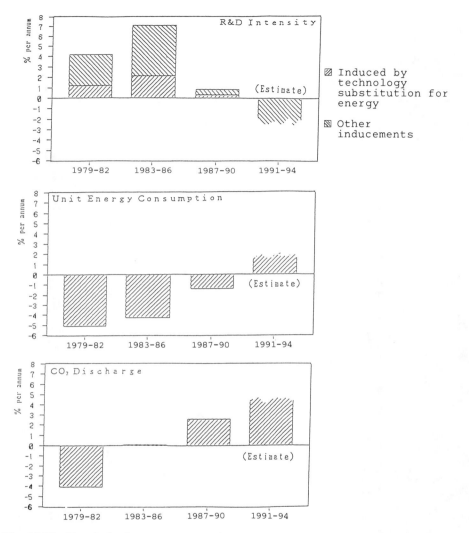

Fig. 10.18 **Trends in the average rate of change in R&D intensity, unit energy consumption, and CO₂ emissions in Japanese manufacturing industry, 1979–1994 (Note: R&D intensity = ratio of R&D expenditure to sales at constant prices; unit energy consumption = ratio of energy consumption to production. Sources: See fig. 10.14)**

and fuel change increase, the priority for waste treatment was expected to decrease. This estimated trend supports the analyses in the previous section and demonstrates the increasing significance of energy conservation and fuel change as the principal measures to counter global environmental constraints.

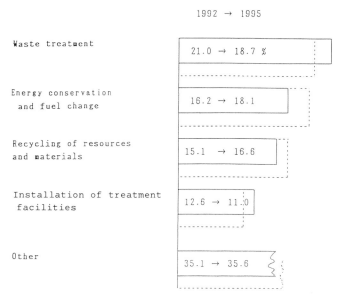

1992 → 1995

Waste treatment: 21.0 → 18.7 %

Energy conservation and fuel change: 16.2 → 18.1

Recycling of resources and materials: 15.1 → 16.6

Installation of treatment facilities: 12.6 → 11.0

Other: 35.1 → 35.6

Fig. 10.19 Principal measures to counter global environmental constraints in Japanese manufacturing industry, 1992 and 1995 (Source: questionnaire to major firms undertaken by the Japan Development Bank in 1992; total number of valid samples, 657)

The New Sunshine Programme

Objectives

The global environmental consequences of energy use are causing mounting concern regarding the sustainability of the world's development future. Given the two-sided nature of the global environmental issue and energy consumption, a comprehensive approach based on R&D programmes on new energy technology, energy conservation technology, and global environmental technology is needed to lead the way to sustainable development by overcoming both energy and environmental constraints simultaneously (MITI, 1992a).

In this regard, MITI decided to establish the New Sunshine Programme (R&D Programme on Energy and Environmental Technologies) in April 1993 by integrating the Sunshine Project, the Moonlight Project, and the Global Environmental Technology Programme, as illustrated in figure 10.20 (MITI, 1992b). This is expected to achieve effective and accelerated achievement of R&D in the fields of energy and environmental technologies by means of co-utilization and sup-

223

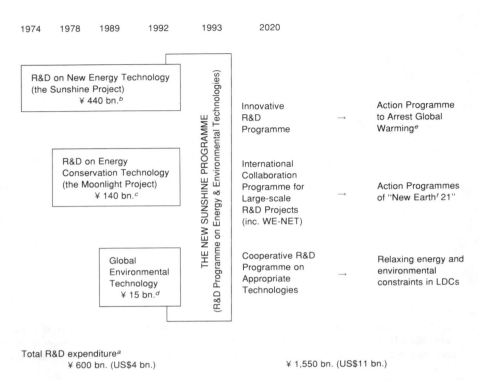

Total R&D expenditure[a]
¥ 600 bn. (US$4 bn.)   ¥ 1,550 bn. (US$11 bn.)

Fig. 10.20 **The basic concept of the New Sunshine Programme (Notes: *a.* total R&D expenditure indicates the accumulation of MITI's R&D budget; *b.* includes R&D on hydrogen, solar, wind, and geothermal energy, and synfuels such as coal liquefaction; *c.* includes R&D on fuel cells and energy storage; *d.* includes R&D on chemical CO_2 fixation and utilization; *e.* action to stabilize per capita and total CO_2 emissions at 1990 levels by the years 2000 and 2010, respectively; *f.* action to restore the Earth over future decades through the reduction of greenhouse gases)**

plementation of such key technologies as catalysts, hydrogen, high-temperature materials and sensors common to new energy, energy conservation and environmental protection. In addition, the New Sunshine Programme is expected to provide a new concept for an environmentally friendly technology system and inspire a new principle to be pursued under global environmental constraints.

The structure of the New Sunshine Programme
The New Sunshine Programme comprises the following three R&D programmes in the field of energy and environmental technologies:
• *The Innovative R&D Programme* – aims to accelerate R&D on innovative technology essential for the achievement of the goal of

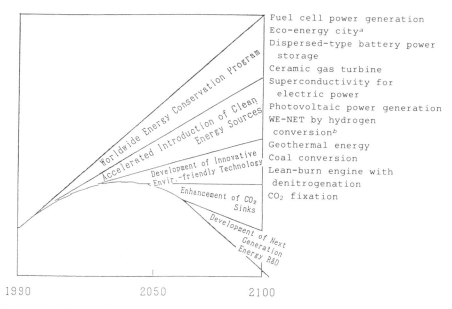

Fig. 10.21 **The development programme of the New Sunshine Programme's projects in conjunction with the action programmes of "New Earth 21" (Notes: *a*. broad-area energy-utilization network system; *b*. world energy network – international clean energy network using hydrogen conversion)**

"The Action Programme to Arrest Global Warming," which is to stabilize per capita CO_2 emissions at 1990 levels by the year 2000.

· *The International Collaboration Programme for Large-scale R&D Projects* – aims to initiate large international R&D projects expected to make a significant contribution to the achievement of the goal of "New Earth 21," which is to restore the Earth over future decades through the reduction of greenhouse gases (fig. 10.21).

· *The Cooperative R&D Programme on Appropriate Technologies* – aims at the development and assimilation of appropriate technologies in neighbouring developing countries through cooperative R&D on technologies originating from the Sunshine Project and the Moonlight Project.

Development programme

Priority projects in the New Sunshine Programme can be classified into two basic types:

1. Acceleration projects, which are expected to lead to practical use in the near future by means of a virtually spiralling cycle (decrease

225

n costs through technological improvement → increase in demand → further decrease in costs through mass production) triggered by an acceleration of R&D.
2. Innovative synthetic system projects, which are expected to achieve an extremely high level of breakthrough by means of a synthesis of key technologies.

Cost and benefit estimates
The budget requirement for the New Sunshine Programme's projects over the period 1993–2020 is estimated at ¥1,550 billion (US$11 billion). Of this amount, ¥54 billion (US$390 million) will be disbursed in JFY 1993, with such investment expected to contribute to reducing Japan's energy and environmental constraints by one-third and one-half, respectively, by 2030.

6. Implications for sustainable development

Increasing constraints of energy and the environment, especially the global environmental consequences of energy use, are causing mounting concern, and it is widely warned that these consequences could limit the ability to sustain future development. Considering the two-sided nature of the global environmental issue and energy consumption, Japan's success in overcoming the energy crises while maintaining economic growth and attaining a dramatic improvement in its technological level could provide useful suggestions on the question of how technology can be utilized to sustain development.

Summarized briefly, these suggestions include the following:

The basic principle of a constrained economy suggested by Industry–Ecology
The following suggestions obtained from Industry–Ecology may be useful as basic principles applicable to a constrained economy:
– recognition of confinement;
– recognition of system;
– recognition of redundancies;
– recognition of dose-response; and
– discipline of self-control.

Technological development as a system
Japan's success with respect to technological development and its effective contribution to economic development can be attributed to

the integration of both internal and external technology in a cyclical system similar to an ecosystem. This suggests that careful consideration, taking into account the global environmental issue as a significant factor of external technology, is especially important in furthering R&D.

A grave situation turned into a springboard
Another important observation is that Japan was able successfully to change a grave situation such as the energy crisis into a springboard for technology development by using the situation as an external stimulus that might dampen "homeostasis." This suggests that integrated efforts directed towards overcoming the global environmental issue could be a springboard for effective R&D and stimulate the potential vitality of industry.

Stimulation to substitute as a basis of a constrained economy
An analysis of trends in the substitution of limited production factors such as energy by technology indicates that Japanese technological development succeeded by focusing on efforts to break through the constraints of the scarcest resources of the 1970s and 1980s. This suggests that a comprehensive approach that challenges the limits of sustainable development by substituting new technology for energy and environmental constraints could lead to a new frontier.

Notes

1. $E = E/IIP \cdot (V/IIP)^{-1} \cdot V$

$$\Delta V/V - \Delta E/E = \Delta(V/IIP)(V/IIP) - \Delta(E/IIP)/(E/IIP) + \eta$$

where E = energy, IIP = index of industrial production, and V = value added.
2. In the analysis of my previous work with respect to the analysis of trends in the substitution of production factors by technology in Japan's manufacturing industry over the past 20 years, the following conclusions were supported (Watanabe, 1992b). Triggered by the sharp increase in energy prices due to the two energy crises, energy has been substituted by technology and also, to some extent, by capital. The sharp increase in energy prices also resulted in an increase in labour prices, which has induced labour to be substituted by technology. Although capital and materials have been complementary to technology, they have been shifting towards substitution by technology. Thus, all of the production factors have been, directly or indirectly, substituted by technology or have been shifting in that direction.
3. *MITI's Vision*, in order to establish a knowledge-intensive industrial structure, stressed the significant role of innovative R&D, which leads to less dependence on materials and energy in the process of production and consumption. It also stressed that such reduced dependence could be possible by means of intensive conservation and recycling of

resources (materials and energy) in a long, global, and *ecological* context, and that R&D aiming to develop "limit-free energy technology" (technology-driven clean energy) was significant.

4. MITI attempted to construct a cyclical system, similar to an ecosystem, which aims to maintain homeostasis (checks and balances that dampen oscillations) through the cycle of producers → consumers → decomposers → abiotic substances → producers (Odum, 1963).

5. A chronology of MITI's efforts can be summarized as follows (MITI, *Annual Report on MITI's Policy*, 1970–1990; MITI, 1972a,b):

1971	May	*MITI's Vision for the 1970s* ("limit-free energy technology" – technology-driven clean energy in an ecological context).
	May	Organization of an ecology research group.
1972	March	First research report by the research group.
	April	Advice by MITI Minister's Secretariat to consider a new policy based on the ecosystem principle.
1973	March	Second research report by the research group.
	April	Advice by MITI Minister's Secretariat to formulate a new policy based on the ecosystem principle.
	May	Start of policy formulation.
	Aug.	Budget requirement of the Sunshine Project.
	Oct.	The first energy crisis.
	Dec.	Government's approval for the Sunshine Project's FY 1974 budget.
1974	July	Start of the Sunshine Project.
1978		Start of the Moonlight Project.
1979		The second energy crisis.
1980		Establishment of the New Energy Development Organization (NEDO).
1983		Start of the fall in international oil prices.
1985		Plaza Agreement (appreciation of the yen).
1987		Start of the "bubble economy."
1988		Start of the Global Environmental Technology Programme.
1991		Bursting of the "bubble economy."
1993		Start of the New Sunshine Programme.

6. The mechanism of MITI's policy system for such stimulation can be summarized as follows (Watanabe and Honda, 1991):
   - penetration and identification of future prospects and strategic areas,
   - formulation and publication of visions,
   - provision of policy measures that stimulate such substitution in order to induce industries to increase their R&D intensity,
   - the potential for further technological development increases as the degree of R&D intensity increases,
   - expectations on the outcome of technological development among industries increase,
   - inducing further investment in R&D activities, and
   - building up dynamism conducive to technological development.

7. MITI's energy R&D can be categorized as follows:
   Unconstrained energy resources: energy conservation, hydrogen, solar, ocean, coal conversion, coal, nuclear
   Constrained renewable energy resources: geothermal, wind, biomass, hydro
   Constrained conventional energy resources: oil and gas

8. Japan's CO_2 emissions in 1990 are distributed as follows (inclusive of CO_2 in the power generation process):
   Industry: 47.6% (manufacturing industry: 43.1%)
   Residential and commercial: 22.6%
   Transportation: 18.5%
   Other: 11.3%

9. $C = C/E \cdot E/I \cdot (V/I)^{-1} \cdot V,$

where $C = CO_2$, $E =$ energy, $I =$ IIP, and $V =$ value added.

$\Delta C/C = \Delta(C/E)/(C/E) + \Delta(E/I)/(E/I) - \Delta(V/I)/(V/I) + \Delta V/V$

where $\Delta(C/E)/(C/E) =$ change in fuel or fuel switching
$\Delta(E/I)/(E/I) =$ change in unit energy consumption or energy conservation
$\Delta(V/I)/(V/I) =$ change in industrial structure.

10. $\ln(E/IIP) = -0.002 - 0.971 \ln(R/S) - 0.141 \ln(Re/R) - 0.131 \ln(Pe)$
   (-11.00) (-2.80) (-2.25)

   Adj. R^2 .950 DW 1.71

where $E =$ energy consumption, $IIP =$ index of industrial production, $R =$ R&D expenditure, $S =$ sales, $Re =$ expenditure on energy R&D, $Pe =$ energy prices.

11. The estimation function for figure 10.17 is as follows:

$\ln(R/S) = -0.56 + 0.65 \ln(\text{Lag2}(RD/I)) + 0.07D$
   (26.68) (3.94)

   Adj. R^2 .987 DW 2.23 D 1986, 1990 $= 1$

where $R/S =$ R&D intensity (ratio of R&D expenditure to sales at constant prices), and $RD/I =$ R&D investment share of total investment.

Bibliography

Baranson, J. 1967. "A challenge of low development." In: *Technology in Western Civilization*, vol. II. New York: Oxford University Press, pp. 251–271.

Christensen, L. R., D. W. Jorgenson, and L. J. Lau. 1973. "Transcendental logarithmic production factors." *Review of Economics and Statistics* 55(1): 28–45.

Clinton, W. J. and A. Gore. 1993. *Technology for America's Economic Growth. A New Direction to Build Economic Strength*. Upland: Diane Publishing Co.

Economic Planning Agency. 1965–1992. *White Paper on the Japanese Economy – Economic Survey of Japan*. Tokyo, annual issues.

Edmonds, J. and J. Reilly. 1983. "A long-term global energy-economic model of carbon dioxide release from fossil fuel use." *Energy Economics* 5(2): 74–88.

Freeman, C. 1992 "A green techno-economic paradigm for the world economy." Paper presented to A Talk Given to the Netherlands Director-General for the Environment, Amsterdam.

Hogan, W. and D. Jorgenson. 1991. "Productivity trends and the cost of reducing CO_2 emissions." *Energy Journal* 12: 67–86.

Lichtenberg, H. R. 1986. "Energy prices and induced innovation." *Research Policy* 15: 67–85.

Meadows, D. H. et al. 1972. *The Limits to Growth*. New York: Universe Books.

Meyer-Krahmer, F. 1992. "The German R&D system in transition: Empirical results and prospects of future development." *Research Policy* 21(5): 423–436.

MITI. 1970–1990. *Annual Report on MITI's Policy*. Tokyo, annual issues.

MITI, Industrial Structure Council. 1971. *MITI's Vision for the 1970s*. Tokyo.

MITI. 1972a. "Ecology and application of its concept to industrial policy." *MITI Journal* 5(2): 63–88.

MITI. 1972b. *Industry–Ecology: Introduction of Ecology into Industrial Policy.* Tokyo.

MITI, Industrial Structure Council. 1982. *Towards the Establishment of Economic Security.* Tokyo.

MITI. 1988. *White Paper on Industrial Technology: Trends and Future Tasks in Japanese Industrial Technology.* Tokyo.

MITI, Industrial Structure Council, Comprehensive Energy Policy Council, and Industrial Technology Council. 1992a. *Fourteen Proposals for New Earth – Policy Triad for the Environment, Economy and Energy.* Tokyo.

MITI, Industrial Technology Council. 1992b. *A Comprehensive Approach to The New Sunshine Program.* Tokyo.

Mowery, D. C. and N. Rosenberg. 1989. *Technology and Pursuit of Economic Growth.* Cambridge: Cambridge University Press, pp. 219–237.

National Institute for Research Advancement. 1983. *Basic Survey on the Economic Analysis of the 1st and 2nd Oil Crises.* Tokyo.

NEDO. 1991. *Survey Report on the Utilization Technology of Carbon Dioxide under Global Environmental Constraints.* Tokyo.

Odum, E. P. 1963. *Ecology.* New York: Holt, Rinehart & Winston.

Ogawa, Y. 1991. "An analysis on factors affecting energy consumption and CO_2 emissions and their regional and sectoral differences." Paper presented to The Workshop of Energy and Industry Subgroup, WG3 of IPCC, Seoul.

US Department of Commerce. 1990. *Japan as a Scientific and Technological Superpower.* Washington, D.C.

Uzawa, H. and M. Kuninori. 1993. *Economic Analysis of Global Warming.* Tokyo: University of Tokyo Press.

Watanabe, C. 1972. "A guideline to the ecolo-utopia: Basic suggestion to Japanese economy in the face of the new crisis." *Analyst* 9: 34–56.

——— 1973. "Ecological analysis of the Japanese economy." *The Economic Seminar* No. 211 (January): 29–43.

——— 1990. "Japanese industrial development." *Australian Journal of Public Administration* 49(3): 288–294.

——— 1992a. "How sustainable is our energy future? Leading a way to overcome the global environmental issue: The crossroad between energy and high technology." Paper presented to the 1992 Australian Institute of Energy Conference, Canberra.

——— 1992b. "Trends in the substitution of production factors to technology: Empirical analysis of the inducing impact of the energy crisis on Japanese industrial technology." *Research Policy* 21(6):481–505.

——— 1992c. "R&D intensity in the Japanese manufacturing industry has changed to a decreasing trend since the bubble economy." *Nihon Keizai Shimbun*, 25 November.

——— 1993a. "The role of energy and environmental technologies for sustainable development. A view from Japan." Paper presented to National Academy of Engineering's Technology and Sustainable Development Symposium, Irvine.

——— 1993b. "An ecological assessment of Japan's industrial technological system." Special Lecture to MIT, Boston.

—— 1993c. "Sustainable success of energy for global warming mitigation and new challenge of materials for waste management." Paper presented to National Academy of Engineering's Industrial Ecology Workshop, Woods Hole.

Watanabe, C. and Y. Honda. 1991. "Inducing power of Japanese technological innovation: Mechanism of Japan's industrial science and technology policy." *Japan and the World Economy* 3(4): 357–390.

—— 1992. "Japanese industrial science and technology policy in the 1990s: MITI's role at a turning point." *Japan and the World Economy* 4(1): 47–67.

Watanabe, C., I. Santoso, and T. Widayanti. 1991. *The Inducing Power of Japanese Technological Innovation.* London: Pinter.

11

Global warming and renewable energy: Potential and policy approaches

Thomas B. Johansson

1. Introduction

Renewed attention is now given to the development and utilization of renewable sources of energy, in response to growing concerns about climate change, acidification, and urban air pollution, and interest in secure and affordable supplies of energy for economic and social development, which was the dominating rationale behind the interest of the 1970s. The growing aspirations of an expanding world population are expected to increase world energy demand, even if strong efforts are made to improve energy efficiency. If this growing world energy demand is to be met with fossil fuels to any significant degree, carbon dioxide (CO_2) emissions will increase considerably, not decrease as implied by the Framework Convention on Climate Change and the reports from the Intergovernmental Panel on Climate Change. For example, CO_2 emissions are projected to grow by 2020 by 41 per cent in the reference scenario and by 93 per cent in the high-growth scenario of the World Energy Council Commission (1993).

The flow of renewable energy to the Earth's land surface is thousands of times greater than mankind's present rate of total energy use. Utilizing only a small fraction of this resource would provide

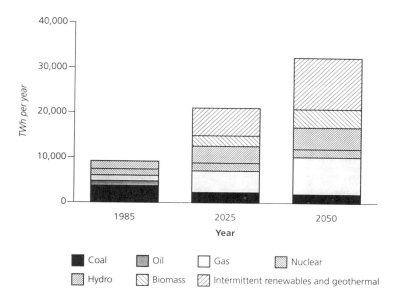

Fig. 11.1 **The renewables-intensive global energy scenario, 1985–2050: electricity generation (Source: Johansson et al., 1993)**

humanity with an alternative and environmentally sound path towards meeting future energy needs. The question is whether this flow of energy can be converted to modern energy carriers such as electricity and liquid and gaseous fuels at acceptable costs in a sustainable manner.

An evaluation of the potential contribution of renewable energies concluded that, given adequate support, renewable energy technologies could meet much of the growing demand at prices lower than those usually forecast for conventional energy (Johansson et al., 1993). By the middle of the twenty-first century, renewable energy could account for three-fifths of the world's electricity market (see fig. 11.1) and two-fifths of the market for fuels used directly (see fig. 11.2). Moreover, making a transition to a renewables-intensive energy economy would provide environmental and other benefits not measured in standard economic accounts (see table 11.1). For example, by 2050 global CO_2 emissions would be reduced to 75 per cent of their 1985 levels provided that energy efficiency and renewables are both pursued aggressively (see figs. 11.3a and 11.3b). And because renewable energy is expected to be competitive with conventional energy, such benefits could be achieved at no additional cost.

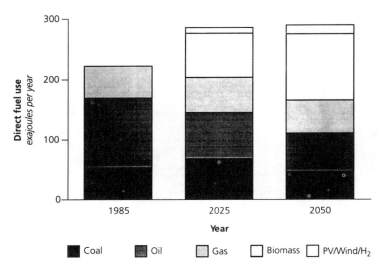

Fig. 11.2 **The renewables-intensive global energy scenario, 1985–2050: direct fuel use (Source: Johansson et al., 1993)**

2. Progress in renewable-energy technologies

Impressive technical gains in renewable-energy technologies and systems have been made during the past decade. Renewable-energy systems have benefited from developments in electronics, biotechnology, materials sciences, and other energy areas. For example, advances in jet engines for military and civilian aircraft applications, and in coal gasification for reducing air pollution from coal combustion, have made it possible to produce electricity competitively using gas turbines derived from jet engines and fired with gasified biomass.[1] And fuel cells developed originally for the space programme have opened the door to the use of hydrogen as a non-polluting fuel for transportation. Indeed, many of the most promising options are the result of advances made in areas not directly related to renewable energy, and were scarcely considered a decade ago.

Moreover, because the size of most renewable-energy equipment is small, the development and use of renewable-energy technologies can advance at a faster pace than conventional technologies. Whereas large energy facilities require extensive construction in the field, where labour is costly and productivity gains difficult to achieve, most renewable-energy equipment can be constructed in factories, where it is easier to apply modern manufacturing techniques that facilitate

Table 11.1 **The benefits of renewable energy not captured in standard economic accounts**

Social and economic development	Production of renewable energy, particularly biomass, can provide economic development and employment opportunities, especially in rural areas, that otherwise have limited opportunities for economic growth. Renewable energy can thus help reduce poverty in rural areas and reduce pressures for urban migration.
Land restoration	Growing biomass for energy on degraded lands can provide the incentives and financing needed to restore lands rendered nearly useless by previous agricultural or forestry practices. Although lands farmed for energy would not be restored to their original condition, the recovery of these lands for biomass plantations would support rural development, prevent erosion, and provide a better habitat for wildlife than at present.
Reduced air pollution	Renewable-energy technologies, such as methanol or hydrogen for fuel-cell vehicles, produce virtually none of the emissions associated with urban air pollution and acid deposition, without the need for costly additional controls.
Abatement of global warming	Renewable energy use does not produce carbon dioxide and other greenhouse emissions that contribute to global warming. Even the use of biomass fuels will not contribute to global warming: the carbon dioxide released when biomass is burned equals the amount absorbed from the atmosphere by plants as they are grown for biomass fuel.
Fuel supply diversity	There would be substantial interregional energy trade in a renewables-intensive energy future, involving a diversity of energy carriers and suppliers. Energy importers would be able to choose from among more producers and fuel types than they do today and thus would be less vulnerable to monopoly price manipulation or unexpected disruptions of supplies. Such competition would make wide swings in energy prices less likely, leading eventually to stabilization of the world oil price. The growth in world energy trade would also provide new opportunities for energy suppliers. Especially promising are the prospects for trade in alcohol fuels such as methanol derived from biomass, natural gas (not a renewable fuel but an important complement to renewables), and, later, hydrogen.
Reducing the risks of nuclear weapons proliferation	Competitive renewable resources could reduce incentives to build a large world infrastructure in support of nuclear energy, thus avoiding major increases in the production, transportation, and storage of plutonium and other nuclear materials that could be diverted to nuclear weapons production.

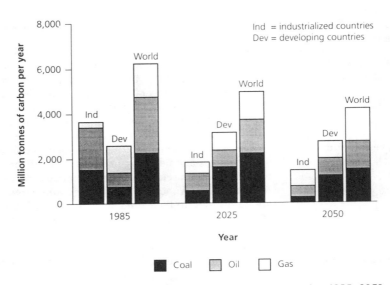

Fig. 11.3 **(a) The renewables-intensive global energy scenario, 1985–2050: Emissions of CO₂ (Source: Johansson et al., 1993)**

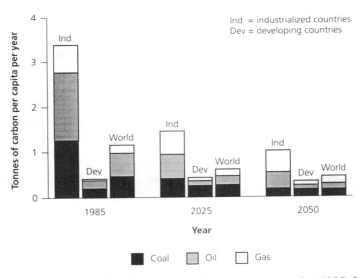

Fig. 11.3 **(b) The renewables-intensive global energy scenario, 1985–2050: Per capita emissions of CO₂ (Source: Johansson et al., 1993)**

cost reduction. The small scale of the equipment also makes the time required from initial design to operation short, so that needed improvements can be identified by field testing and quickly incorporated into modified designs. In this way, many generations of technology can be introduced in short periods. This is reflected in analysis of "learning curves." These show costs as a function of integrated market volume. The examples of photovoltaic modules (Williams and Terzian, 1993) and biomass gasification/gas turbine power generation (Elliott and Booth, 1993) have been discussed.

The advances are described and analysed in Johansson et al. (1993), a volume prepared for the United Nations. Two other important overview volumes in the field are Jackson (1993) and World Energy Council (1993).

3. Constructing a renewables-intensive global energy scenario

The findings are based on a renewables-intensive global energy scenario, which was developed in order to identify the potential markets for renewable technologies in the years 2025 and 2050, assuming that market barriers to these technologies are removed by comprehensive national policies (see "An Agenda for Action" in Johansson et al., 1993: chap. 1). Some global features of the scenario are presented in figures 11.1 to 11.4. Separate detailed scenarios were constructed for 11 world regions.[2]

In constructing the scenario it was assumed that renewable-energy technologies will capture markets whenever (a) a plausible case can be made that renewable energy is no more expensive on a life-cycle cost basis than conventional alternatives,[3] and (b) the use of renewable technologies at the levels indicated will not create significant environmental, land-use, or other problems. The economic analysis did not take into account any credits for the external benefits of renewables listed in table 11.1.

Energy demand

The market for renewable energy depends in part on the future demand for energy services: heating and cooling, lighting, transportation, and so on. This demand, in turn, depends on economic and population growth and on the efficiency of energy use. Future energy supply requirements can be estimated by taking such considerations into account. For the construction of the renewables-intensive energy

237

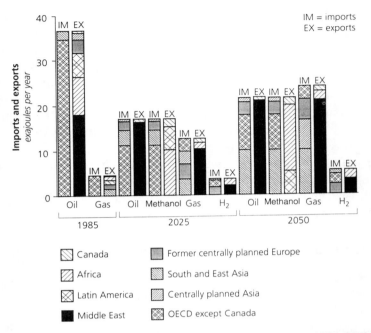

Fig. 11.4 **The renewables-intensive global energy scenario, 1985–2050: Inter-regional flows of fuels (Note: H_2 = hydrogen derived from renewable energy sources. Source: Johansson et al., 1993)**

scenario, future levels of demand for electricity and for solid, liquid, and gaseous fuels were assumed to be the same as those projected in a scenario by the Response Strategies Working Group of the Inter-governmental Panel on Climate Change.

The Working Group developed several projections of energy demand. The one adopted for the renewables-intensive scenario is characterized by "high economic growth" and "accelerated policies" (see fig. 11.5). The accelerated policies case was designed to demon-strate the effect of policies that would stimulate the adoption of energy-efficient technologies, without restricting economic growth. Because renewable technologies are unlikely to succeed unless they are part of a programme designed to minimize the overall cost of providing energy services, the energy-efficiency assumptions under-lying the accelerated policies scenario are consistent with the objec-tives of the renewables-intensive scenario.

The high economic growth, accelerated policies scenario projects

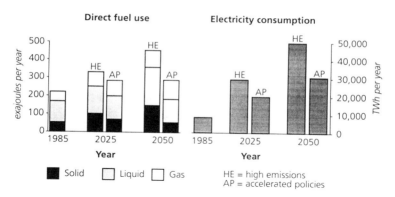

Fig. 11.5 **Alternative global energy scenario developed by the Intergovernmental Panel on Climate Change (Source: Johansson et al., 1993)**

a doubling of world population and an eight-fold increase in gross world economic product between 1985 and 2050. Economic growth rates are assumed to be higher for developing countries than for those already industrialized. Energy demand grows more slowly than economic output because of the accelerated adoption of energy-efficient technologies, but demand growth outpaces efficiency improvements – especially in rapidly growing developing countries. World demand for fuel (excluding fuel for generating electricity) is projected to increase by 30 per cent between 1985 and 2050 and demand for electricity by 265 per cent (see fig. 11.5).

The Working Group's assumptions about energy efficiency gains are ambitious; none the less, cost-effective efficiency improvements greater than those in the scenario are technically feasible, and new policies can help speed their adoption. Structural shifts to less energy-intensive economic activities, for example knowledge-intensive electronics, information technologies, and biotechnology, may also reduce the energy needs of modern economies below those projected.[4]

Energy resources

Construction of a global energy supply scenario must be consistent with energy resource endowments and various practical constraints on the recovery of these resources. Some key elements of a renewables-intensive global energy system are as follows:

• There would be a diversity of energy sources, the relative abundance of which would vary from region to region. Electricity could be provided by various combinations of hydroelectric power, intermittent renewable power sources (wind, solar–thermal electric, and photovoltaic power), biomass power, and geothermal power. Fuels could be provided by methanol, ethanol, hydrogen, and methane (biogas) derived from biomass, supplemented by hydrogen derived electrolytically from intermittent renewables.

- Biomass would be widely used. Biomass would be grown sustainably and converted efficiently to electricity and liquid and gaseous fuels using modern technology, in contrast to the present situation, where biomass is used inefficiently and sometimes contributes to deforestation.
- Intermittent renewables would provide as much as one-third of total electricity requirements cost-effectively in most regions, without the need for new electrical storage technologies.
- Natural gas would play a major role in supporting the growth of a renewable-energy industry. Natural-gas-fired turbines, which have low capital costs and can quickly adjust their electrical output, can provide excellent backup for intermittent renewables on electric power grids. Natural gas would also help launch a biomass-based methanol industry; methanol might well be introduced using natural gas feedstocks before the shift to methanol derived from biomass occurs.
- Most electricity produced from renewable sources would be fed into large electrical grids and marketed by electric utilities.
- Liquid and gaseous fuels would be marketed much as oil and natural gas are today. Large oil companies could become the principal marketers; some might also become producers, perhaps in joint ventures with agricultural or forest-product industry firms.

Renewable energy

In the renewables-intensive energy scenario, global consumption of renewable resources reaches a level equivalent to 318 exajoules per year (EJ/yr) of fossil fuels by 2050 – a rate comparable to total present world energy consumption. Though large, this rate of production involves using less than 0.01 per cent of the 3.8 million EJ of solar energy reaching the earth's surface each year. The total electric energy produced from intermittent renewable sources (some 34 EJ/yr) would be less than 0.003 per cent of the sunlight that falls on land and less than 0.1 per cent of the energy available in the winds. Moreover, the electric energy that would be recovered from hydropower resources, some 17 EJ/yr by 2050, is small relative to the 130–160 EJ/yr that are theoretically recoverable (Moreira and Poole, 1993). The amount of energy targeted for recovery from biomass – 206 EJ/yr by 2050 – is also small compared with the rate (3,800 EJ/yr) at which plants convert solar energy to biomass (Hall et al., 1993).

The production levels considered are therefore not likely to be constrained by resource availability. A number of other practical considerations, however, do limit the renewable resources that can be used. The scenario was constructed subject to the following restrictions.

First, biomass must be produced sustainably (see Johansson et al., 1993: 13 and 593), with none harvested from virgin forests. Some 62 per cent of the biomass supply would come from plantations established on degraded lands or, in industrialized countries, on excess agricultural lands. Another 32 per cent would come from residues of agricultural or forestry operations. Some residues must be left behind to maintain soil quality or for economic reasons; three-quarters of the energy in urban refuse and timber and pulpwood residues, one-half of residues from ongoing logging operations, one-quarter of the dung produced by livestock, one-quarter of the residues from cereals, and about two-thirds of the residues from sugar cane are recovered in the scenario. The remaining 6 per cent of the biomass supply would come from forests that are now routinely harvested for timber, paper, or fuelwood. Production from these forests can be made fully sustainable – although some of these forests are not well managed today.

Secondly, although wind resources are enormous, the use of wind equipment will be substantially constrained in some regions by land-use restrictions – particularly where population densities are high. In the scenario, substantial development of wind power takes place in the Great Plains of the United States (where most of the country's wind resources are found), whereas in Europe the level of development is limited because of "severe land-use constraints" (Grubb and Meyer, 1993).

Thirdly, the amounts of wind, solar–thermal, and photovoltaic power that can be economically integrated into electricity-generating systems are very sensitive to patterns of electricity demand as well as weather conditions. The marginal value of these so-called intermittent electricity sources typically declines as their share of the total electricity market increases. Analysis of these interactions suggests that intermittent electricity generators can provide 25–35 per cent of the total electricity supply in most parts of the world (Kelly and

Weinberg, 1993). Some regions would emphasize wind, while others would find photovoltaic or solar–thermal electric systems more attractive. On average, Europe is a comparatively poor location for intermittent power generation, so that the penetration of intermittent renewables there is limited to 14 per cent in 2025 and 18 per cent in 2050.

An interesting approach to the intermittency of wind energy has been proposed by Cavallo (1994). Wind electricity generated in the US Midwest and transported to major demand centres is projected to cost about 6 cents per kWh at the demand site, with a capacity factor of 70 per cent (this is essentially equivalent to base load generation in conventional power stations). The increased availability is achieved through wind farm oversizing (in relation to transmission capacity), increased hub heights, and compressed air storage.

Fourthly, although the exploitable hydroelectricity potential is large, especially in developing countries (Moreira and Poole, 1993), and hydropower is an excellent complement to intermittent electricity sources, the development of hydropower will be constrained by environmental and social concerns – particularly for projects that would flood large areas. Because of these constraints, it is assumed that only a fraction of potential sites would be exploited, with most growth occurring in developing countries. Worldwide, only one-quarter of the technical potential, as estimated by the World Energy Conference, would be exploited in the scenario by 2050. Total hydroelectricity production in the United States, Canada, and OECD Europe would increase by only one-third between 1985 and 2050, and some of the increase would result from efficiency gains achieved by retrofitting existing installations.

The levels of renewable energy development indicated by this scenario represent a tiny fraction of the technical potential for renewable energy. Higher levels might be pursued, for example, if society were to seek greater reductions in CO_2 emissions. The scenario presented here is based on stringent standard economic criteria, without including a value for the benefits indicated in table 11.1. Cost reductions through research and development and "learning curve" effects would permit a higher utilization, under the same economic criteria.

A renewables-intensive energy future would introduce new choices and competition in energy markets. Growing trade in renewable fuels and natural gas would diversify the mix of suppliers and the products traded (see fig. 11.4), which would increase competition and reduce the likelihood of rapid price fluctuations and supply disruptions. It could also lead eventually to a stabilization of world energy prices. In addition, new opportunities for energy suppliers would be created. Especially promising are prospects for trade in alcohol fuels, such as methanol derived from biomass. Land-rich countries in sub-Saharan Africa and Latin America could become major alcohol fuel exporters.

Conventional fuels

By making efficient use of energy and expanding the use of renewable technologies, the world can expect to have adequate supplies of fossil fuels well into the twenty-first century. However, in some instances regional declines in fossil fuel production can be expected because of resource constraints.

Oil production outside the Middle East would decline slowly under the renewables-intensive scenario, so that one-third of the estimated ultimately recoverable conventional resources will remain in the ground in 2050. As a result, non-Middle Eastern oil production would drop from 103 EJ/yr in 1985 to 31 EJ/yr in 2050. To meet the demand for liquid fuels that cannot be met by renewables, oil production is assumed to increase in the Middle East, from 24 EJ/yr in 1985 to 34 EJ/yr in 2050. Total world conventional oil resources would decline from about 9,900 EJ in 1988 to 4,300 EJ in 2050.

Although remaining conventional natural gas resources are comparable to those for conventional oil, natural gas is presently produced globally at just half the rate for oil. With adequate investment in pipelines and other infrastructure components, natural gas could be a major energy source for many years. In the decades ahead, substantial increases in natural gas production are feasible for all regions of the world except for the United States and OECD Europe. For the United States and OECD Europe, where resources are more limited, production would decline slowly, so that one-third of these regions' natural gas resources will remain in 2050. In aggregate, natural gas production outside the Middle East would increase slowly, from 62 EJ/yr in 1985 to 75 EJ/yr in 2050. However, in the Middle East, where natural gas resources are enormous and largely unexploited, production would expand more than 12-fold, to 33 EJ/yr in 2050. Globally, about half the conventional natural gas resources would remain in 2050.

The renewables-intensive scenario was developed for future fuel prices that are significantly lower than those used in most long-term energy forecasts. It is expected that in the decades ahead the world oil price would rise only modestly and the price of natural gas would approach the oil price (which implies that the natural gas price paid by electricity utilities would roughly double). There are two primary reasons for expecting relatively modest energy price increases: first, overall demand for fuels would grow comparatively slowly between 1985 and 2050 because of assumed increases in the efficiency of energy use; and, secondly, renewable fuels could probably be produced at costs that would make them competitive with petroleum at oil prices not much higher than at present.

4. Public policy issues

A renewables-intensive global energy future is technically feasible, and the prospects are excellent that a wide range of new renewable-energy technologies will become fully competitive with conventional sources of energy during the next several decades. Yet the transition to renewables will not occur at the pace envisaged if existing market conditions remain unchanged. Private companies are unlikely to make the investments necessary to develop renewable technologies because the benefits are distant and not easily captured by individual firms. Moreover, private firms will not invest in large volumes of commercially available renewable-energy technologies because renewable-energy costs will usually not be significantly lower than the costs of conventional energy. And, finally, the private sector will not invest in commercially available technologies to the extent justified by the external benefits (e.g. a stabilized world oil price or reduced greenhouse gas emissions) that would arise from their widespread deployment. If these problems are not addressed, renewable energy will enter the market relatively slowly.

Fortunately, the policies needed to achieve the twin goals of increasing efficiency and expanding markets for renewable energy are fully consistent with programmes needed to encourage innovation and productivity growth throughout the economy. Given the right policy environment, energy industries will adopt innovations, driven by the same competitive pressures that have revitalized other major manufacturing businesses around the world.

Electricity utilities will have to shift from being protected monopolies enjoying economies of scale in large generating plants to being competitive managers of investment portfolios that combine a diverse set of technologies, ranging from advanced generation, transmission, distribution, and storage equipment to efficient energy-using devices on customers' premises.

Automobile and truck manufacturers, and the businesses that supply fuels for these vehicles, will need to develop entirely new products. A range of new fuel and vehicle types, including fuel-cell vehicles powered by alcohol or hydrogen, are likely to play major roles in transportation in the next century.

Capturing the potential for renewables requires new policy initiatives. The following policy initiatives are proposed to encourage innovation and investment in renewable technologies:

- Subsidies that artificially reduce the price of fuels that compete with renewables should be removed; if existing subsidies cannot be removed for political reasons, renewable-energy technologies should be given equivalent incentives.
- Taxes, regulations, and other policy instruments should ensure that consumer decisions are based on the full cost of energy, including environmental and other external costs not reflected in market prices.
- Government support for research on and development and demonstration of renewable-energy technologies should be increased to reflect the critical roles renewable-energy technologies can play in meeting energy, developmental, and environmental objectives. This should be carried out in close cooperation with the private sector.
- Government regulation of electricity utilities should be carefully reviewed to ensure that investments in new generating equipment are consistent with a renewables-intensive future and that utilities are involved in programmes to demonstrate new renewable-energy technologies in their service territories.
- Policies designed to encourage the development of a biofuels industry must be closely coordinated with both national agricultural development programmes and efforts to restore degraded lands.
- National, regional, and international institutions should be created or strengthened to implement renewable-energy programmes.
- International development funds available for the energy sector should be directed increasingly to renewables.
- A strong international institution should be created to assist and coordinate national and regional programmes for increased use of renewables, to support the assessment of energy options, and to support centres of excellence in specialized areas of renewable-energy research.

There are many ways such policies could be implemented. The preferred policy instruments will vary with the level of the initiative (national, regional, and/or international). The preferred options will reflect differences in endowments of renewable resources, stages of economic development, and cultural characteristics.

The traditional approach of market introduction involves the identification and addressing of niche markets, where the comparative advantages of the new technology are the most valuable, leading to experience being gained and costs reduced. An interesting alternative approach has been suggested, where the "learning curve" of photovoltaics is extended into the future. Williams and Terzian (1993) observe that a sufficiently large investment now would bring costs down much faster than for a niche market approach, and would, in fact, be an economically advantageous proposition.

The integrating theme for all such initiatives, however, should be an energy policy aimed at promoting sustainable development. It will not be possible to provide the energy needed to bring a decent standard of living to the world's poor or to sustain the economic well-being of the industrialized countries in environmentally acceptable ways, if the present energy course continues. The path to a sustainable society requires more efficient energy use and a shift to a variety of renewable-energy sources.

Although not all renewables are inherently clean, there is such a diversity of choices that a shift to renewables carried out in the context of sustainable development could provide a far cleaner energy system than would be feasible by tightening controls on conventional energy.

The central challenge to policy makers in the decades ahead is to frame economic policies that simultaneously satisfy both socio-economic developmental and environmental challenges. This analysis demonstrates the enormous contribution that renewable-energy can make in addressing this challenge. It provides a strong case that carefully crafted policies can provide a powerful impetus to the development and widespread use of renewable-energy technologies and can lead ultimately to a world that meets critical socio-economic, developmental, and environmental objectives.

Acknowledgements

This paper draws heavily on work done together with Henry Kelly, Amulya Reddy, and Robert Williams, which has been published in Johansson et al. (1993).

Notes

1. In this study, the term "biomass" refers to any plant matter used directly as fuel or converted into fluid fuels or electricity. Sources of biomass are diverse and include the wastes of agricultural and forest-product operations as well as wood, sugar cane, and other plants grown specifically as energy crops.
2. The regions are Africa, Latin America, South and East Asia, centrally planned Asia, Japan, Australia/New Zealand, the United States, Canada, OECD Europe, former centrally planned Europe, and the Middle East.
3. Assumptions about the cost and performance of future renewable-energy equipment are based on detailed analyses of technologies in Johansson et al. (1993: chaps. 2–22).
4. For example, per capita energy use in OECD Europe is currently about 20 per cent less than in Eastern Europe and the former Soviet Union. In the accelerated policies scenario, per capita energy demand declines in OECD Europe and increases 60 per cent by 2050 in Eastern Europe and the former Soviet Union. In light of the rapid economic and political changes now under way, it is doubtful that these two regions will take such divergent paths.

References

Cavallo, A. J. 1994. "High capacity factor wind turbine-transmission systems." Paper presented at the 13th ASME Wind Energy Symposium, Energy Sources Technology Conference, 23–26 January.

Elliott, P. and R. Booth. 1993. *Brazilian Biomass Power Demonstration Project*. Shell Special Project Brief, September.

Grubb, M. J. and N. I. Meyer. 1993. "Wind energy: Resources, systems and regional strategies." In: T. B. Johansson, H. Kelly, A. K. N. Reddy, and R. H. Williams (eds.), *Renewable Energy: Sources for Fuels and Electricity*. Washington, D.C.: Island Press.

Hall, D. O., F. Rosilio-Calle, R. H. Williams, and J. Woods. 1993. "Biomass for energy: Supply prospects." In: T. B. Johansson, H. Kelly, A. K. N. Reddy, and R. H. Williams (eds.), *Renewable Energy: Sources for Fuels and Electricity*. Washington, D.C.: Island Press.

Jackson, T. (ed.). 1993. *Renewable Energy: Prospects for Implementation*. Stockholm Environment Institute.

Johansson, T. B., H. Kelly, A. K. N. Reddy, and R. H. Williams (eds.). 1993. *Renewable Energy: Sources for Fuels and Electricity*. Washington, D.C.: Island Press.

Kelly, H. and C. J. Weinberg. 1993. "Utility strategies for using renewables." In: T. B. Johansson, H. Kelly, A. K. N. Reddy, and R. H. Williams (eds.), *Renewable Energy: Sources for Fuels and Electricity*. Washington, D.C.: Island Press.

Moreira, J. R. and A. D. Poole. 1993. "Hydropower and its constraints." In: T. B. Johansson, H. Kelly, A. K. N. Reddy, and R. H. Williams (eds.), *Renewable Energy: Sources for Fuels and Electricity*. Washington, D.C.: Island Press.

Williams, R. H. and G. Terzian. 1993. *A Benefit/Cost Analysis of Accelerated Development of Photovoltaic Technology*. PU/CEES Report No. 281, Princeton University, October.

World Energy Council. 1993. *Renewable Energy Resources: Opportunities and Constraints 1990–2020*. London: World Energy Council, September.

World Energy Council Commission. 1993. *Energy for Tomorrow's World*. London: Kogan Page.

12

Energy efficiency: New approaches to technology transfer

William U. Chandler and Marc R. Ledbetter with Igor Bashmakov and Jessica Hamburger

1. Introduction

This paper considers the energy efficiency potential and the priorities for technology in Eastern Europe, the former Soviet Union, and China. These regions are interesting because they produce a combined total of one-third of global energy-related carbon dioxide emissions, and they are undergoing rapid changes of energy and economic policy.

Energy efficiency technology transfer is often cited as a high priority in international development cooperation programmes for Eastern Europe, the former Soviet Union, and China. This priority is warranted by the fact that energy efficiency improvements bring multiple benefits. Efficiency can reduce energy bills for consumers, reduce the capital required for energy system development, and reduce pollutants, including the oxides of carbon, sulphur, and nitrogen. Efficiency, in fact, is perhaps the clearest example of a *sustainable development* strategy because it is the one strategy that contributes to development by providing higher levels of employment, higher standards of living, and better working and environmental conditions.

Igor Bashmakov and Jessica Hamburger contributed sections of this report. William Chandler and Marc Ledbetter are responsible for the integrated piece, its validity or errors.

The three formerly centrally planned regions rank high in energy intensity – no matter how economic output is measured. If we consider rationalization of these economies through restructuring as well as technological energy efficiency improvements, the efficiency potential in the regions is large indeed. Rapid economic and political change in these regions may thus presage major reductions in energy intensity, though this improvement will be offset to some extent by increases in energy used for personal consumption. That trade-off is the subject of a different paper.

Market restructuring is, of course, the first priority for rationalizing energy use in these countries. No other measure to improve the efficiency with which energy is used will have as large an effect. But market restructuring is not enough. Experience in market economies tells us that markets leave vast untapped cost-effective resources of energy efficiency. Strong non-market measures are often proposed to supplement markets, including imposing heavy energy taxes and high performance standards on energy-using equipment. However, it has become increasingly clear that such measures are not always politically feasible. Nor are they always appropriate. Therefore, additional approaches are needed that provide strong incentives to producers and consumers to improve energy efficiency, including measures such as market-pull programmes, integrated resources planning, demand-side management, financing, and partnership between government, non-governmental organizations (NGOs), and business to stimulate efficiency investments.

2. Energy efficiency prospects in three key regions

Eastern Europe

The nations of Eastern Europe rank among the least energy-efficient countries in the world. Per capita energy use in the former Czechoslovakia, for example, exceeds that of Austria, yet former Czechoslovakian GNP per capita is only one-third as high as Austria's (Kostalova et al., 1992). It is this excessive, uncontrolled energy use that more than anything else causes severe air, land, and water pollution in the immediate region. The region, with less than 3 per cent of the world's population, produces 9 per cent of global energy-related greenhouse gas emissions – almost as much as China.

Energy inefficiency constrains economic growth. Consider the case of Poland, which is the world's fourth-largest coal producer and which meets three-quarters of its domestic energy demand with coal. Poland in 1985 allocated one-third of its entire annual industrial capital budget to coal mining alone. Coal production in Poland before the revolution consumed one-fifth of all steel used in the country and nearly one-tenth of all electric power. Coal production is becoming more difficult and expensive year by year as the resource is being depleted. The average depth of mines is now 600 metres, and the required depth of new mines is increasing at a rate of 10–20 metres per year. Reducing the demand for coal simultaneously frees capital for more productive uses elsewhere in the economy (Sitnicki et al., 1990).

The nations of Eastern Europe have had varying degrees of success in reducing their burdens of energy intensity. Poland, as a result of strict price decontrol measures, cut energy intensity by 11 per cent between 1988 and 1990, more than any other East European nation. Energy intensity in the former Soviet Union, in contrast, has increased (Bashmakov, 1992a; see also Makarov et al., 1990).

GDP, unfortunately, dropped dramatically in Poland until 1992. (In 1992 Poland's economy grew at a rate of 5 per cent, faster than any other in Europe.) However, energy use has fallen faster than the economy. Consequently, the amount of capital allocated to energy production has dropped markedly since the economic reforms began, owing primarily to structural change. The share of capital allocated to coal is down from almost 40 per cent of industrial investment to just over 20 per cent. A smaller share of investment for the energy sector means that Poland's crumbling infrastructure – poor telephone service, lack of health care facilities, inadequate public transportation – will suffer less from the misallocation of capital seen for the last 50 years.

Poland has won these gains the hard way – in part by imposing an extremely rapid rate of adjustment to world prices on its citizens. Its policy represents extraordinary political courage. Consider the following changes in energy prices in Poland in 1991–1992 (Slawomir Pasierb, executive director, Polish Energy Efficiency Centre):
– the price of residential natural gas has increased 1,600 per cent;
– the price of residential electricity has increased 1,000 per cent;
– the price of gas to Polish industry has reached US levels.

The price of residential electricity is now at 5 US cents per kilowatt hour, close to the actual cost and equal to the price paid by many US residential customers. Yet annual per capita income in Poland is one-quarter that of the United States. In two years, Poland has made the transition from highly subsidized energy to free prices. In comparison, the United States took 10 years to accomplish the same thing.

In Hungary, energy prices have reached world market levels. The price of gasoline in Hungary, in fact, is twice as high as in the United States. The economy has also fallen dramatically, in 1991 reaching only 70 per cent of the 1988 level. The Hungarian economy is lower in energy intensity than those of other East European nations, however, because it began energy price reform over a decade ago and uses oil and gas, which are easier to use efficiently than coal, to a greater extent. The nation imports about 60 per cent of its total energy supply, primarily oil and natural gas. Hungary is an export-oriented economy, and thus can earn the foreign currency now necessary for purchasing oil and gas (Jaszay, 1990).

The situation has evolved somewhat more slowly elsewhere in Eastern Europe. The Czech Republic, like Poland, is plagued by heavy reliance on coal, which, with lignite, supplies over two-thirds of total energy use. The economy has undergone much slower market reform than in Poland, and prices remain controlled. Nevertheless, restructuring is under way, with prices hundreds of times higher for industrial natural gas and electricity than in 1989. In 1991, Czech and Slovak GDP was 20 per cent below the 1989 level. Similarly, Bulgaria's economy dropped by 11 per cent in 1991, and the number of jobs fell by 14 per cent. Inflation reached 72 per cent on an annual basis. Food now costs about 40 per cent of average household disposable income (Bulgarian Agency for Economic Coordination and Development, 1992). And three-fifths of the Bulgarian industrial sector is operating at less than half of capacity owing to shortages of energy. The nation recently imported 70 per cent of its energy from the former Soviet Union (Dempsey, 1992).

Romania remains far behind the rest of Eastern Europe in economic and energy reform. The nation's economic and political infrastructure still suffers from the legacy of the Ceaușescu regime. In the electricity sector, power shortages remain common and the quality of power is so badly degraded that the frequency drops from the standard 50 Hz to 47.5 Hz. Chronic energy and power shortages since 1980 resulted in the disconnection of the power grid from that of the Council for Mutual Economic Assistance (Comecon). To keep the system operating, the national dispatcher had to resort frequently to brownouts and blackouts, with the brunt of shortages borne by domestic consumers and public lighting even though industry accounted for two-thirds of power use. Present policy, however, is now oriented more toward consumers, and the energy deficit is borne by industry. The present shortage of electric energy supply amounts to 30 gigawatt hours per day – over 40 per cent of total electric power use (Gheorge, 1992).

The energy efficiency potential in Eastern Europe amounts to 15–25 per cent of current energy use. With consumption at about 16 exajoules (EJ), this means that up to 4 EJ of savings is available. The carbon emissions reduction that would be achieved by capturing this potential would total 80 million tons.

Future energy use in Eastern Europe – or in any post-planned economy – is exceedingly difficult to project. In general, future demand will depend on two broad factors: the extent of economic restructuring and the application of modern energy efficiency technology. Without restructuring, economic growth is likely to be anaemic. With restructuring and with energy productivity improvements, growing incomes are likely to push up consumption in the residential and transportation sectors, offsetting demand reductions in the industrial sector. One study suggested that a combination of economic reform and the introduction of energy efficiency technology, however, could enable Eastern Europe to hold energy demand – and carbon emissions – virtually constant (Kolar and Chandler, 1990). However, much more work is needed to clarify the future of energy demand in the region.

The former Soviet Union

The former Soviet Union overall consumes three-quarters as much energy as the United States, yet produces only 30–50 per cent as much economic value. The economy of that region has experienced collapse equal to the Great Depression in the United States in 1929. GDP in the former Soviet republics fell 15 per cent in 1991 and 10–20 per cent more in 1992 – all the way back to 1970 levels (Bashmakov, 1992b).[1] This crisis translates into hardship for 90 million persons – 30 per cent of all former Soviets – who now live below the official poverty line.

Unfortunately, the economic crisis has not yet produced energy efficiency improvements; the energy intensity of the Soviet economy has in fact increased. This problem is explained by the fact that the light manufacturing sector has been hit hard by the reduction in imports, which provided spare parts and other essential inputs, whereas the energy-intensive heavy materials sector has not been affected as much.

High energy intensity in the former Soviet Union is not due to high levels of energy use by consumers, however. Russians live in small apartments: they enjoy only 15 m^2 of household space per capita, compared with 30 and 55 m^2 for West Europeans and Americans, respectively. Electric power consumption per capita in the region is 70 per cent of US levels, but actual direct consumption by consumers is only 10 per cent that of the average US citizen.[2] Similarly in the transportation sector, residents of the former Soviet Union rely heavily on mass transportation.

High Soviet energy intensity grew primarily out of the skewed emphasis on heavy industry and energy-intensive materials, as well as reliance on outdated technology. The buildings sector also lacks individual heating controls in apartments, and all sectors lack economic incentives to conserve heat and hot water. Heavy energy supply investments have become excessive and reduce economic growth. The total annual investments in oil, natural gas, and coal production have reached almost 20 per cent of all investment and 40 per cent of industrial investment.

Restructuring the Soviet economy would have major benefits for energy conservation. Materials use per capita is very high compared with other nations, and market reforms would have two effects. First, less scrap and unnecessary material would be produced. Secondly, materials would be used more efficiently in manufacturing, construction, and packaging as manufacturers compete for price-sensitive markets. Structural reform could save 11 EJ by 2010, or almost one-sixth of current total Soviet energy demand.

The potential energy savings the former Soviet Union could achieve by implementing energy efficiency measures is over 15 EJ (15 quads, or 7.5 million barrels of oil equivalent per day). The largest savings are available in the energy, industrial, and agricultural sectors. The investment required to achieve these potential energy savings is estimated at US$4–6 billion.

Energy consumers would profit substantially from investments in energy-efficiency improvement projects. Potentially avoided capital investments total up to 1.8 trillion roubles (mid-1992 values). In addition, atmospheric pollution could be reduced 10 per cent, including a significant decrease in greenhouse emissions at no additional capital cost.

According to research by Igor Bashmakov, every rouble invested in the production of energy efficiency equipment produces – throughout the economy – five times more jobs than a rouble invested in electricity generation, and seven times more than a rouble invested in the oil and gas industry. Therefore, 29 billion roubles in investments in energy would create as many jobs as 175 billion roubles in energy supply (mid-1992 roubles) (Centre for Energy Efficiency, Moscow, 1992). The difference between 29 and 175 billion roubles of investments represents 40 per cent of the total capital accumulated in residential buildings. In other words, energy efficiency measures could free resources to improve living conditions substantially for the Russian population. If a share of the investment savings were to go to production in light and food industries and residential buildings construction, then simultaneously more jobs would be created and production of consumer goods would increase, resulting in a better level of well-being in the former Soviet Union.

Full implementation of the wide range of energy efficiency improvements with very low costs could reduce CO_2 emissions by 200 million tons of carbon in the former Soviet Union alone in the year 2005, the equivalent of annual CO_2 emissions in France and Italy together. It would be very difficult to find any other country with so large and so cheap a carbon conservation potential and with a relatively well-educated labour force capable of developing and realizing programmes to capture this potential.

China

China has become the world's third-largest energy consumer, using 30.4 EJ in 1991. Consumption and domestic production increased by 5 per cent a year during the 1980s (Wang Qingyi, 1992). As in many developing or planned economies, the industrial sector dominates consumption. In 1991, China's energy was used in the following manner:

    industry – over 68%
    buildings – about 20%
    transportation – about 6%
    agriculture – about 5%

Energy consumption per unit of GNP (energy intensity) in China is twice the average level of other developing countries, and three times that of Western Europe (Zhang Aling, 1992).

Economic reforms begun in 1978 and accelerated since 1990 have led to tremendous growth in energy use and significant changes in China's energy management system. The rest of the economy grew much faster than the energy sector, however, causing energy demand to outstrip supply, especially in power production. During the 1980s, 5 per cent annual growth of energy production and consumption lagged behind explosive economic growth, which averaged 9 per cent per year over the decade, and reached 14.1 per cent in 1992.

A striking characteristic of China's energy economy is low per capita consumption. In 1990, commercial energy consumption per capita in China was only about 25.5 gigajoules (GJ), about 40 per cent of the world average, and less than one-tenth that of the United States. Space heating is prohibited or sharply restricted in large areas of China in order to conserve fuel for industry.

Environmental pollution remains a major problem with and challenge for China's energy industry. Coal combustion, which supplies three-quarters of China's energy needs, is the largest source of emissions. Whereas most countries convert coal to electricity, many Chinese consumers use coal directly, even for household cooking and heating. Excessive, inefficient coal use contributes to a range of global, regional, and local environmental problems.

China still faces severe energy shortages and severe energy-related environmental damage. Energy shortages are caused by a combination of low energy prices, use of inefficient technologies and management practices, rapid economic growth, transportation bottlenecks, and emphasis on energy-intensive industries, such as cement and steel. Insufficient energy supply prevented enterprises from operating at full capacity and caused economic losses. In 1988, 25 per cent of industrial enterprises were operating at low capacity and one-third of the agricultural sector suffered from severe power shortages, resulting in a 400 billion yuan loss in output value.

China made the following gains in energy efficiency in the 1980s (Shen Longhai and Zhou Changyi, 1992):

- Energy consumption per 10,000 yuan of GNP fell from 392 GJ in 1980 to 273 GJ in 1990. Energy intensity decreased by 30 per cent over the decade, an annual average rate of 3.5 per cent. The accumulated energy savings were 7.9 EJ.
- The income elasticity of energy demand was 0.56 during the 1980s. That is, almost half of the incremental growth in the national economy was made possible by energy conservation. Elasticity was reduced by two-thirds compared with the previous 25 years.

• Energy efficiency improvements were achieved in two-thirds of industrial products examined in a government survey. Examples include the production of coal-fired power, steel, cement, aluminium, fertilizer, and crude oil processing.

In addition to price reform and ownership changes, the Chinese government also initiated policies to promote energy efficiency directly. Conservation was formally introduced into China's national economic plan in 1981. Laws and regulations were passed, and the State Planning Commission (SPC) undertook a study of energy consumption and the potential for conservation by enterprises (Shen Longhai and Zhou Changyi, 1992). Efficiency standards were set for a wide range of products, although they currently serve as guidelines, not enforceable regulations.

Funds were allocated to energy efficiency projects, and project implementation procedures were established. Projects are administered by the Energy Conservation Company, part of the State Energy Investment Corporation. The Energy Conservation Company reviews projects, provides soft loans, tax exemptions, and equipment, and solicits matching funds from local governments.

China's conservation measures focused on industry, which consumed almost 19.8 EJ in 1990. Measures were aimed specifically at the chemical, iron and steel, and building materials industries, each of which accounts for about 15 per cent of total industrial energy use, and on widely used equipment such as industrial boilers, fans, and pumps (Wang Qingyi, 1992). The main measures adopted were equipment retrofit; elimination of inefficient equipment; restrictions on wasteful and environmentally harmful production methods; adoption of efficiency standards; utilization of new energy conservation materials and equipment, such as computers to monitor consumption; waste recovery and utilization; and co-generation.

In fertilizer production, for example, significant energy savings were achieved by installing new equipment, using a new method to synthesize ammonia, and using electronic process controls. Large savings were also achieved in the steel industry through the adoption of various energy-efficient technologies and co-generation. Boilers were also made cleaner and more efficient through design changes; the use of co-generation, briquettes, and control mechanisms; and the adoption of fluidized bed and dust removal technology. Large efficiency gains can be made simply by replacing equipment designed and/or made in the 1950s, 1960s, and 1970s with more recent designs.

256

In many cases, the more advanced designs already exist in China, but need to be popularized.

Energy planners in China are pushing for more reforms to promote economic and energy efficiency and environmental protection. Technical assistance can help China implement these reforms by supporting Chinese energy experts and by promoting joint ventures and foreign investment in energy efficiency technologies and services. Assistance in energy efficiency will improve the market for developed nation exports; reduce global carbon emissions; minimize energy-related pollution in China; and accelerate social progress and the development of a market economy in China.

The efficiency potential in China must be viewed in terms of how much future demand *growth* can be reduced. One major study of this potential suggested that year 2025 demand could be cut from a projected level of 75 EJ to 50 EJ (Sathaye and Goldman, 1991).

3. Technology needs

Technological energy efficiency opportunities in the former Soviet Union, Eastern Europe, and China include the use of efficient electric motors; adjustable speed drives for electric motors; automation of and greater use of sensors and controls in industrial processes; advanced boiler controls; combined-cycle power co-generation and other advanced power generation technologies; more sophisticated and improved lighting and refrigeration technologies; and thermal insulation and improved windows in buildings. In the district heating and electric power sector, transmission and distribution losses remain high, and new combined-cycle technologies could eventually cut heat rates in generating plants by 30 per cent or more. Major opportunities also exist in the use of heat meters and thermostatic valves for controlling radiators. More efficient trucks and automobiles are a high priority as the transportation sector grows with increasing income.

Recent developments in energy conversion technologies make possible the cleaner and more efficient use of fossil fuels. These same systems will reduce the cost of renewable energy to competitive levels, thus permitting large reductions in fossil and nuclear energy use over the coming decades (see Chandler, 1990; see also Johansson et al., 1993). These new technologies rely on combined-cycle and gas-turbine system generation of electricity, usually coupled with the use of natural gas or the gasification of coal or biomass. Using Soviet gas in the short term and renewable resources in the longer term would enable the regions to reduce both their economic and environmental costs. Existing gas turbine systems could improve the thermal efficiency of electricity generation from about 30 per cent in the region to 40–50 per cent (Chandler et al., 1990).

Gas turbines could also be used in the short term to take advantage of coal-bed methane. Coal seams in Poland and the former Czechoslovakia are very gassy – that is, they emit large volumes of methane. Tapping this methane before the coal is mined could produce up to 1 EJ (the equivalent of 500,000 barrels of oil per day) in Poland and the former Czechoslovakia. Doing so would make mines safer, reduce gas imports, and reduce emissions of a powerful greenhouse gas to the atmosphere. The US government is actively supporting exploitation of this resource in Eastern Europe and China and, more recently, in Russia.[3]

In China, efforts to improve technology have been targeted mainly on the industrial sector, which accounts for over two-thirds of energy demand. Within this sector, the chief energy consumers are the chemical industry, the iron and steel industry, and the building materials industry. China encouraged the adoption of energy-efficient technologies in these three industries and pushed for the use of efficient boilers, fans, and pumps in all industries. Technology upgrades were facilitated by the establishment of over 200 provincial and local energy efficiency centres. The centres are staffed by about 5,000 technical experts who provide energy audits, technical assistance, and training.

These gains were relatively easy because of China's extremely low efficiency rates, and there is still much room for improvement. In 1988, China consumed at least three times more energy for each unit of economic output than did Japan. Future efficiency gains will be more difficult because they will depend on improvements in management and technological efficiency, not simply on economic restructuring.

4. Policy

Eastern Europe

Energy waste and inefficiency are so widespread that opportunities for improving efficiency abound in nearly every sector and for nearly every end use in Eastern Europe. The limited availability of resources and, just as importantly, the timing of major capital investments and the needs of economically pressed citizens dictate a focused effort. Among the more important considerations that should drive policy focus in Poland are:

• What uses of energy are subject to radical change as a result of economic restructuring, and what is the probability that energy efficiency investments in those uses will be stranded as a result of restructuring? What can be done to reduce this probability?
• What large investments are being made, or will soon be made, in equipment and structures that will significantly affect Poland's energy consumption?
• Because the huge energy price increases that have been imposed on Polish consumers are causing significant hardship, what cost-effective, near-term measures are available to reduce this hardship through improved energy efficiency?
• Where is the market not working well in improving energy efficiency, and what would make it work better?

On the basis of these considerations and others, and on the basis of the particulars of the Polish energy economy, several policy priorities emerge.

Among the more important is application of integrated resources planning (IRP) in the electricity sector. IRP is a flexible planning framework that fairly compares end-use efficiency and load management resources (demand-side management resources, or DSM) against a wide range of supply-side resources. A plan produced through this process will recommend a path for acquiring both supply- and demand-side investments to meet energy needs at the lowest possible costs, considering the risks, reliability, and environmental costs of the resources. Including low-cost DSM resources typically results in large savings over traditional utility planning methods.

A sound integrated resource plan, with a strong DSM component, would help Poland guide the investment of a new US$1 billion power sector loan being negotiated with the World Bank, and would potentially save hundreds of millions of dollars. With the assistance of the US Agency for International Development and the government of Austria, Poland is now preparing such a plan (RCG/Hagler Bailly, 1993).

Application of IRP in the heating sector also holds great promise. As in the electricity sector, Poland's district heating systems are facing large capital investments for repair and upgrading. Before pouring huge sums of capital into systems that have been sized to meet the load in poorly insulated and controlled buildings, it is important to consider the cost-effectiveness of improving these buildings to reduce the heat load on the systems, and thereby take advantage of smaller and less expensive system capacity requirements.

Providing consumers with access to capital is an important policy option. Energy-efficiency loan funds can be created for use by utilities and major industries through revenues from fuel taxes or loans from multilateral development banks. Blocks of financing could be channelled to utilities for distribution to residential, commercial, and industrial consumers through DSM programmes. In the industrial sector, loans could be made available to enterprises for investments increasing energy efficiency in addition to output or productivity. Experience has shown that disbursing such loans requires technical assistance, including:
- energy audits for industry and buildings;
- IRP specialists to advise utilities;
- loan-processing training for banking, utility, and industrial organizations.

Building domestic capability in the manufacture and installation of energy-efficient equipment and materials is also a high priority. East Europeans still depend heavily on domestically produced equipment and materials, but unfortunately these products typically have much lower energy performance than do competing foreign-produced products. Because the foreign products remain significantly more expensive than their domestically produced counterparts (often two to four times more expensive), potential energy savings from more efficient products are usually forgone in favour of much lower purchase prices. The result is a continuing flow of inefficient products into the marketplace. The unfortunate trade-off between very high first costs and energy efficiency need not continue. A concerted effort to encourage the development of domestic capability for producing energy-efficient products, which could take advantage of domestic low-cost labour and materials, is an attractive option for reducing energy consumption, supporting domestic industry, and positioning domestic companies to compete better with foreign producers.

An effective means of speeding development of domestic production capability is to help domestic producers develop markets for their products through "market-pull" programmes that, through a variety of mechanisms, substantially increase the market demand for their products. Market-pull mechanisms might include voluntary efforts in which large consumers and other interested parties offer financial incentives to producers to help cover the development costs of new energy-efficient products.

The Super-Efficient Refrigerator Program in the United States is an example of this type of programme. Also known as a "golden carrot" programme, this programme offered US$30 million in prize money to the winner of a competition among refrigerator manufacturers to produce and sell a refrigerator that consumed no more energy than 75 per cent of the level allowed by the 1993 US refrigerator energy efficiency standard. The programme was created by the Natural Resources Defense Council, the US Environmental Protection Agency, and a group of two dozen utilities. The prize money was provided by the electricity utilities. The winner of the competition was the Whirlpool Corporation, which proposed a refrigerator that uses no CFCs, sacrifices nothing in service, and costs buyers no more than standard models with comparable features (Treece, 1993).

An example of domestic capability building in energy efficiency is already under development in the Polish lighting products industry. The International Finance Corporation is developing a project that is intended to help build the Polish market for domestically produced compact fluorescent lamps. If approved, the project will use funds from the Global Environmental Facility of the World Bank to provide rebates to Polish producers of these lamps. The rebates are targeted at producers rather than consumers so that wholesale and retail mark-ups are applied to a smaller base price, yielding a much lower retail price than would be possible with a consumer rebate. The very low price is expected to overcome the strong reluctance among Polish consumers to purchase a lamp that now exceeds the cost of an incandescent lamp by a factor of 20 to 30. Currently, the only domestic producer of compact fluorescent lamps is Philips Lighting Poland, a joint venture of Philips Lighting and Polam Pila, a Polish producer.

Other domestic production capability programmes should be considered for refrigerators, electric motors, variable-speed electric motor drives, insulation, energy-efficient windows, residential heating equipment, industrial boilers, energy management systems, and other equipment and materials whose domestic producers could make a substantial contribution to domestic energy saving. Much of this capability building could be achieved through the development of joint ventures with non-domestic producers of energy-efficient equipment and materials, but special efforts, such as targeted deal brokering, are needed to speed the creation of the joint ventures.

Consumer information – in the form of appliance energy efficiency labelling – helps overcome a major market failure. New appliances can be labelled for energy efficiency so that buyers can cut their future energy costs. The programme fits within a philosophy of promoting market mechanisms because it promotes the availability of impartial and credible information, a legitimate activity of all forms of government. Most important energy-consuming appliances made or sold in the United States (including refrigerators, water heaters, furnaces, air conditioners, and lighting) must carry labels advising buyers on the energy cost of their operation as well as to meet standards for maximum rates of energy consumption. The European Community, led by Denmark, is actively considering energy efficiency label requirements. Some highly efficient lighting products marketed in Europe already bear annual energy-cost labels. Labelling would help push manufacturers to produce competitive products, and ensure that inefficient products are not "dumped" on the region by foreign exporters.

Of less importance now, but of enormous importance within the next 10 years, are policies to promote energy efficiency in the transportation sector. The countries of Eastern Europe have levels of public transit ridership that most Western countries can only dream about. More than 80 per cent of workers in Prague and Warsaw commute to work by public transportation. These passenger levels are at risk though. Rising incomes and the ease, flexibility, and convenience of commuting by car are pulling people out of public transportation and into cars. Warsaw and Budapest are already experiencing large traffic jams. Warsaw's city centre sidewalks are jammed with cars that make walking difficult. Financially pressed public transit systems, whose fare increases have been tightly controlled, have had difficulty maintaining their level of service. Warsaw's public transit system is so hard pressed that it could not pay its electricity bill for six months in 1991. Should the trend continue, large East European cities could find themselves in the same predicament as their Western counterparts: rapidly growing suburban, low-density sprawl, falling transit ridership, traffic-caused heavy congestion and pollution, and huge transportation and land-use commitments to the automobile. East European nations need to take advantage of their low dependence on the automobile by working to keep public transportation efficient, convenient, and attractive. Keeping riders on public transportation is a far less daunting task than persuading drivers to abandon their vehicles and choose public transportation.

The former Soviet Union

Energy price decontrol in the former Soviet Union is under way. However, privatization and restructuring will take longer. These efforts have not worked well in Eastern Europe, and the new nations formed from the Soviet Union would do well to take this process in manageable steps. The key issue is competition, and competition can be engendered among state-owned enterprises during the transition to private property. The utility sector will require regulation because for the foreseeable future the supply of thermal and electric energy by utilities will remain monopolistic.

Western nations can aid the difficult transition for the new nations of the former Soviet Union in many ways. Macroeconomic assistance is vital; but so is microeconomic assistance. That is, the former Soviet Union will need help in financing energy efficiency measures, particularly the installation of new, highly efficient gas turbines for power generation. Billions in loan guarantees, with the promise of technical cooperation from the private sector, would probably be necessary to make this happen.

In the utility sector, integrated resources planning is a high priority (see Vine and Crawley, 1991). Low-cost exchanges of experts would help transfer this experience. Placing half a dozen foreign IRP specialists in utilities and bringing a similar number of former Soviets to the West would best facilitate this process. Demonstrations could be developed in IRP for a few tens of millions of dollars, and would have the effect, in the long run, of saving billions.

IRP could also be used to great effect in the district heating sector, where large, cost-effective demand-side resources should be allowed to compete against supply-side resources for new investments. Much of this demand-side resource can be developed with relatively *low-technology* measures.

The Russian Federation Ministry of Fuels and Energy and the Ministry of Sciences have articulated principles and mechanisms of government policy in energy efficiency. The main directions they recommend for improving energy efficiency are:
• developing basic energy efficiency legislation, including incentives for investment and standards for energy-consuming equipment; and
• developing a favourable economic environment, including soft

credits for efficiency investments and the creation of a regional loan fund (funded by a 1 per cent value-added tax on energy).

This programme is not particularly aggressive, and, in projections made by a policy group, energy intensity of the economy would not decline beyond the 1990 level even by the end of the century.

China

Despite the rapid expansion of energy production since 1978, per capita commercial energy consumption remains low. The combination of low per capita energy use, inefficient technologies, and an inefficient management system results in a low level of energy services. Chinese energy planners are pushing ahead with a variety of reforms in order to raise the level of energy services while minimizing environmental damage. Priorities include:

- increased importation of efficiency and environmental technologies and services;
- continuation of the break-up of monopoly energy corporations;
- elevation of energy prices to cover production costs and discourage inefficiency;
- elimination of subsidies to money-losing state energy enterprises; and
- integration of conservation and energy supply investment planning, functions that are currently carried out by separate government agencies.

Fundamental changes in China's economic system have already laid the groundwork for these reforms and have been responsible for rapid growth in the economy and in energy use. Since 1978, China has taken great strides away from central planning toward what Party Secretary Jiang Zemin calls a "socialist market economy." State ownership is on the decline as unprofitable state enterprises lose their subsidies and make way for new ventures in the booming non-state sector.

Reform has come later and slower to the energy sector, but appears to be gaining momentum. Energy price reform, ownership changes, and energy efficiency policies are the essential elements of China's attempt to bridge the gap between energy supply and demand.

China's pricing system has been transformed by the introduction of markets, decentralization, and price adjustments. China has created a "two-tier" pricing system as a step on the path to free markets. Under this system, the government gives state enterprises an incentive to increase production by allowing them to sell above-plan output at market prices. It has been estimated that in 1989, on average, 38 per cent of a state enterprise's outputs were sold on the market, and 56 per cent of its inputs were procured on the market (McMillan and Naughton, 1992).

Price reform is sorely needed in the energy sector because prices are too low to cover the cost of production. Irrational pricing has resulted in massive debt. The cumulative debt owed by public coal mines and utilities amounts to 100 billion yuan, and there is no way to pay off the debts within the existing management system (Zhou Dadi, 1992).

In the case of energy products, the pricing system has more than two tiers. For example, there are three crude oil prices in China: the low plan price, the high plan price, and the international market price. The low plan price for oil tripled in 1993, from around US$5 a barrel to US$16.30 a barrel. This price hike brings about two-thirds of China's oil closer to the international price, which is around US$21 a barrel. In addition to raising the low plan price, administrators have also decided that much of the oil formerly assigned to the low-price category will now be sold at the high plan price. The high plan price is actually higher than the international price now because of transportation bottlenecks (Goldstein, 1992). Coal prices have also risen significantly in the 1990s and may soon be deregulated.

Electricity prices are also affected by a variety of market and regulatory mechanisms. Prices are regulated for state-operated power plants and cost based for plants operated by investors, which may be local government, users, or semi-private corporations. The state plants still sell electricity at a relatively low plan price, although the price has been raised somewhat owing mostly to the rising cost of fuel. Non-state plants set prices by calculating interest and profit from the capital investment and operation costs. The price paid by the consumer is often much higher than the price set by the generator, however, because governments at the provincial, municipal, and county level may impose fees to raise funds for electricity development. In addition, all plants are allowed to sell electricity at a higher price if they exceed the planned target.

The shift from planned to market prices has been matched by a shift away from ownership by the central government. Ownership changes have been accomplished through collectivization of state enterprises and the growth of the non-state sector. The non-state sector has grown at an annual rate of 17.6 per cent. Some analysts claim that the non-state sector employed as much as 82 per cent of the total labour force and produced 64 per cent of China's GNP in 1990. Its share of total industrial output expanded from 22 per cent in 1978 to 45 per cent in 1990 (Chen Kang, 1992).

Energy conservation measures were financed through China's policy of replacing oil with coal for domestic use. Instituted at a time when international oil prices were high, this policy allowed China to use hard currency from oil exports to purchase foreign technology that was more energy efficient and to build more coal-fired power plants. The policy may soon be phased out, however, for both economic and environmental reasons. It has been undermined by the drop in oil prices, as well as by the recognition of coal's contribution to air pollution and global warming (Christoffersen, 1992).

If the coal-for-oil policy is abandoned, China will have to find other sources of funding for energy efficiency. One obvious method is for the central government to take funds that are currently designated for expanding supply and reallocate them to conservation. This is not likely to occur, however, until the government adopts a planning method that integrates supply and demand. Meanwhile, the central government has shifted the burden of increasing efficiency to enterprises and local governments. Yet these organizations will have little incentive to invest in efficiency without price reform – that is, the removal of all subsidies for energy prices.

Facilitating joint ventures in energy efficiency simultaneously helps developed nations' firms and promotes economic development and environmental protection in China. Those who are sceptical of the profitability of trade and investment in China might note that Hong Kong, Taiwan, Japan, and South Korea have already taken the lead in profiting from China's booming economy.

The developed nations can promote joint ventures through business information exchange and demonstration projects, and legislative support for energy efficiency policies in China. Information exchange helps foreign companies understand the Chinese market – how to do business, with whom they can collaborate, where siting their operations makes sense, how to conduct banking, how to get their money out of the country. One example of information exchange that has already been funded is the US Department of Energy's electric power mission to three major Chinese cities in June 1993. US participants represented independent power producers, regulated utilities, architectural and engineering firms, and equipment manufacturers. They met with Chinese counterparts to discuss opportunities for cooperation.

Facilitating demonstration projects in areas of foreign expertise is another good way to promote joint ventures. The US Environmental Protection Agency, for example, worked with China's Ministry of Energy to get World Bank Global Environmental Facility funding for a coal-bed methane demonstration project.

Technical assistance can also promote joint ventures through legislative and regulatory support for energy efficiency policies in China. Foreign firms cannot market their practices and technologies until the institutional and legal infrastructure in each country has been put in place. By helping Chinese experts promote IRP as a national policy, the West can increase demand for compact fluorescent light bulbs, metering systems, renewable energy assessments, and building efficiency technologies.

Energy policy must balance supply and demand measures to provide energy services for economic development while protecting consumers and the natural environment. A sustainable energy policy will promote economic development by:

- increasing industrial competitiveness by reducing net production costs;
- reducing net capital requirements by avoiding the need for new mines and power plants;
- improving overall productivity by promoting new technologies to increase labour and capital productivity while saving energy.

Such a policy would help consumers cope with rising energy prices by saving money through conservation. This strategy requires measures to overcome market failures, including: lack of information; split incentives; natural monopolies; and lack of capital due to the economic mismanagement of the former communist system.

Technology transfer will not proceed in any of the three regions without fundamental policy reform. Any rational energy policy must be based on market mechanisms, with limited intervention to regulate monopolies and overcome market failures. The basic mechanisms of a market-based strategy should include:

- market pricing of energy supplies;
- energy supply sector restructuring;
- privatization and re-regulation of transmission and distribution networks for electricity, gas, and heat supply enterprises;
- privatization of energy suppliers.

5. Conclusion

Technology transfer in the regions of the former Soviet Union, Eastern Europe, and China cannot be achieved without significant new efforts in the energy sector. Past energy policy has seriously harmed the region's economic and environmental health by encouraging the development of expensive, polluting supply alternatives for providing energy services. The establishment of market prices and freer markets should be the top energy policy priority for these countries, but adequate time should be allowed for their economies to adapt to these measures, and it should be recognized that market measures alone will not fully exploit the vast energy efficiency resources that exist. Among other policies and programmes that are needed to tap these resources, new models of technology transfer that aggressively promote both production and demand for new technologies are needed. By reorienting their policies to deliver cost-effective energy services through demand-side measures and, early in the next century, new renewable energy supply systems, the regions could achieve a healthier, more prosperous future. This strategy implies:

- moving, with appropriate speed, to establish market prices and freer markets for energy;
- where markets leave large, cost-effective energy efficiency resources untapped, adopting policies and programmes to improve energy efficiency to maximum cost-effective levels;
- to the extent possible, satisfying new energy demand in the medium term with natural gas; and
- developing renewable energy supplies over the long term.

The first element requires energy resources be priced to reflect both their replacement costs and their environmental impacts. The second element requires study and adaptation of the experience gained by other countries in exploiting energy efficiency resources. The third element requires careful development and use of natural gas resources in a way that will permit an easy transition to renewable energy carriers. And the fourth element must rely on a combination of Western research efforts and local measures for encouraging the market penetration of new energy sources.

Notes

1. US GDP fell from about US$1 trillion to US$0.75 trillion (1958 dollars) between 1930 and 1934.

268

2. Russian electricity consumption in 1990 totalled 7,031 kWh per capita, compared with about 10,600 kWh per capita in the United States.
3. Major reports on the potential for developing coal-bed methane have been sponsored by the US Environmental Protection Agency. See Bibler et al. (1992).

References

Bashmakov, I. 1992a. *Energy Conservation: The Main Factor for Reducing Greenhouse Gas Emissions in the Former Soviet Union*. Battelle Pacific Northwest Laboratories, January.
───── 1992b. "Energy conservation: Costs and benefits for the former USSR." Battelle Pacific Northwest Laboratories, March, draft.
Bibler, C., J. S. Marshall, and R. Pilcher. 1992. *Assessment of the Potential for Economic Development and Utilization of Coalbed Methane in Czechoslovakia*. Draft final report prepared for Battelle Pacific Northwest Laboratories by Raven Ridge Resources, 7 March.
Bulgarian Agency for Economic Coordination and Development. 1992. "Year of the iron sheep." *Business Climate Survey of the Bulgarian Economy in 1991*. Sofia, Bulgaria.
Chandler, W. U. (ed.). 1990. *Carbon Emissions Control Strategies: Case Studies in International Cooperation*. Washington, D.C.: World Wildlife Fund & Conservation Foundation.
Chandler, W. U., A. Makarov, and Zhou Dadi. 1990. "Energy for the Soviet Union, Eastern Europe, and China." *Scientific American*, September.
Chen Kang. 1992. "Economic reform and collective action in China." *China Report*, vol. 3, Washington Center for China Studies, May.
Christoffersen, G. 1992. "China's 'comprehensive' energy policy." In: T. W. Robinson (ed.), *Report of a Joint AEI–Johnson Foundation Conference on the Foreign Relations of China's Environmental Policy*. Washington, D.C.: American Enterprise Institute for Public Policy, August.
Dempsey, J. 1992. "Bulgaria far from solving energy equation." *Financial Times*, 27 March.
Gheorge, A. 1992. "A case study of the Rumanian energy economy." Battelle Pacific Northwest Laboratories, January, draft.
Goldstein, C. 1992. "China's oil shock." *Far Eastern Economic Review*, 12 November.
Jaszay, T. 1990. *Hungary: Carbon Dioxide Emissions Control in Hungary: Case Study to the Year 2030*. Battelle Pacific Northwest Laboratories, Advanced International Studies Unit, May.
Johansson, T. B., H. Kelly, A. K. N. Reddy, and R. H. Williams (eds.). 1993. *Renewable Energy – Sources for Fuels and Electricity*. Washington, D.C.: Island Press.
Kolar, S. and W. U. Chandler. 1990. "Future energy demand in Eastern Europe." In: W. U. Chandler (ed.), *Carbon Emissions Control Strategies: Case Studies in International Cooperation*. Washington, D.C.: World Wildlife Fund & Conservation Foundation.
Kostalova, M., J. Suk, and S. Kolar. 1992. *Reducing Greenhouse Gas Emissions in Czechoslovakia*. Battelle Pacific Northwest Laboratories, Advanced International Studies Unit, January.

269

McMillan, J. and B. Naughton. 1992. "How to reform a planned economy: Lessons from China." *Oxford Review of Economic Policy* 8 (Spring).

Makarov, A. A., et al. 1990. *The Soviet Union: A Strategy of Energy Development with Minimum Emissions of Greenhouse Gases*. Battelle Pacific Northwest Laboratories, April.

RCG/Hagler Bailly. 1993. "Demand-side management in Poland: Assessment and pilot program." Draft report, US Agency for International Development, Washington, D.C., June.

Sathaye, J. and N. Goldman (eds.). 1991. *CO_2 Emissions from Developing Countries: Better Understanding the Role of Energy in the Long Term. Vol. III: China, India, Indonesia, and South Korea*. LBL-30060, UC-350. Berkeley, Calif.: Lawrence Berkeley Laboratory, July.

Shen Longhai and Zhou Changyi. 1992. "Overview of economic development, present situation and prospects for environmental protection and energy conservation in China." US–China Conference on Energy, Environment, and Market Mechanisms, Seattle, Wash., and Berkeley, Calif., October.

Sitnicki, S., K. Budzinski, J. Juda, J. Michna, and A. Szpilewicz. 1990. *Poland: Opportunities for Carbon Emissions Control*. Global Environmental Change Program, Battelle Pacific Northwest Laboratories.

Treece, J. B. 1993. "The great refrigerator race." *Business Week*, 15 July.

Vine, E. and D. Crawley. 1991. *State of the Art of Energy Efficiency: Future Directions*. Washington, D.C.: American Council for an Energy-Efficient Economy.

Wang Qingyi. 1992. "The present state and prospects of China's energy conservation technology." US–China Conference on Energy, Environment, and Market Mechanisms, Seattle, Wash., and Berkeley, Calif., October.

Zhang Aling. 1992. "Forecast of China's energy demand." US–China Conference on Energy, Environment, and Market Mechanisms, Seattle, Wash., and Berkeley, Calif., October.

Zhou Dadi. 1992. "Energy management system pricing and market mechanisms in China." US–China Conference on Energy, Environment, and Market Mechanisms, Seattle, Wash., and Berkeley, Calif., October.

13

Decarbonization as a long-term energy strategy

Nebojša Nakićenović

The possibility of less carbon-intensive and even carbon-free energy as major sources of energy during the next century is consistent with the long-term dynamic transformation and structural change of the energy system. Natural gas seems the likely transitional fuel that would enhance the reduction in other adverse impacts of energy use on the environment as well as substantial reductions in carbon dioxide (CO_2) emissions. Natural gas could be the bridge to carbon-free energy sources such as hydrogen (Nakićenović, 1993a).

Global primary energy use has evolved from reliance on traditional energy sources to being based on fossil fuels, first coal and steam then oil and natural gas, and more recently (but to a lesser extent) on nuclear and hydro energy. Figure 13.1 shows the competitive struggle among the five main sources of primary energy as a dynamic substitution process. Fuelwood and traditional energy sources dominated primary energy until 1880. Coal, the major energy source between 1880 and 1960, was the basis for the massive expansion of railroads and the growth of steel, steamships, and many other sectors. Since 1960, oil has assumed a dominant role at the same time as the automotive, petrochemical, and other industries have matured. The current reliance on coal in many developing countries illustrates the gap

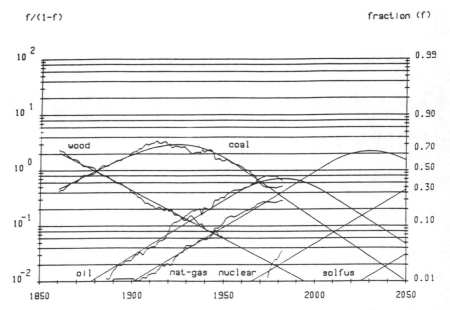

Fig. 13.1 **Global primary energy substitution, 1860–1980, and projections to 2050 (expressed in fractional market shares, *f*. Note: Smooth lines represent model calculations and jagged lines are historial data. "Solfus" is a term employed to describe a major new energy technology, for example solar or fusion)**

between the structure of primary energy supply and actual final energy needs.

During the past two centuries, global consumption of primary energy has increased about 2 per cent per year, doubling on average about every 35 years. As a result, emissions and other environmental effects of energy conversion and end-use have also increased. Current annual emissions are about 6 gigatons (billion tons) of carbon or more than 20 gigatons of CO_2. Most of the anthropogenic atmospheric CO_2 is due to fossil energy use and deforestation. Fossil energy consumption contributed more than two-thirds of all human sources of CO_2. The largest single source of energy-related carbon emissions is coal (about 43 per cent), followed by oil (around 39 per cent) and gas (less than 18 per cent).

In general, the instrumental determinants of future energy-related CO_2 emissions can be described by the Kaya identity. The Kaya identity establishes a relationship between population growth, per capita value added, energy per unit of value added, and CO_2 emissions per unit of energy on one side of the equation, and total carbon dioxide emissions on the other (Yamaji et al., 1991).

$$CO_2 = (CO_2/E) \times (E/GDP) \times (GDP/P) \times P,$$

where E represents energy consumption, GDP the gross domestic product or value added, and P population. Changes in CO_2 emissions can be described by changes in these four factors. Two of these factors are increasing and two are declining at the global level.

At present, the world's global population is increasing at a rate of about 2 per cent per year. The longer-term historical growth rates since 1800 have been about 1 per cent per year. Most of the population projections expect at least another doubling during the next century (see UN, 1992; Vu, 1985). Productivity has been increasing in excess of global population growth since the beginning of industrialization, and thus has resulted in more economic activity and value added per capita. CO_2 emissions per unit of energy and energy intensity per unit of value added have been decreasing since the 1860s in most countries.

The decarbonization of energy and decreases in the energy intensity of economic activities are a pervasive and almost universal development (Nakićenović, 1993b). Since 1860, the ratio of average CO_2 emissions per unit of energy consumed worldwide has been decreasing, owing to the continuous replacement of fuels with high carbon content, such as coal, by those with lower or zero carbon content. Figure 13.2 shows the historical global decarbonization of energy, expressed in tons of carbon (tC) per kilowatt year (kWyr). The reduction in the carbon intensity of the world economy, historically about 1.3 per cent per year, has been overwhelmed by growth in economic output of roughly 3.0 per cent per year. The difference, 1.7 per cent, parallels the annual increase in CO_2 emissions, implying a doubling before 2030 in the absence of appropriate countermeasures and policies.

Analysis of energy decarbonization requires the energy system to be disaggregated into its three major constituents: primary energy requirements, energy conversion, and final energy consumption. The carbon intensity of primary energy is defined as the total carbon content of primary energy divided by total primary energy requirements (consumption) for a given country. As such it is identical to the ratio used to define the carbon intensity of primary energy in the world given in figure 13.2. The carbon intensity of final energy is

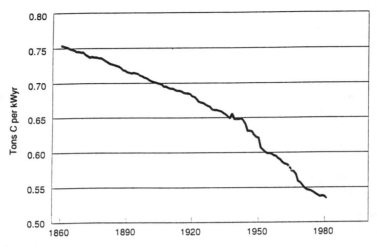

Fig. 13.2 **The global decarbonization of primary energy, 1860–1980**

defined as the carbon content of all final energy forms consumed divided by total final energy consumption. Various final energy forms that are delivered to the point of final consumption include solid fuels (such as biomass and coal), oil products, gas, chemical feed stocks, electricity, and heat. Electricity and heat do not contain any carbon. Thus it is evident on an a priori basis that the carbon intensity of final energy should generally be lower than the carbon intensity of primary energy. In addition, its rate of decrease should exceed that of primary energy decarbonization because of the increasing share of electricity and other fuels with lower carbon content, such as natural gas, in the final energy mix. The carbon intensity of energy conversion is defined as the difference between the two intensities.

Figures 13.3, 13.4, and 13.5 show the carbon intensities of primary energy, final energy, and energy conversion for selected countries, expressed in tons of carbon per ton of oil equivalent (toe). In figure 13.3 the higher carbon intensities of China and India result from higher reliance on coal and traditional sources of energy, which are assumed also to result in net CO_2 emissions owing to deforestation and, in general, unsustainable exploitation. The steep decline in carbon intensity during the 1980s in France is a direct result of its vigorous introduction of nuclear energy.

Figure 13.4 shows the carbon intensities of final energy. The figure indicates a continuous and smooth transition toward lower-carbon and zero-carbon energy carriers, in particular toward increasing shares

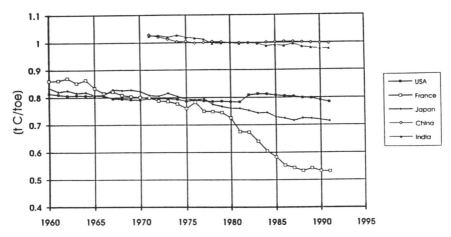

Fig. 13.3 **The carbon intensity of primary energy in China, France, India, Japan, and the United States, 1960–1991**

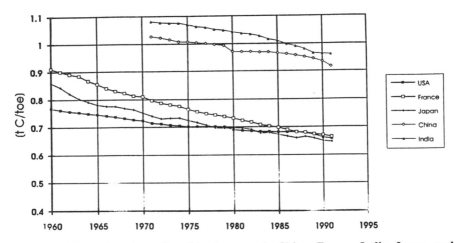

Fig. 13.4 **The carbon intensity of final energy in China, France, India, Japan, and the United States, 1960–1991**

of high-quality, exergetic fuels such as natural gas and, above all, electricity.

The carbon intensities of conversion shown in figure 13.5 present a different picture, with a variety of energy systems and development strategies, despite convergence in the final energy mix. In the developing countries, carbon intensity increases over time, whereas in the

275

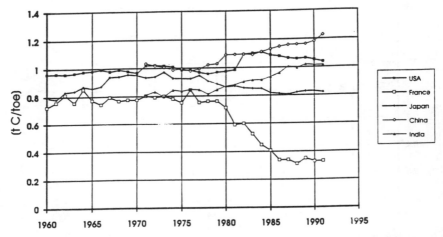

Fig. 13.5   **The carbon intensity of energy conversion in China, France, India, Japan, and the United States, 1960–1991**

industrialized countries it decreases at various rates, most rapidly in France. Should China and India continue to rely heavily on coal, it may not be possible to reduce carbon intensity in these countries. This means that some time in the twenty-first century a trend reversal may be expected, in the carbon intensity of either final energy or primary energy or both. The only bridge between these opposing trends could be even higher shares of electricity. The other alternative is that the future energy system restructures towards natural gas, nuclear energy, biomass, and other zero-carbon options. This would bring the energy systems of these two developing countries in line with those of the more industrialized ones.

Generally, the carbon intensities of primary energy and energy conversion are due to the energy system itself, whereas the carbon intensity of final energy is due to the actual energy required by the economy and individual consumers. Therefore, the former is a function of the specific energy situation in a given country whereas the latter is a function of the economic structure and consumer behaviour. The difference between the two provides deeper insight into the carbon emissions that result from energy and economy interactions and those that are determined by the nature of primary energy supply, conversion, and distribution.

Some degree of decarbonization has also been accompanied by

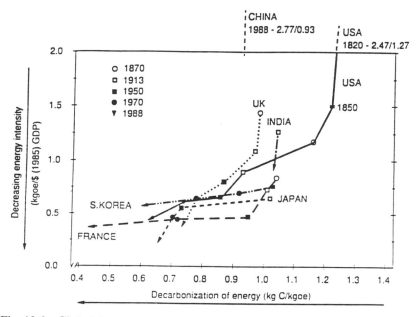

Fig. 13.6 **Global decarbonization and de-intensification of energy, 1870–1988**

lower energy intensities. Energy intensity measures the primary energy needed to generate a unit of value added and is usually measured in terms of gross domestic or national products (GDP or GNP). Energy conversion has fundamentally changed and improved with the diffusion of internal combustion engines, electricity generation, steam and gas turbines, and chemical and thermal energy conversion. Improvements in energy efficiency have reduced the amount of energy needed to convert primary energy to final and useful energy. Figure 13.6 shows declining envelopes of energy intensity, expressed in kilograms of oil equivalent energy per US$ GDP in constant 1985 dollars (kgoe/$(1985)GDP), and decarbonization, expressed in kilograms of carbon per kilogram of oil equivalent energy (kg C/kgoe), in selected nations. It illustrates salient differences in the policies and structures of energy systems among countries. For example, Japan and France have achieved the highest degrees of decarbonization; in Japan this has been largely through energy efficiency improvements over recent decades, while in France it has been largely through substitution of fossil fuels by nuclear energy. In most developing countries, commercial energy is replacing traditional energy forms so that total energy intensity is diminishing while commercial energy intensity is increasing.

Although decarbonization and energy de-intensification are responsible for relative reductions in energy emissions, they are not enough to offset the absolute emissions increases and projected emissions associated with the world's energy needs, especially those required for further economic development. Structural changes in energy systems toward carbon-free sources of primary energy are needed for further carbon intensity reductions. Analysis of primary energy substitution, shown in figure 13.1, suggests that natural gas could become the next dominant energy source and would enhance the reduction of the adverse impacts of energy use on the environment, especially CO_2 emissions.

Natural gas is a very potent greenhouse gas if released into the atmosphere but, after combustion occurs, the amount of CO_2 is much smaller compared with other fossil energy sources. Consisting mostly of methane, natural gas has the highest hydrogen to carbon atomic ratio and the lowest CO_2 emissions of all fossil fuels, emitting roughly half as much CO_2 as coal for the same amount of energy. The historical transition from wood to coal to oil and to gas has resulted in the gradual decarbonization of energy or to an increasing hydrogen to carbon ratio of global energy consumption. Natural gas is also desirable regionally because of its minimal emissions of other air pollutants. Regional assessments suggest that gas resources may be more abundant than was widely believed only a decade ago. New discoveries have outpaced consumption. Additionally, gas hydrates and natural gas of ultra-deep origin indicate truly vast occurrences of methane throughout the Earth's crust.

The methane economy offers a bridge to a non-fossil energy future that is consistent with both the dynamics of primary energy substitution and the steadily increasing carbon intensity of final energy. As non-fossil energy sources are introduced in the primary energy mix, new energy conversion systems would be required to provide other zero-carbon energy carriers in addition to growing shares of electricity. Thus, the methane economy would lead to a greater role for energy gases and later hydrogen in conjunction with electricity. Hydrogen and electricity could provide virtually pollution-free and environmentally benign energy carriers. As the methane contribution to global energy saturates and subsequently declines, carbon-free sources of energy would take over and eliminate the need for carbon handling and storage. This would then conclude the decarbonization process in the world.

The issue of climate warming is a major planetary concern along with the need to provide sufficient energy for further social and economic development worldwide. Methane and later hydrogen offer the possibility for reconciling these objectives. The evolutionary development of the global energy system toward a larger contribution by natural gas is consistent with the dynamics of the past 130 years. The current phase in the development of the global energy system may be just midway through the hydrocarbon era. Decarbonization in the world can continue as methane becomes the major energy source. From this perspective, methane is the transitional hydrocarbon, and the great energy breakthrough will be the production of hydrogen without fossil fuels. In the meantime, the natural gas share in total primary energy should continue to grow at the expense of dirtier energy sources (coal and oil). This transition to the methane age and beyond to carbon-free energy systems represents a minimum-regret option because it would also reduce emissions from economic and energy interactions, especially CO_2 emissions.

Acknowledgements

Some results given in the paper are based on joint research with Gilbert Ahamer and Arnulf Grübler, both from the International Institute for Applied Systems Analysis, Laxenburg, Austria.

Bibliography

Ausubel, J. H., A. Grübler, and N. Nakićenović. 1988. "Carbon dioxide emissions in a methane economy." *Climatic Change* 12: 245–263 (reprinted at International Institute for Applied Systems Analysis, RR-88-7).
Grübler, A. 1991. "Energy in the 21st century: From resource to environmental and lifestyle constraints." *Entropie* 164/165: 29–33.
Grübler, A. and N. Nakićenović. 1988. "The dynamic evolution of methane technologies." In: T. H. Lee, H. R. Linden, D. A. Dreyfus, and T. Vasko (eds.), *The Methane Age*. Dordrecht, the Netherlands: Kluwer Academic Publishers, and Laxenburg, Austria: IIASA.
Marchetti, C. and N. Nakićenović. 1979. *The Dynamics of Energy Systems and the Logistic Substitution Model*. Laxenburg, Austria: International Institute for Applied Systems Analysis, RR-79-13.
Nakićenović, N. 1990. "Dynamics of change and long waves." In: T. Vasko, R. Ayres, and L. Fontvielle (eds.), *Life Cycles and Long Waves*. Berlin: Springer-Verlag.

———— 1993a. "Energy gases – The methane age and beyond." In: D. G. Howell, K. Wiese, M. Fanelli, L. Zink, and. F. Cole (eds.), *The Future of Energy Gases.* Washington, D.C.: US Government Printing Office.

———— 1993b. *Decarbonization: Doing More with Less.* Laxenburg, Austria: International Institute for Applied Systems Analysis, WP-93-076.

Nakićenović, N., A. Grübler, and G. Ahamer. 1993. "Decarbonization of the world, representative countries and regions." Laxenburg, Austria: International Institute for Applied Systems Analysis.

UN (United Nations). 1991. *World Population Prospects 1990.* New York: United Nations, Population Studies No. 120.

———— 1992. *Long-range World Population Projections: Two Centuries of Population Growth 1950–2150.* New York: United Nations.

Vu, M. T. 1985. *World Population Projection 1985.* Baltimore, Md.: Johns Hopkins University Press.

Yamaji, K., R. Matsuhashi, Y. Nagata, and Y. Kaya. 1991. "An integrated system for CO_2/energy/GNP analysis: Case studies on economic measures for CO_2 reduction in Japan." Paper presented at the Workshop on CO_2 Reduction and Removal: Measures for the Next Century, 19–21 March, International Institute for Applied Systems Analysis, Laxenburg, Austria.

Part 5
Energy issues in developing countries

14

The crisis of rural energy in developing countries

Kunio Takase

1. The background of the study

Since the World Commission on Environment and Development published its report entitled *Our Common Future* (WCED, 1987), a number of international conferences have been held to minimize the hazards of indiscriminate exploitation of natural and ecological resources and, at the same time, to eradicate poverty in the developing world. In spite of many agricultural studies on existing environment and resource management in the rural development sector, little effort has been made to analyse and synthesize them into action programmes to form the basis of socio-economic development in the third world.

It was in this context that in 1990 the Japanese Ministry of Agriculture, Forestry, and Fisheries, through the International Development Centre of Japan (IDCJ), initiated a comprehensive four-year study entitled "Global Environment and Agricultural Resource Management." The study has four main focuses, each of which has become a topic of the year with a three-country case-study, as follows:

1. 1990/91: Slash-and-Burn Cultivation (Brazil, Nigeria, and Indonesia)
2. 1991/92: Overgrazing and Land Degradation (Syria, Kenya, and Bolivia)
3. 1992/93: Fuelwood Harvesting and Forestry Degradation (Mali, Honduras, and Nepal)
4. 1993/94: Land Degradation by Soil Salinization and Erosion (Pakistan, Egypt, and Mexico)

This paper is based on the IDCJ Mission's study in 1992/1993. Figure 14.1 is the IDCJ Mission's schematic concept of socio-economic development and global environment, finalized after a series of discussions between the Mission and its partners in the 12 countries and international organizations visited by the Mission.

At the top of the scheme, the Mission placed "population explosion and economic growth" as given propositions of socio-economic development and the main causes of environmental destruction. Three major development sectors ("rural development," "industrial development," and "urban development") are placed at the second level.

The "industrial development" sector has three major environment-related development objectives, namely "wood production," "water resources," and "energy resources." The major energy resources, such as fossil fuels (e.g. coal) and nuclear power, are not free from environmental destruction, resulting in greenhouse effects, acid rain, and nuclear waste. Frequent use of gas is also harmful, because it creates an ozone layer hole. "Wood production" requires cutting trees and inevitably involves the extinction of species, greenhouse effects, forestry degradation, land degradation, and soil erosion, and finally results in grassification and desertification. The "urban development" sector comprises the areas directly affected by population explosion, particularly in developing countries. Inadequate habitation causes health hazards and diseases. Massive unemployment leads to further deterioration in low-income families' living conditions and accelerates urban pollution. These two development sectors are, however, not directly related to agriculture and rural development *per se*, and major international efforts, governmental and non-governmental, are already under way in these problem areas.

The Mission's main focus is, therefore, the "rural development" sector, in which "food production," "enterprise" (income-oriented agriculture), and "fuelwood" (energy source for home consumption) are the major development objectives. In particular, food production has been the top priority in the world since the end of World War II

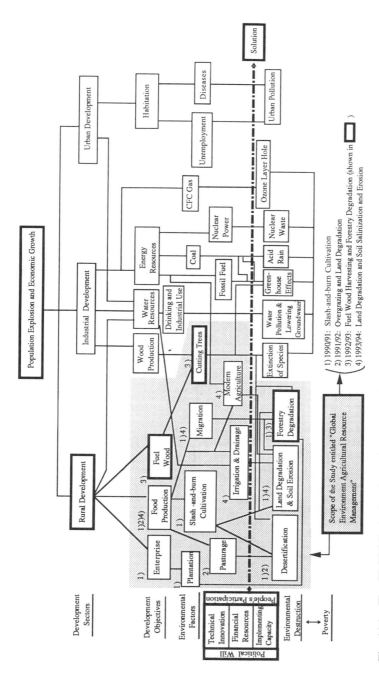

Fig. 14.1 **The IDCJ Mission's schematic concept of socio-economic development and global environment (Note: This diagram is not intended to be exhaustive or definitive in explaining all factors concerning socio-economic development and the global environment, but facilitates a systematic way to carry out the four-year-study without losing sight of the entire conceptual framework)**

285

owing to continuous and accelerating population explosion. It takes different forms, such as slash-and-burn cultivation, pasturage, migration, modern agriculture (supported by chemical products including fertilizers and insecticides derived from "energy resources"), and irrigation and drainage (supported by "water resources"), while agricultural enterprise is often associated with plantations, including non-food products such as rubber, coffee, and fibre crops. These activities, if carelessly planned and implemented (as in many cases in the past), contribute a great deal to environmental destruction including forest degradation, land degradation and soil erosion, and desertification, as shown at the bottom level in figure 14.1. Such environmental destruction is intricately connected to poverty, which further accelerates environmental destruction, thus forming a vicious circle with irresponsible development efforts.

The statistics show that the major causes of forest degradation are slash-and-burn cultivation (45 per cent), overgrazing (30 per cent), and "other," including fuelwood harvesting (25 per cent). The Mission adopted a theme for each year on this basis. In accordance with the emphasis in each year, a step approach was taken (1, 2, 3, and 4) in the scheme, so that the four-year study was able to maintain its systematic approach without losing sight of the overall conceptual framework. It was the Mission's conviction, after the field trips, that "technical innovation," "financial resources," and "implementing capacity" supported by "political will" and "people's participation" (see fig. 14.1) are the minimum requirements to prevent environmental destruction and to maintain compatibility between development and the environment. This schematic concept is considered to be a good starting point for logically organizing many complicated and integrated factors related to the "three Es," namely energy, economy, and environment.

2. Global forest resources

The global forest area is estimated to be in the range 3–6 billion hectares (ha) and its share of the global land area to be between 20 and 45 per cent. The large ranges in these statistics are due to the inaccuracy of the basic data available, particularly in developing countries. Table 14.1 shows forest areas in the world in 1980. The total forest area was 4,300 million ha (32 per cent of total land area) and, in addition, forest in fallow and bushes occupied 1,000 million

Table 14.1 **Global forest resources, 1980**

	Forest area[a] (million ha)	% of total land	Forest area per capita (ha)	Forest in fallow and bushes (million ha)	Total area of woody vegetation (million ha)
World	4,320.5	32.3	0.9	1,030.4	5,350.9
Developed countries	1,967.8	34.8	1.6	0	1,967.8
North America	734.5	37.9	2.4	0	734.5
Europe	158.9	30.5	0.3	0	158.9
Japan	25.3	67.9	0.2	0	25.3
USSR	928.6	41.5	3.5	0	928.6
Others[b]	120.5	13.1	2.3	0	120.5
Developing countries	2,352.7	30.4	0.7	1,030.4	3,383.1
Africa[c]	739.6	25.4	1.6	608.3	1,347.9
Latin America	987.6	48.2	2.8	313.4	1,301.0
China	170.0	17.7	0.1	–	170.0
Asia[d]	272.8	17.8	} 0.3	62.2	335.0
Oceania[e]	182.7	66.3		46.5	229.2

Source: FAO, *Forest Resources 1980*, Rome, 1985.
a. Total of closed and open forest.
b. Australia, New Zealand, Israel, South Africa.
c. Excluding South Africa.
d. Excluding Japan, China, and Israel.
e. Philippines, Indonesia, Brunei, Papua New Guinea, etc.

ha. This makes the total area of woody vegetation 5,300 million ha, or 40 per cent of the total land area of the world.

The total growing stock of wood resources in the world is estimated at 340 billion m^3 and the average wood-growing stock is calculated at 80 m^3/ha. The per capita forest area is roughly estimated at 0.83 ha and the per capita wood-growing stock is 65 m^3. The three main factors controlling forest growth and distribution are temperature, rainfall, and human activities. According to Mather (1990), potential wood production is estimated at 3–12 m^3/ha/year.

In pre-history, forest was believed to cover more than half of the global land area and benefited human life a great deal through hunting and collecting food, and over 90 per cent of the demand for forest resources was for fuelwood. After industrialization in the seventeenth century, however, much wood was used for shipbuilding, house-building, and other industrial products.

In North America, by the nineteenth century about 60 million ha of forest had been opened up, of which 90 per cent was for agriculture, 9 per cent for fuelwood and construction, and the remaining 1 per cent for pasture. About half of this area (30 million ha), however, remained uncultivated as barren land. In 1891, the Forest Reservation Act was promulgated, and in 1905 President Roosevelt made a speech about forest conservation. Russia and the middle European countries also recognized the importance of forest conservation and started taking conservation measures.

In Africa, however, colonial Europeans drove out traditional forest for development and commercial logging. The Mediterranean countries, too, suffered from forest degradation. In China, a slow but gradual deforestation process started in 3000 B.C. and continued until the nineteenth century. Most of its forest area was lost, falling to only 9 per cent of the total land area in 1950. It recovered to 12 per cent of the total land area in 1980 through intensified afforestation efforts.

In Japan, until the end of the nineteenth century, fuelwood and other products had been sufficient for consumption needs. From the end of the seventeenth century man-made forests began to be created in an attempt to compensate for primary forest harvesting, which had reached its limit. The afforestation method undertaken in the Yoshino area (central Japan) was a forerunner of agro-forestry (the technology was known as the Taungya system in Myanmar and later Tumpangsari in Indonesia). Even in 1936, about 15 per cent of agricultural land in the mountain area of Japan, or 77,000 ha, was rotated as shifting cultivation or agro-forestry with integrated utilization of agriculture, fodder, logging, and fuelwood. With these very careful conservation practices, the forest area is still roughly 68 per cent of the total land area even today, which is exceptional.

Figure 14.2 reveals the change in forest areas between 1971 and 1986. In developed countries, the forest areas slightly increased, whereas in developing countries they continued to decrease, especially in the tropical regions. From 1981 to 1990, the average area of deforestation was 16.9 million ha per year (0.9 per cent of the total forest area). In contrast, the area of afforestation was 1.1 million ha per year, which represents only 6.5 per cent of the deforested area. In Asia, the afforestation rate was 12.5 per cent, while in Africa it was 2.5 per cent. It can be concluded that the afforestation efforts are far from adequate and should be increased over tenfold if the forest resources are to be sustainable.

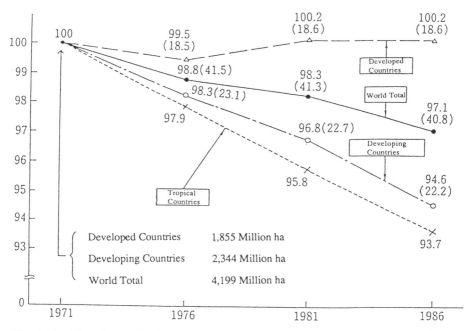

Fig. 14.2 **The change in forest areas, 1971–1986 (1971 = 100; figures in brackets denote volume in 100 million ha. Note: Forest areas include natural forest, artificial forest, and fallow areas for replanting; "tropical countries" = 76 developing countries in the tropical area. Source: FAO,** *Production Yearbook 1987,* **Rome)**

3. Fuelwood and rural energy

Fuelwood and industrial wood

The consumption of wood can be divided into two major uses: industrial wood use (timber, pulp, panel, and paper) and fuelwood for energy use. According to Food and Agriculture Organization (FAO) statistics for 1985 (Mather, 1990), over 80 per cent of wood harvested in developed countries was for industrial use, whereas in developing countries about 80 per cent of wood harvested was for fuelwood. Furthermore, 76 per cent of industrial use occurred in developed countries, whereas 84 per cent of fuelwood was used in developing countries, as shown in table 14.2.

In developed countries, about US$58 billion were earned from timber exports from 2 billion ha of forest, whereas in developing

Table 14.2 **Wood usage, 1985**

	Fuelwood		Industrial wood		Total	
	Volume (m. m³)	%	Volume (m. m³)	%	Volume (m. m³)	%
Developed countries						
Volume (m. m³)	263	16	1,160	76	1,422	45
Per cent	18		82		100	
Developing countries						
Volume (m. m³)	1,384	84	358	24	1,743	55
Per cent	79		21		100	
Total						
Volume (m. m³)	1,646	100	1,518	100	3,164	100
Per cent	52		48		100	

Source: Mather (1990).

countries only US$10 billion were earned from timber exports from 2.3 billion ha of forest. Since most of the fuelwood harvesting was taking place in tropical dry forest and open forest, which was causing serious environmental destruction, the FAO and World Bank started in 1978 to invest in community forest projects. The World Bank's historical lending records in the forestry sector reveal that before 1970 most of the lending was for industrial forestry. However, since its social forestry project started in the Philippines in 1977, 32 projects out of 64 over the next 15 years were for social forestry, 21 projects were for industrial forestry, and 11 projects were for environmental forestry. However, the performance of these projects has been mixed. Recently, more people-oriented projects, with special attention to their ownership and with more incentives for farmers, such as community forestry, farm forestry, and household trees, have become the new fashion.

The demand for and supply of fuelwood in developing countries

The FAO has conducted a systematic survey of fuelwood harvesting in developing countries for the past 40 years and published the results in the *World Forestry Inventory* in 1953, 1958, and 1963. At the UN Conference on New and Renewable Sources of Energy in August

1985, the FAO predicted that the oil crises of 1974 and 1979 would lead to an energy crisis in the third world, and clarified the link between fuelwood harvesting and forest degradation by processing data on the supply and potential sources of fuelwood. This survey was very comprehensive and conducted by local consultants in various regions under the supervision of the FAO. It involved 2.1 billion people in 95 developing countries (of whom 1.7 billion were found to be suffering from shortage) and was carried out from February 1980 to July 1981 (table 14.3).

Fuelwood is the fourth-largest energy source, after only petroleum, coal, and gas. It supplied 5.4 per cent of world energy consumption in 1978 and is the largest renewable source of energy. Demand for fuelwood for cooking and heating varies according to cooking method, climate, lifestyle, and the efficiency of stoves, and ranges from a minimum of 0.5–1.0 m³/ha/year to 3.0 m³/ha/year in the mountain area. On the supply side, the productivity of fuelwood varies from 4.0 m³/ha/year in closed forest to 2.0 m³/ha/year in conifer forest, 1.0 m³/ha/year in savanna forest, 0.5 m³/ha/year in low savanna, 0.1 m³/ha/year in shrubby forest, and 0.1 m³/ha/year in fallow forest. About 1 ha is required for one person's energy per year. To estimate the global balance of fuelwood, 2.3 billion ha of forest in developing countries can supply fuelwood for only 2.3 billion people, but the population of the developing countries has already reached 4.1 billion. Population increase in developing countries will further aggravate the balance of fuelwood supply.

Efficient utilization of fuelwood and alternative energy

Improved cooking stove
Most of the cooking stoves used in developing countries are not heat-efficient and produce thick smoke, which is not good for health. If cooking stoves were improved to be heat-efficient and to produce less smoke, this would be good for rural people. But experience has proved that things are not that simple, because rural people claim that these improved cooking stoves do not warm the inside of the house and they miss the smoke's effect of killing insects. So it is important to develop a variety of improved cooking stoves that meet the varying priorities of rural women and are also economical and easy to use.

Table 14.3 **Areas of fuelwood shortage in developing countries, 1981**

Classification[a]	Item	Africa[b]	North Africa and Middle East[c]	Asia[d]	Latin America[e]	Total[f]
A	No. of areas of shortage	19	0	4	6	29
	Population, 1980 (m.)	55	0	31	26	112
	Study area	Mali (North)	—	Nepal (Mountain)	—	
B	No. of areas of shortage	19	11	10	10	50
	Population, 1980 (m.)	146	104	832	201	1,283
	Study area	—	—	Nepal (Terai)	—	
C	No. of areas of shortage	14	0	5	5	24
	Population, 1980 (m.)	112	0	161	50	323
	Study area	Mali (South)	—	—	—	
Total	No. of areas of shortage	52	11	19	21	103
	Population, 1980 (m.)	313	104	1,024	277	1,718
	No. of areas surveyed	535	268	1,671	512	2,986

Source: Compiled by the International Development Centre of Japan from various FAO materials presented at the UN Conference on New and Renewable Sources of Energy, August 1985.

a. A – Extreme shortage: minimum requirements cannot be met even by over-harvesting.
   B – Shortage: minimum requirements can be met, but over-harvesting may result in extreme shortage in near future.
   C – Shortage in future: production of fuelwood met demand in 1980, but will be short in 2000.

b. In the past, most people lived in the savanna areas, but when the population exceeded 20 persons/km^2, both fuelwood and food (crops and livestock) became short, owing to the low productivity of the forest. However, fuelwood is sufficient where abundant rainfall prevails. Per capita fuelwood demand in Africa is larger than that in Asia owing to different cooking methods.

c. The oil-producing countries do not use fuelwood. However, fuelwood consumption increases as oil consumption increases.

d. Fuelwood provides one-third of total energy in Asia, and as much as three-quarters in the Mekong countries and Nepal. Animal dung and agricultural residuals are also used for both energy and fertilizer, in equal proportions.

e. Sufficient energy supply is maintained by hydropower, petroleum, and replanted forestry in the Andean countries, whereas the energy supply is inadequate in Central America and the Caribbean countries.

f. About 1.7 billion people were suffering from a shortage of fuelwood in 1980. It is predicted that this number will increase to 3 billion by 2000, and the energy situation will worsen.

Charcoal

Charcoal may be considered as an alternative to fuelwood where the forest resource is abundant. Charcoal has the merit of long-life storage and low-cost transportation for its smaller volume and weight (one-third to one-fifth those of fuelwood). Powdered charcoal can also be used as an insecticide and soil conditioner. Furthermore, comparing heat efficiency, charcoal gives out 7,000 kcal/g compared with 3,000 kcal/g from dry fuelwood and 1,000 kcal/g from green fuelwood. In Zambia, a package project, comprising an oval briquette and a clay charcoal stove, is being successfully implemented. On the other hand, in Nepal it is customary for only lower-class people to produce, sell, and utilize charcoal. Finding a way to comply with the culture and customs of the users is a first step for the success of a project. However, charcoal may be used widely in urban areas and more advanced areas in future.

Development of alternative energies

Alternative energies such as solar energy, wind energy, hydropower, and biogas are still far from meeting the large demands of rural energy, because of the immaturity of the technology and its high cost. In developing countries, the practical use of hydropower and thermal power as alternatives to fuelwood for domestic energy is limited. However, the use of kerosene and liquefied petroleum gas (LPG) for lighting and fuel, respectively, is increasing in urban areas because of their low cost, cleanness, and ease of use.

Fuelwood thermal power generation

According to an estimate by the Central Laboratory of Electrical Power in Japan, a fuelwood thermal power station of 50,000 kW capacity requires 5 kcal/g of wood as fuel. To provide fuelwood for this station, willow and poplar are planted on an area of 18,000 ha and one-eighth of that area is harvested each year. The cost of power generation is about ¥10/kWh, which is comparable to the cost of a coal-fired power station (¥10/kWh) or an oil-fired power station (¥11/kWh). In addition, fuelwood is a renewable energy source, in contrast to coal and oil, so this seems a good alternative. However, in developing countries, it is not economical to use fuelwood thermal power for heat energy, because of large losses in transmitting electricity to distant areas in addition to the inherent loss in converting from heat energy to electrical energy and back to heat energy.

4. Sustainable fuelwood management

Basic problems of fuelwood resources

The IDCJ Mission concluded that reliable information and data on fuelwood are even more scarce than for slash-and-burn cultivation (year 1 of its study) and for overgrazing (year 2). The Mission failed to identify a clear-cut project exclusively for fuelwood harvesting. It should be recognized, therefore, that the lack of knowledge and data is one of the biggest constraints in fuelwood management.

It should also be recognized that one of the causes of forest degradation by fuelwood harvesting is a conflict among the following three viewpoints:
1. the farmer considers fuelwood harvesting to be his traditional right inherited from his ancestors;
2. governments stress the importance of forest management as part of the social and economic development of the country;
3. the global viewpoint insists on the importance of forests for the conservation of the global environment in the future.

Although fuelwood harvesting is normally a complement to industrial wood harvesting, because 50 per cent or more of the tree typically remains as a residue after logging operations, in some cases it is in competition with farm land, pasturage, and logging. People are so poor that the price of fuelwood needs to be in effect free of charge. It is therefore difficult to introduce alternative energy sources, such as kerosene and LPG, because they involve a cost. The only advantage of fuelwood as an energy source is its renewable nature, so fuelwood needs to be economical and environmentally friendly. Demand for it will increase, especially in developing countries not particularly blessed with natural resources.

Feasibility study and long-term development strategy

Since fuelwood management is a small part of forest management, it is imperative to confirm the feasibility of total land use (agriculture, pasturage, and forestry) and its conservation. The annual global growth rate of forest is calculated at 2.4–10.0 m^3/capita. This is enough to meet average fuelwood consumption and logging requirements of 2 m^3/capita, which varies from place to place. Forest management can be enhanced by planting carefully selected tree varieties and in carefully selected locations. The record indicates that production of 4–7 m^3/ha/year may be possible in large-scale planting in the Sahel area, at a cost of US$1,000/ha. This is enough to meet the average demand for fuelwood, which should be reviewed by systematic monitoring and evaluation of existing social forestry programmes. This type of research is urgently needed in order to establish the feasibility of forest management in different climatic conditions and with different trees.

As mentioned above, the basic problems of fuelwood resources management are not yet solved. It is necessary to start a comprehensive research programme through international collaboration. For example, it is important to look at energy demand in relation to each energy source and at the status of fuelwood in the global macro economy; and also to determine the feasibility of large-scale and long-term programmes, such as a 50–100 per cent increase in production and a large-scale plantation programme. To develop these programmes, it is necessary to continue financial and institutional international cooperation for at least five years with a firm global political will based on the spirit of the UN Conference on Environment and Development (UNCED). In addition, technology innovation based on environmental science and public participation (research and training) is a core part of this proposal. As far as the Japanese government is concerned, it is necessary to cooperate with the FAO, the UN Development Programme, the Consultative Group on International Agricultural Research, and other international agricultural research institutions, by increasing contributions to and funding for the Global Environmental Facility of the World Bank, as an essential follow-up to the UNCED.

Short-term strategy
As an immediate strategy, the Mission recommended the following programmes: (i) introduction of alternative commercial energy sources; (ii) construction of infrastructure for the transportation of fuelwood; (iii) improvement of the production techniques and marketing of charcoal; and (iv) introduction and dissemination of improved cooking stoves.

A sustainable biological system

Based on the experience of the short-term strategy and an interim review of the long-term strategy, it may be possible to work out an optimum combination of programmes for each area by considering

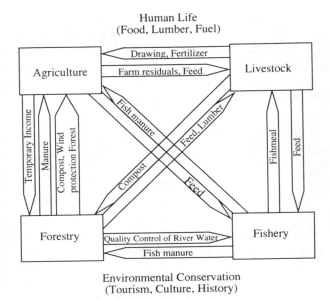

Fig. 14.3 **A sustainable biological system**

cost, environment, and convenience. In order to find alternatives to slash-and-burn cultivation, a number of combinations of biological resources (trees, crops, animals, fish, and human beings) under given natural resources (topography, soil, and water) should be integrated. Figure 14.3 shows such an example. It may well be necessary first to build a minimum social and physical infrastructure to support farmers' daily life, particularly when the area is classified as extremely poor. It is important to draw from a number of research projects and experiments on the selected farming systems and their ecological cycles already undertaken by many international agricultural research centres and, where necessary, to conduct new pilot research. The best alternative would be determined as one, or a combination, of the following categories:

- upland (identification of appropriate farming systems, including agro-forestry, to maintain the physical and chemical properties of soil);
- lowland rice (rotation with legume crops to minimize chemical fertilizer application); and
- forestry (selection of high-value tree species suitable to the given topographic and climatic conditions).

It may not be sufficient to develop technically sustainable agricultural programmes, unless they are accompanied by attractive incentives to farmers. Sustainability in agriculture is largely dependent upon soil management, which involves both short- and long-term improvements. Unless security of tenure is assured, farmers have no incentive to replenish a depleted soil, because it requires a significant investment of money and time (which in certain cases may involve a decade or so). It is essential to take the following socio-economic and institutional factors into account when formulating a sustainable agriculture and rural development programme, because the existence of mass poverty is the main cause of environmental destruction: (i) governments should give their highest priority to "rural transformation," whereby the poorest farmers, including young people and women, are enabled to remain in rural areas; (ii) land tenure should be secure to encourage farmers to supply the necessary inputs; (iii) the farmer's workload should not be unduly heavy; (iv) the natural and economic risks of the programme should be minimized; (v) a reasonable income should be assured, enabling farmers to invest in agricultural resource management without being affected by government pricing policy; and (vi) marketing and transportation systems should be stable and reasonably assured.

5. Beyond the UNCED

The United Nations Conference on Environment and Development (UNCED) in Rio de Janeiro, Brazil, in June 1992, reached broad consensus between: development and the environment; the rich and the poor; and governments and non-governmental organizations (NGOs). The highlights of the Rio Declaration are: (i) all people have equal rights to enjoy a healthy and productive life as the main actors in sustainable development in harmony with nature; (ii) there should be national sovereignty to utilize natural resources in accordance with its environmental and development policy without destroying environments in other countries; (iii) all nations should cooperate to eradicate poverty as an essential target in attaining sustainable development; (iv) priority should be given to the needs of the poorest developing countries suffering from environmental destruction; and (v) developed countries should assume international responsibility for sustainable development and provide technical and financial assistance. The Declaration also touched on: consumption and population control; NGOs' active participation; international law for compensation to the victims of environmental destruction; women's role; ethnic tribes' rights; and demilitarization.

I believe that poverty alleviation (or narrowing the gap between the rich and the poor) is the first step to solving environmental problems, including the crisis of rural energy in developing countries. Based on the broad consensus reached at the UNCED, realistic targets of socio-economic development in harmony with ecology should be sought. As one such indicative target, I have ventured to formulate a long-term projection of poverty alleviation in a programme with controlled population and GNP/capita growth rates, which could narrow the gap between the rich and the poor. I am fully aware of the fact that GNP per capita is not the best indicator of quality of life. However, in the absence of an internationally recognized best indicator, I decided to use it as the second-best indicator of growth. To establish a first approximation, I referred to the *World Development Report 1991* (World Bank, 1991a). Out of 124 countries, 25 countries (19 OECD members, 3 oil producers, Israel, Hong Kong, and Singapore), with GNP per capita of US$6,000 or more, were classified as rich and the remaining 99 countries as poor. Their populations and GNP per capita in 1990 are summarized in table 14.4.

The three most important assumptions as regards reducing the disparity between the rich and the poor relate to: (i) the time needed to reach the goal; (ii) average population growth rate; and (iii) the target ratio of GNP per capita between the rich and the poor. First, I assumed that the target year should be 2040, which is long enough for development purposes and short enough from an environmental point of view. The population assumption is rather difficult. Records show that world population growth decreased from 2.1 per cent in

Table 14.4 **Population and GNP per capita in rich and poor countries, 1990**

	Year	25 rich countries	99 poor countries	Total
Population (million)	1990	900	4,100	5,000
Population growth (%/year)	1965–1973	1.0	2.5	2.1
	1980–1990	0.7	2.1	1.8
	1990–2000	0.6	1.9	1.6
GNP per capita (US$) (weight)	1990	18,700 (23)	800 (1)	3,800
Total GNP (US$ billion)	1990	15,700	3,300	19,000

Source: World Bank (1991a).

1965–1973 to 1.8 per cent in 1980–1990 and it is estimated at 1.6 per cent for the period 1990–2000. In view of these statistics, it would not be unreasonable to target 1.0 per cent as a 1990–2040 average, because in the 25 years 1970–1995 the rate fell by 0.5 per cent (from 2.1 to 1.6). Another encouraging example is Sri Lanka, where population growth, which averaged 2.8 per cent in the 1960s (very close to the magnitude in Africa today), fell during 1980–1990 to 1.5 per cent, and is expected to fall further to a little over 1 per cent in the 1990s.

As for the third assumption, it would be ideal to eliminate entirely the disparity between the rich and the poor by 2040. But it may not be realistic for the poor (US$800) to reach the rich's level (US$18,700) in 50 years, which would require an average annual growth rate close to 7 per cent, provided that the rich's growth rate remains zero for 50 years. After some trials, I reached the conclusion that the disparity in GNP per capita could be targeted to narrow from the present 23:1 to 10:1 in 2040. In this case, the annual average growth rate of GNP/capita would be 3.5 per cent for developing countries and 1.8 per cent for developed countries, which results in GNP/capita in 2040 being US$45,000 for developed countries and US$4,500 for developing countries. If the population growth rate (1.1 per cent for developing countries and 0.6 per cent for developed countries) is added, the necessary GNP growth rate per year would be 4.6 per cent for developing countries and 2.4 per cent for developed countries. The average global GNP growth rate would be 3.0 per cent, which is exactly the same figure as required to achieve sustainable development given in the Bruntland Report. The results of the calculation are summarized in table 14.5. This seems to be an appropriate aim and could be achieved, though it would not be at all easy.

In reality, the trends in economic and population growth will be quite diverse among developing countries. For example, some developing countries may develop quite rapidly and could be in the range of "developed" countries in 2040, and some may not. Thus, the results of this simple calculation are neither to represent the huge, complex, and dynamic process of development, which is beyond the scope of my study, nor to argue that the optimum level of disparity between the rich and the poor is 10:1. Rather, the heart of the issue here is to delineate rough relationships between population and GNP per capita, if the primary goal is to *narrow* the disparity. It is my conclusion that neither the planned economy nor the market economy is capable of overcoming this complex problem in relation to popu-

Table 14.5 **Proposed population and GNP per capita, 1990 and 2040**

	Year		Annual growth (%)	Proposed annual GNP growth (%)
	1990	2040		
Population (million)				
Total	5,000	8,200[a]	1.0	
Developed	900	1,100	0.6	
Developing	4,100	7,100	1.1	
GNP/capita (US$)				
Total	3,800	10,000	2.0	3.0
Developed	18,700 (23)	45,000 (10)	1.8	2.4
Developing	800 (1)	4,500 (1)	3.5	4.6
World total GNP (US$ trillion)	19.0	82.0	3.0	

a. This target may still be ambitious, when compared with the prediction by the UN Fund for Population Activities of 6.4 billion (2001), 8.5 billion (2025), and 10.0 billion (2050).

lation, growth, and poverty, which human society is already facing. We may well need a new philosophy of a "strategically planned market economy" in the twenty-first century.

References

FAO (Food and Agriculture Organization). 1953, 1958, 1963. *World Forestry Inventory*. Rome: FAO.

Mather, A. S. 1990. *Global Forest Resources*. Portland, Oreg.: Timber. Translated by Minoru Kumazaki.

Montalembert, M. R. de and J. Cleent. 1983. *Fuelwood Supplies in the Developing Countries*. Rome: FAO Forestry Paper 42.

WCED (World Commission on Environment and Development). 1987. *Our Common Future*. Oxford: Oxford University Press.

World Bank. 1991a. *World Development Report 1991*. Oxford: Oxford University Press.

——— 1991b. *Forestry Sector Policy Paper*. Washington, D.C.

15

The developing world: The new energy consumer

Anthony A. Churchill

1. Introduction

This paper is an attempt to look ahead at the energy production and consumption patterns of the developing world and the implications for both the countries themselves and the rest of the world.[1] A period of three decades has been selected because anything less would not adequately reveal the underlying trends. The patterns of energy production and consumption are well established and represent a vast amount of capital; change will occur only with changes in basic parameters such as population, economic growth, and technology. The basic database used is that of the report by the Commission of the World Energy Council (WEC), *Energy for Tomorrow's World* (WEC Commission, 1993). This is the most recent summary of the global scene and its scenarios cover a sufficiently long period of time. The data and assumptions of the scenarios presented are all in line with other similar exercises by the International Energy Agency or the Intergovernmental Panel on Climate Change. I refer to this as the "consensus view."

Table 15.1   **Energy demand to 2020: Four scenarios (billion tons of coal equivalent)**

	1990	2020			
		A	B_1	B	C
OECD	4.1	4.9	4.7	4.7	3.6
Central and Eastern Europe/CIS	1.7	2.0	2.4	1.8	1.5
Developing countries	2.9	10.3	8.0	6.8	6.1
World	8.8	17.2	16.0	13.4	11.3

Source: WEC Commission (1993).

2. Energy demand

Consensus views are not necessarily correct; for example, the consensus view on oil prices in the late 1970s looks slightly ridiculous from today's perspective. Table 15.1 summarizes the demand alternatives of the Commission report. Under the high-demand scenario (case A), the consumption of the developing world about doubles in the 30-year period. The alternatives presented differ in the assumptions about economic growth and the rate at which the energy intensity of output changes. The lowest-demand scenario (case C) is what would have to happen if greenhouse gas emissions were to be stabilized at 1990 levels. It is presented as an illustration of how difficult it would be to accomplish this objective. There are no realistic policies that would make this possible.

All of these scenarios imply a substantial shift in the way energy is used in the developing world. They imply a significant break between what is currently happening and what would have to happen if the demand of the developing world were to double only over 30 years – as opposed to doubling every decade as at the present time.

Why should dramatic changes of these orders of magnitude take place? What are the sets of policy changes that would have to be put in place to make this work?

For the most part, these scenarios assume that increasing efficiency brought on by more market-oriented pricing and other policies will permit the continued growth of output with declining inputs of energy. But these are assumptions, not facts – even if the appropriate policy changes were to take place, we have no way of accurately estimating their impact on energy demand. In fact, as I argue below, it is equally plausible to assume that a better set of policies like those generally assumed in these scenarios will increase, not decrease, demand.

Even the high economic growth scenarios are pessimistic. If, on average, the developing world grows only at the rates assumed, the bulk of humanity will continue to live in wretched poverty 30 years from now. These assumptions do not fit the present aspirations of most of the developing world, and two countries alone, India and China, which account for a third of the world's population, are currently growing at rates that are multiples of those assumed. A doubling of the assumed growth rates would nearly double energy demand.

There are alternative ways of looking at the same facts and figures. Rather than focus on global aggregates, let us start with how the individual responds to changes in prices and incomes. If, through changes in policy, technology, or other measures, the production of a service becomes more efficient, it is equivalent to lowering the price of the service. If there is an improvement in the efficiency of the automobile engine so that it is now possible to drive more kilometres for a given fuel input, the price of vehicle kilometres has fallen. Similarly an improvement in the efficiency of the light bulb lowers the cost of the service. The consumer is purchasing the service, not the fuel, and in both cases will experience a decline in price of the service. What is his reaction? Does he purchase more or less? In other words, the amount consumed will vary with the price.

Most of those advocating increased efficiency and conservation as a way of decreasing the quantities consumed implicitly assume that energy services are price inelastic or that consumption does not change with a change in price. A perfectly inelastic demand curve is not supported by the evidence. Estimating price elasticities for energy and other services is notoriously difficult but most of the evidence points to some positive price elasticity – that declines in price will produce increases in the quantity consumed. Whether the increased quantity of the service consumed results in more or less fuel usage depends on the relationship between fuel costs and total service costs. In the United States, for example, improvements in the fuel efficency of vehicles has not produced an aggregate decline in fuel consumption because of an increase in vehicle kilometres. In Japan, in particular, improvements in efficiency have been associated with rising consumption.

Another way of examining the same phenomena is in terms of expansion of markets. The efficiency of electric power production has continued to increase, for example, from less than 4 per cent heat efficiency at the turn of the century to over 50 per cent in today's combined-cycle plants. Real prices have fallen by a factor of at least five. In response to these changes in price, whole new markets have developed for electric power. In many cases it led to the substitution of a convenient and cheap form of energy for the sweat of the human brow.

In the developing world the potential for the expansion of energy services is enormous. The present inefficiencies of energy production and consumption result in high prices for the services, in effect rationing large segments of the population out of the market-place. Take, for example, electric power production. In almost all countries the price of electricity produced by the public sector is subsidized. But the subsidies introduce inefficiencies and in particular they lead to rationing because the subsidies are insufficient to produce the power that would be demanded at these prices. This forces those not lucky enough to be part of the system to seek more expensive alternatives. People using kerosene lamps or handpumps are paying multiples per unit of service compared with those connected to the grid. Even those connected to the grid are forced to take expensive measures to compensate for the poor quality of the service. In Indonesia or Nigeria, where nearly half the electric power production is in inefficient auto generation that is required to compensate for the poor quality of the public supply, the real cost of electricity is two to three times the price that would prevail under an efficient system of public supply. Imagine how much more electric power would be consumed in India if it were efficiently produced and distributed.

Probably even more important than the impact of efficiency on prices is the impact of increased incomes. The present per capita consumption levels of the developing world are between one-tenth and one-twentieth of those of today's industrial countries. In the developed world (although not yet in Japan), we have seen the per capita consumption levels stabilize or even begin to decline. Most of the assumptions behind the low levels of demand growth in the developing world assume a similar pattern, at least at the aggregate level, of a turn-down in the rate of increase in energy use relative to increases in income.

But is this a realistic assumption? Is it correct to take the changes in the developed world and apply them to the developing countries? In other words, what is the income elasticity of energy consumption? The evidence at hand is mixed and it is not an easy parameter to calculate with any certainty. At the aggregate level, most of the empirical studies come out at between 1.5 and 3.0. None shows this to be a declining figure. At a minimum, a per capita income increase of 1 per cent will generate a growth in energy consumption of 1.5 per cent. If one looks at both the planned and present construction of energy facilities in most of the developing world in the 1990s, the figures suggest that countries are working on the assumption that energy demand will grow at twice the rate of income. This is consistent with historical experience.

It is also useful to look at income elasticities from an individual or household perspective. At present, average per capita energy consumption is low in developing countries. The average Chinese, for example, uses less than 400 kilowatt hours (kWh) per capita – compared with the US average of nearly 10,000, or the Japanese of 5,000. In these higher-income countries, growth in GNP is increasingly concentrated in services and less energy-intensive activities. The developing world, in contrast, has yet to go through the stage of income growth in which demand for energy-intensive services is a large part of total consumption. Household demand for basic lighting, transportation, appliances, refrigeration, etc., is at relatively low levels. As income grows, demand for these energy-intensive services is likely to be quite income elastic.

One area of increasing demand that probably has been underestimated is transportation. The developing world is undergoing an unprecedented process of urbanization. In the next 30 years most developing countries will have shifted from being primarily rural to being primarily urban. This urbanization is part of the process of economic growth in which higher productivity in agriculture permits a greater degree of specialization in the production and trade in non-agricultural goods and services. Inevitably this will mean greater demand for the transport of goods, all of which are energy intensive. Add to this demand for personal mobility and you have a potentially explosive growth in the demand for energy related to transport needs.

The rapidly growing countries of East Asia are well into this process where the combination of rapid economic growth and rising incomes is producing double-digit rates of growth for transport services. All of today's developed countries have gone through this stage and there is no reason to expect a different experience in the developing world. Improvements in efficiency of transport will permit this increase in demand to take place at lower income levels.

Assuming modest income and price elasticities and a conservative rate of growth, it is possible to get increases in demand that are multiples of what is generally being projected, even with, or perhaps because of, substantial improvements in energy efficency (Churchill, 1993: 6).

What are the quantitative implications? If energy services are income elastic and using the most conservative of these income elasticities (1.5), a growth rate in per capita income of 2 per cent would produce a growth in energy demand of 3 per cent. To this must be added the growth in population (assume an average of 1.6 per cent over this period), and we now have energy demand growing at 4.8 per cent. How do we take into account the price effects from improved efficiencies or technological progress? Casual observation on the part of many observers suggests that the developing countries are at least 25 per cent less efficient than the developed countries. Let us assume that by the end of 30 years they reach at least the present level of efficiency of the present developed world; that is, real prices will decline by at least 25 per cent. Again, let us make a conservative assumption that consumption will increase more or less in proportion to the decline in prices; that is, demand will be 25 per cent higher than it would have been in the absence of a price decline. We now have the growth of energy demand up to 6 per cent. This is more than five times greater than the growth rates of energy demand implicit in the WEC high scenario and in most other similar "high-case" scenarios, and it is based on using the low end of the estimates of per capita income elasticities.

Different assumptions about growth rates, income and price elasticities, technological progress, and policies can change these results. But it is difficult to see what plausible assumptions about any of these parameters could alter the basic outcome by a factor of five. One could assume declining income elasticities over time, but, given the low initial levels of energy consumption, it is difficult to see why much in the way of declines in this figure can be expected in this period. Present per capita income levels in the major developing countries are one-tenth to one-twentieth of those of the OECD average.

Policy changes can be important. Governments, for example, could choose to try and capture all of the efficiency gains through prices and to soak up the resulting consumer surpluses through the tax system. The practicality of doing so is open to question.

Is this rapid rate of growth in demand likely to be constrained by either supply or financing constraints? It is possible that specific countries will undertake policy and other measures that will restrain the growth in demand by slowing down the rate of economic growth.

But this is hardly a desirable objective. Given appropriate policies, there is no reason to assume that these increases in demand cannot be met within the existing constraints on physical supplies and financial resources.

3. Energy supply

Over the next 30 years there is no reason to assume shortages of the basic raw materials for energy production. The WEC scenarios and most others are consistent in this viewpoint. Particularly with improvements in efficiency and changes in technology, it is likely we face a world of relatively constant energy prices. This is consistent with the historical experience.

The two major economies in the developing world in terms of size are India and China. In both cases these are, and will remain, coal-based economies. Both have large reserves of coal that go well beyond the needs of the next 30 years. There is also no reason to suppose this coal will be produced under conditions of rising costs; as has happened in the past, the combination of improved efficiency and more efficient technologies will permit the production of final energy services at prices that are not too different from today's price. It is interesting to note that the world prices of basic fuels into the energy transformation process have been relatively constant in real terms over the past 100 years.

Some concerns have been expressed about the availability of petroleum. Again, most of the supply projections indicate an adequate supply of petroleum at least for the next 30 years. Reserve estimates tend to be on the conservative side because they generally are based on today's technology, and at present costs of capital it makes little sense to spend resources to "prove" reserves for any extended period.

The issue may be more one of distribution. Undoubtedly the present distribution of these resources creates some concerns, but over the longer term it may not make all that much difference. In the production of electric power or other energy services resulting from the boiler use of petroleum, there are a multitude of substitutes, from nuclear to natural gas. It is only in the transportation area that petroleum products have a strong comparative advantage. But even here substitutes are developing. The cost of producing liquid fuels from natural gas has dropped by almost half in the past 20 years to the point where it is close to that of petroleum-based alternatives.

Substantial resources are being spent on the development of the electrically powered vehicle. Given present trends it is highly likely that a commercially feasible vehicle is within the horizon of the next 30 years. Once this is feasible, there are numerous substitutes for petroleum as a transport fuel.

4. Financial constraints

What about financial constraints? All energy transformation processes are capital intensive, and concerns have been raised about the availability of capital to finance the expansion of energy supplies, particularly in the developing world. The savings required to finance the supplies necessary to meet the type of demands forecast above all lie within historical parameters. Typically, in the energy-intensive stages of economic development, energy investments are about 20 per cent of total investment or between 3 and 5 per cent of GDP. These ratios are not expected to change and the type of demand growth forecast above is consistent with the historical pattern. In other words, economic growth and appropriate policies will generate the necessary resources.

The basic resource – the savings – will be available as part of the growth process. The challenge is in mobilizing those resources. Many countries have structured their energy enterprises so that they are both inefficient and subsidized. In these circumstances, only the government through its taxing powers is able to invest. Individuals will not knowingly invest their hard-earned savings in loss-making businesses. There also are limits on how much foreign savings can be attracted into the sector. At present most of these foreign savings are simply relying on the credit standing of the public sector. In any case it is not possible to finance a sector as large as the energy sector on the basis of foreign savings without running into overall balance-of-payment constraints. In order to mobilize the necessary domestic resources, a fundamental restructuring of many of the institutions in the energy sector is required. This is a process that is now under way in many developing countries.

5. Environmental issues

Most energy transformation processes produce wastes that, if improperly handled, can cause serious environmental consequences. Dealing with these wastes has become an increasingly important issue for all countries. Fortunately the technology exists for mitigating most of the serious problems. In most cases the costs of better environmental practices are a small part of total costs and are within the resources constraints of most developing countries.

In the case of the most serious environmental problem with respect to human health and welfare, that of particulates in the air, the costs are relatively minor and are easy to justify in terms of local costs and benefits. Others create more serious issues for cost–benefit analysis. Cross-boundary pollution from acid rain is one such problem. Emissions from Chinese coal plants, for example, impact on acid rain in Japan and other parts of South-East Asia. It is not clear that it is of benefit for China to spend the resources to eliminate this problem for its neighbours. On the other hand, it should be in the interest of these neighbours to provide some of the resources necessary to eliminate this problem. Given the rate of growth of new plant (some 1,000 MW per month) this will not be a trivial expense – approximately US$2 billion per year. This is not unaffordable, however, by the neighbouring countries.

In most cases the waste problems can be met through the direct application of appropriate technologies to eliminate the wastes rather than trying to achieve the same ends through improvements in efficiency. Figure 15.1 shows the trade-offs between reducing emissions through end-use and other efficiency efforts and removing them directly at source. In all cases, once one moves beyond the obvious measures to stop subsidizing inefficiency, it is cheaper to use existing technologies to remove the pollutants at source. Nuclear power,

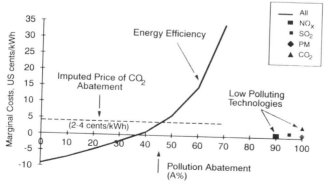

Fig. 15.1 **The marginal costs of pollution abatement in electric power through energy efficiency and low-polluting technologies, with reference to developing countries**

for example, is a cheaper alternative (assuming it can be operated safely) for removing CO_2 than draconian policies to improve energy efficiency.

The one potential problem for which there is no immediate solution is that of greenhouse gas emissions. Over the coming decades almost all of the additional greenhouse gas emissions will be coming from the developing countries. India and China alone will account for about two-thirds of the increase. There is little alternative for these economies but to burn coal and neither one is likely to sacrifice economic growth in response to global concerns about the atmosphere. It is also unlikely that the rest of the world will be willing to contribute sufficient resources to these countries to offset the extra expenses that moving out of coal would entail. Shifting India and China from coal to nuclear power, assuming it were technically possible, would cost around US$15 billion per year over the next two decades.

Improved efficiency and conservation measures will have a limited impact. The 1992 *World Development Report* (World Bank, 1992) estimated that, under the best of assumptions regarding efficiency, savings of 20 per cent over the next 20 years were a possibility. These best of assumptions may not take place and, as has been suggested above, the cost reductions that are brought about by these efficiency measures may, in fact, increase demand.

If global warming proves to be a serious problem – there is still sufficient uncertainty about it to warrant some caution in spending too much in the way of resources to deal with it – then reliance will have to be placed on technologies as yet unavailable.

Is this an unreasonable expectation? Should we try to solve tomorrow's problems with today's technology? What are the potential alternatives that may become available in the next 30 years? To assume that technology will not change is an unreasonably conservative assumption that is contrary to the historical evidence. Technological change is continuing at a rapid pace. One has only to consider the world of 30 years ago to speculate on the potential magnitude of the changes ahead of us. In the production and consumption of energy there has been a steady improvement in overall efficiencies.

If we look ahead for the next 30 years, it would not be unreasonable to assume a continued or similar pace of development. A number of new technologies are close to commercial feasibility. Solar energy, whether in the form of photovoltaics or thermal, is a renewable technology that offers considerable potential. If costs continue to

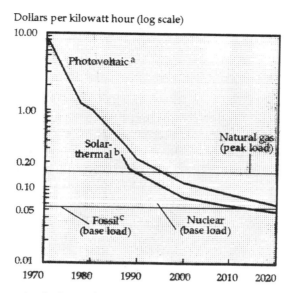

Dollars per kilowatt hour (log scale)

Fig. 15.2 **The cost of alternative means of generating electric power in high-insolation areas, 1970–2020 (Data after 1990 are predicted; future costs of fossil fuel and nuclear generation are uncertain, being affected by such factors as demand shifts, technological change, environmental concerns, and political conditions, which may act in opposite directions. Notes: *a.* Excluding storage costs. *b.* Including storage costs – on the basis of hybrid natural gas/solar schemes through 1990 and heat storage thereafter. *c.* Natural gas and coal)**

decline at even half the pace of the past 20 years, solar energy could well become competitive with fossil fuels in the next 20 years (see fig. 15.2). Using electric power to produce hydrogen or the direct production of electric power from fuel cells are all technologies that could prove commercially feasible in the near future. Continued improvements in existing fossil fuel technologies, particularly in using natural gas, are also well within the realm of possibility. Nuclear power is also a possible contender if costs and safety concerns can be met.

Will these technologies be available to the developing countries? Inevitably they will be followers: only rich societies can afford to be at the margins of technological progress. Latecomers have the opportunity to capture the gains without bearing many of the risks and costs. In most developing countries the greatest benefits will come from using already tried and true technologies.

311

The key to the transfer of technology lies in the ability or absorb-tive capacity of the recipient. Study after study shows that the great-est gains in productivity come not from the technologies, *per se*, but rather from the organizational and institutional changes that are required to utilize the technologies efficiently.[2] If labour and man-agement practices are unchanged, little may be gained from intro-ducing new technologies. Unfortunately, the monopolistic structure of most energy enterprises, with their poor incentive systems, does not always permit the most benefits to flow from the introduction of new technologies. More competitive markets in which investors have a clear financial stake in the successful adoption of available tech-nologies appear to be the direction in which countries will have to move if they are to take advantage of the substantial and growing volume of new technologies.

6. Conclusions

Within the next three decades the developing countries are set to become the world's major energy consumers. This growth is to be welcomed because it will be the result of economic growth, with its promise of a better life for some of the world's poorest populations. This growth will not be automatic; substantial institutional changes are required in the energy sector, particularly to improve efficiency and mobilize capital. Nor will it always be as environmentally benign as one would wish. The most serious problems with respect to human health and welfare are essentially local in nature and can be dealt with within the constraints of existing technology. Should global warming prove to be a serious problem, it will have to be dealt with using tomorrow's technology.

Notes

1. Much of the analysis developed for this paper is given in further detail in Churchill (1993).
2. There are many examples of this in World Bank (1989).

References

Churchill, A. A. 1993. *Energy Demand and Supply in the Developing World 1990–2020: Three Decades of Explosive Growth. Annual Bank Conference of Development Economics.* Washington, D.C.: World Bank, May.

WEC (World Energy Council) Commission. 1993. *Energy for Tomorrow's World – The Realities, the Real Options, and the Agenda for Achievement*. London: Kogan Page.

World Bank. 1989. *Technological Advance and Organizational Innovation in the Engineering Industry*. Washington, D.C.: World Bank, Industry and Energy Department, Working Paper No. 4, Industry Series, March.

————— 1992. *World Development Report 1992*. Oxford: Oxford University Press.

313

16

The role of rural energy

Jike Yang

1. The energy consumption of peasant households in China

The damage caused by biomass burning

Each year, about 500 million tons of biomass fuel are burned by rural households. This figure is one-third of China's total energy consumption. In the plains region, where there is a large population and limited arable land, biomass is used as a substitute for fuelwood. In the townships of mountain regions, distances to fuelwood harvesting sites are much greater than before. In the dry area of north-west China, the fuelwood shortage is becoming a serious problem. If we calculate rural household energy consumption in terms of standard agricultural output values, energy consumption per 10,000 yuan output is 9 tons of coal equivalent (tce). This figure is far higher than the energy consumption level of China's consumer goods industry and close to the average level of heavy industry. It is therefore important in the Chinese rural economy to cut this figure to 4.5 tce. This target could be achieved by widespread use of the straw-saving stove, the biogas stove, and the solar stove (known as the "three stoves").

The coefficient of heat conversion of rural biomass burning is as low as 10–15 per cent. Taking a typical rural family relying mainly on straw burning as an example, the average effective thermal quantity needed every day for five people is about 3,100 kilocalories (kcal); in mountain areas where rural families rely on fuelwood, this figure is about 4,200 kcal. Compared with the straw- or fuelwood-saving stove, with a coefficient of heat conversion as high as 30–40 per cent, at least 50 per cent of biomass is wasted. Given that there are 192 million rural families in China, the total annual loss is about 280 million tons of biomass, which is equivalent to 77 million tce.

Another big loss from biomass burning is that the organic nitrogen content in biomass is released into the air as oxides of nitrogen and cannot return to the soil as fertilizer. Compared with the biogas digester, in which the organic nitrogen content in biomass can be saved and returned to the soil, the annual loss of organic nitrogen from biomass burning in China is equivalent to 5 million tons of ammonium sulphate or 6 million tons of ammonium carbonate. In energy-deficient rural areas, large-scale biomass collection and burning is causing serious damage in terms of the ecological balance and further shortages of biomass resources. A vicious cycle is thus formed leading to serious problems such as soil degradation in plains areas, deforestation in mountain areas, and devegetation in the grasslands.

Corrective action

As described later in this paper, at every level of official and non-official organizations, remarkable efforts have been made in order to reduce rural energy expense and to tap new energy sources. In many regions, the serious problems of household energy are being solved or ameliorated. A beneficial ecological cycle is gradually being formed.

Straw- and fuelwood-saving stove
In order to prevent huge energy losses from small stoves, the Department of Agriculture has introduced the straw- and fuelwood-saving stove in several hundred counties. It is becoming very popular and is spreading quickly among peasants. A statistical survey was conducted in Fuyang County, Anhui Province, with a random sample of 107 rural families. The results show that the household straw-saving stoves have greatly increased the coefficient of heat conversion, a quarter of them up to 20–30 per cent, half of them up to 30–40 per cent, and the other quarter up to 40–50 per cent. This shows that peasants have indeed mastered this innovation. If applied to the

whole country, by 2000 huge amounts of biomass equivalent to 7.5 million tce would be saved. By solving the household energy problem, eco-agriculture could be developed in China. A 100,000 km "green great wall" has been planted in 20 counties in the plains of northern Anhui Province, and crop yields have increased every year.

The biogas digester

Biogas is not only used for cooking, heating, and lighting in rural households, but also has ecological benefits. Through anaerobic fermentation, elements of hydrogen and carbon are separated from nitrogen, phosphorus, potassium, boron, molybdenum, zinc, and iron, which are used as both fuels and fertilizer. The methane gas produced in rice fields as a pollutant can be converted into a useful fuel in a biogas digester. Therefore biogas technology utilizes biomass energy and also provides one of the best environmental protection measures.

Fuelwood forestry

There are many fast-growing tree shrub species that could be selected for fuelwood forestry. In this selection process local conditions must be considered and breeding experiments conducted. For instance, a shrubby legume called purple-spike locust is a good choice because its branches can be used for fuel or for making baskets and lining mine tunnels, the leaves and twigs can be used for feed, and the green plough-under becomes a good organic nitrogen fertilizer owing to its nitrogen-fixing capability. It is a perennial plant and it is hardy. In addition to optimized species selection, a combined configuration of trees, shrubs, and grasses should be adopted for maximum utilization of solar energy through photosynthesis.

Eco-agriculture

The eco-agriculture idea could be realized in the plains areas by keeping one-third of the land for crops while using another third for forestry, and another third for forage grasses for livestock raising, and by rotating usage of the land. In the alluvial plain of the Yellow River and Hui River, this idea is gradually being realized. Rural families are making a lot of money by selling timber and fuelwood products from plains forestry. Combined with the straw-saving stove, the rural fuel shortage has been solved. Further consideration should be given to the comprehensive utilization of the remaining biomass,

316

as both fuel and raw materials for the chemical industry. The economic benefits of plains forestry are invaluable.

Solar energy
The annual average solar radiation on earth is 120 kcal/cm^2. Over two-thirds of China it is more than 140 kcal/cm^2, and in Qinghai, Gansu, Xinjiang, and Tibet it is more than 200 kcal/cm^2. This renewable energy could be put to daily use by technologies such as the solar stove, which collects heat by focusing sunlight, and the water heater using the black-body conversion technique. In rural areas, solar energy can be utilized not only for cooking and heating, but also for growing rice seedlings, incubating, greenhouse planting, and drying processes. Solar energy stoves are becoming a valuable compensating energy source in energy-shortage areas, especially in north-west China which has higher than average solar radiation intensity. In China, there are 66 counties, cities, and districts and more than 30 research and development institutes and manufacturers engaged in developing, utilizing, and introducing solar energy. A new solar energy industry is beginning to appear.

Overall achievements by 1992
The Department of Energy and Environment of the Ministry of Agriculture has provided me with some figures on the rural energy situation. By the end of 1992, about 150 million rural families in China had replaced their old stoves with straw- or fuelwood-saving stoves and 5 million rural families had installed biogas digester pits. The capacity of small hydropower stations was over 14.42 gigawatts (GW) and annual power generation was 44 terawatt hours (TWh). Fuelwood forests covering 4.5 million hectares had been planted. Around 140,000 rural families had installed solar stoves, and solar water-heating devices with a total effective area of 1.55 million m^2 had been installed. Energy-efficiency technologies for use in kiln combustion and in tea and tobacco drying had been developed. Altogether, in China's rural areas, the energy saved and new energy developed is equivalent to 8 million tce, making this a leading project in terms of the investment to energy output ratio. More than 1,000 technical personnel in over 100 research institutes have been working on rural energy development. By 1992, over 2,700 enterprises, 1,400 township-level petrol stations, and over 16,000 construction teams in the rural energy industry had been established.

2. The energy consumption of township enterprises in China

The boom in township enterprises is a significant step in the reform of China's rural economic system. Along with the rapid development of rural enterprises, more peasants are leaving their land to go to nearby towns to work in these enterprises and other trades or professions. This will create more energy demand. The development of township enterprises will reduce the labour available for farming and accelerate the growth of intensive farming practices. On the other hand, owing to the imbalance between the supply of and demand for commercial energy sources, rural energy development is urgently needed. Another important factor is that a prosperous township economy provides more financial support to the development of rural energy resources. Rural energy development is fundamental to township enterprises and, in turn, it relies on the vigour and prosperity brought by newly emerged township enterprises.

The rapid growth in township enterprises is creating many social, economic, and environmental problems, of which the problems of energy and environment are the most serious. The energy shortage in rural households has been partly solved. One reason is that more straw is available with increasing rates of growth in agriculture. Other reasons are the widespread use of straw-saving stoves, biogas digesters, and solar stoves and the cultivation of fuelwood forestry. The energy shortage in township industries, however, is becoming increasingly serious, and there are growing demands for commercial energy sources such as coal, petroleum products, and electricity. The implications raise several issues.

The value of low energy consumption in agriculture

Agriculture in the United States is totally mechanized, 90 per cent of it being petroleum powered. For each kcal of farm product, 15 kcal of energy is invested. Hence during periods of oil price crisis, American farmers could not make ends meet even if the output of their farm products was increased, and subsidies from the government were required to support their farming activities. In developed countries where agricultural mechanization is adopted as a measure to promote productivity, this might be a common situation. A serious problem of energy efficiency is also induced by such practices. Many international economists take a critical view of oil-powered agriculture and have suggested that China's agriculture should emphasize land productivity rather than labour productivity through petroleum-powered agriculture.

The dependence of agricultural production on commercial energy in China is far less than in developed countries. Although agricultural machinery power has reached well over 300 GW in China, it accounts for less than 40 per cent of the total power used in agriculture. The rest is still provided by manual and animal labour. It is likely that rural household energy will continue to rely on all sorts of biomass energy and other renewable energy sources. Commercial energy consumption per 10,000 yuan of agricultural output is only 1.0 tce for agriculture, which is much less than the figure of 5.5 tce per 10,000 yuan for heavy industry, and also less than the 1.2 tce per 10,000 yuan for light industry. The low consumption of commercial energy by agriculture is an advantageous feature that could also be introduced into the processing and transportation of farm products. Biogas-fuelled small power stations and farm trucks are typical examples. The benefits in terms of society and the environment are significant.

The high energy intensity of township enterprises' consumption

A team investigating township enterprises' energy consumption sampled 22 counties in different parts of China. The statistical data show that energy consumption per 10,000 yuan output ranges from 1.1 tce in Ningbo County, Zhejiang, to 16.7 tce in Xingyang, Henan. The median is 7.9 tce in Rongcheng, Shandong. This median figure is 2.6 times higher than the figure for China's light industry. A major factor in township enterprises' high energy consumption is the building materials industry. In Xingyang County, the coal consumption by the building materials industry is as high as 60 tce per 10,000 yuan output, accounting for 23 per cent of the county's total coal consumption, whereas in Ningbo County the figure is 5.5 tce, accounting for only 7 per cent of the county's total coal consumption. Thus, in addition to energy saving by technology and management, attention also needs to be paid to structural energy saving for township enterprises.

The energy-saving potential of household handicraft industries

The characteristics of household handicraft industries are:
1. They are labour intensive and could combine into enterprises with a substantial scale of production.
2. They could be divided into many specialities and distributed among

households, thus reducing energy consumption and increasing the economic benefits.

3. They comprise many production levels and could cooperate voluntarily to produce a series of products.
4. The techniques are simple and easy to learn. This makes it easier to switch types and kinds of product whenever demand in the market changes and therefore to increase competitiveness.

The concept of "one town, one product" has recently been spreading. This involves handicraft products from thousands of rural households, all powered manually. For instance, in the region of Dabie Mountain where bamboo trees are abundant, a handicraft processing industry is emerging. Bamboo shoot fibre is shredded by rural households. This material, with high tensile strength and good elasticity, can be used as a good-quality filling in the furniture industry, so it is in great demand in domestic markets. These energy-saving household rural handicraft industries not only support various light industries, but also dramatically increase the incomes of poor rural families through hard work and utilization of local resources without damaging the environment.

Employing surplus rural labour

By 2000, China will have a surplus of 70 million entering the labour market. In addition, 110 million peasants will transfer from farming to other trades. This labour corps is certainly too huge to be absorbed by China's cities. One solution would be to coordinate their labour, capital, and farm products with other productive elements such as investment capital, government subsidies, and new technologies. In this way, it might be possible to give them a good chance to be employed in various kinds of nearby township service or light industries rather than looking for jobs in cities far away from their homeland.

China's rural population increase will also increase the demand for energy, and the rise in peasants' standard of living will further increase this demand. It is obvious that problems of energy, population, employment, and environment are closely interconnected. Given the potential for expansion of township industries and the pressure to absorb more surplus labour from the surrounding rural regions, we must try our best to control the population by all effective measures.

Increasing energy supply shortages

It is expected that there will be 300 million people working in township industries by 2000. If each worker's output amounts to 3,000 yuan, and assuming average energy consumption per 1,000 yuan drops from the present 790 kilograms of coal equivalent (kgce) to 310 kgce, the commercial energy supply will amount to 200 million tce. In China, 37 per cent of villages still lack a power supply, and average rural power consumption amounts to only 60 kWh per capita, which is only 1 per cent of US consumption. The total power capacity of farm machines (mainly tractors) is 150 GW, but the average yearly worktime is a mere 300 hours owing to insufficient supplies of diesel fuel. The yearly energy requirements of villages and towns in 2000 are estimated to be 300 TWh of power and 20 million tons (Mt) of diesel fuel. In view of the fact that demand for energy in urban areas is increasing faster than that in rural areas, the ever-increasing shortage of energy supply in city industry will make township industries lag further behind. It will therefore also be difficult to fulfil demand in rural areas.

The value of emerging service industries in townships

If China's more than 60,000 townships could each develop a competitive product that suits local conditions, then all service industries supporting the development of this product should play their part in order to enable it to sell well in the market. As the practice of "one town, one product" becomes more widespread, linked occupations such as industrial plantation, livestock farming, storage, manufacturing, transportation, marketing, information, construction, finance, insurance, researching, consulting, and other service industries are also increasing. Most of these occupations belong in the category of tertiary industries, and would provide jobs for young workers. If an average of 3,000 workers in each town could be absorbed into these trades, 180 million workers could be employed and the problem of their influx into cities could be avoided. In terms of energy consumption, no more than 100 kgce per 1,000 yuan GDP would be needed to support these service industries, and their output–input ratio would be one of the highest. However, effective training of managers in each business category should have priority. It would be logical for them to come from cadres willing to change jobs as well as from educated young people returning to their own villages and towns.

The potential energy output of human and animal power

There are 300 million rural labourers in China providing energy equivalent to 18 GW. Suppose each of them works 250 days per year and 8 hours per day, their total work would be equivalent to 36 TWh. However, other than manpower-operated machines such as bicycles and sewing machines, neither R&D institutes nor machine industries have paid much attention to the development and production of similar machines or equipment that are highly efficient but consume little commercial energy other than manpower. A large part of this energy is wasted owing to the use of inefficient old-fashioned equipment, although this situation is improving since the opening of commodity markets everywhere.

As for the number of draught animals, this is expected to increase from a recent figure of 80 million to 200 million by 2000. The energy output of 80 million animals is equivalent to 33 GW. Suppose they work 140 days per year and 8 hours a day, their total work would be equivalent to 37 TWh. The same amount of work of 37 TWh would consume 17 million tons of diesel oil per year if generated by diesel engines. Research shows that the average draught animal's yearly work is only 70 days or 16.5 TWh, with an efficiency less than 50 per cent. However, the energy of animals is indirectly derived with great efficiency from solar energy and should not be neglected in rural agro-industrial activities. In some developing countries such as China and South-East and South Asia, they are still major power suppliers for farming. Quite a few environmental workers consider the efficient use of animal power in rural areas instead of petroleum as a matter of progress rather than retrogression.

The advantages of small-scale hydropower plants

Small-scale hydropower potential in China amounts to 150 GW, of which 70 GW can be exploited. Construction of new small hydropower stations is planned to add 25 GW by 2000, using less than one-third of the total potential. Analysis of available data reveals that the capital requirement of these stations was 1,250 yuan per kW, which is affordable by rural communities. Since they satisfy the essential requirements of both economy and technology, these new stations should be constructed as soon as possible. With a national effort, capacity of 45 GW could be constructed. Such a power supply would greatly facilitate industrial development for township enterprises in mountainous regions. For power stations where over 60 per cent of their drainage area is covered by vegetation, it would be feasible to raise funds on liberal terms from the local community or bank for their construction.

The capacity of numerous small hydropower stations would add up to quite a large figure despite their individual small scale. The power from each plant could be consumed locally, thus avoiding the necessity to invest in long-distance transmission lines. In addition, small stations could be constructed in far less time than is required for large projects. They could also have the benefit of providing flood-control and irrigation for local regions if integrated with other water and soil conservation projects. Fuelwood harvesting would end if the hydropower supply were used for cooking, as already happens among about 20 per cent of local inhabitants in China's 700 counties where hydropower is available. Hydropower is used, too, in township enterprises such as pottery, tobacco, and tea industries for their thermal energy demands. The outcome of all these measures is that: forests are preserved, the environment is protected, and tourists are attracted.

3. The benefits of energy efficiency improvements and the use of new and renewable natural resources

Reduced use of synthetic fertilizers

There are several ways to reduce expenditure on energy and to tap new resources in China, such as the development of straw- or fuelwood-efficient stoves, biogas digesters, solar stoves, and fuelwood forestry. All these measures could save large amounts of biomass from being burnt. The renewable biomass thus saved could be digested either in biogas pits or by herbivore animals to produce valuable organic fertilizers to be returned to arable land after the production of biogas or animal products. This is a good way to reduce the amount of synthetic fertilizers used in farming, and to maintain the quality of the soil, which is an important factor in sustaining high yields on arable land. Biogas has another function of killing rats and pests in grain bins, thus lessening the loss of grain in storage.

Maintenance of soil quality

It has become common knowledge that excess use of synthetic fertilizers has a destructive effect on soil quality, and their diminishing returns on China's arable land have already given warning to the government as well as to peasants. Since the development of renewable energy sources in rural areas produces large quantities of organic fertilizers to replace synthetic fertilizers, this in turn is of great help to the development of sustainable eco-agriculture. In fact, whatever the model of eco-agricultural system, it must be built on the basic reconstruction of rural renewable energy resources.

Increased rural incomes from backyard-farming

In China's vast areas of farming districts, family-size backyard-farming is popping up everywhere. Although the type of business varies, the outcome is quite similar; i.e. the family works harder and makes more money – both of which are good for the rural socio-economy. For instance, a typical family in Funan County has installed a biogas digester pit in their backyard. Depending on the supply of biogas, jobs such as cooking, seedling and vegetable cultivation, fertilizing, pest control, grain storage, and animal feeding keep the whole family a lot busier but also a lot richer than before.

Amelioration of the energy shortage

China has a large variety of biological resources, yet on a per capita basis they are quite low and they are far from completely and comprehensively utilized. Their economic potential is limited, and wastage is considerable. If people could make full use of them, their potential outcome would be tremendous. In hundreds of projects set up by China's National Committee of Science and Technology, many have been enabled to develop this potential under prevailing conditions in China's rural areas. One of the problems that has arisen is, of course, the inadequate supply of energy for farm production. In view of the fact that the supply of commercial energy to rural and township agro-industry is likely to be limited for rather a long time, this increases the importance of developing rural renewable energy resources such as solar energy, wind energy, biomass energy, tidal energy, geothermal energy, etc. to higher levels as the best solution to this energy shortage.

The sustainable development of rural agro-industry

A high proportion of peasants have made a fortune from domestic livestock rearing. Pigs, cows, cattle, rabbits, geese, fish, crabs, and silkworms are the prevailing products in Funan, Feixi, Jieshou, Fuyang, Lu'an, Jiashan, Wuhe, and Jinzhai counties, respectively, in Anhui Province. In Funan County, biogas enthusiast Shen Chaojun invented the technology of using fermented liquid drawn from biogas digester pits as an additive to raise pigs with great success. Another technological invention worth mentioning here is the successful inter-planting of wheat and paulownia trees in the vast East Henan and North Anhui regions. This new method of combining farming and forestry not only increases peasants' incomes, but also greens the rural areas and humidifies the micro-climate. Rural families could benefit from using liquid from a biogas digester pit to raise pigs, or from a biogas lamp, a manpowered sewing machine, and a biogas iron to run a garmentwork business. It is clear that different kinds of renewable energy resources could aid the sustainable development of rural agro-industry in developing countries such as China's vast rural areas.

The dispersion of culture and industry from urban centres

There are many links between urban and rural areas. Apart from commodity trading, communications and transportation, information transmission, technology transfer, and the export of training and labour services, the dispersion of culture and industry from urban centres into the surrounding rural areas also needs consideration. According to business research, the most economic industrial layouts are those of light industry and the textile industries, and in particular the food industry. For example, the primary processing of products such as tobacco, tea, and sweet potato (mostly dehydration processes) is carried out *in situ*, whereas subsequent processing and packaging into finished products occur in township factories. Those factories require an adequate supply of raw materials from the surrounding rural areas to keep both sides in business.

Reduced energy intensity

Past agro-industrial development in China involved incompatible demands for economic inputs for agriculture and energy development. This is the main reason for the declining output–input ratio in agriculture in recent years. Considering that agriculture and energy are China's two focal strategies, a joint strategy appears even more important. From the point of view of outputs and inputs, rural energy development has a large output–input ratio. It has already been seen that the straw- or fuelwood-efficient stove can improve thermal efficiency by 30 per cent at very little expense. In comparison, a coal mine project to produce 4 million tons would require an input of 800 million yuan and a construction period of 8 years. The same thermal value could be saved by installing millions of efficient stoves in rural families at a fraction of both the inputs and time required in investment and research and development. It is no exaggeration to say that the output–input ratio of this rural project would rank first not only among all energy-efficient projects, but also among all other industrial projects.

Other socio-economic, environmental, and resource benefits

The spectrum of research and development of high and new technologies in the field of energy conservation in China's rural areas has broadened quite a lot since 1978. The socio-economic, environmental, and resource benefits have thus been greatly improved.

For example, ever since improved pig-raising started in Funan County of Anhui Province, there has been an upsurge in the combined construction of biogas digester pits, pigpens, and latrines, which is spreading far and wide. Peasants have found that the addition of fermented liquid from the pit to feeds makes pigs disease resistant and gives them a better appetite. This is because bacteria and the eggs of parasites are completely killed in the process of anaerobic fermentation in the sealed pit, and nutritious ingredients such as the B vitamins and amino acids are produced in the same process. For instance, lysine, which is lacking in natural pig or chicken feed, shows up in the pit liquid samples. If these developments were further combined with the sinking of water wells and water filtration measures, both environmental and health conditions in rural areas would be greatly improved.

4. Summary

Rural energy consumption in China is spreading from household to industry nowadays, and is leading to a nationwide energy shortage.

Thus, the rapid advance of township industries is incompatible with the present energy supply, which must be treated as an important element in the national reconstruction of more than 60,000 townships in China. In spite of there having been a good start in the development of renewable energies in rural areas, a large amount of work still remains to be accomplished in order to develop the land sustainably, not only for ourselves but also for coming generations. As the statistics show, although China leads the world with some 5 million biogas digester pits having already been constructed, this is a tiny figure in relation to China's 192 million rural families. If the total energy content of the biomass accumulated through photosynthesis were to be fully utilized, this would tap a hundred-fold larger amount of energy resources. Other statistics show that only a quarter of the 20 GW capacity of small-scale hydropower stations in east and south China's seven provinces had been exploited. Furthermore, the 300 counties with successful rural electrification experiments represent only 17 per cent of the total number of counties in China.

Acknowledgements

Statistical data on the development of rural energy and environment after 1988 were submitted by Deng Keyun, head of the Department of Energy and Environment, Ministry of Agriculture of China, to the Committee on Environmental Protection, National People's Congress of China. Statistical data on the development of small-scale rural power after 1988 were submitted by Zheng Xian, head of the Department of Hydropower, Ministry of Water Conservancy of China, to the Committee on Environmental Protection, National People's Congress of China.

Comments on part 5

Yujiro Hayami

I have little disagreement with Dr. Takase on the issues covered by his comprehensive and well-balanced review. Therefore, I will mention only one critical issue that is not covered, that is the need to design institutions that are compatible with the incentives of local people to conserve natural resources in developing economies. I will draw on two examples of forest conservation programmes that I observed in South-East Asia.

The first example relates to a programme of privatization of forest land management in Viet Nam. Since 1981, Viet Nam has moved from the socialist-style cooperative-managed farming system to a household-managed system. The cooperative farms were subdivided and allocated to individual households to be privately managed. It is well known that this reform has resulted in major increases in crop yields, especially for rice. More recently, Viet Nam has begun to experiment with a programme that transfers forest land to individual household management. Under this programme, state-owned forest lands hitherto managed by cooperatives are allocated on long-term leases to individual households if they agree to reforest and manage them properly and to hand over a share of the timber harvests as ground rent.

328

In comparison with arable land, forest land is less amenable to private management by a single household, partly because of the externalities involved in the use of forest land and partly because of the difficulty of demarcating it into distinguishable parcels for exclusive use by individuals. To my surprise, despite the theoretical difficulties involved in the privatization of forest management, this scheme appears to be highly successful. Reforestation has been speeded up, and forest conservation has been strengthened. Usually, a hill neighbouring a farmer's residence is allocated to his household, so that protection of the forest against fire and timber theft can be efficiently accomplished by the family with little opportunity cost. Further, when land is allocated that is a long way from home, farmers have built temporary huts where family members stay to guard the plot. It was also remarkable to find in the site we visited that the boundary between allocated sectors was clearly demarcated by an open space, sometimes marked by stones, which was used as an access road into the forest.

Typically, households that are allocated forest land plant seedlings of eucalyptus, pine, and acacia, mainly using family labour during the slack season for farming activities. For a few years they grow upland crops between the seedlings, then, as the trees become taller, the forests begin to provide employment and income from thinnings and prunings for fuel and other uses as well as from grazing for animals.

It is too early to judge the success of this household-managed forestry system. It appears, however, that this scheme has great potential for solving the difficult problem of how to achieve the socially optimum conservation of forest resources while producing current income and employment for local people not only in Viet Nam but also in other developing economies in the third world. In many developing countries, such as Indonesia, Thailand, and the Philippines, most forest land is under state ownership and management. Yet, partly because of the weak administrative capacity (and, often, corruption) of public agencies and partly because of the difficulty of organizing local communities for collective action, serious depletion of forest resources has been ubiquitous.

To reverse this trend it is necessary, but not sufficient, to strengthen government administrative capacity and community organizational power. A crucial requirement is incentives for individuals to undertake resource conservation efforts in a way consistent with social welfare criteria. The household management of forest lands in Viet

Nam appears to represent a highly promising example of "incentive-compatible" institutional arrangements.

In contrast, an institutional design based on a miscalculation of local people's incentive mechanism can result in devastating failures in natural resource management. Such a case was observed in a reforestation project in the Philippines about a decade or so ago. This project attempted to mobilize local people's labour for reforestation by paying a fee per seedling planted. This scheme speeded up reforestation, but, as hills and mountains in nearby villages were planted with seedlings, people found their employment opportunities disappearing. They therefore began to destroy the seedlings by setting fire to them at night.

The effective design of institutions for the conservation of natural resources in the third world must be based on a full understanding of human behaviour and incentive systems in local communities.

Part 6
Long-term strategies of developing countries

17

Leapfrogging strategies for developing countries

José Goldemberg

1. Introduction

In the past it was generally accepted that economic growth, as measured by gross domestic product (GDP), was linked to the growth in consumption of raw materials and energy and in the unpleasant consequences of consumption, namely pollution.

If such linkages were to last for many decades the consequences for mankind would be disastrous. At present, only approximately a quarter of the world population (concentrated in the OECD countries) has reached a standard of living that can be considered acceptable. Of the remaining three-quarters – spread over more than 100 countries – only a small fraction has reached a reasonable standard of living; the remainder are at a level little above absolute poverty.

In the developing world (low-income economies[1]), GDP/capita is at least 10 times smaller than that in the OECD countries, and consumption of raw materials and energy is also at least 10 times smaller. Such disparities in income will not last forever. The economies of a number of very populous developing countries are growing rapidly and – barring unexpected set-backs – their GDP/capita will approach that of the developed countries. This will result in great strains

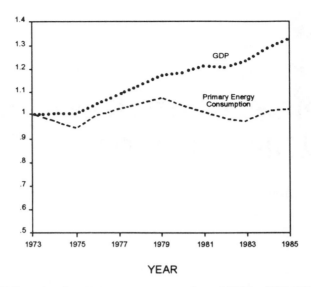

Fig. 17.1 **GDP and primary energy consumption: OECD, 1973–1985 (1973 = 1.** **Sources: energy data –** *BP Statistical Review of World Energy*, **London, June 1986;** **GDP data –** OECD, *National Accounts of OECD Countries, Vol. 1*, **Paris, 1985)**

on access to raw materials and energy, as well as an increase in pollution.

Efforts to delink GDP growth and consumption/pollution are, therefore, a high priority in the strategies of many governments. Figure 17.1 shows the evolution of primary energy consumption and of GDP for OECD countries in the period 1973–1985 relative to 1973.

The delinking of energy and GDP growth occurs for several reasons:

– the saturation of consumer goods markets – in industrialized societies economic activity has moved towards services not heavy industry;
– a shift towards the use of less energy-intensive materials;
– a shift from traditional, inefficient non-commercial fuels to such energy sources as electricity, liquid and gaseous fuels, and processed solid fuels;
– the adoption of new and more energy-efficient technologies.

These trends have not so far spread significantly to developing countries although successful efforts are being made in some of them.

Projections of primary energy consumption give an idea of what might happen in the future. However, depending on the assumptions

334

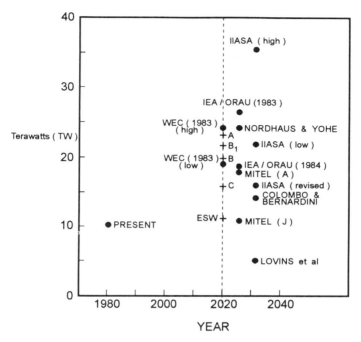

Fig. 17.2 **Projections of primary energy consumption, 2020–2030 (Note: A = WEC Commission high-growth case, B = reference case, B₁ = modified reference case, C = ecologically driven case)**

made, the results can be quite different (as shown in fig. 17.2). More recently, projections such as the ones prepared by the World Energy Council (WEC) tend to cluster at the lower end of such projections (Goldemberg et al., 1987; WEC Commission, 1993).

As far as pollution is concerned, the situation is more complex because some pollutants are associated with low income, such as concentrations of particulate matter, and others with high income, such as CO_2 emissions, as shown in fig. 17.3 (World Bank, 1992). The goal of many governments is to achieve an evolution over time of the type shown in fig. 17.4.

2. The prospects of success in delinking GDP and energy

The way energy is used in different countries and the efficiency of its use are usually quantified by an indicator called *energy intensity*, that

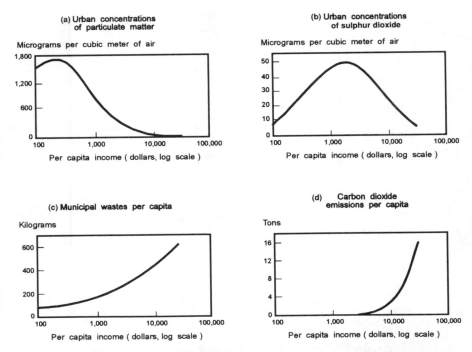

Fig. 17.3   **Environmental indicators at different country income levels. (a) Urban concentrations of particulate matter. (b) Urban concentrations of sulphur dioxide. (c) Municipal wastes per capita. (d) Carbon dioxide emissions per capita (Source: World Bank, 1992)**

is, the ratio between energy consumption (E) – measured in kilojoules (kJ), BTUs, or tons of oil equivalent (toe) – and GDP measured in US dollars. Long-term studies of the evolution of energy intensity in a number of countries (Martin, 1988) indicate that this ratio climbs during the initial phase of development when heavy industrial infrastructure is put in place, reaches a peak, and then decreases (fig. 17.5).

Only commercial energy consumption is considered in figure 17.5. Other factors besides technology, such as geography, population, and history, play a role in the evolution of energy intensity. This is why it is difficult to compare the evolution of different countries. It is quite clear, however, that latecomers in the development process follow the same pattern as their predecessors but with less accentuated peaks: they do not have to reach high E/GDP ratios in the initial stages of

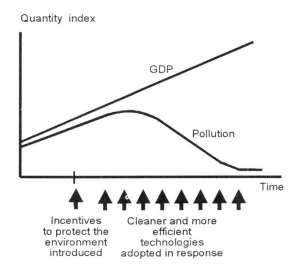

Fig. 17.4 **Evolution over time of the growth in GDP and pollution**

industrialization because they can benefit from modern methods of manufacturing and more efficient systems of transportation developed by others. In other words, what was once considered an iron link between energy and GDP growth is not a general feature of modern economies. This was true even before the oil crisis of 1973, and rising oil prices only accelerated the pace of structural change in the industrialized countries.

In contrast, as figure 17.5 shows, energy intensity in the developing countries is increasing. The adoption of outdated technologies foisted on them by the industrialized countries seems to be part of the reason. Other reasons might be the transfer of "dirty industries" or highly energy-intensive industries (such as aluminium smelters) to developing countries. A notable exception to the prevailing increase among the developing countries is China, where energy intensity is diminishing rapidly. As a whole, however, the energy intensity of the world is decreasing, as shown in figure 17.6.

One way for developing countries to avoid environmental and economic stress is to leapfrog the technologies used by industrialized countries in the past. This means incorporating energy-efficient technologies early in the development process.

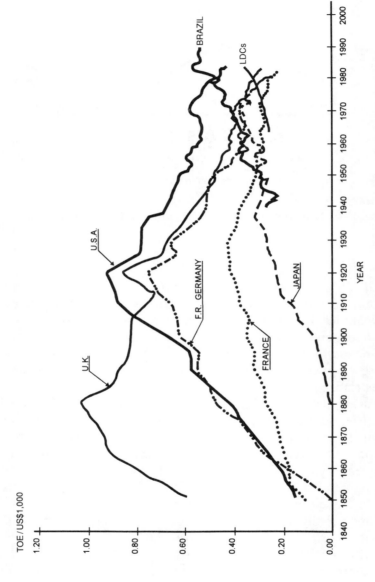

Fig. 17.5 **The evolution of energy intensity in various countries (Source: Martin, 1988)**

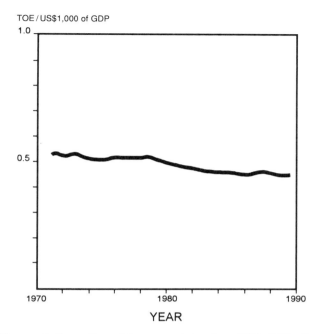

TOE / US$1,000 of GDP

Fig. 17.6 **The evolution of world energy intensity, 1970–1990 (Source: World Energy Council,** *Survey of Energy Resources,* **London, 1992)**

The result could be a decrease in the yearly growth of energy consumption without hampering development. In Brazil, for example, action planned for the period 1990–2010 is expected to lead to a 30 per cent reduction in projected energy consumption by the end of this time-span, compared with what it would be if no action were taken (Brazilian Ministry of Infrastructure, 1991).

Brazil's energy system relies heavily on renewable resources such as hydropower and biomass (fuelwood, charcoal, ethanol, and biogas from sugar cane): 62.7 per cent of all energy used is renewable and 37.3 per cent is non-renewable in the form of oil, gas, and coal. Energy consumption in Brazil has grown quite rapidly – 4.8 per cent a year in the past decade. At this rate, total consumption would grow from 183.6 million metric tons of oil equivalent (Mtoe) in 1990 to 473.6 Mtoe in 2010, i.e. a 2.6-fold increase. The new energy matrix of the Brazilian government incorporates energy conservation, an increase in the consumption of natural gas, and the continued use of biomass coupled with modern technology (including gasification for

Table 17.1 **Brazil's growth in GDP and energy consumption: Historical trend and new energy matrix, 1990–2010**

	Historical trend	New energy matrix
GDP, annual growth rate	4.3%	4.3%
Energy consumption, annual growth rate	4.8%	3.8%
Increase in energy consumption (year 2010/1990)	473.6 Mtoe/183.6 Mtoe = 2.6	386.6 Mtoe/183.6 Mtoe = 2.1

electricity generation using highly efficient gas turbines). Under the new plan, the present consumption of 183.6 Mtoe would grow to 386.6 Mtoe in 2010, which is 30 per cent below the historical trend (table 17.1). This would result in savings of US$85 billion in investments and a 30 per cent reduction in CO_2 emissions.

Another way to look at the energy intensities of different countries is to analyse the way they change not with time but with GDP, as shown in table 17.2 and figure 17.7 (WRI, 1993). East European countries were excluded because they use energy very inefficiently. Energy intensity increases very slowly as income per capita increases, which means that highly industrialized countries have incorporated modern and efficient technologies into their infrastructure.

3. The prospects of success in delinking GDP and pollution

Appreciable success has been achieved in delinking GDP and certain types of pollution as GDP increases. Figure 17.8 shows the evolution of GDP and emissions of particulates, lead, and sulphur oxides, which are all linked to fossil fuel consumption. Reductions in nitrogen oxides have not been achieved (World Bank, 1992).

Another area where progress has been made is solid waste, which is becoming increasingly important owing to problems of disposal (WRI, 1993). Table 17.3 presents data on municipal solid waste per capita for a number of countries. The amount of waste per capita increases by a factor of 4 when one goes from low- to high-income countries owing to the increasing importance of packaging. In analogy with the energy intensity indicator one can introduce a "solid waste intensity" indicator (the ratio of solid waste to GDP) and plot this indicator as a function of GDP. Figure 17.9 shows that countries

Table 17.2 **Energy intensity in selected countries (ranked by GDP/capita)**

Country	Energy use (million BTU/capita)	GDP/capita ($PPP/capita)	Energy intensity (million BTU/$PPP)
China	24.3	2,656	0.009
Peru	21.7	2,731	0.008
Iraq	29.7	3,510	0.008
Colombia	35.1	4,068	0.009
Argentina	61.5	4,310	0.014
Brazil	47.4	4,951	0.010
Chile	43.7	4,987	0.009
Portugal	55.3	6,259	0.009
Greece	90.7	6,764	0.013
Ireland	102.8	7,481	0.014
Spain	82.5	8,723	0.009
Saudi Arabia	176.9	10,330	0.017
Israel	83.7	10,448	0.008
Oman	95.4	10,573	0.009
New Zealand	187.7	11,155	0.017
Austria	144.2	13,063	0.011
Belgium	189.0	13,313	0.014
Netherlands	188.7	13,351	0.014
Italy	115.3	13,608	0.008
United Kingdom	150.1	13,732	0.011
Denmark	138.9	13,751	0.010
France	149.3	14,164	0.011
Japan	127.8	14,311	0.009
Germany	178.8	14,507	0.012
Finland	222.4	14,598	0.015
Sweden	265.8	14,817	0.018
Singapore	138.4	15,108	0.009
Australia	214.7	15,266	0.014
Kuwait	230.7	15,984	0.014
Norway	369.7	16,838	0.022
Switzerland	155.4	18,590	0.008
Canada	399.7	18,635	0.021
USA	308.9	20,998	0.015

Source: WRI (1993).

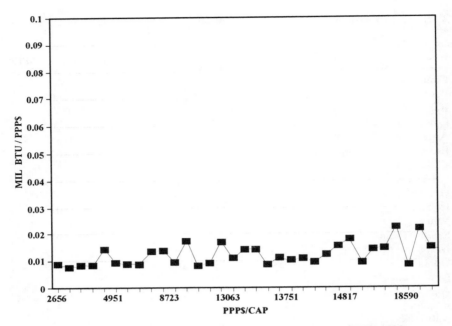

Fig. 17.7 **Energy intensity vs. per capita GDP (Source: WRI, 1993)**

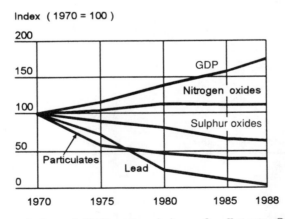

Fig. 17.8 **The evolution of GDP and emissions of pollutants: OECD countries, 1970–1988 (Note: GDP and emissions of nitrogen oxides and sulphur oxides are OECD averages; emissions of particulates are estimated from the averages for Germany, Italy, the Netherlands, the United Kingdom, and the United States; lead emissions are for the United States. Sources: OECD, 1991; US Environmental Protection Agency, 1991)**

342

Table 17.3 **Solid waste intensity in selected countries (ranked by GDP/capita)**

Country	Waste (lbs/capita/day)	GDP/capita ($PPP/capita)	GDP/capita/day ($PPP/capita/day)	Waste intensity (lbs/$PPP)
Liberia	1.1	937	2.57	0.43
Kenya	1.1	1,023	2.80	0.39
Côte d'Ivoire	1.1	1,381	3.78	0.29
Indonesia	1.3	2,034	5.57	0.23
Romania	1.3	3,000	8.22	0.16
Iraq	2.4	3,510	9.62	0.25
Colombia	1.2	4,068	11.15	0.11
Poland	1.3	4,770	13.07	0.10
Bulgaria	1.3	5,064	13.87	0.09
Hungary	1.6	6,245	17.11	0.09
Portugal	1.5	6,259	17.15	0.09
Trinidad & Tobago	1.1	6,266	17.17	0.06
Former USSR	1.3	6,270	17.18	0.08
Greece	1.5	6,764	18.53	0.08
Czechoslovakia	1.1	7,420	20.33	0.06
Ireland	2.0	7,481	20.50	0.10
Spain	1.9	8,723	23.90	0.08
Saudi Arabia	2.4	10,330	28.30	0.08
Israel	2.4	10,448	28.62	0.08
Oman	2.4	10,573	28.97	0.08
New Zealand	4.0	11,155	30.56	0.13
Austria	1.3	13,063	35.79	0.04
Belgium	2.0	13,313	36.47	0.05
Netherlands	2.6	13,351	36.58	0.07
United Kingdom	2.2	13,732	36.64	0.06
Italy	1.5	13,608	37.28	0.04
Denmark	2.6	13,751	37.67	0.07
France	4.0	14,164	38.81	0.10
Japan	2.0	14,311	39.21	0.05
Germany	1.8	14,507	39.75	0.05
Finland	2.4	14,598	39.99	0.06
Sweden	2.0	14,817	40.59	0.05
Singapore	1.9	15,108	41.39	0.05
Australia	4.2	15,266	41.82	0.10
Kuwait	2.4	15,984	43.79	0.05
Norway	2.9	16,838	46.13	0.06
Switzerland	2.2	18,590	50.93	0.04
Canada	3.7	18,635	51.05	0.07
USA	3.3	20,998	57.53	0.06

Source: WRI (1993).

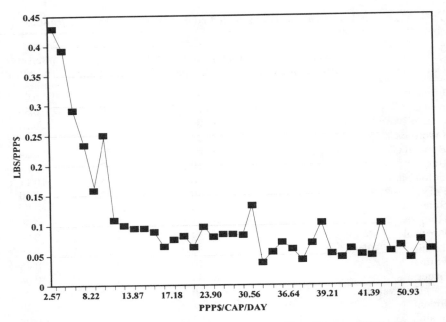

Fig. 17.9 **Solid waste intensity vs. GDP/capita/day (Source: WRI, 1993)**

with high per capita incomes produce much less waste per unit of GDP than do countries with low per capita incomes. Low-income countries produce an inordinate amount of waste considering their per capita incomes, whereas industrialized countries have incorporated efficient technologies that have reduced waste.

A serious pollution problem in developing countries involves indoor emissions of particulates and other pollutants originating in fuels used for cooking (WHO, 1992). The results are shown in table 17.4 and are quite alarming. As far as particulates are concerned, table 17.5 shows that firewood gives off larger amounts than coal briquettes. The SO_2 concentrations given off by various fuels are shown in table 17.6. This demonstrates that a switch from coal to liquefied petroleum gas (LPG) would represent enormous progress as far as SO_2 emissions are concerned. Regarding particulates, the same would be true if firewood were to be replaced by LPG.

Table 17.4 **Indoor air concentrations of pollutants in developing countries**[a]

Pollutant	Concentration	WHO daily exposure guidelines
Total suspended particulates (TSP)	$1–120$ mg/m^3	0.12 mg/m^3
CO	$10–50$ mg/m^3	10 mg/m^3
NO_2	$0.1–0.3$ mg/m^3	0.15 mg/m^3
Benzo-alpha-pyrene	$1–20$ μg/m^3[b]	0.001 μg/m^3

Source: WHO (1992).

a. India, Nepal, Nigeria, Kenya, Guatemala, and Papua New Guinea.
b. At these concentrations there is a link with cancer in 1 out of 100,000 people after a lifetime's exposure.

Table 17.5 **Concentrations of total suspended particulates in kitchens from various fuels**

Fuel	Concentration (mg/m^3)
Firewood	0.79
Briquettes	0.49
LPG	0.19
Biogas	0.18
Outdoors	0.18

Source: WHO (1992).

Table 17.6 **Concentrations of SO$_2$ in kitchens from various fuels**

Fuel	Concentration (mg/m^3)
Coal briquettes	0.49
Firewood	0.04
Biogas	0.02
LPG	0.02
Outdoors	0.01

Source: WHO (1992).

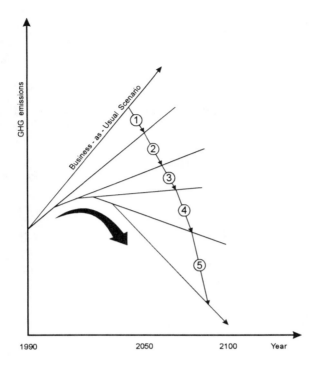

1 - Intensified energy conservation programs , CFCs phase - out .

2 - New & renewable energy sources.

3 - CO_2 fixation & re - utilization technology.

4 - Reforestation , stopping desertification , enhancing oceanic sinks .

5 - Future energy technologies : enhanced nuclear, fusion , space solar power generation.

Fig. 17.10 **Strategies to reduce greenhouse gas emissions**

4. Conclusions

In developing countries, pollution reduction seems to be closely connected to modernization. Growth along traditional lines would produce unbearable amounts of pollution, but the data show that industrialized countries have achieved important reductions in emissions
per unit of GDP. This evidence is not so dramatic in the case of emissions causing the greenhouse effect (mainly CO_2). Greater progress
in the future will require a combination of the strategies described in
figure 17.10.

Note

1. The World Bank classification of countries is as follows:
   - *Low-income economies* are those with a GNP per capita of US$610 or less in 1990.
   - *Middle-income economies* are those with a GNP per capita of more than US$610 but less than US$7,620 in 1990. A further division, at GNP per capita of US$2,465 in 1990, is made between lower-middle-income and upper-middle-income economies.
   - *High-income economies* are those with a GNP per capita of US$7,620 or more in 1990.

References

Brazilian Ministry of Infrastructure. 1991. *Brazilian Energy Matrix*. Brasilia.

Goldemberg, J., T. B. Johansson, A. K. N. Reddy, and R. H. Williams. 1987. *Energy for a Sustainable World*. New Delhi: John Wiley.

Martin, J. M. 1988. "L'intensité énergétique de l'activité économique dans les pays industrialisées." *Economies et sociétés – Cahiers de l'ISMEA* 22(4), April.

OECD (Organization for Economic Co-operation and Development). 1991. *The State of Environment. Annual Report*. Paris: OECD.

US Environmental Protection Agency. 1991. *National Air Pollution Emission Estimates 1940–1989*. Research Triangle Park, N.C., Report EPA-450/4-91-004, March.

WEC (World Energy Council) Commission. 1993. *Energy for Tomorrow's World – The Realities, the Real Options, and the Agenda for Achievement*. London: Kogan Page.

WHO (World Health Organization). 1992. *Indoor Air Pollution from Biomass Fuel*. Geneva: WHO.

World Bank. 1992. *World Development Report 1992. Development and the Environment*. Oxford: Oxford University Press.

WRI (World Resources Institute). 1993. *Environmental Almanac*. Washington, D.C.: WRI.

18

A development-focused approach to the environmental problems of developing countries

Amulya K. N. Reddy

1. Industrialized countries and global environmental degradation

The developing countries, with three times more population than the industrial countries, have been, and continue to be, far less responsible for "polluting" the global atmosphere with greenhouse gases (GHGs). However, their contribution to the concentration of greenhouse gases in the atmosphere is rising. For example, a general consensus exists that, "during 1988, almost three-quarters of the CO_2 from fossil-fuel combustion was released in industrialized countries. But when non-industrial sources are included (e.g., burning of forests and other land-use changes) the contribution of industrialized countries was about 56%. ... Analysis of the available data suggests that the historical fossil-fuel related emissions from developing countries represent only about 14% of the global total, as compared to 28% of current fossil-derived CO_2 emissions" (Grubb et al., 1992: 310).

Thus, in a world stratified into rich and poor countries, the bulk of the degradation of the global atmosphere has originated primarily from the rich industrialized countries but the contribution from the poor developing countries is increasingly rapidly.

2. Environmental degradation in dual societies

Most developing countries, however, are internally stratified. They consist of dual societies with small élites living in little islands of affluence amidst vast oceans of poverty inhabited by the more populous masses. The élites and the masses differ fundamentally in their consumption patterns and therefore in their impacts on the environment. Environmental degradation is none the less evident at both ends of the income spectrum (Reddy, 1986) – the rich pollute owing to the wasteful over-use of resources and the poor degrade the environment by surviving at its expense. Thus, the global phenomenon of non-uniform and skewed contributions to atmospheric degradation is mirrored within developing countries.

Further, attention is now being drawn to the fact that the nature of the environmental degradation caused by the élites and the masses is also different (José Goldemberg, personal communication, May 1993). For example, the rich are responsible for CO_2 pollution from automobiles and electricity generation, CFCs from refrigerators, etc. In contrast, the poor are responsible for deforestation in those countries and regions where cooking fuel is obtained by felling trees and where forests are cleared for agriculture to gain access to land in a highly skewed land ownership regime. In addition, the kerosene burnt by the poor for illumination contributes to CO_2 emissions.

Thus far, the contribution of the various income strata to national emissions in developing countries has not been scrutinized and unravelled. In fact, these emissions have not even been disaggregated crudely into the contributions of the rich and the poor. The basic problem seems to be that adequate information is lacking on the emissions from various end-use devices such as automobiles, two-wheelers, three-wheelers, buses, trucks, electric lighting, and kerosene lighting.

Nevertheless, an impressionistic conclusion is that the poor in developing countries contribute only marginally to the greenhouse gas emissions from these countries. This has two implications of major significance:
1. an emphasis on basic-needs-oriented development with a direct attack on poverty involves virtually no conflict with global environmental concerns;
2. however alarming and ominous the high population growth rates of the poor in developing countries may be from an economic growth point of view, these growth rates do not threaten the global

atmosphere as much as the smaller growth rates of industrialized-country populations and of the rich in developing countries.

3. A developing-country perspective on environmental problems

Most developing countries view the challenge of development to be far more important than the threat of climate change. Thus, if they address the threat of climate change at all, they would prefer to tackle it along with the advancement of, or as a bonus from, development. This bonus principle, which is the other side of the coin of the "no regrets" principle, requires that the short-term measures that advance development in developing countries yield the *bonus* of combating climate change.

This does not mean that developing countries can ignore all environmental issues. Invariably, local environmental concerns and developmental tasks are intimately intertwined. Business-as-usual economic growth in developing countries with dual societies has led neither to basic-needs-oriented development nor to environmentally sustainable patterns.[1] Economic growth catering to the élites and neglecting the poor – involving a variety of subsidies, price distortions, inefficiencies, etc. – has resulted, as pointed out, in environmental degradation caused by both segments of the dual society. Environmental degradation impedes and frustrates sustained development. More directly, the hardest-hit victims of environmental degradation are the poor, not only because they cannot commute or move away from pollution, but because their poorer health status makes them more vulnerable. Thus, an attack on poverty – an essential requirement of development (if not of blind economic growth) – has necessarily to include environmental protection.

The relative lack of responsibility of the developing countries for the degradation of the global atmosphere and the environmental degradation arising from élitist growth patterns suggest a step-by-step environmental approach for developing countries, apparently first enunciated by Yokobori (personal communication, 1993):

Step 1: Address local environmental problems such as unsafe rural water supplies, kerosene consumption for lighting, indoor particulate pollution due to smoke from fuelwood stoves, and urban vehicular pollution due to two-, three-, and four-wheeler personal transportation.
Step 2: Tackle regional environmental problems such as acid rain or river pollution.

Step 3: Focus on national environmental problems.
Step 4: Turn attention to global environmental problems such as greenhouse gas accumulation in the atmosphere.

Such a step-by-step approach will be more politically saleable within developing countries. This is because zeroing in on global environmental problems right at the initiation of environmental awareness is often viewed as succumbing to a stratagem of the industrialized countries to get the developing countries to fix a mess that the rich countries created. In addition, the equity pay-offs from this approach are substantial, because those who suffer most from environmental degradation become the first beneficiaries. There is also historical justice in this step-by-step approach because it demands that developing countries first address the problems that they themselves created and only then become environmentally altruistic by turning to problems that the industrialized countries created. Finally, an emphasis on the initial step(s) very often yields as a bonus environmental benefits corresponding to subsequent step(s), in particular global environmental benefits. Thus, a reduction in local urban vehicular pollution caused by two-, three-, and four-wheeler personal transportation also results in a reduction in GHG accumulation in the global atmosphere.

4. The crises of energy systems

The step-by-step approach begs the question of how environmental problems are to be addressed. It is submitted here that the best way of addressing an environmental problem is invariably not directly, but indirectly via the implementation of a development objective, particularly the energy component of such an objective. This is because energy production and consumption are major causes of environmental degradation. Hence, attempts to address environmental problems must preferably begin with an analysis of energy systems. However, the energy systems of developing countries are trapped in several crises, if a crisis is defined as a situation that does not permit continuation of old patterns of behaviour.

First, there is the *environmental* crisis, which involves *local* and *global* impacts. In the case of electricity, for instance, the local impacts consist of submergence of forests by hydroelectric projects, acid rain and other forms of atmospheric pollution from thermal power projects and vehicle use, and radiation hazards from nuclear power plants. The global impacts occur through increasing concentrations of greenhouse gases in the atmosphere, which have raised the spectre of global warming. In the case of petroleum products, vehicular pollution is choking third world metropolises and making life impossible. The transport systems of developing countries are blindly replicating all the mistakes of the systems in the industrialized countries, by being iniquitous, energy intensive, highly polluting, and harmful to the global atmosphere.

In addition, the electricity systems of developing countries face a serious *capital* crisis, because the capital requirements of the energy systems are three to five times greater than can be provided by the suppliers of capital. This unbridgeable gap, first highlighted at the level of the whole developing world by the World Bank in 1989 (Churchill and Saunders, 1990), also exists at the country level and within countries at the state level (Reddy, 1993). In India, the energy sector has been compared to the demon, Bakasura, of Indian mythology who had an insatiable appetite and, however much he was fed, wanted even more to eat. As for the petroleum consumption patterns of developing countries, they have serious capital, foreign exchange, and balance-of-payments implications, as shown by recent studies on the energy–debt nexus in Brazil, India, and Mexico (Rammanohar Reddy et al., 1992).

The environmental and capital crises are related, because the industrialized countries are pressurizing the developing countries to cut their emissions and adopt environmental measures as a *quid pro quo* for capital. This link between the capital and environmental aspects of the energy crisis may be unfair, but it is *Realpolitik*. It is often interpreted by developing countries as a conflict between environmental protection and the advancement of development.

Finally, there is the *equity* crisis. Even though energy systems are expanded in the name of development, they tend to bypass the poor. For example, in the state of Karnataka in South India, estimates show that half the population do not benefit directly from the electricity system primarily because their homes are not electrified although the village is (Reddy et al., 1991).

5. Overcoming the crises of energy systems through a new paradigm for energy

In the final analysis, the environment–development conflict and the crises threatening the energy systems of developing countries stem from the conventional energy paradigm or mind-set determining the thinking of energy decision makers. This mind-set is based on the so-called energy–GDP correlation according to which GDP increases can be achieved only by increases in energy consumption. In this paradigm, the magnitude of energy consumption becomes the indicator of development. And, once projections are made of energy requirements in the future, attention shifts to increasing supplies to meet these requirements.

The way out of the crisis is through a new paradigm for energy (Reddy, 1990) in which it is recognized that what human beings and their individual and collective activities require is not energy *per se* but the work that energy performs and the services that energy provides: illumination, warmth, "coolth" (to coin a word), mobility, etc. In this approach, although development requires, particularly for the poor, a substantial increase in energy services, such increases can be achieved not just by increasing the supply of energy to the devices (lamps, heaters, air conditioners, vehicles, appliances, etc.) but also by increasing their efficiency. It was efficiency improvements that led to the decoupling of GDP growth from energy consumption that characterized the economies of many OECD countries (particularly Japan) during the 1980s (Boyle and Taylor, 1990; Yamaji, 1991).

Efficiency improvements have associated costs, but very often the costs of saving energy are only one-third to one-half the costs of generation. Nevertheless, the costs of saving energy must be carefully compared with the costs of producing energy. Also, the magnitude of energy that can be saved must be taken into account. All this means that it is necessary to identify a *least-cost mix* of saving and generation options for energy.

Thus, the new challenge to the energy systems of developing countries is to reduce the coupling between GDP growth and energy consumption by identifying and implementing a least-cost mix of saving and generation options for increasing energy services, particularly for the poor. Energy, therefore, must acquire a human face and become an instrument of development, the crux of which must be poverty eradication. Energy planning must acquire a development focus and an end-use orientation directed towards energy services. Energy for whom? Energy for what? Energy how (efficiently)? These become central questions in the new approach.

What is required, therefore, is a development-focused end-use-oriented service-directed (DEFENDUS) paradigm for energy. A commitment to poverty eradication and development must guide the construction of energy demand and supply scenarios and the evolu-

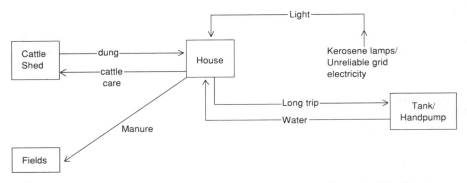

Fig. 18.1   **The traditional system of obtaining water, light, and fertilizer**

tion of energy systems that in turn should become the basis of environmental protection and management. The slogan must be: "From the needs of the poor and the imperatives of development to the design and implementation of efficient energy systems and thereby to a better environment!"

The remainder of this paper will be devoted to illustrations – at the village, state, and national levels – of this approach.

6. How Pura village triumphed over the Tragedy of the Commons

Pura is a typical village in the drought-prone part of Tumkur District in the Deccan part of Karnataka State in South India. It has a human population of about 470 (in approximately 90 households) and approximately 250 cattle. The traditional system of obtaining water, illumination, and fertilizer (for the fields) in Pura village is shown in figure 18.1. It implies a low quality of life characterized by poverty and environmental degradation in the form of unsafe water from an open tank, considerable effort to get this unsafe water, and inadequate illumination from traditional fossil-fuel-based kerosene lamps or from unreliable, low-voltage grid electricity.

This traditional system was replaced in September 1987 with the present Community Biogas Plants system (Reddy and Balachandra, 1991; Rajabapaiah et al., 1993). The main components and the flows of inputs/outputs are shown in figure 18.2. The operation of the system consists of the activities implicit in figure 18.2. Apart from the delivery of dung to the plants and the removal of sludge, all the other

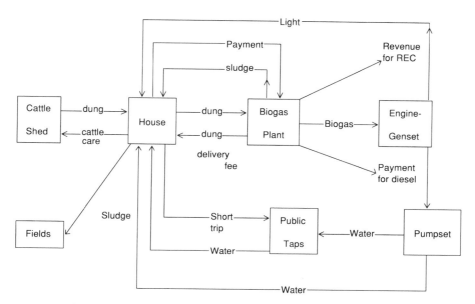

Fig. 18.2   **The present Community Biogas Plants system at Pura**

activities – involving the operation of the biogas plants, the electricity generation and distribution subsystem, and the water supply sub-system – are carried out by two village youths who are employed by the project.

A comparison of the present Community Biogas Plants system with the traditional system of obtaining water, illumination, and fertilizer shows that the households are winners on all counts. Not only have the households lost nothing, but they have gained the following:

– better and safer water,
– less effort to get this improved water,
– better illumination,
– cheaper illumination for the households using kerosene lamps,
– improved fertilizer, which has greater nitrogen content and is less conducive to the growth of weeds compared with farmyard manure,
– a dung delivery fee to those (mainly women and children) who deliver the dung to the plants and take back the sludge.

Thus, there has been a step towards development – a significant improvement in the quality of life and a diminution of some characteristics of poverty – along with an upgrading of the environment.

In addition, the village (as a collective) through its Grama Vikas Sabha (Village Development Committee) has gained in the following ways:
• training and skill upgrading for two of its youths in the operation and maintenance of the biogas system,
• challenging jobs for these two youths,
• revenue for the village, to the extent that the total payment received for the system outputs delivered inside the houses exceeds the expenses for diesel and dung delivery fees,
• a powerful mechanism that initiates and sustains village-scale co-operation, without which the village would revert to a less pleasant way of life in the matter of water and illumination,
• a distinct improvement in the quality of life with regard to water (and therefore health) and illumination,
• a small but significant advance in checking the growing erosion of self-reliance, thanks to the realization that the current status and the future development of the energy system can be decided and implemented by the village, i.e. their future in this matter is in their hands.

Since Pura village has witnessed both an increase in individual benefits as well as the advancement of community interests, it is appropriate to mention here the discussion of individual gain versus community interests in the famous "Tragedy of the Commons" described by Hardin (1968). In that description, the personal benefits that each individual/household derives from promoting the further destruction of the commons (i.e. community resource) are larger and more immediate than the personal loss from the marginal, slow, and long-term destruction of the commons – hence, each individual/household chooses to derive the immediate personal benefit rather than forgo it and save the commons.

The Pura Community Biogas Plants system illustrates a principle that may be termed the "Blessing of the Commons" (Reddy, 1992)[2] – the converse of the "Tragedy of the Commons." According to the "Blessing of the Commons," the price that an individual/household pays for not preserving the commons far outweighs whatever benefits there might be in ignoring the collective interest. In other words, *there is a confluence of self-interest and collective interest* so that the collective interest is automatically advanced when individuals pursue their private interests. In the case of Pura, non-cooperation with the Community Biogas Plants results in access to water and light being cut off by the village, and this is too great a personal loss to compensate for the minor advantage of being a loner.

With the growing experience and awareness of the defects of state control, operation, and maintenance (regulation) of the commons, the privatization (deregulation) option, with its emphasis on the market, is being offered as a solution to the problem of monitoring and control of common resources and facilities. The market may be an excellent allocator of people, materials, and resources, but it does not have a very successful record in dealing with equity, the environment, the infrastructure, and the long term. In this debate, it is invariably forgotten that the type of individual initiative subject to *local* community control necessary for the "Blessing of the Commons" situation is a distinct third option that has very attractive features. There must have been many examples of "Blessing of the Commons" (the maintenance of village tanks, common lands, woodlots, etc.) that have contributed to the survival of Indian villages for centuries in spite of the centrifugal forces tearing them apart.

In Pura, this third option has successfully maintained and operated water-supply and electrical illumination systems for several years without external control. It has ensured the careful husbanding of resources and enlisted the cooperation of every one of the households in the village. It has performed better than the centralized electricity system in terms of the reliability of supply and of the collection of dues. And, above all, it has shown that the path to environmental improvement must start via energy with an attack on poverty as the basis of a development strategy.

7. The DEFENDUS electricity scenario for Karnataka

Apart from causing local atmospheric pollution (in the form of particulates and thermal pollution of water) and regional pollution (in the form of acid rain), the generation of electrical power is the most important source of CO_2 GHG emissions: table 18.1 shows that it accounted for as much as 40 per cent of India's 1989/90 emissions (Sathaye and Reddy, 1993). Hence, any concern for CO_2 emissions must address the problem of environmentally more benign electricity scenarios. An example of how this can be done is briefly described for the state of Karnataka (Reddy et al., 1991).

In 1987, a committee for the Long-Range Planning of Power Projects (LRPPP) set up by the government of Karnataka State in South

Table 18.1 **India's carbon dioxide emissions, 1989/90**

Sector	Million metric tons	%
Coal[a]		
Steel	51.2	9.7
Power	213.0	40.3
Railways	12.3	2.3
Cement	20.5	3.9
Sponge iron	1.8	0.3
Fertilizer	10.2	1.9
Soft coke	5.7	1.1
Others	51.0	9.7
Lignite	19.1	3.6
Coal subtotal	384.8	72.8
Oil[b]		
Light distillate		
Liquefied petroleum gas	6.8	1.3
Mogas	10.7	2.0
Special boiling point hexane	0.4	0.1
Others	0.6	0.1
Sub-subtotal	18.4	3.5
Middle distillate		
Kerosene	25.6	4.8
Aviation turbine fuel	5.5	1.0
High-speed diesel	64.4	12.2
Light diesel oil	4.7	0.9
Mineral turpentine oil	0.4	0.1
Jet propulsion oil	0.3	0.0
Others	0.3	0.0
Sub-subtotal	101.1	19.1
Heavy ends		
Furnace oil/TDO	14.3	2.7
Low-sulphur heavy stock	13.8	2.6
Sub-subtotal	28.1	5.3
Refinery fuel	8.2	1.6
Naphtha	2.1	0.4
Asphalt	–	–
Lubes	1.4	0.3
Petroleum coke	1.2	0.2
Wax	0.4	0.1
Miscellaneous	0.8	0.2
Sub-subtotal	14.0	2.7
Oil subtotal	161.6	30.6
Forests	−17.6	−3.3
TOTAL	528.8	100.0

Sources: coal – Mitra (1992); oil – Mehra and Damodaran (1993); forests – 1986 data from Makundi et al. (1992).

a. Emissions figures assume 90% conversion.

b. Emissions figures allow for 1.5% carbon unburnt.

India (19 million hectares and home to 37.1 million people) projected that the state would require a sixfold increase in electricity supplies by the year 2000 from the 1986 consumption of 7.5 terawatt hours (TWh) of electricity to 47.5 TWh and from the 1986 installed capacity of 2,500 megawatts (MW) to 9,400 MW. This sixfold increase would require the construction of a 1,000 MW super-thermal plant and 2,470 MW of nuclear power facilities. The infrastructure would also have to be expanded by constructing transmission lines, new rail facilities, etc. The bill for this projected increase in supply would be an annual carrying cost of US$3.3 billion, which could be achieved only by spending more than 25 per cent of the state's budget and borrowing from the central government and international sources.

Despite this investment and expansion of supply, the committee was frank enough to warn that energy shortages would not be eliminated; shortages would continue into the next century, with little hope of improvements thereafter. In fact, that would be an appropriate epitaph for the conventional paradigm for energy.

In response to the LRPPP projection, a DEFENDUS scenario was constructed, not just with the objective of increasing supplies, but with a

- a focus on *development*, through the electrification of all homes and a shift to non-energy-intensive employment-generating industries;
- a focus on *end-use efficiency*, through efficiency improvements, replacement of electricity with other heat sources, and load management;
- a focus on *augmenting electricity supply*, through the reduction of transmission losses, implementation of co-generation in sugar factories, use of non-conventional sources, and decentralized electricity generation at the village level.

This alternative scenario requires far less increase in supply – only 17.9 TWh of electricity and an installed capacity of 4,000 MW – and resulted in the shelving of the LRPPP projection. Since the requirements of electricity and installed capacity are only about 40 per cent of those in the conventional LRPPP projection, the annual bill for the DEFENDUS scenario is only US$618 million, i.e. one-third. In other words, it is very expensive to keep poor people poor; it is much cheaper to make a direct attack on poverty. Further, because of a reduced reliance on centralized generation, with its long gestation times, the gestation time of the DEFENDUS scenario is significantly less. Finally, the efficiency improvements, electricity substitution measures, and decentralized sources greatly lessen the environmental impacts of the alternative scenario.

Champions of efficiency and renewables have been arguing for the past decade or so that alternative scenarios are much quicker, cheaper, and environmentally sounder than conventional plans. In the past, however, these recommendations have invariably been based on emotional pleas and hand-waving arguments. Now the situation is different. The mix of efficiency, renewables, and clean centralized sources constituting the DEFENDUS scenario is the result of rigorous quantitative exercises that have survived presentations at local, national, and international forums.

The DEFENDUS electricity scenario for Karnataka has shown that an emphasis on development objectives in the construction of electricity scenarios would lead to lower CO_2 emission levels than if these objectives are ignored. An environmentally more benign approach would be a bonus from the pursuit of basic-needs-oriented development.

8. A strategy for the reduction of India's oil consumption

India's serious balance-of-payments problems, which are a major developmental obstacle, are overwhelmingly due to its rapidly growing oil consumption (Rammanohar Reddy et al., 1992).

India's transport sector is a major oil consumer, but, quite unlike the industrialized countries, the country's transport runs mainly on diesel, consumption of which has been growing at about 8.6 per cent per year and accounts for 70 per cent of the oil used in the transport sector. Diesel consumption is mostly by trucks, which are far less energy efficient than railways in hauling high-bulk-density goods. Despite this, the share of total freight transported by trucks has increased enormously because of the low price of diesel, which has been subsidized and pegged at a price slightly above that of kerosene. Diesel prices cannot be increased without roughly equal increases in kerosene prices because, if the price of kerosene is very much lower than that of diesel, trucks adulterate their diesel fuel with kerosene and immediately create a kerosene shortage. This causes great hardship to the poor because kerosene is used almost wholly in the household sector. For the same reason, kerosene prices cannot be increased under present conditions.

Though electric lighting is far more energy efficient than kerosene lamps, the number of non-electrified kerosene-illuminated homes in

India is increasing at the rate of about 1 million households per year. Under these conditions, India has been forced to increase kerosene consumption at a rate of 7.8 per cent per year.

India's problem of growing oil consumption is, therefore, primarily a problem of the two middle distillates, diesel and kerosene (in that order). Together, they account for as much as half of its oil consumption, and incidentally account for the bulk of India's imports of petroleum *products*.

In contrast, gasoline is currently a small problem because it represents less than one-tenth of oil consumption. However, it is a rapidly growing problem in India because the decision makers have not only failed to provide the funds necessary for public transportation but also encouraged the proliferation of mopeds, scooters, motorbikes, cars, and three-wheeler autorickshaws. De facto, the planners and government have "chosen" personal and hired vehicles as the preferred mode of intra-city passenger movement.

On the basis of this analysis, a four-pronged strategy for resolving India's oil crisis and advancing the country's development has been suggested.[3] It is based primarily on reducing demand for diesel, kerosene, and gasoline. The strategy consists of:

Prong 1: implementing efficiency improvements in the use of petroleum products.

Prong 2: shifting passenger traffic from personal vehicles to public transportation.

Prong 3: shifting freight traffic from road to rail, through the removal of subsidies on kerosene and diesel once homes have been electrified and kerosene replaced as an illuminant.

Prong 4: replacing oil with alternative non-oil fuels, particularly biomass-derived fuels.

Prong 1, namely efficiency improvements in the transport sector, can be achieved straight away by better house-keeping and by long-term measures such as improvements in the fuel efficiency of the truck fleet. In the case of gasoline, a reduction in consumption also requires Prong 2, i.e. a change in the modal mix for passenger traffic away from personal vehicles to public transportation through overall measures such as massive investment in infrastructure for public transportation. For *intra-city* passenger movements, special supplementary measures such as major increases in the number of buses and, where possible, suburban trains are also necessary.

The crux of Prong 3 of the proposed strategy is a massive programme of *home* electrification. When *all* homes are electrified, kerosene becomes unnecessary as an illuminant. To make kerosene completely redundant, additional measures are required for replacing kerosene as a cooking fuel in cities. Once this is done, the subsidy on diesel can be removed and its price can be brought on par with that of gasoline.

The increase in diesel prices is necessary, but not sufficient, to decrease truck freight; it would, however, create a favourable environment in which supporting policy measures could be adopted. For the railways to exploit the situation and increase their freight haulage, there must be substantial investments in the improvement of the railways' freight operations. These funds can come from the diversion of the implicit subsidies on kerosene and diesel.

The combination of this strategy of shifting freight from trucks to rail along with a strategy of shifting short-distance inter-city passenger traffic from diesel locomotives to buses could reduce diesel demand in the transport sector from about 36 million tonnes in the year 2000 projected by the Planning Commission of the Government of India to about 21 million tonnes, which is only about 10 per cent above present consumption.

Even with this combination of strategies, the oil problems would not be eliminated. Intra-regional or short-haul traffic would still require road transport and, therefore, a considerable amount of oil. So, in order to advance the objective of sustainable development, the possibility must be explored of completely eliminating the dependence of road transport on non-renewable oil resources. In other words, a comprehensive oil-reduction strategy requires, over the longer term, Prong 4, which is the much more radical solution of shifting to alternative fuels for road transportation.

Producer gas and biogas have limited scope for use in road transport. Since natural gas is not only more abundant than oil but also much cheaper, far less polluting, and as easily distributed, the compressed natural gas (CNG) option is an attractive alternative for urban fleets of vehicles – buses, taxis, city delivery vehicles. Although hydrogen produced by solar photovoltaics may well turn out to be the transport fuel of the future, it is only the liquid fuels – ethanol and methanol – that are widely applicable alternative fuels in road transport. They could be distributed through the nationwide network already established for gasoline and diesel. Mixtures of ethanol and gasoline – so-called "gasohol" – could be used widely as gasoline extenders. And pure methanol, although never used extensively, is, like pure ethanol, an excellent fuel for internal combustion engines.

Producer gas, biogas, ethanol, and methanol can all be obtained from *biomass* sources. A synergistic coupling between the transport sector and the agricultural sector would therefore be possible whereby "fuel farms" are established to supply fuel for transportation in the same way that rural farms produce food for urban demands.

The fuel–food conflict can be avoided by turning to non-agricultural land for cellulosic resources, particularly fuelwood, to produce methanol and/or ethanol. But this solution to the oil crisis could aggravate the domestic fuelwood problem, particularly for the poor. Domestic cooking fuel is one of the basic energy needs, and the satisfaction of this need has to be an essential feature of an overall development-oriented energy strategy. Hence, the solution to the oil crisis must be compatible with the solution to the fuelwood problem.

One way of achieving a compatible solution would be to extend the synergism between the agricultural and transport sectors to include the domestic sector, in two steps. The first step is based on the fact that, if alternative high-efficiency fuels were provided for cooking, or the efficiencies of fuelwood stoves were radically improved, then the resulting drastic reductions in fuelwood consumption could free a vast fuelwood resource base for the production of liquid fuels for the transport sector. In villages, either biogas stoves, or fuelwood-efficient stoves, or a mix could be introduced. In cities and towns, the LPG option could be adopted because there is considerable scope for the expansion of LPG supplies. And, once the pressure on forests as a source of cooking fuel decreases, conditions become established for managing the growth of forests and dramatically improving their fuelwood yields. In other words, silvicultural practices – agriculture in the general sense – can be implemented to increase fuelwood availability. This is the second step in the extension of the synergism; it consists of including agriculture in the domestic–transport synergism.

In all, therefore, the provision of high-efficiency cooking fuels and/ or devices in rural and urban areas would make available large amounts of wood provided that all the firewood being used today for cooking can still be collected. This saved fuelwood could be converted into methanol. If diesel fuel in trucks and buses were replaced with methanol, then the only diesel demand from the transport sector would come from the railways, and this demand would be quite small.

In the case of India, therefore, it appears that the country has been engulfed by a grave oil crisis because it has ignored two crucial basic needs of poor households: efficient energy sources for lighting and for cooking. The oil strategy proposed here shows that, by providing

Table 18.2   **India's oil-related carbon dioxide emissions, 1989/90**

	Million metric tons	%
High-speed diesel	64.4	39.8
Kerosene	25.6	15.9
Furnace oil/TDO	14.3	8.8
Low-sulphur heavy stock	13.8	8.5
Mogas	10.7	6.6
Refinery fuel	8.2	5.1
Liquefied petroleum gas	6.8	4.2
Aviation turbine fuel	5.5	3.4
Light diesel oil	4.7	2.9
Naphtha	2.1	1.3
Lubec	1.4	0.9
Petroleum coke	1.2	0.7
Miscellaneous	0.8	0.5
Other light distillates	0.6	0.4
Special boiling point hexane	0.4	0.2
Mineral turpentine oil	0.4	0.2
Wax	0.4	0.2
Jet propulsion oil	0.3	0.2
Other middle distillates	0.3	0.2
Asphalt	–	0.0
Total	161.6	100.0

Source: see table 18.1.

electric lighting and efficient cooking fuels/devices to all homes, India could move towards a virtually oil-free road transport system and drastically reduce its dependence on oil, which in turn would accelerate development.

What are the environmental implications of the strategy outlined above? The combustion of petroleum products accounted for about 30 per cent of India's CO_2 emissions in 1989/90, as against 70 per cent in the case of coal (table 18.1). A disaggregation of the CO_2 emissions from these petroleum products is given in table 18.2, from which it can be seen that high-speed diesel, kerosene, furnace oil, low-sulphur heavy stock, gasoline, and refinery fuel are the "A" class items accounting for 85 per cent of emissions. It is clear from table 18.2 that diesel and kerosene, which accounted for 55 per cent of India's oil-related CO_2 emissions, should be the first targets of an emissions-reduction strategy. But the achievement of a reduction in CO_2 emissions is the automatic result – a bonus – of the pursuit of a basic-needs-oriented oil strategy that leads to a significant reduction, and even elimination, of the consumption of precisely these petroleum products. And it is not only CO_2 emissions from oil that are reduced; local vehicular pollution is reduced by shifting passenger traffic from personal vehicles to public transportation. Hence, in the case of oil too, the pursuit of development objectives via energy-efficient strategies is tantamount to addressing local and global environmental concerns.

The lesson is simple: "Look after the people by producing and using energy efficiently, and the environment will look after itself!"

Notes

1. The ruling élites of countries with dual societies would of course like to persist with business-as-usual economic growth but they would adopt environmentally benign technologies in the interests of the global environment if the incremental costs were paid for from external sources. (A cynical third world environmentalist once described the attitude of developing country governments to the industrialized countries in the following words: "If you don't give us money, we won't do anything for the environment; if you give us money, we will do anything!")
2. See the report by Sinha and Herring (1993).
3. Presentation at the PETRAD Seminar on The Role of Petroleum in Sustainable Development, Penang, Malaysia, 7–11 January 1991, International Programme for Petroleum Management and Administration (PETRAD) in cooperation with ECON, Centre for Economic Analysis, Norway, and PETRONAS, Malaysia, and revised in the light of comments and discussions at the Seminar.

   A simpler two-pronged version of the strategy proposed here was presented more than a decade ago in Reddy (1981a,b). The two-pronged strategy was updated and incorporated in Goldemberg et al. (1988).

References

Boyle, S. K. and L. Taylor. 1990. "Energy conservation in Japan." Association for the Conservation of Energy for Greenpeace International, July.

Churchill, A. A. and R. J. Saunders. 1990. "Financing of the energy sector in developing countries." Paper presented at the 14th Congress of the World Energy Conference, 14–22 September, Montreal.

Goldemberg, J., T. B. Johansson, A. K. N. Reddy, and R. H. Williams. 1988. *Energy for a Sustainable World*. New Delhi: Wiley-Eastern Limited.

Grubb, M. et al. 1992. "Sharing the burden." In: I. Mintzer (ed.), *Confronting Climate Change – Risks, Implications and Responses*. Cambridge: Cambridge University Press.

Hardin, G. 1968. "The Tragedy of the Commons." *Science* 162, December: 1243–1248.

Makundi, W., J. Sathaye, and O. Masera. 1992. "Carbon emissions and sequestration in forests." Berkeley, Calif.: Lawrence Berkeley Laboratory, LBL Report 32119.

Mehra, M. and M. Damodaran. 1993. "Anthropogenic emissions of greenhouse gases in India, 1989–90." In: R. K. Pachauri (ed.), *Climate Change: An Indian Perspective*. New Delhi: Tata Energy Research Institute.

Mitra, A. P. (ed.). 1992. "Greenhouse gas emissions in India (1992 update)." Scientific Report No. 4. New Delhi: Council of Scientific and Industrial Research and Ministry of Environment and Forests.

Rajabapaiah, P., S. Jayakumar, and A. K. N. Reddy. 1993. "Biogas electricity. The Pura Village case study." In: T. B. Johansson, H. Kelly, A. K. N. Reddy, and R. H. Williams (eds.), *Renewable Energy – Sources of Fuels and Electricity*. Washington, D.C.: Island Press, pp. 787–815.

Rammanohar Reddy, C., A. D'Sa, and A. K. N. Reddy. 1992. "The debt energy nexus: A case study of India." *Economic and Political Weekly* 27(27), 4 July: 1401–1416.

Reddy, A. K. N. 1981a. "A strategy for resolving India's oil crisis." *Current Science* 50(2), 20 January: 50–53.

——— 1981b. "India - A good life without oil." *New Scientist* 91(1261), 9 July: 93–95.

——— 1986. "Principles of environmentally sound development." *Vichara* 2(26), Indian Institute of Science.

——— 1990. "Development, energy and environment – A case study of electricity planning in India." PARISAR Annual Lecture, Pune, India.

——— 1992. "The Blessing of the Commons." Paper presented at the International Conference on Common Property, Collective Action and Ecology, August, Centre for Ecological Sciences, Indian Institute of Science, Bangalore.

——— 1993. "Electricity planning in India: Current approach and resulting problems." International Energy Initiative Workshop on Electricity, Environment and Development, 2 and 3 September.

Reddy, A. K. N. and P. Balachandra. 1991. "The economics of electricity generation from the Pura Community Biogas system." In: B. R. Pai and M. S. Rama Prasad (eds.), *Power Generation through Renewable Sources of Energy*. New Delhi: Tata/McGraw-Hill Publishing Company, pp. 66–75.

Reddy, A. K. N., G. D. Sumithra, P. Balachandra, and A. D'Sa. 1991. "A development-focused end-use-oriented electricity scenario for Karnataka." *Economic and Political Weekly* 26(14 & 15), 6 & 13 April: 891–910 and 983–1001.

Sagawa, N. 1985. "Japanese experience in energy conservation." In: K. Thukral and R. K. Pachauri (eds.), *Energy Policy Issues*. New Delhi: Allied Vikas Publishers, pp. 61–84.

Sathaye, J. and A. K. N. Reddy. 1993. "Climate change and India's socioeconomic development." In: P. Hayes and K. Smith (eds.), *Global Greenhouse Regime: Who Pays?* London: Earthscan Publications.

Sinha, S. and R. Herring. 1993. *Economic and Political Weekly* 28(27–28), 3–10 July: 1425–1432.

Yamaji, K. 1991. "Role of electricity in minimizing environmental impacts." In: *Electricity and the Environment*, Proceedings of a Senior Expert Symposium on Electricity and the Environment, held in Helsinki, Finland, 13–17 May 1991. Vienna: Atomic Energy Agency, pp. 97–112.

19

Economic development, energy, and the environment in the People's Republic of China

Fengqi Zhou

1. Economic development and the increase in energy consumption

China's internal reforms and its opening up to the outside world during the 1980s pushed the Chinese economy to new heights, resulting in an average annual GNP growth rate of 9 per cent between 1981 and 1990. Thus China has one of the most rapidly developing economies in the world today. If the GNP rate continues to increase at 6 per cent until 2000, the national economy is expected to quadruple by the end of the century.

At the beginning of 1992, the Chinese government decided to make the transition from a low-efficiency and highly centralized planned economy to a high-efficiency market economy, and to establish a socialistic market system with Chinese characteristics. Since then, the annual increase in GNP has been 13 per cent. Judging from these developments, the average annual increase in GNP in the 1990s will probably reach 8–9 per cent.

In 1990, total primary commercial energy consumption in China was 987 million tons of coal equivalent (Mtce), consisting of coal (76.2 per cent), petroleum (16.6 per cent), natural gas (2.1 per cent), and hydroelectricity (5.1 per cent). Final energy consumption by sector was: industry 68.5 per cent, residential 16.0 per cent, and others 15.5 per cent.

During the 1980s, primary commercial energy consumption grew at an annual rate of 5.1 per cent. Energy consumption per capita increased from 0.614 tce in 1980 to 0.869 tce in 1990 – an average annual growth rate of 3.5 per cent.

Total electricity generation in 1990 was 621.1 terawatt hours (TWh), of which thermal power provided 494.4 TWh (79.6 per cent). The annual growth rate of electricity generation was 7.5 per cent during the 1980s. In 1990, the total energy used for electricity generation was 212 Mtce, in which coal, fuel oil, and diesel accounted for 89, 7, and 3 per cent, respectively. Final electricity consumption by sector was: industry 78.2 per cent, residential 7.7 per cent, agriculture 6.9 per cent, and others 7.2 per cent. Electricity consumption per capita increased from 306 kilowatt hours (kWh) in 1980 to 549 kWh in 1990, with an average annual growth rate of 6.5 per cent.

Depending on the rate of growth of the economy, the Energy Research Institute has made a forecast of energy demand for the year 2000. If the coefficient of elasticity of primary energy consumption is 0.45 (it was 0.56 in the 1980s), and the annual average rate of energy conservation is 4 per cent, the aggregate of primary energy consumption will be 1,450 Mtce, including 1,500 Mt of raw coal, 165 Mt of crude oil, 25 billion m^3 of natural gas, and electricity generation of 1,350 TWh, including 240 TWh of hydropower and 10 TWh of nuclear power.

2. The environmental challenge of energy development

The main energy-related environmental problem in China is urban air pollution caused by the burning of large amounts of coal. In 1990, coal consumption in China was 1,055 Mt, 80 per cent of which was burnt directly, which caused serious air pollution.

In 1990, total emissions of particulates were 13.24 Mt in China, 70 per cent of which were from coal combustion. The daily average concentration of total suspended particulates in China's cities is 387 $\mu g/m^3$, and it is higher in the northern cities than in the southern cities.

In 1990, total SO_2 emissions were 14.95 Mt in China, 90 per cent of which were from coal combustion. The daily average concentration of SO_2 in cities was 93 $\mu g/m^3$. These massive emissions of SO_2 are leading to serious SO_2 pollution in urban areas. In a quarter of cities in northern China, the SO_2 concentration has exceeded level 3 of the national standard (which is 100 $\mu g/m^3$). In southern China, especially in the south-western area, there is acid rain in some regions. In the worst places, the pH value of precipitation is below 4.

It is estimated that CO_2 emissions from fossil fuel combustion were 564 MtC in 1990, 85 per cent of which were from coal combustion. In addition, overconsumption of biomass energy, vegetation loss, and the failure to return large amounts of straw to the land resulted in soil erosion and a reduction in organic content. The national area of soil erosion has reached 150 million hectares, and the national average organic content in farmland is below 1.5 per cent.

Given that coal consumption is predicted to reach 1,500 Mt in 2000, air pollution will continue to get worse. The right strategy and effective measures are needed to control serious air pollution.

3. An energy efficiency strategy

Energy conservation and improvements in energy efficiency are the best means of harmonizing the development of energy and protection of the environment.

China has made considerable progress in energy conservation. From 1980 to 1990, the average annual increase in commercial energy consumption was 5.1 per cent, whereas the average annual growth rate of GNP was 9.0 per cent, giving an elasticity of energy consumption of 0.56. Energy consumption per 10,000 yuan GNP decreased from 13.36 tce in 1980 to 9.3 tce in 1990, a drop of 30 per cent. This represents an average annual energy conservation rate of 3.7 per cent, and a cumulative saving of over 280 Mtce. Nearly two-thirds of this was saved indirectly through changing macroeconomic structures; the rest was saved directly by industrial enterprises.

Goldemberg suggested in chapter 17 that energy intensity in developing countries is increasing, with the notable exception of China, whose energy intensity is clearly declining. This indicates a de-coupling of energy consumption and economic growth (see fig. 19.1).

Improvements in energy efficiency are at the core of efforts to reduce air pollution and greenhouse gas emissions. During the 1980–1990 period, it is estimated that, as a result of energy conservation, there was a reduction in particulate emissions of 0.5 Mt and in SO_2 emissions of 0.55 Mt every year.

China's development target calls for further reductions in com-

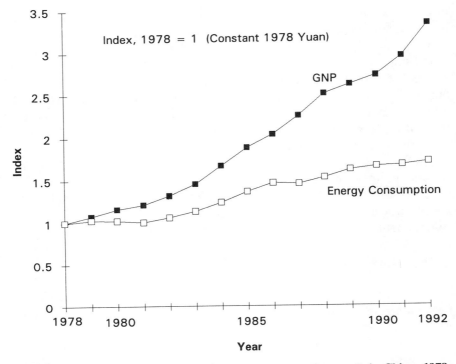

Fig. 19.1 **De-coupling energy consumption and economic growth in China, 1978–1992**

mercial energy intensity of at least 35–40 per cent per unit of GDP from 1990 to 2000. This further energy saving can be achieved, but there are major obstacles to be overcome. Success will require both further substantial structural savings and an acceleration in technical reform to increase energy efficiency.

4. A strategy of clean coal technologies

China is one of the few countries that uses coal as its major energy source. In 1990, coal accounted for 76.2 per cent of primary energy consumption, supplying 70 per cent of fuel for electricity generation, 60 per cent of raw materials for the chemical industry, and 80 per cent of residential fuel utilization. It is estimated that, by the year 2010, coal will still account for 66.7 per cent of consumption, and even in 2050 the share of coal will be above 50 per cent. This coal-dominated energy structure is unlikely to change in the near future unless there is a breakthrough in new energy technologies.

The important role of coal is determined by the state of its reserves. Because proven reserves of coal comprise 90 per cent of the total proven reserves of primary energy in China, it would be impossible not to use it. The best strategy would therefore be to spread "clean coal technologies" (CCT), which is the general name for technologies that increase energy efficiency and reduce pollution. In the United States and Japan, CCT has played a leading role. China has also paid great attention to it in recent years and made some progress. Ten kinds of CCT have been studied and ranked according to assessments of technological and economic characteristics: coal selection, briquette coal, coal water mixture (CWM), advanced combustor, fluidized bed combustion (FBC), integrated gasification combined cycle (IGCC), flue gas treatment, coal gasification, coal liquefication, and fuel cells.

China is a developing country and it would be impossible to halt or delay economic development. However, we should show responsibility towards the world and posterity, by making every effort to reduce the effects of energy development on the environment. We should admit that clean coal is the "future energy" and that developing clean coal technologies is an important strategy.

Comments on part 6

Hoesung Lee

The papers in part 6 all emphasize the importance and desirability of pursuing an energy-efficient development path. Professors Goldemberg and Reddy both argue for the de-linking of energy and GDP growth in developing countries through the adoption of energy-efficient technologies early in the development process. They provide examples from Brazil and India that demonstrate the possibility of moving toward energy-efficient growth, although the Brazilian example is of future plans for such growth and the Indian example is a small village development experience. They conclude that developing countries should be able to leapfrog old technologies to achieve an energy-efficient growth path.

I agree with their conclusions for energy-efficient growth strategies for developing countries. It is difficult to take issue with a growth proposal that has energy efficiency at its core, especially when energy efficiency improvements are one of the most cost-effective ways to reduce carbon dioxide emissions. But how do we achieve the goal of an energy-efficient growth path? One can observe many practical barriers standing between reality and the goal. These are what I shall comment on.

372

The energy/GDP ratio is lower in industrialized countries because, as the authors indicate, (a) energy efficiency in each individual sector is better than in developing countries, and (b) the economy is dominated by energy-efficient industries. This implies that the first task for the developing countries is to improve end-use energy efficiency. More specifically, they need to find out why energy-efficient technologies are not used as much in developing countries as in the industrialized countries. Developing countries may enjoy latecomers' advantages, as suggested by Professor Goldemberg, but the prospects for improving energy/GDP ratios are not bright.

In most developing countries, energy prices are subsidized to keep them considerably below costs. In these circumstances, it is likely that an energy-intensive industrial structure will be sought. As a result, the physical energy input per unit of output – the energy/GDP ratio in aggregate – will be higher than otherwise.

However, this does not necessarily imply that energy expenditures per unit of output will also be higher. What matters in the investment decision is energy expenditures, not the quantity of energy use. A high energy/GDP ratio reflects an energy-inefficient outcome, but, given low energy prices, it makes good business sense to have high energy intensity. This is why the inefficient outcome is sustainable.

In order to achieve a lower ratio for energy/GDP in developing countries, energy prices should be rationalized. But this is easier said than done. Energy prices in developing countries reflect a complex mixture of economic, social, and political interdependencies. The task then is how to induce the adoption of energy-efficient technologies in a situation of low energy prices. Market competition and energy efficiency regulations play a critical role.

Experience in Korean manufacturing industries indicates that the more the industries are subject to competition, especially export competition, the higher the energy efficiency in those industries. Energy efficiency standards are also effective and complement market competition. Industries are, however, generally reluctant to see the tightening of efficiency standards.

In conclusion, in order to realize an energy-efficient growth strategy, the following conditions must be satisfied:
• no energy price subsidies
• market competition
• energy efficiency regulations.

Contributors

Akihiro Amano
Dean, School of Policy Studies,
Kwansei University,
Sanda-shi,
Japan

William U. Chandler
Director, Advanced International
Studies Unit,
Pacific Northwest Laboratories,
Washington, D.C.,
USA

Anthony A. Churchill
Senior Advisor, Washington
International Energy Group,
Washington, D.C.,
USA

William R. Cline
Senior Fellow, Institute for International
Economics (IIE),
Washington, D.C.,
USA

John P. Ferriter
Deputy Executive Director,
International Energy Agency (IEA),
Paris,
France

José Goldemberg
Professor, Instituto de Electrotécnica e
Energia,
Universidade de São Paulo,
Brazil

Yujiro Hayami
Professor, School of International
Politics, Economics & Business,
Aoyama Gakuin University,
Tokyo,
Japan

Thomas B. Johansson
Professor, United Nations Development
Programme,
New York,
USA

374

Rajashree S. Kanetkar
TATA Energy Research Institute,
New Delhi,
India

Mohamed Kassas
Professor, Department of Botany,
Faculty of Science,
University of Cairo,
Giza,
Egypt

Yoichi Kaya
Professor, Jyukankyo Research
Institute,
Tokyo,
Japan

Lawrence R. Klein
Professor Emeritus, Department of
Economics,
University of Pennsylvania,
Philadelphia,
USA

Marc Ledbetter
Senior Programme Manager, Battelle
Pacific Northwest Laboratories,
Portland,
USA

Hoesung Lee
Former President, Korea Energy
Economics Institute, Kyunggi-do,
Korea

Hung-yi Li
Senior Research Economist, Institute
for Policy Analysis,
University of Toronto,
Canada

Warwick J. McKibbin
Professor, Department of Economics,
Research School of Pacific Studies,
The Australian National University,
Canberra, Australia

Senior Fellow, Brookings Institution,
Washington, D.C.,
USA

Nebojša Nakićenović
Project Leader, Environmentally
Compatible Energy Strategies Project,
International Institute for Applied
Systems Analysis (IIASA),
Laxenburg,
Austria

Sozaburo Okamatsu
Adviser, The Long-Term Credit Bank of
Japan,
Tokyo,
Japan

R. K. Pachauri
Director, TATA Energy Research
Institute,
New Delhi,
India

Peter Pauly
Professor of Economics,
University of Toronto,
Canada

Amulya K. N. Reddy
President, International Energy
Initiative,
Bangalore,
India

Kenneth G. Ruffing
Chief, Economics and Finance Branch,
Division for Sustainable Development,
Department for Policy Coordination and
Sustainable Development,
United Nations,
New York,
USA

Giuseppe M. Sfligiotti
Chairman, Italian Member Committee,
World Energy Council,
Rome,
Italy

Kunio Takase
Executive Director, International
Development Centre of Japan (IDCJ),
Tokyo,
Japan

375

Contributors

Tatsushi Tokioka
Director, Climate Prediction Division,
Climate and Marine Department,
Japan Meteorological Agency,
Tokyo,
Japan

Chihiro Watanabe
Professor, Department of Industrial
Engineering and Management,
Tokyo Institute of Technology,
Tokyo,
Japan

Senior Advisor to the Director on
Technology, IIASA,
Laxenburg,
Austria

Kenji Yamaji
Professor, Department of Electrical
Engineering,
Tokyo University,
Japan

Jike Yang
Vice-Chairman, Environment and
Resources Protection Committee,
National People's Congress,
Beijing,
China

Keiichi Yokobori
President, Asia Pacific Energy Research
Centre,
Institute of Energy Economics,
Tokyo,
Japan

Fengqi Zhou
Director, Energy Research Institute,
State Planning Commission,
Beijing,
China

Index

DATE DUE

12/01/08			